Business Ethics:
Violations of the Public Trust

Robert F. Hartley
Cleveland State University

JOHN WILEY & SONS, INC.

New York • Chichester • Brisbane • Toronto • Singapore

ACQUISITIONS EDITOR	*Timothy Kent*
MARKETING MANAGER	*Carolyn Henderson*
PRODUCTION SUPERVISOR	*Micheline Frederick*
DESIGNER	*Kevin Murphy*
MANUFACTURING MANAGER	*Andrea Price*
COPY EDITING SUPERVISOR	*Richard Blander*
ILLUSTRATION COORDINATOR	*Jaime Perea*
COVER DESIGN	*Hothouse Designs, Inc.*

This book was set in Palatino by V & M Graphics, Inc. and printed and bound by Courier Stoughton. The cover was printed by Phoenix.

Recognizing the importance of preserving what has been written, it is a policy of John Wiley & Sons, Inc. to have books of enduring value published in the United States printed on acid-free paper, and we exert our best efforts to that end.

Copyright © 1993, by John Wiley & Sons, Inc.

All rights reserved. Published simultaneously in Canada.

Reproduction or translation of any part of
this work beyond that permitted by Sections
107 and 108 of the 1976 United States Copyright
Act without the permission of the copyright
owner is unlawful. Requests for permission
or further information should be addressed to
the Permissions Department, John Wiley & Sons, Inc.

Library of Congress Cataloging in Publication Data:

ISBN 0-471-54591-0 (pbk)

Printed in the United States of America

10 9 8 7 6 5 4 3 2 1

KING ALFRED'S COLLEGE
WINCHESTER

174.4
HAR 0164676

Preface

If ever there was a time when we could afford to take ethical behavior in business for granted, that time has long since passed. *Business Ethics: Violations of the Public Trust* confronts this critical issue head-on, presenting real cases, cases from which all of us can learn. These are real scenarios and dilemmas faced by real companies. In them, we are privy to the major causal factors behind the ill-advised actions as well as to the consequences of these misdeeds. *Business Ethics* starkly reveals both causes and effects, dissecting the carcass of some of the most noteworthy violations of the public trust in recent history.

The text is organized into three parts: Part I deals with classic cases dating back several decades; Part II, with more recent controversies. These cases range from those of great corporate culpability, to those where naivete or carelessness led to trouble; from those whose consequences were monumental in terms of human suffering, to those of less drastic consequence but that were still abusive, unethical, and illegal. Some of the cases involve substantial controversy: the text examines what is proper conduct, and are the criticisms against the company's decisions truly justified? Part 3 examines the other side of ethical dilemmas: what happens when an ethical controversy in handled responsibly. Part 3 also offers some conclusions and attempts to answer the question, what can be learned?

Each chapter is a complete case unto itself. Each chapter contains one or more boxed elements, either an *Issue* or *Information* topic, which is linked to a key term within the nearby chapter text.

Wherever possible, the reader is invited to participate in the various issue resolutions and role-play scenarios. We hope to stimulate and challenge the student by providing thought-provoking sidelights as well as topics for discussion, questions, and research ideas. We invite the students to place themselves in the shoes of those principally involved and ponder how they might have reacted. For example, would they have become "whistleblowers" and publicized the company's misdeeds at the risk of job and career?

To this end, the end-of-chapter material offers a boxed *What Can Be Learned* section and provides *Learning Insights, Issue Insights,* conclusions, and explanations. This section is then followed by *For Thought and Discussion, Invitation to Role-Play,* and *Invitation to Research.*

We have tried to present the cases as objectively as possible by not condemning without a hearing, by seeking extenuating circumstances or explanations, or by looking for whatever good might have accompanied the bad.

My hope for this book is that it promotes awareness—by our students as well as by business people and the concerned public—of how ethical misconduct can develop insidiously, and how devastating the consequences can be for all involved. In particular, our students, the business leaders of tomorrow, ought to fully realize the importance of considering the ethical consequences of business decisions—or else! This book may be used in a great variety of courses, both undergraduate and graduate, from a management principles course, to strategic management, business policy, business and society, business ethics, marketing, as well as any number of other courses where the issue of ethics is a topic to be discussed.

And therein, we should find deeper learning experiences both from the firm's perspective and that of society. From such mistakes we may learn to avoid similar mistakes in the future, as well as learn to better cope should an ethical dilemma arise in our own business experiences.

It is my hope, and even expectation, that a better ethical climate lies ahead, one of more substance and more beneficial to society and to its business participants.

A number of persons have provided encouragement, information, advice, and constructive criticism. I appreciate the help and support of my colleagues at Cleveland State University, particularly Ram Rao, John Gardner, and Margaret Bahniuk. I also thank the following reviewers who have given me their valuable suggestions and insights: John Bunch, Kansas State University (Manhattan, KS); Al Gini, Loyola University (Chicago, IL); Howard Smith, University of New Mexico (Albuquerque, NM).

I appreciate the encouragement of my editor at Wiley, Tim Kent, and his assistant, Ellen Ford. Finally, my thanks to Richard Blander, Senior Copy Editor, for his helpful input in the careful review of the manuscript.

Robert F. Hartley

Contents

Business Ethics:
Violations of the Public Trust

CHAPTER 1

Introduction and Perspective

GENERAL PERSPECTIVE

In this book, we are not on a witch hunt. We are not seeking to sensationalize corporate misdeeds, to blacken the image of business. Far from it. Rather, we want to identify the factors that lead to misconduct, their dire consequences both for the firm and for society, and how these experiences might help us avoid similar mistakes in the future. We will also examine certain cases where the alleged misconduct is open to question, is controversial, and as such deserves an objective appraisal. We will be wearing two hats: that of concerned citizens and that of should-be-concerned executives.

The book offers this thesis:

The interests of a firm are best served by scrupulous attention to the public interest and by seeking a *trusting relationship* with the various publics with which a firm is involved. In the process, society also is best served.

These various publics are a firm's customers, suppliers, employees, and stockholders, the financial institutions, the communities in which they dwell, and the various governments—local, state, and federal. And to these groups must be added the press, which cannot always be relied upon to deliver objective and unbiased reporting but is influenced by the firm's reputation and its relations with the other publics.

Any philosophy or course of action that doesn't take the public interest into consideration is vulnerable in today's business environment. Compared to earlier decades, today's firms face more critical public and governmental scrutiny and an environment in which regulatory and litigious actions are a constant possibility. Perhaps the best measure of how far we have come toward a more enlightened business climate is this: a firm that violates the public trust today stands to be surpassed by competitors more eager to please customers and develop a trusting relationship with its various publics.

The overwhelming majority of business dealings are noncontroversial, but the abuses receive the publicity, harming the image of business. Whenever corporate misdeeds are publicized, blame often falls on business schools: allegations resound that the schools have paid short shrift to ethical topics in their zeal for coldly analytical tools and processes. Admittedly, ethical behavior is difficult if not impossible to fully teach. Perhaps the best we can do is to expose you, our students, to ethical problems and examples of unethical conduct and encourage you to seek higher moral standards. We can make you aware of various ethical dilemmas and temptations. And we can show you the consequences of bad practices, as has been done in this book. We hope the exposure will bring a new generation of more scrupulously honest and concerned executives.

In this book we seek to discover what can be learned from the mistakes made by well-known firms in order to help prevent similar mistakes and errors of judgment in the future. We should learn from mistakes. Such learning can come from insights regarding both *avoidance* and *response* decisions.

A firm should learn, from its own mistakes or from those of other firms, to be wary, to take care to *avoid* situations and actions that might harm its trusting relationship with its various publics. For example, the A. H. Robins Company (discussed in Chapter 9) blundered into an aggressive promotional strategy with a product inadequately tested for safety, one which was to prove harmful and even life threatening to thousands of women. Robins, as it happened, also blundered badly with its response to this situation: first, denial, and then a vain effort to cover up.

Sometimes a firm faces a catastrophe, suddenly and without warning. That's what happened to Union Carbide (discussed in Chapter 11) when one of its chemical plants in Bhopal, India leaked 40 tons of toxic chemicals. Although the company quickly rushed aid to the victims, it was bitterly condemned for complacency and loose controls that permitted the accident to happen in the first place.

In the first case described in this book (Chapter 2), General Motors is shown obdurately refusing to admit that its Corvair is an unsafe car. It maintained that "drivers, not the car, caused the accidents." And it went on to try to discredit Ralph Nader, its harshest critic. Eventually, public opinion became so incensed at the callousness of a major firm refusing to spend a few dollars per car to make it safer that protests were triggered against all kinds of business practices. The resulting movement, known as *consumerism*, led to the greatest increase in legislation and regulation at all levels of government, all aimed at preventing abuses in the marketplace and in the environment.

Many learning experiences can be found in these and the other examples described in this book: for example, how to avoid the worst scenario, if possible, and how best to respond, if the worst scenario can't be avoided.

ETHICS

Ethics refers to standards of right conduct. Unfortunately, there is often not complete agreement as to what constitutes ethical behavior. At the extremes, of course, there is not much dispute. But many practices fall into a gray area, where opinions may differ as to what is ethical and what is unethical and unacceptable. Here are examples from this gray area: using high-pressure tactics to persuade people to buy; misleading customers into thinking they are getting a bargain; cheating on expense accounts; exaggerating advertising claims; giving expensive "gifts" to clients or potential clients. As another example, how would you feel about more pollution if it would contribute to full employment in your community? These issues can become complicated and confusing. For example, opening a business on Sundays may be viewed by strict adherents of some religious doctrines as unethical, but it is accepted by most people as a convenience to customers and a desirable and customer-oriented business practice.

Other actions clearly violate the socially accepted norms of behavior. Examples include competitive espionage; bribery; falsifying costs for defense contractors; deceptive and outright falsehoods regarding product claims; callous disregard for the health and welfare of customers, employees, and the general public; environmental pollution on a grand scale.

Unfortunately for some business firms that have chosen to "walk on the edge," what society once tolerated as acceptable behavior is rapidly becoming unacceptable. Society expects, and is now demanding, much more ethical conduct, whereas it had previously regarded questionable practices with apathy or ignorance.

Ethics and the Law

The relationship between ethical conduct and the law is sometimes confusing. Some would rationalize that actions within the law are therefore ethical and perfectly justifiable. But an "if it's legal, it's ethical" attitude disregards the fact that the law "codifies only that part of ethics which society feels so strongly about that it is willing to support it with physical force."[1] Many practices are within the law, such as firing an employee just before retirement benefits become vested, or charging a naive customer more than a fair price; yet many people would see these as unethical practices.

Can actions be ethical but illegal? Violating the fair trade laws, which at one time prohibited retailers from offering certain brands below a designated price, is a case in point. If a firm engages in illegal price cutting, is this unethical? Is the violation of blue laws (local laws prohibiting doing business on Sundays) unethical? Many people see these acts as ethical, even though they are against the law. The law is not infallible.

Quasi-legal Practices

Certain practices can be condemned at the extreme but may be tolerated in moderation. Ethical as well as legal considerations may be involved, especially in matters such as gift giving, which at the extreme becomes commercial bribery. The attempt to influence an employee by a gift of some sort can be considered an unfair method of competition under the Federal Trade Commission Act. Various state and federal laws specifically prohibit the bribing of governmental employees. And the Foreign Corrupt Practices Act of 1977 makes it a criminal offense to offer a payment to a foreign official to obtain foreign business. No other industrialized nation has imposed this restriction on its business executives. And this law has been criticized as making it more difficult for American firms to compete in those foreign environments where bribery is a way of life.

What constitutes *commercial bribery*? The free lunch? Free football tickets? The bottle of Scotch or the fruit basket at Christmas time? Probably not. These are traditional gifts and are commonly accepted industry practices. But where does one draw the line? It is merely one more step to the cash gift, the paid "business" vacation, the expensive gift, such as a fur coat or a car. Because "modest" hospitality or gifts can escalate into a semblance of bribery and can affect objective business judgment, some firms have a policy that purchasing agents and other executives may not accept even token gifts or free meals.

---

[1] John H. Westing, "Some Thoughts on the Nature of Ethics in Marketing," in *Changing Marketing Systems*, Reed Mayer, ed., 1967 Winter Conference Proceedings (Chicago: American Marketing Association, 1968), p. 162.

Ethics and Profits

Many businesspeople assume that the more strictly one interprets ethical behavior, the more profits suffer. Certainly, the muted sales efforts that may result from toning down product claims or resisting customer hints and even demands (especially in some foreign countries) for bribes or kickbacks may hurt profits. Yet, a strong argument can also be made that scrupulously honest and ethical behavior is better for business and for profits. Well-satisfied customers tend to bring repeat business. (This is the source of our thesis that it is desirable to develop trusting relationships with not only customers but also personnel, suppliers, and the other publics with which a firm deals.) An unbending disavowal of the unethical practices of bribery, kickbacks, false claims, and padded expenses may help restore a healthier business environment for an entire industry. The firm's reputation for honest dealings can be a powerful competitive advantage. Ethical conduct is compatible with maximizing profits in the long run, although in the very short run, disregard of high moral principles may yield more profits.

Incentives for Questionable Practices

The perception that unethical and shady practices will yield more sales and profits (or are necessary even for reasonable profits) still prevails. Given this attitude, certain factors or conditions can be identified that tend to motivate those less than desirable practices, whether illegal or merely ethically questionable, such as (1) overemphasis on performance (by both the individual and firm); (2) intensity of competition; (3) expediency, indifference, or both; (4) custom; and (5) what we might term "groupthink."

Overemphasis on Performance. In most firms, job promotion and higher pay depend on achieving greater sales and profits. This is true not only for individual employees and executives but for departments, divisions, and the entire firm. The value that stockholders and investors, creditors, and suppliers place on a firm depends to a large extent on growth. And the evidence of growth is increasing sales and profits. The better the growth rate, the more money available for further expansion by investors and creditors at attractive rates. Suppliers and customers are more eager to do business. Top-quality personnel and executives are also more easily attracted. This emphasis on quantitative measures of performance, however, has some potential negative consequences:

> Men are not measured on the basis of their moral contribution to the business enterprise. Hence, they become caught up in a system which is characterized

by an ethic foreign to and often lower than the ethics of man. There is always the temptation for the business [man] to push harder even though there are infractions of the "rules of the game."[2]

Top management cannot always be blamed for employees' questionable behavior. An ambitious manager, or perhaps an employee interested in substantially increasing his or her immediate income, can be tempted to make a strong short-term showing at the expense of scrupulously honest behavior.

Intensity of Competition. An intensely competitive environment, especially if coupled with a firm's inability to differentiate products substantially or to cement segments of the market, can motivate unethical behavior. The actions of one or a few firms in a fiercely competitive industry may generate a follow-the-leader situation, requiring the more ethical competitors to choose lower profits or lower ethics.

Expediency and Indifference. The attitude of expediency and indifference to the customers' best interests accounts for some questionable practices. These attitudes, whether permeating an entire firm or affecting only a few individuals, are hardly conducive to repeat business and customer loyalty—the trusting relationship we have advocated. They are more prevalent in firms with many small customers and in those firms where repeat business is relatively unimportant, such as the marketing of used cars, home repairs, and recreational land. Here, unfortunately, deceptive practices and even fraud are not uncommon.

Custom. The adage *caveat emptor*, "let the buyer beware," applied to many business dealings until the last few decades but today generally does not. Now customers are more knowledgeable and demanding, competitors are more intense and eager to develop good relationships, and government is often involved. Yet, the tradition of considering the marketplace as an arena of psychological conflict between buyer and seller endures.

The Groupthink Mentality. As we will examine in Chapter 2, the phenomenon of "groupthink," executives acting in the committee environment, may dictate courses of action (including a lack of concern for safety or environmental dangers) that no executive alone would possibly condone. Such a psychological mindset is not unrelated to the lynch-mob mentality of ages

---

[2]Robert J. Holloway and Robert S. Hancock, *Marketing in a Changing Environment* (New York: Wiley, 1968), p. 212.

past. But it reflects the decision-by-committee syndrome in which the lowest-common-denominator action can be agreed upon in an environment where no one person can be held responsible.

ORGANIZATION OF BOOK

The cases in this book are well known, and are the most widely publicized examples of alleged corporate misdeeds that have yet come to light. Despite the press coverage, however, there is the need for a more objective and less sensationalized treatment if we are to better understand the parameters leading to the problems. We need a balanced and undistorted perspective to analyze the contributory factors and the questionable reactions, and thereby gain a learning experience that may help avoid similar mistakes in the future or else better cope with unexpected adversities.

Some cases involve great culpability, callousness, and blame. Other firms had the problem thrust upon them unexpectedly; they may have been careless or exercised poor judgment, but the intent was hardly damning. In some cases the social consequences were drastic and deadly, such as in the Bhopal disaster and the Dalkon Shield. In other cases, consequences were far less severe, and anything negative could even be disputed as blown out of proportion by social activists, as in the alleged targeting of strong beer and certain cigarette brands to the ghetto. Figure 1.1 presents a matrix based on culpability and severity of the consequences of the misdeeds, and the cases in the book are plotted on this matrix.

Classic Ethical Violations (Part I)

The body of the book has been divided into classic and contemporary ethical mistakes. Chapter 2, the first case in the book, describes the classic confrontation between Ralph Nader and General Motors over its "killer" car, the Corvair, a confrontation that led to widespread consumer repudiation of business practices that ignored public safety and the environment.

The second case shows the consumer movement continuing to grow in strength and effectiveness because of a chemical manufacturer's unconcern about environmental pollution. Union Carbide, in the 1960s and early 1970s, finally capitulated to public hostility and the effective marshaling of media and governmental pressure. The tradeoff between jobs and the environment was decided in favor of the environment.

In Chapter 4, deceptive promotional claims made by the producers of STP were finally challenged by the media and eventually by the Federal Trade Commission in the early 1970s. But this was after a useless product (as most petroleum engineers and automotive experts agreed it was) had

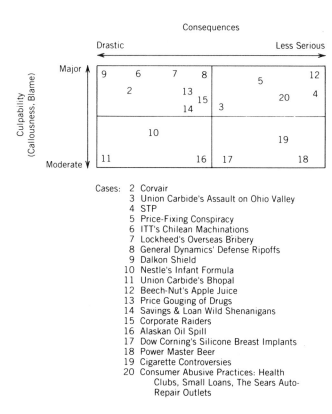

Figure 1.1 Positioning of cases as to culpability and severity of consequences.

achieved widespread success because of its association with the macho image of racing and race car drivers.

In the late 1950s, electrical equipment manufacturers conspired to fix bids and prices in the greatest ever violation of the Sherman Anti-Trust Act. This widely publicized conspiracy, which resulted in jail sentences for some executives, was one of the first cases to have major impact on the nation's thinking regarding business ethics.

Chapter 6 describes the machinations of ITT, a multinational corporation, in its attempts to protect its holdings in Chile in the early 1970s, even to the point of trying to influence and then overthrow the Chilean government—in particular, its president, Salvador Allende. The CEO of ITT, Harold Geneen, apparently believed the end (preserving ITT property in a small Third World country) justified the means (whatever it took to save the firm's holdings). ITT's abuses of power and its interference in a foreign government brought critical scrutiny of all multinationals and how they might need to be constrained.

In the mid-1970s, revelations surfaced that Lockheed, a major defense contractor, had made millions of dollars in bribes to foreign officials, even to a prince and a prime minister. Chapter 7 discusses major facets of the controversy concerning overseas payoffs.

Abuses by other defense contractors are examined in Chapter 8. One of the worst violators of Defense Department trust, General Dynamics, is singled out. Massive cost overruns, fraud, bill padding, bribery—these are some of the allegations against General Dynamics during the 1970s and 1980s. Sadly, most other defense contractors were also culpable. And who paid the bills? Of course, we the people.

Chapter 9 shows marketing at its very worst. A. H. Robins Company rushed to market its intrauterine contraceptive, the Dalkon Shield, without adequate and unbiased testing. As serious medical injuries became known, the company resorted to denial and cover-up and continued to promote the device aggressively. Eventually, by the mid-1980s, a host of lawsuits finally toppled the company, but not before thousands of women suffered serious injuries, even deaths, from the Shield.

In the Nestle case, we see that good and evil can exist simultaneously. Nestle's infant formula, marketed in underdeveloped Third World countries, was both a blessing and a curse in countries that did not always have the sanitation necessary to make the product safe. But worldwide criticism of Nestle in the 1970s and into the 1980s eventually led to boycotts and overwhelming public pressure for reforms.

Contemporary Ethical Controversies (Part II)

Union Carbide's Bhopal, India plant suffered a monumental catastrophe in 1984. Some 2,500 deaths occurred, with upwards of 300,000 people injured. With hindsight, the accident could have been prevented or at least greatly minimized. How much should a firm be blamed for consequences it could hardly have imagined, but which the public perceived it should have?

In the case of Beech-Nut (a subsidiary of Nestle), corporate executives pleaded guilty in 1988 to willful violations of the food and drug laws by selling adulterated apple products—to babies. Although health and safety was not an issue, a cheapened product was fraudulently foisted on consumers because the company was in dire shape profitwise.

Chapter 13 examines certain controversial pricing practices within the pharmaceutical industry, with closer looks at Burroughs Wellcome, which priced AZT, the first drug authorized by the Food and Drug Administration for use against AIDS, at a level that would cost users $10,000 a year; and at Hoffman-La Roche, which priced Valium and Librium many times over cost. Especially with AZT, public outcries reached a crescendo against such "price gouging." Is there any justifications for such high profit margins on drugs that are important, even essential, to well-being and life itself?

An entire industry comes under scrutiny in the savings and loan chapter. As of the early 1990s, the debacle is still unraveling. The final bailout figure is estimated in the hundreds of billions of dollars. The case represents the ultimate repudiation by management of its responsibility to stockholders and depositors. Admittedly, management was not alone in culpability; state and federal regulators and an easily influenced and naive Congress must also share the blame. But the monumental scope of the "betrayal" is still not comprehended by most Americans.

Chapter 15 describes two of the corporate "raiders" who characterized the 1980s, a decade in which many solid companies were taken over by other firms that financed the acquisitions by borrowing heavily, usually with so-called junk bonds. Robert Campeau acquired two of the country's most prestigious department-store corporations and, because of severe financial overextension, brought these famous stores into bankruptcy, but not before he had slashed thousands of jobs. His excesses brought to a screeching halt the era of leveraged buyouts and hostile takeovers. Who benefited? Not the employees or the managers, not the consumers, not even Campeau, who was forced into personal bankruptcy. The only winners were the lawyers and investment bankers who collected huge fees.

England's Sir James Goldsmith, who had earned the reputation of being an "asset stripper," set his sights on Goodyear Tire and Rubber Company, the major tiremaker in the world. Although the company and its resident city and state were successful in fighting off Goldsmith's takeover attempt, Goldsmith made $93.75 million in "greenmail" when he consented to be bought off by Goodyear. Legal blackmail on a grand scale!

Chapter 16 describes the Alaskan oil spill and the issue of "how much corporate responsibility for environmental protection"? Just after midnight, on March 24, 1989, the worst maritime environmental disaster in U. S. history began as a huge oil tanker, the Exxon Valdez, ran aground. Although Exxon eventually spent $2.5 billion in cleanup efforts, these payments did not allay the criticisms. And yet the blame for the disaster was not uniquely Exxon's.

In the next four chapters, we examine cases that as recently as the summer of 1992 were still front-page news. In Chapter 17, Dow Corning and its silicone breast implants triggered perhaps the greatest medical controversy since abortion. Critics and supporters of breast implants squared off, with

Dow Corning and the Food and Drug Administration (FDA) in the middle. There was plenty of blame for everyone, but was the issue as black as the opponents of breast implants and their lawyers claimed, and was Dow Corning as culpable?

In Chapter 18, an effective marketing strategy is roundly criticized. The sin was targeting a somewhat stronger beer, a malt liquor, to ghetto youth via promotion by rock stars, billboard advertising, and a name that critics maintained was highly suggestive in the most negative sense: PowerMaster. At the height of the controversy, ministers led their flocks on billboard white-washing campaigns. Yet more sober observers raised the question of why black consumers could not be allowed the same right to make their own buying decisions as whites.

In Chapter 19 we examine the most current controversies facing the beleaguered tobacco industry. The issue of targeting particular brands to the ghetto is again a focus of critical black ministerial attention. So is the successful Joe Camel cartoon character, which has been particularly appealing to children, thereby promoting smoking by young people, or so the critics maintain. Criticisms of the aggressive efforts of cigarette companies in targeting Asian and Eastern European countries as alternative markets, now that cigarette consumption is falling in the United States and Western Europe, are described and evaluated.

In Chapter 20, three examples of abusive practices toward consumers are examined: health clubs, small loan firms (with ITT again in the limelight), and auto repairs, with Sears' Auto Centers the scapegoat for the industry. High pressure, deception, bait and switch, padding bills—these are the types of abuses that consumers and state attorneys general are casting critical eyes upon.

Conclusions (Part III)

The last case in the book, Chapter 21, was intended as a contrasting model of how a firm can handle adversity in a responsible, caring, yet highly effective manner for its own long-term interest. In 1982, Johnson & Johnson suddenly discovered that a number of capsules of its most important and profitable product, Tylenol, had been deliberately contaminated with cyanide poison. The perpetrator was never found, but this conscienceless act was thought by many to be a death blow for Tylenol. But it was not. In fact, the company's reputation for being a trusted corporate citizen was enhanced by the way it responded to the crisis.

However, as this book goes into final production, Johnson & Johnson is now being charged with "unconscionable" pricing of a cancer drug, charging a hundredfold higher for it than for an older veterinary version of the drug. One wonders whether any firm is immune to temptations to violate the public trust.

In our concluding chapter we summarize and categorize the many insights that can be drawn from these cases. Again, the great value of these cases is the learning that can be gained and transferred to other firms, other industries, other times—learning that can help guide executives in avoiding ethics-related mistakes and coping better and more responsibly with crisis situations.

Where possible, we have depicted the major personalities involved in these cases. We invite you to imagine yourself in their positions, facing the temptations, the problems, and the decisions they faced. What would you have done differently, and why? We invite you to participate in the discussion questions and role-playing episodes that appear within and at the end of each chapter. We urge you to consider the pros and cons of alternative actions and to be objective in your analysis and proposals.

One

CLASSIC ETHICAL
VIOLATIONS

2

General Motors' Corvair vs. Ralph Nader: Triggering the Age of Consumerism

Ralph Nader precipitated a new era in business-society relations. His best-selling book *Unsafe at Any Speed* was an indictment of the safety of General Motors' rear-engine Corvair. Spawned in an age of apathy by carmakers toward highway deaths, the book had two enduring consequences.

1. It fanned consumer resentment toward certain business practices, a militancy to be known as *consumerism* and which was to have major implications for marketers and business in general (see the information box discussing consumerism).
2. It compelled General Motors to eventually withdraw the Corvair from the market when the company realized that carmakers could no longer escape blame for downplaying safety using the old rationale that drivers, not cars, caused accidents.

Nader has been a major force for change, but GM contributed to Nader's influence by not only disregarding customer safety but also attempting to discredit and intimidate him.

HORROR SCENARIOS

John Bortolozzo was a California Highway Patrol officer. In 1961, while patrolling in Santa Barbara, he noticed a Chevrolet Corvair approaching in the opposite lane. Approvingly he noted its observance of the 35-mile-per-hour speed limit. Suddenly he stiffened. The Corvair suddenly veered to the left and then turned over!

He rushed to the wreck and saw an arm with a wedding band and a wristwatch lying on the ground. He extricated an injured woman while trying to stop the blood gushing from the stub of her arm. He remembered that the woman was calm, only murmuring, "Something went wrong with my steering."[1]

Officer Bortolozzo later testified in a suit brought by the driver, Mrs. Rose Pierini, against GM that in his opinion the design of the Corvair caused it to go out of control and flip over. At that point, GM decided to settle the case. Mrs. Pierini was awarded $76,000.

In 1962, Doreen Collins was driving her fiancé's 1960 Corvair on a narrow two-lane highway. Suddenly it swerved out of control and hit a 16-ton truck head-on. Her fiancé and a child were killed. She brought suit claiming that the car was "inherently defective." While the judge seemed sympathetic, GM lawyers argued that the fault lay with Miss Collins, who was an inexperienced driver. She had driven the Corvair for only four months and had only a learner's driving permit. They claimed that she had panicked and that the accident had nothing to do with any defect in the car. The jury acquitted GM of responsibility

In a celebrated Florida case, two state legislators were driving on U.S. 19 when their 1962 Corvair overturned and killed one of them. In a trial that lasted six weeks, General Motors was again acquitted of any negligence.

More suits were to follow. By mid-1969, 150 had been brought against GM, with most of these settled out of court.

GENERAL MOTORS AND THE CORVAIR

In the mid-1960s, General Motors was the behemoth of American industry. In 1966, it employed 734,600 people in the United States, with a payroll of $5.1 billion. That year its net profit was $2.1 billion after taxes, the highest profit ever recorded by a U.S. firm. This came from sales of $20.7 billion, representing 5,348,568 cars sold. The Chevrolet Division led the company, with sales of 2,417,177 cars.

Chevrolet introduced the Corvair in 1959. The car featured an aluminum air-cooled engine mounted in the rear, with a swing-axle independent rear suspension. The Corvair gave the U.S. consumer an affordable sports car reminiscent of European sports cars, in particular the Porsche, but without their huge price tags. It was hailed as the most exciting innovation since automatic transmissions.

---

[1]This is described in Ralph Nader's *Unsafe at Any Speed* (New York: Grossman, 1965), p. 5.

HISTORICAL PERIODS OF CONSUMER MILITANCY (CONSUMERISM) IN THE UNITED STATES

Dates	Precipitator	Consequences
Early 1900s	Harvey W. Wiley and "poison squad" of 12 healthy young men who were fed adulterants daily with marked deterioration of health publicized dangers of preservatives then being used in food.	Law forbidding adulteration and misbranding of foods and drugs sold in interstate commerce.
	Upton Sinclair's book, *The Jungle*, depicted unsanitary conditions in meat-packing plants.	Law providing for federal inspection of slaughtering, packing, and canning plants that shipped across state lines.
1930s	Drug elixir sulfanilamide was introduced without adequate safety testing, and 100 people died.	Food, Drug, and Cosmetic Act of 1936.
Mid-1960s	Ralph Nader's book, *Unsafe at Any Speed*, and Rachel Carson's *Silent Spring* were published.	A plethora of consumer protection and environmental laws at all levels: federal, state, and local.

INVITATION TO DISCUSS
The period of consumer militancy starting in the mid-1960s has lasted far longer than those of earlier periods—it is still evident today. Why has it had such staying power?

In designing the car, General Motors wanted a small, light-weight car with good fuel economy that would seat six passengers comfortably while giving a ride comparable to a standard Chevrolet sedan. With the rear-engine, reardrive design, the floor hump for the drive shaft could be eliminated. Engineers chose the swing-axle rear suspension for lower cost, ease of assembly, ease of service, and greater simplicity of design. Production costs were thereby lowered.

However, the design had a potential hazard. On the 1960–1964 Corvairs, the rear wheel was mounted on the control arm, which hinged and pivoted on an axis near the center of the vehicle. In a sharp turn, this could cause the outside wheel to tuck under and cause steering difficulties. Until the 1964 Corvair, only the shock absorbers limited this problem, but this is not a function shock absorbers are designed to perform. Tire blowouts, wind gusts, cornering maneuvers, and the second leg of S-shaped curves could cause the wheels to tuck under. At this critical point, it took an expert driver to take the corrective action to avoid trouble. But the Corvair was promoted as a sports car particularly appealing to youth. In trying to take curves at high speeds, the young and inexperienced drivers were especially vulnerable.

Yet, these cars were tested on proving grounds, in laboratories, and otherwise analyzed by engineers to provide information about any design limitations before being put into production. Actually, a considerable internal controversy arose among GM engineers about what some felt were serious design flaws. But Ed Cole, Chevrolet's general manager, who was also an engineer and product innovator, was "enthralled with the idea of building the first modern, rear-engine American car."[2]

The problem with the Corvair suspension was so bad that several enterprising companies realized that money was to be made from the flawed design. For example, EMPI, a California company, developed and marketed an accessory specifically for installing beneath the rear control arm of Corvairs. This stabilizer was quite effective in keeping the rear wheels in optimum contact with the roadway.

Ford, which was also considering a rear-engine compact to compete with the Corvair, had suspicions that the Corvair design was flawed. In 1959, it acquired a Corvair that it tested on the Ford proving ground for comparison with the Ford Falcon. The engineering report stated:

> These pictures have shown only that the Corvair exhibited instability under extreme cornering conditions, under which the Falcon remained stable . . . While the average driver of the Corvair will not encounter difficulty under most normal driving conditions, there are frequently encountered emergency conditions such as slippery pavement or emergency maneuvering in which the Corvair falls considerably short of our handling standards.[3]

MOUNTING CRITICISM

By the early 1960s, criticism began mounting. The legal department at GM was inundated with lawsuits. But GM executives and associates were also becoming victims. The son of the general manager of the Cadillac Division

[2]J. Patrick Wright, *On a Clear Day You Can See General Motors* (Grosse Pointe, Mich.: Wright Enterprises, 1979), p. 54.
[3]"Corvair's Second Case," *Time*, Sept. 10, 1965, p. 37.

was killed in a Corvair. The son of an executive vice president was critically injured. So was the niece of Semon (Bunkie) Knudsen, head of the Pontiac Division. And the son of an Indianapolis dealer was killed in the car.[4]

Still, nothing was done to make the car safer until the 1964 models. Then, at the insistence of Knudsen, then head of Chevrolet, top management of GM relented and authorized installation of a stabilizing bar in the rear that counteracted the tendency of the car to flip. John DeLorean, former GM executive, noted that the cost of the modification was about $15 per car. But for years the top brass refused to permit this because it was "too expensive."[5] What price is a human life worth?

In May 1965, Dr. Seymour Charles, a General Motors stockholder and founder of Physicians for Automobile Safety, made a plea to management to recall all remaining 1960–1963 Corvairs so that the stabilizing parts could be installed. This was the first time a shareholder had ever publicly raised the question about unsafe vehicle design. Charles estimated that the recall would cost $25 million, equivalent to one-half of one day's gross sales, or less than five days net profits to GM at that time.[6] But GM refused to act.

The book, *The Investigation of Ralph Nader*, reported that the attorney in charge of general litigation for GM was in favor of recalling the 1960–1963 Corvairs. He had driven the car on the proving grounds at General Motors, and it had rolled over, although he was apparently not injured. However, three weeks later, at the age of 54, he died of a cerebral thrombosis. It is not known if the accident contributed to his death. One can only speculate on what might have happened if this attorney had lived and pressured for recall.[7]

It remained for the power of the press, in particular the soon-to-appear best-seller of Ralph Nader, to stimulate corrective action.

RALPH NADER

Ralph Nader was born in 1934, so he was not much more than 30 years old when he came to national prominence. He was 6 ft 2 in., slender, and unmarried. He graduated from Princeton University magna cum laude in 1955, and from Harvard Law School with distinction in 1958.

He served a six-month tour of active duty in the Army Reserve and then entered private law practice in Hartford, Connecticut. After four years, he left commercial law and went to Washington to pursue the cause of what he liked to call "public interest law." He was particularly interested in

[4]*On a Clear Day*, p. 55.
[5]*Ibid*. p. 56
[6]"Profits vs. Engineering: The Corvair Story," *Nation*, Nov. 1, 1965, p. 295
[7]Thomas Whiteside, *The Investigation of Ralph Nader* (New York: Arbor House, 1972).

automobile safety, but the field was not very lucrative. He supported himself by occasional lectures and articles on auto safety for the *New Republic* and the *Nation*. In 1963, he also began writing on auto safety for the *Christian Science Monitor*. Then he came to the attention of Daniel P. Moynihan, who was assistant secretary of labor, and began consulting for him as a writer and researcher. Just before the end of 1964, Senator Abraham A. Ribicoff's Subcommittee on Executive Reorganization invited Nader to become an unpaid adviser during the preparation of upcoming safety hearings.

During the summer of 1964, Richard Grossman, a book publisher, was looking for a writer to prepare a book on auto safety. Nader was mentioned as someone very knowledgeable about this subject. The resulting book, *Unsafe at Any Speed*, was published in 1965.

In his book, Nader accused the auto industry, as well as the traffic safety establishment, of failure to protect the public from poorly designed automobiles and charged the government with failing to set adequate safety standards for cars. Although others had written on the subject of auto safety, Nader cast blame on the entire industry's concerted negligence in depriving the public not only of safe vehicles but also of basic information concerning the vast numbers of defective cars capable of causing highway deaths. He focused his attack on one particular car: the 1960 through 1963 models of the Corvair. He accused GM of "one of the greatest acts of industrial irresponsibility in the present century," in describing the Rose Pierini suit against GM.[8]

> A great problem of contemporary life is how to control the power of economic interests which ignore the harmful effects of their applied science and technology. The automobile tragedy is one of the most serious of these man-made assaults on the human body. The history of that tragedy reveals many obstacles which must be overcome in the taming of any mechanical or biological hazard which is a by-product of industry or commerce. Our society's obligation to protect the body rights of its citizens with vigorous resolve and ample resources requires the precise, authoritative articulation and front-rank support which is being devoted to civil rights.[9]

The press quickly disseminated the allegations in the book. Nader was immediately thrust into the limelight, with frequent interviews and television appearances. On January 6, 1966, he held a press conference in Detroit concerning auto safety and his criticisms of the auto manufacturers. He had invited each of the four major auto firms to send representatives to debate him. None showed up.

---

[8]Ralph Nader, *Unsafe at Any Speed* (New York: Grossman, 1972), p. 4.
[9]*Ibid.* p. ix.

The next day he went to Des Moines, Iowa, to participate in a hearing conducted by State Attorney General Lawrence Scalise. During these proceedings Nader became suspicious that he was being followed. He informed Scalise, who assigned state officials to investigate. No evidence could be found to support Nader's uneasiness, but this was the beginning of General Motors' harassment of Ralph Nader, an action that was to backfire on GM and lend credence and support to Nader's allegations.

THE INVESTIGATION OF RALPH NADER

Written in late 1965, a memorandum to investigators instructed:

> Our job is to check his life and current activities to determine what makes him tick, such as his real interest in safety, his supporters, if any, his politics, his marital status, his friends, his women, boys, etc., drinking, dope, jobs—in fact, all facets of his life.[10]

The principals were Aloysius Power, General Motors' general counsel, and Vincent Gillen, a former FBI agent who ran a detective agency in New York. James Roche, the president of General Motors, was thought to be implicated but was able to convince later congressional investigations that he knew nothing about the extent and direction of the probe of Nader. Roche admitted to hiring detectives to investigate Nader but stated that it was only to determine whether Nader was involved in any of the Corvair cases still pending.

The harassment of Nader began in January of 1966 and continued until March. It included surveillance, late-night telephone calls, and apparent efforts to lure Nader into compromising situations with young women. Nader's friends and associates from his Connecticut hometown of Winsted were questioned about his drinking habits, driving record, sex life, attitudes toward Jews, political beliefs, and credit rating. His unlisted Washington, D.C., telephone would ring in the middle of the night and "ominous-sounding voices" would ask him, "Why don't you go back to Connecticut, buddy-boy?" Gillen was to admit to the Senate subcommittee that he had been told "to get something, somewhere on this guy to get him out of their hair and shut him up."[11] The press was quick to side with Nader and to criticize the "intimidation." They raised the question of the right of General Motors to pry into a person's private life.[12]

---

[10]"GM Hired the Dick," *New Republic*, March 19, 1966, pp. 8–9.

[11]"Auto Safety: Nader Again," *Newsweek* 69, No. 8 (Feb. 20, 1967): 85–86.

[12] For example, James Ridgway and David Sanford, "The Nader Affair," *New Republic*, Feb. 18, 1967, p. 9; Elinor Langer, "Auto Safety: Nader vs. GM," *Science*, Apr. 1, 1965, p. 48; and "Private Eyes vs. Public Hearings," *Newsweek*, Apr. 4, 1966, pp. 77–78.

After the hearing information came out, Nader sued GM for $26 million in an invasion of privacy suit; he also sued Vincent Gillen for $100,000 on the same charge. Immediately GM abandoned Gillen, but this proved to be a serious blunder on GM's part. Gillen decided to cooperate with Nader's attorneys, as long as the civil suit would be dropped. Gillen had taped all conversations he had with GM's executive counsel and proved that GM was indeed trying to harass and discredit Nader. In 1970, Nader accepted a settlement out of court for $425,000, which according to Nader's attorney was the largest such settlement for an invasion-of privacy action. After legal fees, Nader was left with $284,000, which he put into consumer advocacy programs, including a renewed attack on the Corvair.[13]

Thus, General Motors' inept handling of the Nader affair put the company back into the villain's role it had been trying to shake off regarding product safety and made a hero of one of its most determined critics.

CONSEQUENCES FOR GENERAL MOTORS

The publicity given the Corvair case and Ralph Nader brought General Motors a tarnished image, a reputation of deceit, dishonesty, and uncon-cern for customer safety. Sales and profits were affected. And lawsuits by Corvair owners proliferated.

In May 1969, 10 years and 1,710,018 sales later, the last Corvair came off the assembly line at General Motors' Willow Run, Michigan, plant. During 1960, its first full year of production, 229,985 cars had been sold. By 1964, Corvair sales were down to 193,642 cars. In 1965, Nader's book was published, and in 1966 only 88,951 Corvairs were sold. By 1968, sales had dropped to 12,977. Also during this time, competition was increasing from European and Japanese imports, as well as from other sporty cars such as Ford's Mustang, but more than anything else Corvair was done in by the attacks of Ralph Nader.

In view of Corvair's plummeting sales after 1965, why did General Motors continue to manufacture the car as long as it did? Legal reasons may have accounted for this. Dropping the car might have been construed as an admission of guilt in view of all the pending court cases and public and congressional questions of the automobile's safety.

The Corvair blunder had far-reaching repercussions. President Lyndon Johnson proposed the Traffic Safety Act, authorizing the secretary of commerce to set safety standards. Detroit was to be given two

---

[13] Ed Cray, *Chrome Colossus: General Motors and Its Times* (San Francisco: McGraw-Hill, 1980), p. 427.

years to increase safety or the government would step in. The act was passed by the Senate on June 23, 1966, and signed into law by the president on September 5, 1966, as the National Traffic and Motor Vehicle Safety Act of 1966. The new law required that (1) the secretary of transportation establish appropriate federal automobile standards, (2) civil sanctions be imposed on manufacturers who produce vehicles or parts of vehicles not meeting these standards, and (3) the manufacturer be required to notify its customers of any defects or flaws later discovered in the vehicle.

Thus, an important initial step was taken to improve automobile safety for the general public. This was to lead to other advances, such as padded dashes, passive restraints, antilock brakes, and air bags.

FACTORS BEHIND THE DEBACLE

We can identify these major factors that led General Motors down the path of the Corvair disaster:

Ignoring or Condoning the Risks

Here we see a classic disregard for the customer, except as a source of revenue. The objective was to design cars to make sales and to maximize profits. Safety was not a top priority; keeping costs down and maximizing profits was.

In the late 1950s, GM wanted to build a car that could compete with the smaller, lighter, European cars, yet be priced low enough for widespread demand. By 1959, four years after the initial decision, the Corvair was introduced. Perhaps this was too short a time to develop an innovative product as complex as a car. The profit motive persuaded the company to rush the car to market, despite "a few imperfections."

Since its beginning, the automobile industry had had no standard safety regulations. The automakers primarily depended on the Society of Automotive Engineers to set safety standards. But one might suspect that this body was not entirely objective, since members were employed by the key automakers, who were eager to produce vehicles at the lowest possible cost. Stringent safety standards would increase manufacturing costs, and the jobs of SAE members might even be in jeopardy. Perhaps there was a crucial lack of communication between the engineers and the top-level executives most interested in bottom-line results. We are left to wonder why no engineer spoke out or became a whistleblower, given driving-test evidence of product instability and possible danger. (See the information box discussing *whistleblowing*.)

WHISTLEBLOWING

A whistleblower is an insider in an organization who publicizes alleged organizational misconduct. Such misconduct may involve unethical practices of all kinds, from fraud, restraint of trade, bribes, coercion, to unsafe products and facilities, as well as violations of other laws and regulations. Presumably, the whistleblower has exhausted the possibilities for changing the questionable practices within the normal organizational channels and as a last resort has taken the matter to public officials and/or the press, which is often panting for sensational evidence of misconduct.

Since whistleblowing may result in contract cancellations and lost jobs, those who become whistleblowers may be vilified by their fellow workers and ostracized by their firms. This makes whistleblowing a course of action only for the truly courageous whose concern for societal best interest outweighs their concern for themselves. (However, there is sometimes a thin line between an employee who truly believes the public interest is jeopardized and the individual who has a gripe or is a fanatic. There are some who believe management is condoning misconduct when in fact such misconduct may be isolated and without management awareness or acceptance.)

Ralph Nader, in a 1972 book on whistleblowing, suggested that corporate employees have a primary duty to protect society that exists over and above secondary obligations to the corporation. He gives examples of whistleblowing heroes, as well as courses of action for other would-be whistleblowers.[14]

INVITATION TO DISCUSS
Do you think you could ever be a whistleblower? Under what circumstances?

Intimidation of Ralph Nader

GM added immeasurably to its problems by its injudicious investigation of its major critic. Perhaps such an investigation could have been supported *if* it had been a routine attempt to ensure that no conflict of interest existed between Nader and one or more plaintiffs in lawsuits against GM. But it went too far—beyond the bounds of the ethical to the point of invasion of privacy and harassment. The rationale behind the overzealous probe was to protect General Motors' reputation and discredit Ralph Nader. In fact, the investigation tarnished GM's reputation and made Ralph Nader a hero.

---

[14]Ralph Nader, Peter Petkas, and Nate Blackwell, *Whistleblowing* (New York: Bantam Books, 1972).

Lack of Top Executive Communication and Control

The president, James Roche, apparently relied on the general counsel to handle the matter of Nader. Roche claimed he did not know what the general counsel was really doing, and apparently he received no progress reports concerning the investigation. The general counsel, James Powers, did not exercise close restraints on the chief investigator, Vincent Gillen. So we have a situation of a president of a major corporation and his chief attorney not being on top of what was actually happening in the field, until too late.

Perhaps the directives by top management were unclear or were poorly understood. Certainly, the increasing popularity of Nader and his mounting criticisms may have been interpreted by subordinates as pressure to intensify this probe, so that they went beyond the bounds of what was proper and expected by management. On the other hand, protestations of ignorance by top executives may have simply been buck-passing, an attempt to escape blame.

WHAT CAN BE LEARNED?

Learning Insight. *One person can make a difference.*

Since the notorious Corvair case, we have come to realize that business cannot be relied upon to protect us from safety deficiencies in its own products. The government has thus become actively involved. Ralph Nader is not single-handedly responsible for the changes in product safety regulations, but his well-researched book and his consumer-interest efforts have helped bring this about. Even General Motors back in 1965 must have realized his potential influence or they would have ignored him.

The example of Ralph Nader shows us that the small can successfully shake the mighty. Our importance in the scheme of things has suddenly achieved a new meaning and vitality—because of Nader. Exercising the power of the individual, however, is not for the weak and timid but for the courageous and persevering.

Learning Insight. *Apathy toward society promotes governmental intervention.*

For decades, automobile manufacturers ignored many car safety considerations—even though it was technologically possible to make cars safer—because adding safety features would raise production costs. Furthermore, the industry had the mind-set that safety did not sell, that customers would not pay extra to lower their risk of injury or death. That mind-set was not totally unfounded, because we see even today that some people resent the requirement that motorcyclists wear safety helmets. (The issue of cost versus safety is somewhat muddled by the propensity of some people to equate greater risk with masculinity.)

Eventually, business and public apathy toward the best interests of society is often violently overcome, perhaps by best-selling books such as *Unsafe at Any Speed* and Rachel Carson's *Silent Spring* or by investigative reporters. As public apathy shifts into a smoldering, and then more vehement, resentment, government eventually imposes regulations on the industry. The following diagram illustrates the common progression:

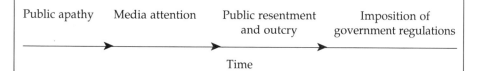

| Public apathy | Media attention | Public resentment and outcry | Imposition of government regulations |

Time

We see this classic pattern in the Corvair case, which resulted in the National Traffic and Motor Vehicle Safety Act of 1966.

What can a firm do about this scenario? The obvious answer is to be fully responsive to *serving* the customer. Serving implies several things.

1. Meeting customers' needs as efficiently as possible, both to hold costs down without sacrificing reasonable quality standards and safety and also to maximize customer utility from the product or service.

2. Protecting the general public—society—from unsafe or environmentally dangerous products or manufacturing facilities.

For the auto industry, an unsafe product, such as a Corvair that is uncontrollable under certain circumstances, endangers not only the customer who bought the car but innocent people who are exposed to an accident-prone situation.

The threat of litigation should motivate most firms today to exercise reasonable prudence in their products and operations. But the final motivation to correct any inherently dangerous situation should be the threat of governmental intervention. Such intervention is not always objective or most effective. It may vary from the extremes of punitive and bureaucratic nit-picking to weak and inadequate protection. At the very least, government regulation involves compliance, red tape, and constraints. Yet, many would see this as the just desserts of firms who are careless with the public welfare.

Learning Insight. *Emphasis on maximizing short-term profits can lead to flawed business practices.*

While a firm needs to make a profit in order to survive and prosper, the single-minded pursuit of maximizing immediate profits can be perilous. It often is incompatible with the customer's best interest as well as the longterm success of the firm. We saw this starkly with the Corvair. We will encounter other cases in which short-term concern with maximizing—or protecting—profits has led to abusive practices and cover-ups, as well as public disgrace.

Most firms are in the business for the long haul; such business depends on continued customer satisfaction and protection. Such a mission may mean sacrificing some profits and increasing some costs in order to solidify relationships and ensure customer satisfaction in the future.

Learning Insight. *Top management is ultimately responsible.*

Top management is ultimately responsible and accountable for what goes on within the organization no matter how large the organization may be. This is a sacred principle of leadership and authority. Top management is quick to take credit—and be rewarded with huge bonuses—for a firm's success; to repudiate any responsibility for the organization's failings or misdeeds is hardly appropriate. So, the protestations of ignorance of the Corvair-Nader affair by top GM brass should in no way excuse them. (We will encounter other buck-passing by top executives in some of the cases that follow.) But while top management may not know the details of any misdeeds, they are instrumental in fostering a climate in the organization of unconcern for customer welfare and scrupulously honest conduct, subordinating everything to short-term profit maximization. Yes, the ultimate responsibility for corporate violations of the public trust should rest with top management.

Learning Insight. *Mechanistic attitudes sometimes prevail in executives suites.*

Something seems to happen to the conscience and the moral sensitivity of top executives. They commission actions in their corporate personas that they would hardly dream of doing in their private lives. John DeLorean, former GM executive, was one of the first to note this dichotomy:

These were not immoral men who were bringing out this car [the Corvair]. These were warm, breathing men with families and children who as private individuals would never have approved this project for a minute if they were told, "You are going to kill and injure people with this car." But these same men, in a business atmosphere, where everything is reduced to terms of costs, profit goals, and productive deadlines, were able to approve a product most of them wouldn't have considered approving as individuals.[15]

We will encounter this same mechanistic mind-set, devoid of a human context, in a number of other cases. We have to raise the question: Why this lockstep obsession with sales and profit at all costs? See the following information box for a discussion of this question.

WHY THE QUESTIONABLE ETHICAL DECISIONS OF "GROUPTHINK"?

The callousness regarding the Corvair, despite increasing evidence that it was a "killer" car, would, as John DeLorean pointed out, probably never have prevailed if an individual was making the decision outside the corporate environment. But bring in *groupthink*, which is decision-by-committee, and add to this a high degree of organizational loyalty (versus loyalty to the public interest), and such callousness can manifest itself. Why can the moral standards of groupthink be so much lower than individual moral standards?

Perhaps the answer lies in the "pack mentality" that can characterize certain committees or groups highly committed to organizational goals. All else then becomes subordinated to these goals, being a single-minded perspective. Within any committee, individual responsibility for decisions is diluted since this is a committee decision. Furthermore, without the contrary arguments of a strong "devil's advocate" (i.e., one who argues the opposing viewpoint, sometimes simply to be sure that all sides of an issue are considered), a follow-the-leader syndrome can take place, with no one willing to oppose the majority views.

But there is more to it than that. Chester Barnard, a business executive, scholar, and philosopher, noted the paradox: people have a number of private moral codes that affect behavior in different situations, and these codes are not always compatible. Codes for private life, regarding family and religion, may be far different from codes for business life. Throughout the history of business, it has not been unusual to find that the scrupulous and God-fearing churchgoer is far different when he or she conducts business during the week: a far lower ethical standard prevails during the week than on the Sabbath. Nor has it been unusual to find that a person can be a paragon of love, understanding, and empathy with his or her family but be totally lacking in such qualities with employees or customers. (Even tyrants guilty of the most extreme atrocities, such as

---

[15]*On a Clear Day*, pp. 5–6.

Hitler and Saddam Hussein, have been known to exude great tenderness and consideration for their intimates.)

It takes a strong personal code of ethics to control one's conduct in the presence of strong contrary desires or impulses.[16]

INVITATION TO DISCUSS:
What does it take for a person to resist and not accept the majority viewpoint? What do you think would be the characteristics of such a person? Do you see yourself as such a gadfly?

FOR THOUGHT AND DISCUSSION

1. Can the president or CEO of an organization disavow himself or herself of the illegal or unethical actions of subordinates?
2. How can an organization's orientation be changed from short-term to long-term profit maximization? Be as specific as possible.
3. How do you account for the fact that the engineering staff of GM was negligent in revealing the dangerous deficiencies of the Corvair? How could a better customer orientation be fostered?
4. How do you account for the way the Ralph Nader investigators exceeded the bounds of moral and ethical conduct? How would you design controls to prevent such abuses from occurring again?
5. The two earlier periods of consumer militancy were short-lived. The present one has lasted over 20 years, even though it is not as well-publicized today as in the past, that's because the worst of the perceived problems have been corrected. How do you account for the long-lasting consumerism of today compared to the short-lived agitation at the turn of the century and in the 1930s?

INVITATION TO ROLE PLAY

1. Place yourself in the role of an engineer at Chevrolet's Corvair unit. You have strong reasons to believe the car is unsafe, but higher management is unresponsive to your concerns. What do you do now?
2. Place yourself in the position of James Roche, the president of GM. You want to instill in your massive organization greater concern for the customer. Discuss how you would go about fostering and controlling such an orientation and commitment among your executives and workers. What problems do you see?

---

[16]Chester I. Barnard, *The Functions of the Executive* (Cambridge, Mass.: Harvard Univ. Press, 1938), p. 263.

INVITATION TO RESEARCH

1. Update the activities of Ralph Nader after the Corvair episode. What conclusions do you draw from his career?
2. Review Nader's book on whistleblowing and, in particular, his recommended courses of action for would-be whistleblowers. In your opinion, how practical are these actions? Do you think you could be a whistleblower? Why or why not?

3

Union Carbide: Assault on the Ohio Valley

Ralph Nader also became involved in an environmental dispute concerning a major polluter, Union Carbide Corporation. Nader helped pressure the company and governmental bureaucracy toward remedial action after some 20 years of worsening air pollution and after a Nader-sponsored book, *The Vanishing Air*, published in 1970, highlighted this and other national environmental concerns.

THE OHIO VALLEY POLLUTION PROBLEM

The Ohio River between Ohio and West Virginia flows through a relatively narrow valley with rounded hills rising 200 to 300 feet above the valley floor on either side. The scenic valley is partially protected from strong winds, but this tends to cause pollutants to accumulate in high concentrations. The valley had become a home to large metal-processing and chemical plants. And these have created pollution, both from their manufacturing processes and from the combustion of coal used to meet their energy requirements.

Union Carbide began its operations in the Ohio Valley in 1950, with the opening of an electrometallurgical plant in Riverview, Ohio. This was shortly followed by plants in Alloy, West Virginia, Anmoore, West Virginia, Marietta, Ohio, and Institute, West Virginia. While the plants made a major contribution to the economy of this area, it was not long before pollution problems became evident. As early as 1951, a citizens' committee was formed to fight air pollution, and in 1954 it pressured Union Carbide to install dust control equipment. However, air pollution grew worse as the industry expanded, and in 1964 a county health department complained that Union Carbide was causing a major problem to local residents with its emissions of heavy soot.

In March 1967, officials from the Department of Health, Education and Welfare (HEW) convened an interstate conference in Parkersburg, West Virginia, to examine air pollution problems in the area around Parkersburg and Marietta. During the conference, federal officials presented a 15-year documentation of high air pollution levels (high enough to cause injury to vegetation and property), soot and ash, foul odors, and high incidences of cardio-respiratory disease. Local citizens pleaded for help. But in spite of strong evidence, the question of emissions was never resolved, and the first Parkersburg conference proved to be fruitless. As the Nader-sponsored book described the result:

> The agency [the National Air Pollution Control Administration (NAPCA)] had allowed itself to be hornswoggled by the Union Carbide Corporation, the region's number one environmental enemy, the Ohio State Department of Health, and Ohio Congressman Clarence Millart. The indifference of the Secretary and the timidity of the West Virginia Air Pollution Control Commission helped to make the "take" complete.[1]

UNION CARBIDE INTRANSIGENCE

From the beginning, Union Carbide had exhibited a cavalier attitude and apparent lack of concern about environmental degradation. The company repudiated any assumption of social responsibility for the worsening Ohio Valley contamination. But the battle lines were being drawn. By 1970, environmentalists were to label Union Carbide's ferro-alloy plant in Alloy, West Virginia, "the world's smokiest factory." Dense layers of soot-laden smoke streamed constantly from the plant, dumping masses of black grit on nearby communities. In all, it was alleged that the factory poured out more health-endangering particles in one year than the total emitted by all of New York City.[2]

Eventually, Union Carbide was to become a symbol of corporate resistance to pollution controls. It was to find itself the center of a controversy

---

[1]John C. Esposito and Larry J. Silverman, *Vanishing Air* (New York: Grossman, 1970), p. 123.

[2]"Union Carbide's Big Cleanup Job," *Business Week*, Nov. 9, 1974, p. 184.

that pitted one of the nation's largest corporations against local citizens, environmentalists, and the federal government. It was to receive national attention after it denied agents of the federal government's National Air Pollution Control Administration (NAPCA) entry into its Marietta plant.

The Runaround

On August 29, 1967, five months after the first Parkersburg conference, NAPCA sent a letter to Union Carbide plant manager G. G. Borden asking for permission to inspect the Marietta plant. Borden replied on September 7, 1967, that he was "giving the matter careful consideration, but with vacations, etc., [he was] unable to help at that time."[3] Four months went by with no further reply. NAPCA repeated its request on January 11, 1968. Union Carbide replied 20 days later that at this time they were already spending a considerable amount of money on antipollution devices. However, no specifics were mentioned, and NAPCA's request for an inspection was completely ignored.

NAPCA then sent its request to Union Carbide's chief executive officer. The company responded by sending Dr. J. S. Whitaker, its Coordinator for Environmental Health, to meet with NAPCA in April 1968. Whitaker informed the agency that the requested information already had been supplied to the Ohio State Department of Health, and that it would be more appropriate to obtain this information from them. But the Ohio State Department of Health denied all knowledge. So the runaround continued.

In October 1969, a second conference was held at Parkersburg. Studies cited there noted that emissions of particulate matter from the Union Carbide plants alone had increased substantially. Increasing complaints from local residents were primarily focused on Union Carbide. The firm was accused of emitting 44,000 pounds per day of particulates and 22,000 pounds per hour of sulfur oxides. However, Carbide boycotted the conference on the grounds that it was working with state authorities, not federal agencies.[4]

Pressure Mounts

In the fall of 1970, a series of severe air pollution episodes brought Union Carbide once again to national attention. The *New York Times* began running articles describing the controversy between Union Carbide and the local residents. People in the Ohio Valley were beginning to publicly voice their indignation and fears. In Anmoore, West Virginia, site of Union

---

[3]As reported in *New York Times*, July 6, 1970, p. 26.
[4]"Along the Ohio: A Test of Will," *Chemical Week*, Feb. 10, 1971, p. 47.

Carbide's Carbon Products Division, Mr. and Mrs. O. D. Hagedorn started a newsletter devoted exclusively to Union Carbide's activities, or lack thereof. The newsletter was distributed to local citizens through merchants, and copies were sent to the West Virginia Air Pollution Control Department, the local plant manager, company offices in Charleston, West Virginia, and the chairman of the board of Union Carbide in New York City.

Still no response. Then the Hagedorns took matters one step further and filed a class action suit against Union Carbide and federal and state air pollution control officials. The complaint was joined by 50 other families from a town of 1000. They contended in the $100,000 suit that they had been denied their constitutional right to a decent place to live because of the pollution created by Union Carbide.[5]

Now Ralph Nader became involved. He wrote letters and organized citizen meetings in Union Carbide factory towns. He was also successful in getting higher taxes levied against Union Carbide by these towns in an effort to make the firm pay for some of the damage caused. In 1970, *Vanishing Air*, a book by a Nader study group, condemned with specific examples the growing environmental problem and the lack of sufficient concern across America.

In 1970, the government's power against polluters was strengthened by the Clean Air Act of 1970 and the newly formed Environmental Protection Agency (EPA). The administrator of the EPA, William D. Ruckelshaus, singled out Union Carbide as a test case in the government's efforts to get industry to comply with the Clean Air Act. The state of West Virginia also joined in setting stringent standards and regulations on the emissions of particulate matter from many manufacturing processes.

Eventually, Union Carbide yielded to federal and state pressure. On January 14, 1971, it agreed to clean up the pollution caused by the Marietta plant in compliance with government requirements. This was the first major victory for the new EPA and the end of a six-year dispute.

The EPA set three requirements:

1. Immediate procurement of low-sulphur coal so as to achieve a 40 percent reduction in sulphur oxide emissions.
2. Construction of taller smokestacks no later than April 1972 to eliminate the downwash by wind of soot, sulphur dioxide, and other emissions.
3. Installation of scrubbers by September 1974 to further reduce sulphur oxide emissions by 74 percent.[6]

---

[5]As reported in *New York Times*, Jan. 9, 1971, p. 11.
[6]*Ibid.*

However, even at this late date, Union Carbide still resisted compliance. Now it turned its attention to stimulating public pressure against such compliance. On January 19, 1971, the date set by the EPA for a written commitment to meet the prescribed requirements, the company announced the impending layoff of 625 employees at its Marietta plant in order to comply with the federal requirements. Union Carbide claimed that the only way it could meet the fly-ash reduction was to shut down one boiler, and thus the need to lay off 125 employees. Furthermore, the company saw no way to meet the April 1972 deadline for reduction of sulphur emissions other than by cutting production, which would result in the layoff of 500 additional workers.

This was an extremely sensitive issue: jobs. (See the Issue box for a discussion of clean air versus jobs.) Most of the workers at the Marietta plant lived in West Virginia, where per capita income was the lowest in the nation and the unemployment rate was nearly twice the national average. For many people living there, smokestacks meant jobs and income. Factory smoke was even called "gold dust."

Then Ralph Nader entered the picture again, calling the job threat environmental blackmail in a letter to Senator Edmund Muskie, chairman of the Senate subcommittee on air and water pollution. Senator Muskie expressed deep concern and promised an investigation. The Securities and Exchange Commission also became involved. A petition had been brought before it alleging that Union Carbide was misleading stockholders regarding its pollution record, thus violating securities laws.

UNION CARBIDE CRIES "UNCLE"

The mounting pressure began to have an effect. At Union Carbide's annual meeting in April 1971, pollution and what to do about it was the main order of business. Moreover, in an attempt to improve public relations and its public image, Carbide announced a massive reorganization. Chairman Birney Mason, Jr., and Vice-Chairman Kenneth H. Hannan resigned; F. Perry Wilson became chairman of the board. Dr. J. S. Whitaker, coordinator of environmental health, and the man many blamed for holding back the data and locking out government inspectors, was subordinated to a new environmental director, Philip Huffard, and the ferro-alloy division received a new president.

By spring 1972, Union Carbide had apparently reversed its intransigent position. It committed itself to spending some $50 million over the next several years to clean up pollution from its plants in Anmoore, Alloy, and Marietta. At the Marietta plant, $10 to $15 million had already been invested in abatement. This plant was now burning low-sulphur coal and had

---

ISSUE: CLEAN AIR VERSUS JOBS

A major issue in the environmental arena is the question of jobs versus clean air (or water). When the costs of complying with government standards are too high, facilities either have to shut down or downsize. This means lost jobs. Making the issue particularly troubling is that often such decisions involve a small town where the factory in question is the major employer. If it is forced to shut down because of stringent environmental standards, the economy of the town can be devastated. The closing can have a powerful multiplier effect: many other businesses, retail and service, depend on support by factory workers. So do city tax revenues, thus affecting the school system and other city services. Real estate values plummet as the economic base is eroded. In such small towns, often no alternative employer exists.

So, there is a lot at stake when any government agency comes down hard on polluters. Does this mean that economic protection should carry a higher priority than environmental protection? The issue should be viewed in terms of relatives rather than absolutes. Perhaps the EPA and other agencies and pressure groups have sometimes been guilty of thinking too much of absolutes. To demand a certain level of air or water purity may outweigh economic considerations. Just as refusing to make any technological improvements because of costs may outweigh legitimate environmental concerns.

The issue is so complex that reasonable people often disagree profoundly. Yet, perhaps we should shy away from extreme positions on either side. To have a bit more air purity at the cost of many jobs and many millions of dollars may be unreasonable. But our planet must be protected for ourselves, our children, and future generations. Jobs may have to be sacrificed when environmental degradation has become extreme. Diehards would support the polluting Union Carbide did in the 1960s because it protected jobs, but the majority would see this as going too far in savaging the environment. Of course, Union Carbide was a well-heeled corporation, not some marginal firm. It could afford the costs of pollution-control equipment and lower-sulphur coal. Public support for Carbide's position faded greatly in this dispute.

INVITATION TO DISCUSS
Given the situation of a plant being the major employer in a small town, how might the issue of jobs versus cleaner air be resolved? What options do you see?

---

shut down one of its boilers. The shutdown was attributed to decreased demand for the plant's products, which included ferro-chrome, electrolytic chromium, ferromanganese, vanadium alloys, and silicon. Two hundred and fifty employees had been laid off, not the threatened 625, and these layoffs were all attributed to the slowdown in demand. At the Alloy plant, $30 million was now committed to antipollution devices, which represented 95 percent of all plant investment over a five-year span. And in Anmoore, the Hagedorns had discontinued their newsletter. Now, Union Carbide's new chairman stated: "[Environmental considerations] have become a part of every corporate business decision from site selection to production, sales, and distribution."[7]

ANALYSIS

The Union Carbide affair in the Ohio Valley was of immense proportions. It involved a wide range of governmental agencies, from the EPA and HEW to the SEC, as well as agencies from two states, Ohio and West Virginia. It brought much bad publicity to the corporation, both locally, in the form of the Hagedorn newsletter, and nationally, from the *New York Times* to *Business Week*. By polluting the air with 45,000 tons of emissions of sulphur dioxide alone, not to mention the tons of soot and fly ash spewed into the air every year, the lives and health of the area's 220,000 residents were seriously endangered. Marked increases from earlier years were found not only in respiratory illnesses but also in skin disorders, allergies, headaches, eye irritations, and psychological depression. Greater costs were also incurred in maintaining homes and other properties because of the grime and the corrosive attributes of the pollutants.

Why the Long Delay in Correcting the Situation?

The plants were almost 30 years old before they were brought into compliance. How was Union Carbide able to delay a crackdown for so long? Several factors accounted for the insensitive procrastination:

1. At the time the plants were initially constructed and became operational in the 1950s, the environment was by no means the issue it was later to become. Not until the mid-1960s, triggered partly by Rachel Carson's *Silent Spring*, did the general public and the government fully begin to realize the present and potential dangers of the various kinds of pollution. And while pollution was occurring in the 1950s and before, it became much more serious with increased production and prosperity.

2. Although Union Carbide's sales were in excess of $3 billion, only 20 percent of its sales consisted of consumer items such as antifreeze, batteries, and plastic kitchen bags. This suggested less vulnerability

---

[7]Fred C. Price, Steven Ross, and Robert L. Davidson, *Business and the Environment* (New York: McGraw-Hill, 1972), p. 49.

to consumer pressures for reform. The company appeased its stock-holders with self-flattering pronouncements. And it used evasive tactics in dealing with the government.

3. Before 1970, no federal regulatory agency had the power to coordinate environmental-protection matters; these were diffused in a number of agencies, with most efforts uncoordinated and toothless. Only in 1970, with the Clean Air Act and the establishment of the Environmental Protection Agency, was serious regulatory power put in place. Since the EPA was a new organization, not yet having won a major confrontation, Union Carbide apparently underestimated its authority. This soon changed: the EPA won its first major confrontation, against Union Carbide.

4. Not only did Union Carbide underestimate the power of federal regulation, it also underestimated the impact of the media, the influence of consumer groups and Nader, and the determination of the local population.

Was Union Carbide the Complete Villain?

Union Carbide had been one of the first chemical firms to install an emission-control system. In 1951, when the Marietta plant opened, its smelting furnaces were equipped with scrubbers that trapped about 75 percent of the particulate emissions. And it continued to invest in new pollution-control technology during the 1960s.

We can wonder whether a more honest and direct approach by Carbide, explaining to the public and the governmental agencies about the serious costs and technological problems involved with meeting the EPA's deadlines, might have avoided much of the controversy. Both costs and technology were problems for Union Carbide at that time. Since 1965, pressures on company profits had been intensifying. It was just coming out of one of the worst financial periods in its history. Part of this was due to a major capital expansion program that had begun in 1965. By 1969, Carbide had spent $1.5 billion on new facilities. Yet, despite increased sales, earnings during this time had plummeted nearly 22 percent because of an untimely combination of factors: faulty construction, an extremely poor operating performance, and a squeeze on chemical prices.

Union Carbide was naturally reluctant to assume any additional financial burdens at that time, particularly ones that would not produce earnings. Compliance with EPA's recommendations promised to run into the millions of dollars, despite the smelting furnaces having already been equipped with scrubbers: after more than a decade, this equipment needed upgrading. Then, too, the real pollution problem was not the smelting furnaces but the generating plant that fired the furnaces. Every day, it poured out thousands of pounds of sulphur dioxide, which came from the high-sulphur coal that Carbide, in order to keep costs down, mined from its own nearby coal fields and burned at the rate of one million tons a year.[8]

By switching to a low-sulphur coal, Carbide's $4.5 million annual coal bill, which was 20 percent of total production costs, would increase 50 percent. Raising the height of the stacks would cost another $1 million, and the new scrubbing system for the power plant would cost between $8 million and $10 million.[9] On the other hand, Carbide's corporate capital expenditures for the 1971–1975 period were projected at $225 million. In light of this, the projected expenditures for emission controls were hardly daunting.

Untried technology was another problem. At that time, no scrubbing system had been developed that would curtail sulphur dioxide emissions on such a large scale. Carbide was experimenting with such a system but still needed time to work out the problems. The EPA, however, was unyielding. Ruckelshaus, the EPA administrator, decided to take a tough stance with Carbide because of its irresponsible behavior in the past; he refused to grant any more delays. (See the Issue box for a discussion of the *cost-benefit analysis* that theoretically should guide requirements for pollution-control expenditures.)

ISSUE: THE COST-BENEFIT ANALYSIS

A cost-benefit analysis is a systematic comparison of the costs and benefits of a proposed action. Only if the benefits exceed the costs would we normally have a "go" decision. The normal way of making such an analysis is to assign dollar values to all costs and benefits, thus providing a common basis for comparison.

Cost-benefit analysis has been widely used by the Defense Department in evaluating alternative weapons systems. And in recent years, such analysis has been sporadically applied to environmental regulation and even to workplace safety standards.

Theoretically, cost-benefit analysis is a very attractive way to determine environmental cleanup actions. For example, is it socially worthwhile for a firm to spend X million dollars to meet a certain standard of clean air or water? Such an analysis has the potential to determine how much should be spent for environmental protection or cleanup; it has the potential to show that, at some level of

[8]"A Corporate Polluter Learns the Hard Way," *Business Week*, Feb. 6, 1971, p. 53.

[9]"Union Carbide to Shut Part of Power Plant in Pollution Dispute," *Wall Street Journal*, Jan. 20, 1971, p. 1.

expenditure, costs will exceed the benefits, with further regulatory requirements not cost-effective.

Actually, using cost-benefit analysis to make environmental cleanup decision has serious flaws. Many of the costs, such as for improved scrubbers or taller smokestacks, can be specifically determined. But placing a dollar value on the anticipated benefits is often a problem. How much is a clear sky worth? A fishable lake? How many extra years of life may result, and what are these worth? (Even the value of a human life is subject to great differences of opinion.) Value judgments for such benefits can differ greatly. We are left with hard quantifiable numbers on the one hand and fuzzy subjective values on the other.

INVITATION TO DISCUSS:

Let's examine the intriguing possibilities, but also the major problems, in a specific cost-benefit analysis:

Estimates place the cost of installing new scrubbers at $17.5 million. If the benefits exceed the cost of this investment, the company will be forced to comply by the government. Environmental engineers estimate that the scrubbers would improve air quality by 25 percent, resulting in less haze, less respiratory distress, less property deterioration (resulting in less maintenance), better all-around health, and generally a more asthetically pleasing environment.

Discuss the specific process by which you would assign dollar values to these benefits.

WHAT CAN BE LEARNED?

Learning Insight. *Business has a symbiotic relationship with society.*

Despite business' preoccupation with profit, in reality a firm has a symbiotic relationship with society. Each benefits from the well-being of the other. Society can hardly allow a firm to falter and go bankrupt because of strict regulations and expenditure demands. To do so would mean the loss of jobs and economic support to the community and the state. But—and this is not as widely realized by business leaders as one might hope—the firm also benefits from a prosperous, safe, and pleasant community. Although the economic impact of such a pleasant environment may not be so directly calculated in terms of the bottom line, an environmentally desirable community provides a more pleasant lifestyle for the firm's executives, makes it easier to attract able employees and executives, makes for pleasant relationships with the community and the press, and in general brings harmony to the business-societal relationship. The example of Union Carbide and its adversarial relationships in the 1960s and early 1970s shows the problems of a business-societal relationship that has gone sour.

Learning Insight. *Woe to the firm today that is insensitive to society's needs and demands.*

With the enactment of the Clean Air Act and other regulatory measures, and with the establishment of the Environmental Protection Agency, the public now has outlets for its concerns, which means it has clout. Any firm, large or small, that ignores or procrastinates on meeting the public's concern will surely be brought to heel. Our society has been more militant since the advent of consumerism in the mid-1960s. The general public is more concerned, less easily satisfied, unwilling to be put off, and quicker to voice its concerns. And not only will the government—federal, state, and local—listen to these concerns, but the press is quick to respond to a newsworthy issue and often, through investigative reporting, leads the way in uncovering abuses. The legal profession is always willing—indeed, eager—to encourage complaints and damage suits, especially against those organizations with "deep pockets." The environment for business is very different today than it was a few decades ago. Woe to the insensitive or myopic firm today.

Learning Insight. *The issue of "jobs versus protection" is still unresolved.*

Both sides of this issue have been argued aggressively and emotionally. Logically, the answer lies somewhere in the gray area of moderation. Economic considerations are necessarily important to many communities. If a plant is closed because of regulatory demands, the community's very existence may be threatened. It may become a backwater inhabited mostly by the elderly, while younger families seek employment elsewhere. On the other hand, how much environmental degradation can we tolerate? These are decisions with big stakes. The solution often leaves neither position satisfied; each must sacrifice for the overall best recourse.

Major problems arise when one side or the other gains an advantage. And in our pluralistic society this often happens, not because of the merits of one position over another but because of that side's greater eloquence, its ability to attract media attention, its greater resources, or its militancy.

Learning Insight. *Environmental planning should be an important part of a firm's total planning process.*

Because of the threat of regulatory scrutiny and punitive action, or simply because of the recognition that environmental protection is an important part of our and our children's quality of life, firms need to study the impact their decisions will have on the environment. They must consider decisions that will minimize social and environmental injury.

This may mean that plant design and site selection should be given very careful scrutiny. If Union Carbide had not located its ferro-alloy plants in a valley, the pollution would not have been maintained in such great concentrations. Also, by raising the height of the smokestacks between 50 and 100 feet, much of the emissions would have been disseminated. And if low-sulphur coal had been used from the beginning, emission contaminants would have been greatly reduced.

Careful attention to environmental impact lowers the risk of blocked or rejected projects. Potential problems can be identified and corrected, thus minimizing unforeseen and costly surprises. Environmental planning reduces the potential for lengthy conflicts, such as the one Union Carbide experienced. Such adverse publicity can be costly in terms of community goodwill, employee morale, as well as the company's reputation with customers and the general public.

This kind of planning needs input from a variety of sources. Often, the people directly involved in the project are too close to it to see the potential problems. Workers themselves can be a source of information. At Union Carbide's Marietta plant, for example, workers' concern for the dust within the plant itself resulted in the construction of a 45-foot wall on the operating floor between the air shafts to eliminate the dust problem.[10] Outside consultants may need to be utilized. And governmental input may be needed, since an agency such as the EPA may be involved in monitoring and regulating.

FOR THOUGHT AND DISCUSSION

1. "Environmentalists are going too far! Unless they are checked, they will destroy our free enterprise system." Evaluate this statement.
2. What do you think accounted for Union Carbide's intransigence? Would a firm today likely be as unyielding?
3. Do you have any criticisms of Ralph Nader in this episode?

---

[10]As reported in *New York Times*, May 28, 1972, p. 2.

4. In the 1960s and early 1970s, other factories in the Ohio Valley and the Kanawha Valley of West Virginia were contributing to air pollution. Do you think Union Carbide was unfairly singled out? In other words, should not all of the polluters have been confronted?

INVITATION TO ROLE PLAY

1. Put yourself in the position of the mayor of Marietta, or Anmoore, or Alloy in the late 1960s. Increasingly, some citizens are complaining about the local Union Carbide plant. What course of action might you take? Discuss as many options and their implications as you can.
2. You are the plant manager of the Marietta plant in the late 1960s. You are being publicly condemned for the filthy air your plant is creating. How would you react to this situation? Be as specific as you can, with a full rationale for your recommendations.

INVITATION TO RESEARCH

1. Research Union Carbide's efforts with respect to the environment since the early 1970s. Has it changed?
2. How serious a problem is air pollution today?

CHAPTER 4

STP: Oh, Such Product Claims

This is the story of a notable marketing success that resulted from linking an automotive product with the macho image of a reference group that many potential customers thought worth emulating—all brought about and supported by heavy advertising. Almost a classic marketing success. Except for one thing. The product really offered consumers no benefits—the experts spoke of it derogatorily as "mouse milk," and what could be more impotent than that? Eventually, bad publicity surfaced about the product, and the Federal Trade Commission took action against the company for misleading advertising.

THE PRODUCT

The principle product of the STP Corporation in the 1960s was STP, a brand of lubricating oil additive supposed to improve car performance (in addition, the firm marketed STP Gasoline Treatment and STP Diesel Fuel Treatment). The name STP means "Scientifically Treated Petroleum." It was sold in 15-oz cans at around $1.50 a can and was poured into the crankcase of a car, preferably with every oil change, as a supplement to the motor oil itself.

While the ingredients of STP remain a closely guarded secret, the major component of all additives is a polyisobutylene polymer dissolved in petroleum oil. Such a polymer-oil solution is called a viscosity-index (VI) improver. This helps motor oil retain its normal thickness despite the large temperature changes that result from hard driving. In other words, with a VI improver, hot oil thins less than it normally would, thus helping lubrication over a wide temperature range.

So far so good. STP promotional messages stressed that the additive would help reduce oil consumption, free sticking valves, make engines run more smoothly, and prevent many other repairs. There was even the strong intimation that the use of a can of STP with every oil change would forestall the expense of a valve and ring job. So intriguingly simple it all seemed: only pour this elixir in the crankcase of a car and make its ailing engine healthy and powerful again.

Unfortunately, there were those who disputed such claims, among them most petroleum engineers, who had labeled these additives "mouse milk." These experts were in general agreement that there was rarely any benefit for a normal engine. The auto firms likewise were critical of STP and similar additives: "No one has ever presented any scientific data to prove that additives do anything good," noted Ray Potter, supervisor of fuels and lubricant research at Ford.[1] The automakers had even found that regular use of the polyisobutylene compounds could sometimes clog small oil passages and cause engine damage, and they refused to recommend the use of additives in their owners' manuals.

So, what do we have here? A product of dubious benefit, with experts in almost complete agreement of its worthlessness, at least under normal driving conditions. How can such a product wrest a niche in the marketplace? But it did, and with gusto.

ANDY GRANATELLI

The success of STP is really the story of Andy Granatelli, who became president of STP Corporation in 1963. How he moved STP from a smallish $9 million in sales in 1963 to sales of $85 million and profits of almost $12 million by 1970 has to make him one of the most astute marketers to come around—or one of the best promoters.

Granatelli had gained a public reputation as a race car driver and a person closely connected with racing. When he was only in his early thirties, he made his first million with a company called Grancor, which developed and sold parts and supplies for racing cars. In 1958, he sold Grancor and became owner of Paxton Products, which made superchargers and similar items. In 1961, he sold Paxton to the Studebaker Company (later to become Studebaker-Worthington in a 1967 merger). He stayed on to run the

[1]"Big Profits in Little Cans," *Time*, Aug. 8, 1969, pp. 70–71.

subsidiary, but in 1963 he was persuaded to take over as president of the STP Division of Studebaker.

Heretofore, additives had been marketed as something to keep "clunkers" operating a little longer. And this was a limited market segment, one with little growth potential in an era of prosperity. Granatelli changed this image for STP. He surmised that if speed could sell cars and tires, it should be able to sell additives as well. "One of the first things Andy realized," said a company executive, "is that to expand sales he had to expand the market. . . . Andy changed the image of STP from an additive to a performance product by promoting it through racing, on the theory that if race drivers used it on $50,000 cars to keep engines cool and maintain lubrication, the general public would buy it for the same reason."[2]

Granatelli offered extra money to race drivers who would paste STP decals conspicuously on their cars and even on their jackets and coveralls. He subsidized "STP cars" at major races. A major coup came when an STP-sponsored car driven by Mario Andretti won the Indianapolis 500 on May 30, 1969. The implication was that STP was the vital ingredient enabling Andretti to achieve the extra performance. Publicity gained for STP from the decal-decorated car and pictures of Granatelli alongside Andretti was worth millions to the company.

Something more subtle than simply a performance product was operative under Granatelli's management: the mystique of fast cars and of the macho men who drove them—*a reference group* that a certain segment of the car-driving public looked up to and wished to emulate. (See the information box for more on *reference groups.*) Hence, these customers could easily be persuaded to buy a product indelibly identified with this group.

Granatelli poured on the advertising to promote the race-driver image, the "Racer's Edge," as STP publicly called it. The 1969 advertising budget was $10 million. This was an amount equal to 20 percent of the previous year's sales, an advertising-to-sales ratio matched by only a handful of firms, and these chiefly in the drug and cosmetics industry, such as Colgate-Palmolive, J. B. Williams, and Alberto Culver. The advertising hit three radio networks, two TV networks, and some 30 auto buff magazines, with ads featuring the STP motto the "racer's edge" and pictures of Granatelli and race cars and drivers. Dolly Granatelli, Andy's wife, participated in very successful radio and TV commercials. By 1969, STP was spending 18 cents more per can for advertising than it spent on the can and the contents.

The great sleeper in all of this was the STP logo. It helped to fuel the burgeoning popularity of the product. In its ads starting in 1966, STP

---

[2]As quoted in "The Wheeler Who Deals in STP," *Business Week*, May 31, 1969, p. 57.

REFERENCE GROUPS

Reference groups, according to consumer behavior researchers, are those groups, or less commonly, those individuals, with whom a person identifies. The group then becomes a standard or a point of reference; an individual looks to these people when forming or evaluating his or her norms, personal values, status, and behavior, both in purchasing and otherwise. A person's reference groups may be those to which he or she belongs; these are called *membership groups*. But a reference group may also be those types of people the individual aspires to be like, or admires, a group the individual does not belong to and perhaps never will, such as athletes, astronauts, the jet set, or race car drivers. As we can see with STP, these "referents" may have considerable influence on purchasing behavior and brand preference.

INVITATION TO DISCUSS
Not all products are influenced by reference groups. What characteristics make a product more, and less, susceptible to reference group influence?

offered the little decals free with a coupon. Kids by the thousands began swamping the company for this newest status symbol. The appeal spread to adults, with stickers being plastered on trucks, passenger cars, tractors, and even limousines. By the end of 1967, STP had to hire six secretaries solely to answer the 4000 requests a day for free stickers. By 1969, the company was giving away 50 million a year. Requests were pouring in from toy makers, confectioners, electronics firms, clothiers, and others to use the STP logo on products. Granatelli readily gave his permission to use the logo without charge, seeing this as a powerful way to broaden recognition of the product and brand. Eventually, the opportunity to tap some of the demand for the logo was realized, and the company established a mail-order marketing organization to handle a full line of STP jackets, caps, overalls, T-shirts, and such.

Sales sprinted ahead. See Table 4.1 for the sales and profit performance from 1963, when Granatelli first took over, to 1970, when the zenith was reached. Note the almost 50 percent spurt in sales in one year, 1969, and the over 50 percent gain in profits, a phenomenal achievement.

The identification of STP with speed resulted in an unwanted by-product that developed in California early in 1968. A particularly potent hallucinogenic drug widely used by hippies was dubbed STP.

As the decade of the 1960s drew to a close, Granatelli could not help but be optimistic about the future. He could see great potential in expanding the product line, first with a cooling system additive and then

Table 4.1   Sales and Profit Growth of STP Corporation, 1963–1970

Year	Sales (000)	Change (%)	Net Income (000)	Change (%)
1963	$ 9,340	—	$ 1,733	—
1964	12,781	36.8	2,439	40.7
1965	18,475	44.6	3,537	45.0
1966	20,828	12.7	4,037	14.1
1967	30,886	48.3	4,807	19.1
1968	44,000	42.5	6,000	24.8
1969	65,335	48.5	9,052	50.9
1970	85,936	31.5	11,601	28.2

Source: STP Annual reports.

spreading into other markets, particularly the industrial and marine markets. Furthermore, Granatelli saw tremendous opportunities abroad, and overseas sales indeed had tripled in a single year. In Japan, sales of STP exceeded the sales of any single state of the Union, while selling at more than twice the price in this country. Granatelli could happily observe: "There's only one other symbol used more than STP, and that's Coke. But they've been around longer than we have."[3]

COMPETITION

Were there any competitors of STP? There were, but they had all been left far behind. Wynn and Bardahl were the two oldest firms in the field. Bardahl advertised its product as a preventative of repairs, although compared to STP it did little advertising. The Bardahl product image was that of a steady, dependable product, but without glamour. Wynn's Friction Proofing was similar to Bardahl in image and market position. Wynn was founded by a lawyer in 1939; he had mixed a home brew "friction proofing" in a 55-gallon drum and sold bottles of it to local garages. Both Wynn and Bardahl had broad product lines; Wynn had 26 related products and Bardahl 18.

PHA Hi-Performance Oil Treatment was the least well known of the four major oil additives, although the company tried to project a top-quality performance image. Stud, a Union Carbide product, was the latest entry into the oil additive field. It had rapidly climbed to the No. 2 market position behind STP, primarily on the strength of an aggressive advertising campaign "guaranteeing to equal or exceed the performance of any oil treatment or your money back." While the formula for each additive was a

[3]*Ibid.*, p. 57.

closely guarded secret, the major ingredient, polyisobutylene, was the same, and the results were similar.

WHY THE STP SUCCESS?

How can we account for the phenomenal success of STP? Was it primarily due to the willingness to spend heavily on mass media advertising? Was it primarily due to race car drivers publicly promoting it? What role, if any, did the popularity of STP decals have on the success of the product?

In order to test certain hypotheses regarding the image and appeal of STP, one researcher asked students and other car owners to write down the two or three associations that most readily came to mind on seeing the letters "STP." The following responses predominated.[4]

Granatelli	Racing
Racer's edge	Indianapolis 500
Speed	High performance
Sports cars	Names of various high
Andretti (who won the	performance and sports cars,
1969 Indianapolis 500)	such as Charger, Corvette, etc.

Clearly STP had succeeded in developing an association between its product and the professional racing community and higher performance cars—in other words, with a reference group that a significant portion of younger car-owning consumers admired or wished to emulate. The overwhelming and unexpected popularity of the STP logo became a highly visible indication of an individual's wish to be identified with this reference group.

That the product itself, offered at a premium price many times higher than the cost of production, was of dubious benefit remained disregarded in the glamour associated with the aura of professional racing. So, STP furnishes tangible evidence that reference group influence, when carefully chosen and strongly promoted, can be a significant marketing tool.

CLOUDS ON THE HORIZON

By the late 1960s, despite a rate of sales and profit growth that seemed to be not only continuing but even intensifying, some communications began appearing that revealed the general uselessness of STP and other oil additives

---

[4]Research conducted by Sidney C. Wooten, Jr., "Self-Concept Theory, the Symbolic Value of Products, and Consumer Behavior: A Study in Interrelationships." Unpublished MBA thesis, George Washington University, Jan. 1971, pp. 84–86.

for most passenger car engines. For example, *Time* and *Business Week* had articles about this in 1969.[5] Although these publications were directed to people who were not typical customers of STP, still the articles presaged more adverse publicity to come.

Then, in July 1971, *Consumer Reports,* the respected consumer advocate magazine, published a harsh indictment of STP.[6] Not only did it charge that STP oil additive was a useless concoction, it also warned that the product could be harmful to engines and might even void a new car warranty.

While *Consumer Reports* agreed that STP helped engine oil retain its normal thickness despite large temperature changes, it noted that major oil refiners had already taken care of this with their multiviscosity oils (labeled 5W-20, 10W-30, and so on) and that adding STP tended to make the oil thicker than desirable. For example, a 20W motor oil was found by testing to have been changed to a 40W with the addition of the recommended amount of STP. While admitting that this would help old, oil-burning engines by making loose mechanical joints and fittings quieter and seemingly tighter and perhaps even reduce oil consumption, *Consumer Reports* stated that any 40W or 50W oil would do this and would be far cheaper. With a normal engine, such a thick oil mixture would cause hard starting and noticeable drag in cold weather, and the engine would not be properly lubricated. Furthermore, *Consumer Reports* noted that because STP can change the viscosity of a new car's oil to a much thicker grade than auto manufacturers recommended, a new car warranty could be voided. General Motors and Ford officials were quoted specifically as to how the use of additives would affect a new car warranty.

> General Motors: If in the analysis of a warranty repair there is evidence that the use of additives is responsible for, or has contributed to the vehicle malfunction or part failure, this fact would be taken into consideration in determining General Motors' responsibility.

> Ford: If supplementary additives . . . modify the properties of the lubricants so that they no longer meet Ford specifications, then warranty terms may be affected.[7]

Granatelli quickly responded. He called the *Consumer Reports* article "an attempt to sabotage the successful business of our company with a twisted set of alleged facts assembled by incompetents."[8]

---

[5]"Big Profits," pp. 70–71, and "The Wheeler," pp. 31–32.
[6]"STP, Does Your Car Really Need It?" *Consumer Reports,* July 1971, p. 422.
[7]*Ibid.*
[8]As quoted in "FTC Tries to Dull the Racer's Edge—STP," *Iron Age,* June 21, 1973, p. 17.

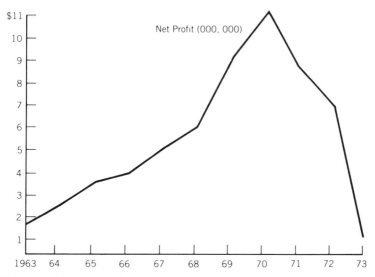

Figure 4.1. STP Corp. profits during Granatelli, 1963–1973. (*Source:* Published company reports.)

STP on the Ropes

Despite Granatelli's counterattack, both earnings and stock prices of STP plunged. The stock, which had peaked at almost $60 early in 1971, was down to $3 in 1973. Profits, by 1973, had fallen to barely $1 million from the $11.6 million of 1970. Figure 4.1 shows the rise and then the collapse of income during the Granatelli years of 1963 through 1973.

To add to Granatelli's troubles, now the Federal Trade Commission (FTC) began looking into a 22-page petition filed early in 1973 against STP by the Center for Automotive Safety, a Ralph Nader–inspired consumer group. The petition asked the FTC specifically to order the company to:

1. Stop asserting unfair and deceptive claims for STP oil treatment.
2. Substantiate all future advertising claims relating to STP oil treatment.
3. Refund to buyers of the product funds obtained through unfair and deceptive advertising.

Granatelli stated: "We believe this unknown group [the Center] is simply seeking publicity by the device of bringing totally unfounded and irresponsible charges against us."[9] When asked whether STP Corp. planned to

[9]*Ibid.*

issue scientific data to support its advertising claims, Granatelli responded, "I take offense at having to defend myself against an unknown group of two or three guys out to get publicity."[10]

In 1973, the Federal Trade Commission finally charged the company with deceptive advertising, and the same year, Granatelli left STP.

Coming Back

Although Granatelli's reign was over and the glory days were gone, the company doggedly began making a comeback from the lows of 1973. The comeback, however, was not without more charges of deceptive advertising and false and unsupported claims. Sales and profits rose somewhat in 1974 and began climbing steadily after that, although they were still well below the peaks attained in 1970.

The complaint initiated by the FTC in 1973 was settled in September of 1976: the company agreed with the FTC consent order not to use false and misleading advertising and to support any claims for the oil additive with competent and reliable scientific tests or other objective data. Two of the FTC commissioners, including the chairman, dissented from the consent order. Chairman Lewis A. Engman criticized the acceptance by the FTC.

> I dissent because this order is too weak. Though the consent order prohibits claims that are not substantiated, I have the statuary "reason to believe" that STP Oil Treatment is of no significant value to the majority of cars which regularly use the proper grade of oil. I accordingly have difficulty in accepting an order which does not explicitly require STP to qualify its future claims.[11]

However weak the consent order was seen to be, STP still did not abide by it. The FTC was forced to sue the company in 1978 for violation of the two-year-old cease and desist order. The new complaint charged as false STP's advertisements that its oil treatment reduced oil consumption by 20 percent in certain road tests. An agreement concerning this was negotiated by the FTC and STP Corp. and made public in February 1978, with STP agreeing to a record-setting $500,000 fine plus another $200,000 to be spent for a *corrective advertising* campaign. (See the information box for a discussion of *corrective advertising*.) Under the terms of the settlement a notice was to be placed in 14 publications, most of them with heavy business readership, such as *Wall Street Journal, Business Week, Forbes,* and *Harvard Business*

---

[10]*Ibid.*
[11]"Legal Developments," *Journal of Marketing,* Oct. 1976, p. 119.

CORRECTIVE ADVERTISING

In the late 1970s, the Federal Trade Commission began taking a militant stand against ads that smack of deception or unfounded claims. One of the alternatives the FTC has in dealing with such unsatisfactory advertising is corrrective advertising.

Corrective advertising may be required in order, theoretically, to eliminate the "residue" effects of misleading advertising in the past. The first such order, issued against ITT Continental Baking Company, required that 25 percent of Continental's advertising budget for one year be given to FTC-approved advertisements that Profile Bread was *not* the effective weight reducer that previous ads had represented. The makers of Ocean Spray Cranberry Juice were also required to correct possible misrepresentations of their products as having the food energy of orange or tomato juice, and 25 percent of the budget was specified for this purpose. Listerine was required to "correct" advertising claims that it had made for over 50 years (that it was a cold and sore-throat remedy) with $10.2 million worth of ads stating that "Listerine will not help prevent colds or sore throats or lessen their severity."

Although one would expect corrective advertising aimed at nullifying false impressions to severely penalize a firm, evidence suggests that firms are not really harmed. Perhaps this is partly due to the innocuous wording of many of these ads; furthermore, any advertising promotes the name of the company, and the fine print is often not read.

INVITATION TO DISCUSS
Puffing is mild exaggeration and is usually deemed acceptable advertising. What in your judgment would be acceptable puffing for Listerine? For STP?

Review; the only consumer-oriented magazines on the schedule were *Esquire, Guns & Ammo, National Geographic, Newsweek,* and *People.* The ads were to be mostly full-page, reading as follows:

> FTC Notice: As a result of an investigation by the Federal Trade Commission into certain allegedly inaccurate past advertisements for STP's Oil Additive, STP Corporation has agreed to a $700,000 settlement.

The notice also included a statement by STP that

> Agreement to this settlement does not constitute an admission by STP that the law has been violated.[12]

[12]As reported in "Legal Developments in Marketing," *Journal of Marketing,* Oct. 1978, p. 91.

The new STP chairman, Craig A. Nalen, said that he doubted the corrective ads would have any impact at all on STP sales. "Nowhere is there any challenge to the efficacy of the product," he said. "It's merely a question of some defective tests done years ago."[13] Despite the critical publicity, the FTC did not probe into whether the products worked but was only concerned with the lack of documentation for STP's advertising claims. The products of STP were not reformulated, and *Consumer Reports* did not change its negative position.

Nevertheless, Nalen brought STP back to increasing profits. Nalen himself was a former marketing executive with General Mills. He at first shunned an offer to run STP: "I was skeptical about the products as much as anybody else. It took a lot of head scratching for me to decide to go to STP."[14] However, he was finally persuaded to take the job as a result of studies made by an independent laboratory and several "lubrication experts" about whom Nalen said: "Their analysis showed that STP oil treatments result in a reduction of oil consumption and wear rate."[15] The next steps were to sign the consent agreement with the FTC and begin the slow job of rebuilding the company's battered image.

Costs were substantially reduced by trimming the sales force from 180 to 100 and by eliminating a policy of giving discounts to dealers for shelf space. A number of new products were test marketed and then introduced, including a multigrade diesel oil claimed to be good for at least 50,000 miles, a passenger-car oil good for 12,000, and a synthetic compression oil for machinery. The channel of distribution was shifted from service stations and garages to supermarkets, with 65 percent of STP products sold in supermarkets by 1977, compared with only 30 percent five years before. Extensive advertising was continued—for example, a $200,000 four-page ad in *Readers Digest*—using test results to document the claims made for the additive. Actor Robert Blake, who played the role of a supercop on the TV show "Baretta," replaced the flamboyant Granatelli as the company's television pitchman. Table 4.2 shows the gains in sales and profits during this rebuilding period.

In 1978, giant Esmark, Inc., offered to acquire STP from parent Studebaker-Worthington, which owned 60 percent of the stock, for about $117 million, paying $22.50 for each share of STP stock. Studebaker-Worthington agreed to vote its holdings for the merger. Philip Thomas, vice

[13]"Corrective Ads for STP Publicize Settlement Costs to Business Execs," *Advertising Age*, Feb. 13, 1978, p. 1.
[14]As quoted in "What Craig Nalen Did to Turn STP Around," *Business Week*, Jan. 10, 1977, p. 38.
[15]*Ibid.*

Table 4.2   STP Corp. Sales and Profits, 1973–1976

Year	Sales	Net Profit
1973	$54,605,000	$1,033,436
1974	62,377,000	3,453,000
1975	65,269,000	3,882,000
1976	69,737,000	6,627,000

Source: Published company reports.

president of corporate communications for Esmark, called STP "a fantastic company and a perfect fit" for Esmark. He said Esmark had conducted intensive tests on STP oil treatment before it began serious negotiations on the acquisition and, as a result, was convinced that "the product works."[16]

About the time the merger was finalized, STP began national advertising for a new product, "Son of a Gun," a pump spray that it claimed would restore and beautify vinyl, rubber, leather, and wood. Carrying a suggested $2.95 price, Son of a Gun was promoted via 30- and 60-second network commercials to both male and female audiences—the first time the company had promoted a product to women as well as men. STP Oil Treatment, which had not been advertised for about a year, also began to be backed by new TV ads, with Robert Blake in his continuing role as STP's spokesman. The company had fully recovered from the dark days at the turn of the decade.

WHAT CAN BE LEARNED?

We can consider the STP case from two perspectives: that of consumers and that of company executives. From both viewpoints, we see rather awesome implications, as well as reasons for caution.

Issue Insight. *Can advertising sell a weak product?*

Can it be that if the marketer chooses the proper reference group and image for a brand, and advertises it heavily and confidently, virtually anything can be marketed, whether or not it is effective? We know that advertising can induce people to try a product for the first time. But, unless the product is satisfactory and meets their expectations, they will not buy it again: this is practically a marketing truism. Yet, the STP example seems to disprove it. The answer lies in the user's inability to correctly assess the effectiveness of STP. Who could say that one's car was helped or hindered

[16]"STP Presents Its New Parent with a New 'Son'," *Advertising Age*, Mar. 27, 1978, p. 30.

by it? Certainly, any judgment could only be made over a long period of use. But many products are like this: their performance and quality cannot be easily and quickly assessed because of their complexity or hidden ingredients, or because the results occur over a long time.

Is effective promotion, then, more important in the marketing mix than a good product? If this were generally true, it would be a disaster to us as consumers; it would destroy our confidence and put us at the mercy of the marketplace. Fortunately, the STP example does not represent the norm; products that do not meet the expectations aroused by advertising are in jeopardy—usually.

For marketers, the challenge of finding the best image, the most effective promotional appeal, can be intriguing. Even the best product needs the proper promotional effort to induce people to try it.

Issue Insight. *Was the FTC correct in its general stance against deceptive practices?*

Where do we draw the line? Was the action of the FTC against STP (as well as against other firms) too harsh? Were the regulators too zealous? Does every advertising claim have to be supported with unimpeachable test results? Are hard sell and image building to be completely ruled out so that the helpless consumer can be protected, even from a careless purchase of a $1.50 can of oil additive? Or, to take the other side, does the FTC's action in permitting a rather innocuous consent agreement—soon to be violated—and a less than $1 million settlement represent a cop-out? Do measures such as these have any deterrent value? As you can see, the issues are hard to resolve and cannot be resolved to everyone's satisfaction.

So, what can we conclude from the STP example? If simply leading consumers on with alluring advertising claims and macho images is so bad, where do we draw the line—at every exaggeration, at every optimistic statement? We must also be somewhat sobered by the realization that almost anything under the sun can be proven—that STP is good for cars, that cigarettes do not cause lung cancer, that a certain dentifrice retards tooth decay—even if the "proofs" are of questionable validity.

Issue Insight. *Is corrective advertising a deterrent to deceptive advertising?*

The penalty of mandatory corrective advertising as a "remedy" for past advertising abuses ought to be considered by firms before they make careless, unsubstantiated claims. Although it appears that corrective advertising heretofore has not had much adverse effect on the firms involved, the possibility remains that a firm's reputation could be harmed by corrective advertising. The marketing environment today prescribes more honest practices, even though there appear to be those who can somehow circumvent them. Honest marketing benefits both consumers and firms: consumers are able to rely on more honest claims and more effective products, and firms derive some protection from the unscrupulous efforts of competitors.

FOR THOUGHT AND DISCUSSION

1. Critique the FTC corrective advertising resolution.
2. How would you, as an STP executive, answer the charge that STP was only "mouse milk"?
3. Do you think another oil additive firm could have successfully pursued a different image than that of STP for its brand?
4. Do you think STP decals should have been dispensed so freely? Why or why not?
5. Discuss the image of the Stud brand of oil additive versus STP's image.
6. Was the success of STP in the 1960s attributable primarily to its willingness to spend much more on advertising than its competitors? Why or why not?
7. To what degree should advertising claims be regulated by the FTC or other governmental agencies? Be as specific as you can, and defend your position.

INVITATION TO ROLE PLAY

As a STP company spokesperson, how would you answer the charge before the Federal Trade Commission of deceptive advertising? Defend your position as persuasively as possible.

INVITATION TO RESEARCH

1. Update the status of STP today. Is it still available? What does it promise? Who is the marketer, and how profitable is the firm?
2. What is the role of corrective advertising today? Is it still being used?

5

The Famous Price-Fixing Conspiracy of the Electrical Equipment Industry

When the price-fixing conspiracy of the electrical equipment manufacturers was revealed in 1959, it was the biggest conspiracy of its kind in U.S. business history—especially in the impact it had on the nation's thinking regarding business ethics.

Twenty-nine companies—including such giants as General Electric, Westinghouse, and Allis-Chalmers—were found guilty of conspiring to fix prices in deals involving some $7 billion of electrical equipment. The products involved in the conspiracy included power transformers, power switchgear assemblies, turbine generators, industrial control equipment, and circuit breakers. The companies were fined $1,924,500. Particularly notable in this case was that 52 executives were prosecuted and fined about $140,000. Even more startling was that seven of the defendants received jail sentences. This was a first under federal antitrust laws.

On top of all that, almost 2000 private action, treble-damage cases were brought as a result of the court findings. In one of these alone, damages of $28,800,000 were awarded.

SUSPICION

In May of 1958, the *News Letter* of the Tennessee Valley Authority (TVA) announced that it had again received identical secret bids for three contracts it had advertised to the electrical equipment industry. Julian Granger of the *Knoxville News Sentinel* latched on to this surprising announcement and, digging deeper, found that TVA, during the preceding three years, had received identical bids by over fifty suppliers on a wide variety of contracts. Granger ran a series of articles revealing that:

- TVA records showed 24 instances of identical bids from 1956 to 1959.
- Some of the bids were exactly the same down to the hundredths of a cent.
- At least 12 of the bids quoted the same delivery price, even though the distances from factories varied from hundreds to thousands of miles.
- General Electric and Westinghouse were responsible for more of the identical bids than any of the other electrical manufacturers.
- The records showed that between 1950 and 1956, General Electric and Westinghouse bids on power transformers showed almost identical price increases six times.
- The same companies did the same thing regarding turbines 10 times during the years 1946 to 1957.[1]

Somehow, nothing came of this. Then, in the beginning of 1959, TVA awarded a contract for a hydroelectric turbine generator to a British firm, C. A. Parsons & Co., Ltd., General Electric, Westinghouse, and Allis-Chalmers bid $17.5 million, but Parsons came in with a $12 million bid, winning the contract. As a result, TVA was heavily criticized by the U. S. electrical industry for not doing business with American firms.

By the middle of 1959, TVA felt that it had taken enough criticism. Electrical equipment prices had risen substantially faster than most other prices, and perhaps this augured well for more public concern with possible abuses in this industry since it translated into higher electrical bills. Two other factors increased the likelihood that TVA's bidding system would receive public attention: (1) it operated the largest generating capacity in the United States, with an enormous budget for electrical power equipment, and (2) Tennessee Senator Estes Kefauver chaired the Senate Subcommittee on Antitrust Activities, which was highly concerned with the setting of prices. Kefauver's subcommittee found a prime investigative opportunity in this industry's pricing practices.

THE INVESTIGATION AND INDICTMENTS

The subcommittee began an investigation in preparation for holding hearings, and the Department of Justice convened a federal grand jury in

---

[1]John Herling, *The Great Price Conspiracy* (Washington: Robert B. Luce, Inc., 1962), pp. 1–2.

Philadelphia. Subpoenas were issued to all major electrical equipment man-ufacturers to produce documents on their pricing and bidding procedures from 1956 on. These documents were to include copies of written, as well as oral, communications between companies—anything that had to do with the terms of sale involving 14 types of electrical equipment.[2]

Westinghouse publicly announced its total cooperation but stated that identical bids had no sinister significance: "Where free competition exists, prices will often be the same and manufacturers will compete on the basis of quality, service, and product preference."[3]

At issue was a violation of antitrust laws. The Sherman Antitrust Act states that:

> Every contract, combination in the form of trust or otherwise, or conspiracy, in restraint of trade or commerce . . . is declared illegal; . . . Every person who shall make any contract or engage in any combination or conspiracy . . . shall be deemed guilty of a misdemeanor, and, on conviction thereof, shall be pun-ished by fine not exceeding fifty thousand dollars, or by imprisonment not exceeding one year, or both said punishments. . . .[4]

Previously, firms had not worried much about antitrust violations being discovered. These were deemed to be "gentlemanly crimes," and any fines levied were considered the cost of doing business.[5] It was unheard of for anyone to be sent to jail. However, things were changing for violators. In 1955, Congress had passed legislation giving the federal government the right to sue for damages.[6] Prior to 1955, it was almost impossible for the government to be awarded damages.

Actually, the industry's transgressions had not gone unnoticed. The Justice Department, as early as 1950, had started putting together a case against the industry. Small companies had complained about being under-cut in their bidding; but when they did not bid, the price stayed high. Government agencies complained of receiving identical bids. And then came the TVA complaint.

Finally, in February 1960, 44 manufacturers and 28 company executives were charged with conspiring to fix prices and bids and divide markets. The indictments were very specific, naming the dates and places of meet-ings of the conspirators.

[2]"TVA Bids Stir Up Anti-Trusters," *Business Week*, July 11, 1959, p. 30.

[3]Herling, p.7.

[4]Sherman Act, 15 U.S.C. sec. 1 (1958).

[5]James M. Claubault and John F. Burton, Jr., *Sherman Act Indictments* (New York: Federal Legal Publications, 1966), pp. 7–8.

[6]Clayton Act, 15 U.S.C., sec. 4a (added by the Act of July 7, 1955, 69 Stat. 282–283).

Pressure was brought to bear on the defendants, who apparently felt they would receive more lenient treatment by pleading guilty, since that would save the court the expense and time of taking each indictment to court.[7] Allis-Chalmers, the third largest manufacturer, decided to cooperate fully in the investigation and prosecution of these cases. Additional indictments were soon handed down.

THE CONSPIRACY

It began in 1945, near the end of World War II. Many of the electrical equipment manufacturers met to discuss ways to get around pricing constraints imposed by the wartime Office of Price Administration (OPA). The group attempted to prove to the OPA that industry price increases were needed. The executives involved apparently assumed that if the public was not gouged, then such meetings were not illegal. However, in 1946, attorneys for the industry became aware of these meetings and warned that any discussion of prices was illegal, regardless of whether the public was being gouged. General Electric's management then forbade any person involved in pricing decisions to attend such industry meetings—but not in time to save GE from involvement in 13 antitrust suits between 1940 and 1950.

After World War II, the industry changed greatly. Growth in the number and size of small companies took market share away from industry giants. Now, customers had more of a choice among suppliers, but the products were very similar in design and quality. Consequently, price became the dominant selling point for the first time, and competitive bidding became the rule for most major equipment purchases. The industry's competitive situation was no longer the cozy environment it had been before, and profit planning became more difficult. In an effort to stabilize market conditions, executives from the various companies again met.

So we had a situation where subordinates were meeting secretly and dividing up markets while top executives in firms such as General Electric and Westinghouse were preaching the free enterprise system and marketplace competition. For example, Ralph Cordiner.

Ralph J. Cordiner was Chairman of the Board of General Electric. As an example of his supposed position regarding competition, here is the gist of Mr. Cordiner's comments to the Senate subcommittee on 5.215, a bill designed to enhance competition in a number of industries (and protect the public against the effects of monopolies and unwarranted price increases): "The contrast between East Berlin and West Berlin, one a regulated economy

---

[7]"The Admissibility and Scope of Guilty Pleas to Antitrust Treble Damage Actions," *The Yale Law Journal*, Vol. 71, 1961–62, pp. 684–686.

and the other a free economy, is a vivid demonstration of what happens to the consumer when the competitive incentive of a free market is replaced by the restrictions of a regulated economy."[8]

Cordiner was a hard-driving executive who had once left General Electric to become President of Schick because he was impatient with his career progress at GE. Later, as CEO of GE, he had reorganized the behemoth into 110 units, each responsible for its own marketing, pricing, and profit performance. He also established a new system of rewards based on profit performance, which made it a short step for zealous subordinates to collude with other companies to preserve market share and profitability. The organizational climate was receptive to this kind of implicit encouragement. For example, executives of the High Voltage Switchgear Division—which accounted for 25 percent of all sales—were of the opinion that "collusion was illegal, but not unethical."[9]

The most publicized conspiracy involved power switchgear assemblies. The corporations would allocate their bids to government agencies by a set percentage: "GE, 39 percent; Westinghouse, 35 percent; Allis-Chalmers, 8 percent; Federal Pacific Electric, 7 percent. . . ."[10] The bids would automatically rotate every four weeks, with the high bidder during one period becoming the lowest bidder during the next period. This was known as the "phase-of-the-moon" formula.

The "quadrant" system was worked out by the power switching equipment group. As the name suggests, the country was divided into four areas, with four companies assigned to each area. One person was designated chair of each quadrant and took charge of allocating bids within that quadrant. Other groups drew lots or flipped a coin to see which company would take low bid on a contract or take the lead in a price change.

A masterful intrigue permeated the conspiracies. Phone calls were made using only first names, letters were sent using no return address, and only first names and code numbers were used to identify conspirators. Executives avoided being seen traveling or eating together; any notes of meetings were to be destroyed. (One executive, Nye Spencer of the I-T-E Circuit Breaker Company, did not destroy all of his notes. He was advised by the I-T-E attorney to turn them over to the grand jury. This is one of the very few recordings of these events that was ever found.)

[8]John Fuller, *The Gentlemen Conspirators* (New York: Grove Press. 1962), p. 35.

[9]Richard Austin Smith, "The Incredible Electrical Conspiracy," *Fortune*, April 1961, pp. 132–134.

[10]Indictment, Case No. 20399—U.S. v. Westinghouse Electric Corp., quoted in "How 29 Companies Got in Trouble, " *Reader's Digest*, May 1961, p. 134.

THE TRIAL

Hearings on the grand jury indictments began on February 6, 1961. 40 companies and 52 individuals were named as either conspirators or coconspirators. Not one of them pleaded not guilty; all pleaded either guilty or *nolo contendere*, which means literally "no defense"—that is, that the defendant will not defend against the charges. Of major interest: none of these defendants were top executives.

In the court procedure that was followed, Judge J. Cullen Ganey heard recommendations for sentences from Justice Department lawyers. These had been determined on the basis of the defendants' degree of participation in the conspiracy, their importance in their companies regarding pricing policy, and, most important, their degree of cooperation with the investigation. Judge Ganey expressed his opinion: "This is a shocking indictment of a vast section of our economy. . . . Companies have shockingly mocked the capitalistic system before the world."[11] Then the views of the new Attorney General, Robert Kennedy, were read: "I strongly recommend that sentences at least as severe as those recommended are imposed."[12]

In this ominous setting, the roll call of the cases began. Defense attorneys spoke imploringly for the defendants, telling of their outstanding services to their communities, their church activities, stressing that they were acting on orders from upper management and that this was their first offense. As the Judge began to impose jail sentences along with fines, the lawyers urged him to have mercy on their clients. They pointed out that the defendants' families would be adversely affected and that the age and health of their clients should be mitigating factors. One went so far as to plead with the Judge not to put his client in jail "with common criminals who have been convicted of embezzlement and other serious crimes."[13]

The roll call went on for two days. Almost $2 million in fines were levied, nearly half of that to General Electric and Westinghouse alone. The government requested jail sentences for 30 of the 52 defendants; 23 actually received sentences, but 16 were suspended with five-year probations. Seven executives received 30-day jail sentences. The sentences handed down were more severe than those imposed in any other cases dealing with one industry in the previous 70 years of antitrust enforcement.

[11]"Dedication to What?" *The New Republic*, Feb. 13, 1961, p. 2.
[12]Herling, p. 197.
[13]"When the Story Broke," *The New Republic*, Feb. 20, 1961, p. 7.

AFTERMATH

The electrical equipment manufacturers were not to be let off so easily. The press had been strangely silent prior to the sentencing. (The *New Republic* even wondered: "Can the press be thinking of all that advertising?"[14]) But now the stories broke, and the negative publicity flowed, tarnishing corporate images and placing executives and corporate directors on the defensive. People overwhelmingly agreed with Judge Ganey's statement that "One would indeed be naive to believe that such a vast conspiracy was not known to those in charge."[15] And the *New York Herald Tribune* asked: "If they did not know what was going on, why didn't they?"[16] Business school professors wondered if too much attention had been given in school to subject matter and too little to the future business people's moral development. Meantime, the National Association of Electrical Manufacturers (NEMA) doubled its public-relations budget.

The consequences for the individuals involved were not as traumatic as they had first feared. Those GE executives who lost their jobs because of their involvement—even those who went to prison—were readily offered equivalent jobs in other corporations. The business community accepted them with open arms. Judge Ganey even canceled five-year probationary sentences after 11 months, despite the Justice Department's strenuous arguments against this.

A major negative consequence was these. companies' vulnerability to civil damage suits. Some 1800 treble-damage suits were brought by public utilities as well as by the government. Notably, in the first case that came to trial, Philadelphia Electric received an award of $28,800,000. Even though manufacturers began to settle claims out of court, the ultimate cost was estimated to be about $400 million. While some of these costs could be deducted from gross income for corporate tax returns, approximately $200 million could not be. Added to this was the not inconsequential cost of hiring legal counsel.[17]

ANALYSIS

The incentives for the illegal actions described in this case stem from several sources. Without doubt, top management was exerting strong pressure on lower executives to improve their performance, particularly with regard

[14]"Dedication to What?" p. 2.
[15]*Ibid.*
[16]From an editorial reprinted in *Reader's Digest*, May 1961, p. 134.
[17]Clair Wilcox, *Public Policies Toward Business*, 3rd ed. (Homewood, Ill.: Richard D. Irwin, Inc., 1966), p. 101

ISSUE: IS ANTITRUST ENFORCEMENT DESIRABLE ON BALANCE?

The aim of antitrust legislation and regulation has been to protect competition, to ensure that it is fair and equitable and that the large firms do not have an unseemly advantage over their smaller competitors. Ultimately, the general public's best interest is at stake. Collusion and price fixing would seem anathema to the public interest. But is the issue that clear-cut?

For example, in this case, some smaller electrical manufacturers complained that their survival in their industry was jeopardized as a result of the convictions. They had agreed to the conspiracy with a live-and-let-live attitude. But when the conspiracy was eliminated, they said, prices were cut so low that their financial situation became desperate. They wanted a legal way to stabilize the market at fair and reasonable prices; otherwise, they claimed, they would be driven from the market and competition would be diminished, thus counterserving the intent of the antitrust laws.

But is protection of small, marginal firms really in the general public's best interest? Consumers want more for their money, which means the highest-quality goods at the lowest prices. Efficient production and state-of-the-art technology are part of this. Agreements to fix prices and divide up the market are not, since they lead to prices not set by the market, which tend to be artificially high.

Consequently, we are left with the trade-off between adequately protecting and preserving smaller businesses that may be relatively inefficient and marginal and the best interests of the general public. It may well be that sacrifice of some of these businesses may be best for society and the economy in the long run. But human suffering accompanies business failure.

INVITATION TO DISCUSS

Do you agree that smaller firms should be allowed to go under so that larger, more efficient firms can give consumers somewhat lower prices? Should there be any exceptions to this rule or regulation?

to the areas under their responsibility. This was prevalent, not just in one company, but in the largest firms throughout the industry. Collusion with executives in other firms seemed to be a practical way to at least stabilize profits.

Added to the strong pressure to maintain or increase profits was the growth of competitors that occurred after World War II. Since there was little chance to differentiate among the various companies' products, there were more firms chasing down the same customers with similar products, a situation bound to bring trauma to their industry. Since the smaller firms were more vulnerable because of their limited resources, their opportunity to join the larger firms in price fixing and market sharing agreements must have seemed like a lifeline. The result was that the practice became practically industry-wide.

These illegal actions would not have been condoned in a strictly enforced antitrust climate. But a rather blasé attitude toward antitrust and collusion characterized the industry at that time, with many executives seeing collusion as ethical, though illegal. This attitude changed with the harsh penalties imposed by Judge Ganey.

Finally, we are left to marvel at how the top executives of these companies were able so adroitly to escape blame or prosecution. General Electric's Ralph Cordiner denied that he ever knew anything about his company's price-fixing activities. We have seen this same top-management repudiation of responsibility in other cases. But do stockholders not have a right to expect that their chief executives, as well as their boards of directors, should know what is going on in their areas of responsibility? After all, leaders of any group set the tone for that group.

WHAT CAN BE LEARNED?

Learning Insight. *Price-fixing is one of the easiest cases to prosecute.*

Conspiracies to fix prices are direct violations of the Sherman Act. The government does not need to prove that competition was injured or that trade was restrained. All that needs to be proven is that a meeting took place with agreements to fix prices, bids, or allocate market share. Although the penalties for price conspiracies in the electrical equipment industry did not used to be that great, they have greatly increased since 1961. Given the ease of prosecution, one would think that no prudent executive would ever take such a risk. Yet, there have been sporadic instances of price-fixing since then, including major supermarkets in one metropolitan area. Is there no learning experience?

Learning Insight. *Employees at all levels should have free and confidential access to company lawyers to answer questions on possible illegalities.*

Lawyers tend to err on the side of caution. If consulted, they are likely to disapprove of questionable statements and practices. As early as 1946, GE company attorneys had warned of the danger of meetings to discuss prices and price strategies. Later, when the conspiracy intensified, company lawyers were not informed and, indeed, executives were told to keep price-meeting information away from them. If an open-door policy—that is, easy access to legal counsel—is communicated to an organization, illegal practices should be prevented or at least quickly curbed. Activities that might lead to vulnerability to lawsuits ought to be nipped in the bud.

Learning Insight. *Heavy pressure from top management to meet performance goals sets up a climate for illegal (and unethical) actions.*

Time and again, we see that undue pressure for performance motivates less than ethical, even illegal, behavior by those "under the gun." This is the basis for the position that top management cannot escape blame for its subordinates' actions: top management has set up the climate for such actions by insisting on performance at all costs. What is the remedy? Is it that top management should repudiate performance pressures? That operating results are not to be aggressively pursued and rewarded? Of course not.

Admittedly, there is a thin line between overemphasizing performance at all costs and encouraging good performance within the bounds of acceptable—even wholly ethical—behavior. Where is that line? Unfortunately, this cannot be answered with certainty. A climate of moderation, of performance geared to acceptable social standards, is the answer— rather than aggressive behavior unconcerned or contemptuous of what is ethical and legal. This is not a wholly satisfactory answer, since we are dealing with qualitative components: the extremes are more easily identified. But there is a large middle ground or gray area, where opinions differ as to what is acceptable and what is not. At what point does top management's pressure for performance become excessive? Are all individuals susceptible to the same pressures? At what point does reasonable pressure to produce become distorted by employee misperception? We are left with an unsatisfactory resolution to the problem of performance pressure vs. ethical and legal behavior.

Learning Insight. *It is difficult to avoid corrupt and unethical behavior when "everyone else is doing it" and "you have to do it to get by."*

Alas, there is yet another major incentive for unethical practices: that you have to do it or you'll be competitively vulnerable. It is hard to deny that unethical practices lead to higher profits in the short term. Of course, in the longer term, this is seldom the case, thanks to governmental detection and consumer resentment. But, with so much performance measured by short-term results, the temptation is to do well in the short term and hope to be promoted or transferred before any transgressions are uncovered.

The "follow the leader" philosophy is hard to resist. It is so tempting to "go with the flow." Yet, somewhere, someone has to act courageously, has to be either a leader or a whistleblower, if our society is to reach high ethical and environmental standards. It must be shown conclusively—through legal means and public pressure—that society will exact the highest toll on conspirators and unethical individuals and firms. It must be shown that only ethical behavior will permit satisfactory profits in the long run.

FOR THOUGHT AND DISCUSSION

1. Do you think the penalties imposed on the firms and on the individuals were too strong, too weak, or about right? Explain your position.
2. Should TVA also have been indicted for tolerating this price-fixing conspiracy for so many years?
3. What is your position regarding top management's culpability for the misdeeds of their subordinates? Should Ralph Cordiner, the CEO of GE, have escaped blame and prosecution? Why or why not?
4. "After decades of mild punishment for price-fixing violations, it was vastly unfair to suddenly raise the punishment—without warning." Evaluate this statement.

INVITATION TO ROLE PLAY

1. Place yourself in the role of Judge Ganey. You have heard strong arguments for clemency, yet the durability and the extent of the conspiracy is undeniable. What would you do under these circumstances?
2. You are a middle-level executive responsible for pricing at Westinghouse. You are confronted with a conspiracy of sweeping proportions. What would you do (assuming there is no indication of government suspicion)?

INVITATION TO RESEARCH

Investigate any other price-fixing scandals that occurred after this celebrated case. How do you account for the lack of "learning experience"?

6

ITT: Heavy-Handed Interference in a Foreign Government

On October 24, 1970, Dr. Salvador Allende Gossens was elected President of Chile. This election brought Chile its first Marxist regime and seemed the spearhead of a socialist philosophy in a country that had been proud of its democratic society.

On March 21 and 22, 1972, Jack Anderson, a well-respected American newspaper columnist, published an outline of a series of secret documents he had obtained from International Telephone and Telegraph Company (ITT) files. The documents revealed the efforts that ITT and the Central Intelligence Agency (CIA) had made to stop the election of President Allende in 1970, and the unsuccessful efforts they made to overthrow him in 1973.

ITT, attempting to protect its Chilean property from government expropriation, intruded in the affairs of a foreign country to an extent unacceptable by the mainstreams of business, government, and society both here and abroad. At issue: What right does a multinational corporation have to interfere in the governance of countries in which it is doing business?

THE COMPANY

The beginnings of ITT (originally called IT&T) were in 1920. It specialized in the newly emerging communications industry, operating outside the United States, although its headquarters were in New York City. By 1960, it was 51st on *Fortune's* list of the country's largest 500 corporations. Growth surged even more during the 1960s, much of this through the acquisition of 54 U.S. companies and 56 companies abroad. By 1971, ITT was 8th on the *Fortune* 500. It had over 250 divisions, business groupings, and subsidiaries operating in 80 countries. Some 350,000 people were employed by ITT in such industries as insurance, chemicals, food production, automotive parts, and hotels. Yet, the company had a checkered past, and more questions were being raised about its activities as it moved toward its half-century mark.

In 1923 founders Colonel Sosthenes Behn and his brother purchased a small Puerto Rican telephone company at a distress price. Partly due to his Spanish background, Behn got the contract to run the Spanish telephone network from the dictator of Spain, Primo de Rivera. In the years that followed, Behn made more acquisitions around the world, turning ITT into an international conglomerate. The firm's reputation was somewhat tainted by its close ties with Nazi Germany in the 1930s and by its overall attitude of self-serving expediency—virtually out of the reach of government controls. Colonel Behn retired in 1956, but the company's mind-set changed little under his successor.

Harold S. Geneen

In 1959, Harold Geneen was chosen to be ITT's president. He had previously been executive vice president of Raytheon, and when he left Raytheon, its stock dropped 6½ points, a graphic indication of the business community's perception of his competence.

Geneen, a former accountant, used this background and his ambitious drive to become a veritable financial wizard. (Today, in his eighties, he is still wheeling and dealing, but on a smaller scale than when he was chairman of a multibillion dollar corporation.) It was his habit to put in 16-hour workdays, and he expected the same dedication from his subordinates. His word was law, and he tended to set near-impossible goals for his top executives and was ruthless in his demands. In his first decade at the helm of ITT, some 50 senior executives either quit or were fired.

Geneen was paid over $800,000 in 1971, more than two-and-a-half times as much as the next-highest-paid ITT executive. He had an apartment off Fifth Avenue, a winter house at Key Biscayne, and a summer home on Cape Cod. He regularly logged 100,000 miles a year in his private jet, which was about the size of Air Force One.[1]

---

[1]Richard J. Barnet and Ronald E. Miller, *Global Reach* (New York: Simon and Schuster, 1974), p. 52.

Geneen revamped ITT's financial system so that he could analyze each company's profitability and exert close operational control. He decided to obtain more investments in the United States in order to reduce what he saw as the increasing pressures on operations abroad. However, to expand within the United States, ITT was limited to making acquisitions, because of American Telephone and Telegraph (AT&T)'s having competitive rights to the U.S. market. Consequently, Geneen set out on an aggressive acquisition campaign, which was to add greatly to the company's growth over the coming decade.

The major acquisitions during the 1960s included Sheraton (hotels), Continental Baking (bakeries), Aetna Finance (consumer finance), Avis (car rentals), Apcoa (airport parking), Levitt (construction), Canteen (vending foods), Hartford (insurance), and Rayonier (chemicals). Geneen's acquisition spree encountered few obstacles, but the Justice Department did oppose ITT's acquisition of the American Broadcasting Company; in 1968, Geneen reluctantly backed away. In the late 1960s, the Justice Department also began contesting some of the completed acquisitions, including the Canteen, Hartford, and Avis mergers. But with top-level political connections in Washington, the company suffered no other major setbacks.

Controversy: the Dita Beard Affair

While ITT was battling with the Justice Department's antitrust investigations, scandal was brewing over the location of the 1972 Republican National Convention. The White House wanted it to be held in San Diego but was having trouble raising the money to do so. Conveniently, Bob Wilson, the key Republican congressman from the San Diego area, was a good friend of Geneen. Geneen's Sheraton division had just completed a new hotel complex in San Diego, and the promotional benefits of hosting the convention would be substantial. ITT pledged $200,000 to the Republicans, and the convention committee approved the site, despite ITT's ongoing antitrust proceedings. Dita Beard was a top lobbyist for ITT. When a highly incriminating memo written by her surfaced, it revealed a secret deal between ITT and Attorney General John Mitchell to settle the antitrust suit involving the Hartford acquisition in ITT's favor: Mitchell pledged a positive influence on the decision.

ITT IN CHILE

If the antitrust cases against ITT, the exposure of a $200,000 bribe to the Republicans, and the questionable settlement arrangement between Dita Beard and the U.S. Attorney General were not enough to keep Geneen occupied, he certainly outdid himself in Chile. On March 22, 1970, Jack Anderson published a column that revealed ITT's manipulations in Chilean internal affairs and its relations with the CIA and the White House in this regard. Anderson had compiled a very thorough study of this affair, which was later used by a Senate subcommittee investigating ITT. According to Anderson, ITT had tried to prevent Salvador Allende from being elected in Chile, and, with the CIA, had encouraged economic chaos and a military coup in Chile, and had offered $1 million to the White House to be used against Allende.[2]

Chile

Chile is situated along South America's western coast. It is only 110 miles wide but some 2600 miles long. It is a land of extremes. The northern third is desert, the Andes Mountains are in the east. A fertile valley dominates Chile's central region, where most of its nine million people live. South of the valley, the land breaks down into thousands of tiny islands leading to Cape Horn and Antarctica.

Chile had had stable political institutions until a 1972 military coup, which deposed and killed Allende. But great inequalities existed: 3 percent of the population received 40 percent of the nation's income. Fifty percent of the working population earned just 10 percent of total income. With such extremes of wealth and poverty, it was not surprising that 40 percent of all Chileans suffered from malnutrition and one-third of all deaths were children.

ITT's Holdings in Chile

Despite Chile's small population and unpromising economic potential, ITT's global reach extended there, including the Chilean Telephone Company, the Standard Electric Company, two Sheraton hotels, and some smaller holdings. The telephone company, in particular, was highly profitable, earning some $10 million annually. By 1970, it employed 6000 workers and was valued by ITT at more than $150 million. Yet, these holdings comprised only a small fraction of ITT's worldwide assets and earnings.

Despite ITT's small stake in Chile, by the end of the 1960s, it began to fear that its properties, in particular the phone subsidiary, would be nationalized and taken over, with the Chilean government offering ITT only a small fraction of its value. (This had already happened in Peru, a neighbor of Chile.) The reason for this newfound fear in a country noted for its stability was the political emergence of Dr. Salvador Allende Gossens, who was a Marxist.

---

[2]Anthony Sampson, *The Sovereign State of ITT* (Briarcliff Manor, N.Y.: Stein and Day, 1974), p. 253.

Allende

Allende was born in 1908, the son of a well-to-do lawyer. His formal education was in medicine, but his career soon veered away from that. In 1933, Allende helped found Chile's Socialist party. Four years later he was elected to the Chilean Congress. He was later appointed to the country's Cabinet, where he gained national recognition for his humanitarian concerns.

Allende's early political years were marked by strict adherence to the Constitution. This put him at odds with Chile's Communist party. After election to the Senate in 1945, he embarked on 25 years of unbroken political service. His rallying cry was that Chile was a nation whose promise had not been fulfilled.

Defeated for the presidency in the 1964 elections by Christian Democrat Eduardo Frei, Allende suspected that his time had come in the 1970 elections. Reforms promised by Frei had not materialized, and in 1968 the Christian Democrats lost their popularity and their majority in Congress.

In the 1970 presidential elections, Allende, the Popular Unity Coalition candidate, won 36 percent of the votes, former President Jorge Alessandri won 35 percent, and the new Christian Democrat candidate, Radomiro Tomic, won only 17 percent. Under the Chilean Constitution, because no candidate had won a majority, the choice of president thus had to be decided by congressional elections seven weeks later. (It was during these seven weeks that most of the ITT memos revealed by Anderson were written.) On October 24, 1970, the Congress voted 153 to 35 in favor of Allende for president.

President Allende had campaigned for a program of extensive land reform and rapid nationalization of basic industries that were controlled by foreign capital. On September 29, 1971, Chile took over the telephone company (CHILTELCO) after several months of negotiations and offers, all rejected by ITT. Chile declared that CHILTELCO's service was deficient, that it was charging too much, that its profits were too high, and that the country was too dependent on ITT for investment decisions.[3]

At this point, there was a sizable disagreement in the negotiations as to the value of the phone company: ITT put the value at $153 million, Chile put it at $24 million. The Chileans proposed a group of international adjudicators, but ITT would not accept this. ITT proposed an international auditing firm that the Chileans would not accept. By March 1972, the Chilean ambassador in Washington had just come up with a new formula

---

[3]U.S. Senate Committee on Foreign Relations, Subcommittee on Multinational Corporations, *ITT and Chile: 1970–1971* (Washington, D.C.: U.S. Government Printing Office, 1973), p. 811.

to determine the fair value. Then Anderson's column appeared, transforming the whole situation.

SPECIFICS OF ITT'S INTERFERENCE IN CHILE'S AFFAIRS

For a long time, Chile was a secure base for foreign corporations, a far cry from the revolutionary nationalism of its neighbors. The election of Christian Democrat Eduardo Frei in 1964, with his pledge to reform without antagonizing the big corporations, was comforting. The likelihood was that Geneen and other industrialists had contributed to Frei's campaign fund, although this was not proven.

Anderson's publication of secret documents obtained from ITT files provided strong proof that ITT had been involved with the Central Intelligence Agency (CIA) in attempting to stop Allende's election to the presidency in 1970, as well as in his 1973 overthrow.

Two days after the first Anderson column appeared, the Senate Foreign Relations Committee formed a special subcommittee, the Multinationals Subcommittee, chaired by Senator Frank Church. On June 21, 1973, the subcommittee, issued a 1000-page report charging that ITT had "overstepped the line of acceptable corporate behavior." If the scheme to defeat leftist Dr. Salvador Allende had been fully implemented, said the report, "it could have resulted in bloodshed and possibly civil war."[4]

The subcommittee criticized Geneen for having offered $1 million to the CIA for its help in supporting the conservative candidate. If such actions came to be accepted as normal, the report said, "no country would welcome the presence of multinational corporations."[5] The subcommittee report continued: "The attitude of the company was best summed up [by ITT Senior Vice-President Edward J. Gerrity, Jr.,] when he asked: 'What's wrong with taking care of No. 1?'"[6]

The report concluded:

[T]he highest officials of ITT sought to engage the CIA in a plan to manipulate the outcome of the Chilean presidential election. In so doing, the company overstepped the line of acceptable corporate behavior. . . . The pressures which the company sought to bring to bear on the U.S. Government for CIA intervention are incompatible with the formulation of U.S. foreign policy in accordance with U.S. national, rather than private interests.[7]

[4]"The Probers Are on ITT's Doorstep Again," *Business Week*, June 23, 1973, p. 29.
[5]*Ibid.*
[6]*Ibid.*
[7]*ITT and Chile*, p. 520.

CONSEQUENCES

In Chile, the Anderson disclosures came just as negotiations between ITT and the Chilean government had reached a critical stage. Allende made the most of it. A week after Anderson's column, the Chilean Congress decided to investigate the past activities of ITT and the CIA. A month later, at a vast pro-government rally of 200,000 people, Allende announced that he would ask the Chilean Congress to nationalize the telephone company, and the Congress duly approved. In December 1972, Allende addressed the United Nations General Assembly in New York City. ITT, he said, had

> driven its tentacles deep into my country and proposed to manage our political life. I accuse the IT&T of attempting to bring about civil war. . . . [the big corporation has been] cunningly and terrifyingly effective in preventing us from exercising out rights as a sovereign state.[8]

The United Nations Economic and Social Council unanimously adopted a resolution calling for a study group to examine the role and impact of transnational corporations in developing countries.

The relations between the United States and Chile worsened, intensified in August 1973 by a large anti-U.S. campaign mounted by the Chilean press, radio, and television media. The United States was charged with influencing the nationwide truckers strike and other labor strikes that were bringing the nation to economic paralysis.

World critical attention was focused even more on Chile after a military coup on September 11, 1973, which led to the death of President Allende. A military junta, headed by Army Commander General A. Pinochet Ugarte, took control.

Because of the unreimbursed takeover of the Chilean phone company, ITT filed a $92.5 million claim with the Overseas-Private Investment Corporation (OPIC). On April 9, 1973, the claim was denied, presumably because of the adverse publicity from ITT's role in Chile. A lengthy court battle ensued, and on January 1, 1975, a $39 million cash settlement was reached by binding arbitration. Still, this was far short of ITT's reimbursement hopes.

The image of the big U.S. multinational firm intruding on the affairs of a small developing country—including allegations that it had tried to plunge Chile into a civil war—brought worldwide criticism. This led to violent actions against some of ITT's property. For example, a building occupied by ITT in Zurich, Switzerland was extensively damaged on September 16, 1973. Two days later, a time bomb demolished four rooms in the Latin-American

---

[8]Tad Szulc, "ITT Under the Gun" *The New Republic*, Aug. 6, 1977, p. 20.

section of an ITT building on Madison Avenue in New York City. Minutes before the explosion, the *New York Times* was informed by an unknown caller that it was in retaliation for crimes against Chile. On October 6, 1973, fire damaged an ITT warehouse in Milan, Italy to the extent of $12 million.

At their annual meeting in May 1973, ITT stockholders were divided in their support of management. Some praised the company's increasing profitability. (Indeed, ITT was racking up record profits: a 45 percent increase in 1972.) Others sharply criticized Geneen. The former bishop of the Methodist Church in Chile, for example, denounced the company's role in Chile by asking Geneen, "Is it legal and ethical to throw a nation into chaos to preserve ITT's profitable ventures?"[9] (See the following Issue box.)

The ITT Chilean "adventure" was to have longer-term consequences. Partly because of the negative publicity engendered by these actions and by other large corporations' payoff scandals, such as Lockheed (discussed in the next chapter), Congress passed the *Foreign Corrupt Practices Act* in 1977. This controversial act was designed to clean up business dealings between multinationals and foreign officials and politicians.

Attempts to Indict ITT and CIA Officials

In 1977, a federal grand jury in Washington, D.C. held a nine-month investigation into the activities of ITT and the CIA. Harold Geneen, Edward J. Gerrity (vice-president of ITT), and former CIA Director Richard Helms were also considered for indictments for perjury during the multinationals subcommittee hearings.

Helms was quoted as saying that, if he were indicted, he would "bring down" former Secretary of State Henry Kissinger, who was one of the architects of the American anti-Allende efforts that contributed to the bloody military coup in September 1973.[11]

In 1978, the Department of Justice brought charges of lying and obstructing against Gerrity for denials that he had done anything to try to stop Allende in 1970. But Geneen escaped being charged, and Richard Helms had already pleaded guilty to a misdemeanor charge for lying to Congress on the same matter. He got off with a small fine.

We can speculate that Geneen had the "protection," also enjoyed by Helms, of being able to expose "national security" secrets if he was forced into a legal defense.[12] Prudence perhaps dictated immunity from prosecution.

---

[9]Michael C. Jensen, "Stockholders Challenge ITT's Use of Influence in U.S. and Abroad," *New York Times*, May 10, 1973, p. 65:3.

[11]Szulc, p. 21.

[12]Norman Birnbaum, "ITT, Equal Justice and Chile," *The Nation*, April 1, 1978, p. 356.

ISSUE: DO WE HAVE A RIGHT TO EXPECT THE HIGHEST MORAL CONDUCT FROM OUR BUSINESS LEADERS?

How much moral adherence, and even leadership, do we have a right to expect from our business leaders? Do they owe anything to society, or is the arena simply one of the law of the jungle or the Darwinian idea of survival of the fittest?

The Darwinian philosophy held sway during the last century. We would hope that it is passé today. Yet, some executives are dinosaurs, throwbacks to an earlier business climate. And Geneen epitomized this attitude.

Have we as a society sufficiently progressed today that we can rely on altruism and a conscience imbued with social moralism to bring out the most socially desirable actions by executives and their corporations? Even if governmental laws and regulations are slackened, it is difficult for most of us to see granting business firms unfettered scope, not even in foreign adventuring. While some executives will see the public's best interest as completely compatible with their own and their firms', others will view the absence of constraints as opportunistic.

Furthermore, short-term bottom line performance still prevails in most firms, and this does not always result in the best actions from society's viewpoint. While more responsive actions might lead to greater long-term results, stockholders and creditors demand more immediate gains, as does industry stature.

INVITATION TO DISCUSS
What ideas do you have for fostering a more ethical and moral stance in U.S. corporations? (This assumes, of course, that you think improvement is desirable, and possible.)

Despite all the information, no indictments were brought in the ITT-Chile case. Essentially, Geneen and his associates escaped with only some bad publicity, although the corporation itself did not fare so well.

ANALYSIS

ITT gambled and lost when it attempted to interfere in the Chilean situation. Besides the Senate subcommittee's condemnation, the company incurred substantial property damage around the world and was penalized in its reimbursements for the financial losses it incurred during the expropriation period. The abuses of power seemed to come home to roost, especially when we consider the fate of other multinationals doing business in Chile at the same time. Xerox was not nationalized. RCA Victor settled for a minority interest in its electronics and phonographic records plants. General Tire sold its shares to the government and continued providing technical assistance. But none of these firms tried to promote sabotage or harassment of the Chilean government.

By most standards, ITT's conduct was reprehensible, resulting in a tainted public image and the loss of millions of dollars in property damage and lost insurance claims. Still, the main victims were Chile, and most of all, Salvador Allende, who lost his life. The promising future of this brilliant and dedicated public servant, even though he had Marxist leanings, can hardly be compared to the minimal losses of a multibillion dollar corporation.

Admittedly, the blame was not all ITT's. The U.S. government—particularly the CIA, but also the offices of the Secretary of State and the President—also interfered in the internal workings of a foreign government. ITT and Washington had a commonality of interest in stopping Allende—and later removing him. Unfortunately, these efforts went beyond honorable means.

But was ITT all that culpable? Are we blaming a firm unjustly? Does a firm not have a right to protect its property, whether in the United States or abroad? As with many ethical and legal issues, it is all a matter of degree. The general consensus is that ITT overstepped the boundaries of acceptable behavior in Chile. But how much influence may a corporation, in its own interests, legitimately exert on foreign policy? The Senate subcommittee raised this question.[13]

ITT, as well as other multinational corporations, should have the right to seek its best interests through the political and legal processes. And this certainly includes lobbying, which is a fact of life, regardless of the issues involved with it. (See the following information box on *lobbying*.) But ITT went beyond this in attempting to influence foreign affairs in covert and intrusive ways.

As an example of the controversy of diplomatic redress of private corporative grievances, Robert G. Hawkins, of New York University's Graduate School of Business Administration, believes that parent companies should not expect "substantial sanctions" by the United States against foreign countries. But then he argues that the U.S. government should be involved in, and even negotiate, property rights for American companies abroad since "the government is at least responsible for protecting the property rights of its citizens."[14] So we see the ambivalence and controversy of this aspect of business/government relations.

---

[13]"The Question the ITT Case Raises," *Business Week*, March 31, 1973, p. 42.
[14]*Ibid.*

LOBBYING

Lobbying may be defined as the efforts of a corporation, trade association, or other interest group to influence government in its behalf. Lobbyists predominately work in Washington, with perhaps 20,000 legislative advocates, government or public-relations consultants and lawyers so engaged. Lobbying is conducted within the legislative and executive branches of government, with Congress and the administrative agencies main targets. The judicial branch, notably the Supreme Court, is generally insulated from special-interest lobbying.

Lobbying has been widely condemned. Certainly, it advances the views of the special-interest groups, which are often opposed to the "public interest." Critics maintain that in attempting to influence key legislators and government officials, it is only a short step to corrupt practices, of which the most flagrant are bribery and payola. More insidious favors are less susceptible to detection. These include: helping legislators with their heavy research work loads, helping them with their speeches and public appearances, and advising them on public relations and campaign strategies. Many observers are concerned that the general public's interests tend to be subordinated because it lacks an effective lobbying presence.

Lobbyists do perform a useful function. They provide legislators with technical information about bills and with information about the attitudes of constituents and those most concerned about specific pending legislation. Of course, if a lobbyist supplies biased or misleading information, legislative decisions are compromised. But proponents of lobbying are quick to point out that lobbyists who do that are quickly shunned. Most legislators want to hear a balanced presentation regarding key issues.

INVITATION TO DISCUSS
On balance, how would you assess the growing popularity of lobbying? Do you think it should be curbed? If so, how?

WHAT CAN BE LEARNED?

Learning Insight. *A multinational should be wary of assuming a heavy-handed posture in foreign environments, especially in Third World countries.*

The less-developed countries, many of which are governed by dictators antagonistic to the United States' power, see multinational corporations as the embodiment of that power in their country. They look on foreign businesspeople with distrust, see them as exploiters of the their raw materials and labor—in other words as what are called economic imperialists.

In such an environment, the U.S. multinational firm needs to tread warily, and exercise the greatest caution in order not to jeopardize its position and its property. As a result of ITT's heavy-handed activities in Chile, demands for restraints on multinational firms reached all-time highs. Just when it seemed that the suspicion and resentment were diminishing, the Bhopal accident occurred in 1984 (discussed in Chapter 11). Now, in the 1990s, attitudes are becoming more positive. But the possibility for a new crescendo of negative sentiments, leading to harsh restraints and expropriations, is always present.

Learning Insight. *Corporate self-interest is vulnerable in Third World countries.*

Multinationals can contribute greatly to developing countries by raising their standards of living, their level of education and employment, their social stability, and indeed their whole quality of life. For the most part, these goals are fully compatible with the firms' goals. But they may not always be compatible with the firms' short-range goals. If a corporation sees its self-interest more tied to short-range profit goals, it may be vulnerable to hostile governments. At best, it will be doing business in an uncertain environment. Immediate self-interest may have to be sacrificed. Although there is always some risk of expropriation in Third World environments, this risk can be reduced by an amicable posture, one that is supportive of the host country. Of course, there is always more risk than in stable societies.

Learning Insight. *U.S.-based multinationals' actions in foreign markets have a direct effect on the image on the United States itself.*

Like it or not, the image of the United States is affected by the practices—especially the negative practices—of its U.S.-based firms. ITT, with its unacceptable interference in foreign governance; Nestlé, with its aggressive promotion of a product that was dangerous unless properly used; and Union Carbide, with its naive acceptance of foreign subsidiary safety standards—all these deficiencies and abuses discredit the image of the United States and promote the idea of the "Ugly American."

This should infuse U.S. multinationals with an added responsibility. They are representatives of the U.S. government: their actions, good or bad, contribute to the prestige (or lack of prestige) of the United States as a whole. Such responsibility should not be treated lightly by our multinationals. They are the conveyors of the public image, not only of themselves, but of their country of origin.

Learning Insight. *Top Management's loose ethics should be resisted by lower management, but they usually are not.*

So many times in this book, we have found that ethical and social responsibility abuses have been either instigated or encouraged by top management. What is lower management to do in this situation? Cotton to it, stubbornly oppose it, whistleblow? With few exceptions, lower management follows along, and even surpasses the questionable standards of higher management. Are we as individuals unable to form our own positions about questionable practices? Are we like driven sheep, swayed greatly by those in higher office? If this indeed is true, it is a sad commentary. In the corporate world, there is a vast need for those who are not willing to follow the crowd and accept the lowest common denominator of conduct. But, this is very difficult to do, as we have seen with the whistleblowers. Let us resist being "dumb, driven sheep" when the cause is right and correct conduct is at stake.

FOR THOUGHT AND DISCUSSION

1. A corporation doing business in a foreign country has the right to protect its investment at all costs. Comment on this statement.
2. Is it not appropriate that Marxist and communist governments should be opposed, even if such opposition takes aggressive forms? Discuss.
3. Discuss the pros and cons of multinationals operating in foreign countries, from the perspective of the countries involved.

INVITATION TO ROLE PLAY

As the public-relations director of ITT at the time of this controversy, what would you have advised Geneen concerning his Chilean activities? How would you handle his criticism of your position of "hands off"?

INVITATION TO RESEARCH

Has ITT been guilty of any other questionable dealings, both in the past and more recently? If so, what is your conclusion about the present posture of the company?

CHAPTER 7

Lockheed Corporation: Overseas Bribery Gone Rampant

In September, 1975, the Senate Committee Hearings on Multinational Corporations, chaired by Senator Frank Church, released the stunning news that the Lockheed Corporation had made more than $200 million in secret payments to foreign agents and government officials in the Netherlands, Italy, Japan, Turkey, and other countries. As months wore on and more and more details emerged, a sense of outage grew in the nation and the Senate. The morality of a major U.S. defense contractor was impugned, as was the morality of the entire defense industry, even U.S. corporations in general. The Foreign Corrupt Practices Act of 1977 was a direct result.

SCANDALS

The Prince

Prince Bernhard, husband of Queen Juliana of the Netherlands, was highly respected. He had fought bravely with the Dutch Army when the Nazis invaded Holland during World War II. He commanded a Dutch brigade when the Allies retook Holland in 1944. After the war, he was a dedicated booster of the Netherlands around the world. He had founded the World Wildlife Fund, was inspector general of the Dutch Armed Forces, and was on the board of the KLM Royal Dutch Airlines, among other highly visible positions.

But he was vulnerable to temptation, temptation wielded by Lockheed. With his apparently expensive tastes, this paragon of nobility and public service succumbed to monetary inducements designed to promote the sale of Lockheed Starfighters. The total contract involved between $150 and $200 million. The contact between Prince Bernhard and Lockheed was an ex-KLM agent who had been employed by Lockheed as a salesman. The negotiated commission for the Prince was $1 million.[1]

The Japanese Connection

Lockheed's involvement with Japanese bribes began in 1958 when the company engaged Yoshio Kodama, who had strong ties with Japanese governmental officials. With his help, Lockheed gained the contract for a Japanese Air Force jet.

In 1972, Lockheed again hired Kodama. And he succeeded in securing a $1.3 billion contract with All-Nippon Airways, for which he asked for and received about $9 million from Lockheed from 1972 to 1975. Much of the money allegedly went to then prime minister Kukeo Tanaka and other government officials who interceded with All-Nippon Airlines for Lockheed.

In August 1975, an investigation by the U.S. government led to Lockheed's admission that it had made $22 million in secret payoffs.[2] Senate investigations in February 1976 publicized the company's involvement with Japanese government officials. Such revelations forced Prime Minister Tanaka to resign. Japan subsequently cancelled the billion-dollar contract with Lockheed. By September 15, 1976, 18 individuals, including Kodama and Tanaka, were arrested as a result of their involvement with Lockheed.

Other Payoffs

Lockheed's payoffs extended to a number of other countries as well, although these did not generate as much public scrutiny and shock as the disclosures from the Netherlands and Japan. Bribes in such countries as Saudi Arabia and Iran were thought to be a "way of life" in those parts of the world. But there was also evidence of payoffs to Italy ($2 million paid to land a $60 million contract for C-130s), Spain ($1.3 million), South Africa ($9 million), as well as Greece, Mexico, Nigeria, Turkey, and Columbia.[3]

---

[1]Yerachmiel Kugel and Gladys W. Gruenberg, *International Payoffs*, Lexington, MA: Lexington Books, 1977, pp. 59–60.

[2]"Lockheed Says It Paid $22 Million to Get Contracts," *Wall Street Journal*, Aug. 9, 1975.

[3]"Payoffs: The Growing Scandal," *Newsweek* Special Report, Feb. 23, 1976, pp. 26–33.

MECHANISM OF PAYOFFS

Payments, whether they be bribes, kickbacks, political contributions, or donations and gratuities of various kinds, may be paid directly to the recipient who wields the desired amount of influence. However, this presents a higher degree of risk than a more indirect connection.

Payments more often are made through intermediaries. A subsidiary corporation may be used, its accounting records not being consolidated with the parent company. In this way, the payoff can be disguised as an expense for services and goods never provided. The subsidiary may be a dummy corporation established only for the payoff function. With this arrangement, the parent company pays sales commissions to the dummy, with no knowledge and no direct link to any payoffs.

Sales agents are the more common mechanism for channelling payments. They can be completely legitimate, and even when they're not, their "commissions" on large purchases such as airplanes—though a quite low percentage of the total contract—can amount to a substantial dollar figure. In many foreign environments, such agents maintain their contacts through personal favors, and thereby facilitate and expedite transactions and favorable decisions. An unusually high commission, which suggests part is turned over to third parties, is suspect, but the evidence is often not clear-cut whether the commission exceeded reasonable bounds for the services rendered.

THE COMPANY

During World War II, Lockheed produced 20,000 combat planes, mainly P-38 fighters. In Korea, its F-80 Shooting Stars ruled the skies. Later it built the U-4 spy plane and the F-104 fighter, the latter being the mainstay of NATO's air defense. Its Agena rocket was used in more than 200 space launchings, and the Polaris submarine-fired missile—completed two and a half years ahead of schedule— had been an essential part of our nuclear deterrent. The more advanced Poseidon missile, at its test firing, induced a Russian tracking ship to nearly collide with a U.S. destroyer as the Russian ship raced to pick up some hopefully tell-tale debris.

After Lockheed's history of successfully developing highly sophisticated products, its contract to build the military transport C-5A, the world's largest plane, seemed relatively simple. But the heavy weight of the plane required major new technological ground to be broken, and this, combined with inflation and other factors—there were charges of bad management— led to a 40 percent cost overrun. Lockheed stood to lose $500 million. Furthermore, the Air Force cut orders for the giant cargo plane. Lockheed experienced other problems with its defense contracting. For example, its Cheyenne hybrid craft, capable of hovering like a helicopter or flying at 250 mph, developed defects, and one of them crashed. This resulted in the contract being cancelled, leaving Lockheed with $124 million in unreimbursed costs and product payments.

Although economic and technological problems led to Lockheed's difficulties, political and bureaucratic factors compounded the problems. The C-5A was the first and most disastrous of the TPP (total package procurement) contracts, in which a contractor had to bid on the whole contract from designing to final production, thereby attempting to forecast costs before the product had even been invented. The political climate also hurt Lockheed: the Air Force's deviousness toward a congressional committee investigating military spending had hardened congressional opposition to costly military programs and raised further criticism of the military-industrial complex.

So, going into the 1970s, Lockheed was a financially troubled company, despite its importance to national defense. Bankruptcy itself threatened in 1971.

Lockheed had wanted to reduce its dependence on the military by entering the commercial jet aircraft market. So it developed a three-engine, wide-body jet: the L-1011. About $400 million was spent on this development, and Lockheed had to obtain an additional $400 million credit line from a group of banks.

The engines were to be built by Rolls-Royce of Britain, but this company went bankrupt. Lockheed now had no engines for the L-1011, and at that late date, there was no chance to switch to another supplier and still meet its delivery schedules. Now Lockheed itself faced bankruptcy, with the heavy costs already incurred and almost $300 million in canceled orders.

The company was only saved when the government stepped in to provide a bailout: a $250 million guarantee for Lockheed's loans. With the federal government standing behind the loans, agreeing to pick up the tab in case of default, creditors would now consent to loan Lockheed the cash it needed to survive. (See the following Issue Box for a discussion of the controversy concerning *bailouts*.)

In order for Lockheed to survive, its overseas sales had to expand greatly, particularly for the C-130 Hercules transport. Foreign sales had grown nicely: from $146 million in 1970 (when the political payments began) to $650 million by 1974. Sales to Iran and Saudi Arabia were particularly high, but both countries received substantial payoffs. In the meantime, Lockheed had used $195 million of the loan guarantees provided by the U.S. government. Thus, the government found itself in a quandary: Securities and Exchange Commission (SEC) requirements that Lockheed make a detailed

---

ISSUE: WAS A BAILOUT FOR LOCKHEED JUSTIFIED?

The debate by Congress on the Lockheed bailout was extensive. The two sides were divided on philosophical and practical grounds. Those opposing the bailout saw this as undermining the very purpose of a competitive economy, by sustaining a marginal firm and incompetent management.

Those in favor of the bailout argued that the bill would cost the government nothing since the government would have first claim on the company's assets should it fail. They cited the 60,000 jobs lost if the company folded, and the $500 million in lost income taxes. A further powerful argument was that the company was essential to national defense.

The practical arguments prevailed over the ideological. Lockheed survived and became profitable, and the government eventually earned $26.6 million in fees on the deal.

In early 1980, Chrysler, facing a similar situation, won $1.5 billion in federal loan guarantees. In later years, the government has stepped in to save banks and savings and loans; in some instances, as we will see in the Savings and Loan case, these firms were riddled with scandal and mismanagement.

INVITATION TO DISCUSS
Are some companies too important to be allowed to fail? Where do we draw the line on size and importance? How small should a firm be for government aid to be denied? Is this fair?

---

disclosure of its payments to foreign political organizations, officials, and agents thus jeopardizing Lockheed's visibility could affect the government-guaranteed loans.

THE INVESTIGATION UNFOLDS

Lockheed's threatened bankruptcy in 1971, in which the government was induced to provide $250 million in loan guarantees, saved the company. But the guarantee had a major negative consequence: all the company's operations were now open to scrutiny, and questionable acts involving international payoffs soon surfaced.

At the time Congress was considering the loan guarantee, hearings before the Senate Banking Committee dredged up initial evidence of payoffs to win contracts. When the story first broke, Lockheed maintained its right to bribe, and refused to disclose the information sought by Congress and the SEC, unless ordered to do so by the courts.[4]

[4]"Lockheed's Defiance: A Right to Bribe?" *Time*, Aug. 18, 1975, p. 128.

In subsequent hearings before Senator Frank Church's subcommittee on multinational corporations, the full extent of the bribery began to unfold. President Gerald Ford expressed "deep concern" about the widening scandal, and he ordered further investigation. The SEC intensified its investigation, not only of Lockheed but of other multinationals, and so did the IRS, with 300 agents searching through corporate books as well as records in foreign countries.[5]

It soon became clear that top corporate officers of Lockheed were involved in the payoff operation. And it also became clear that although a number of multinationals were involved in overseas payments, Lockheed, with $250 million, was far and away the biggest culprit. (The biggest spenders after Lockheed were Northrop, with $30 million, and Exxon, with $27 million; other sizable spenders were Raytheon, GTE, and Gulf Oil.)[6]

The Defense Department continued to place multimillion-dollar orders with Lockheed, despite the bad press. And Congress refused to withdraw government contracts as a sanction for misconduct, thus showing the vital importance of Lockheed to the military establishment (and the government's desire to keep the firm viable so it could repay the loan). But in 1977, Congress was so moved by the unfolding of the scandal that it passed the Foreign Corrupt Practices Act, designed to clean up business dealings and ban most types of foreign payoffs. (See the following information box on the *Foreign Corrupt Practices Act of 1977*.)

However, Daniel J. Haughton, chairman of the board, and A. Carl Kotchian, president, were forced to retire. A new administration and a revamped board led by outsiders sought to undue the damage and clean up the image of a tainted company.

In June 1979, Lockheed pleaded guilty to concealing the Japanese bribes by falsely writing them off as "marketing costs."[7] Under the Internal Revenue Code, no deduction is allowed for payments constituting illegal bribes or kickbacks. Lockheed also pleaded guilty to four counts of fraud and four counts of making false statements to the government. Of course, it could not be specifically charged with illegal bribery since the Foreign Corrupt Practices Act had not been enacted at the time of the misdeeds.

---

[5]"Payoffs: The Growing Scandal," *Newsweek* Special Report, Feb. 23, 1976, p. 26.

[6]Securities and Exchange Commission, *Report on Questionable and Illegal Corporate Payments and Practices*, Exhibits A and B, submitted to U.S. Congress, Senate, Committee on Banking, Housing and Urban Affairs, May 12, 1976. Some estimates of the extent of the illegal payments are much lower; the discrepancy seems to result from whether to consider sales-type commissions as illegal payments or as cover-ups for bribes.

[7]"Lockheed Pleads Guilty to Making Secret Payoffs," *San Francisco Chronicle*, June 2, 1979.

ISSUE: THE FOREIGN CORRUPT PRACTICES ACT OF 1977

This act makes it a criminal offense to offer a bribe to a foreign government official, and it authorizes the harshest penalties ever imposed on executives and
business firms. For example, companies may be fined $1 million, and individ-
uals face fines of $10,000 and five years in jail.

Although the law mandates high ethical standards when U.S. firms deal in foreign environments, it has been subject to strong criticism. Opponents claim that the
law is too restrictive, that the accounting requirements are too burdensome, and
that the penalties are so severe as to discourage many companies from attempting
to do business overseas. But the biggest criticism has to do with competitiveness:
U.S. firms lose to competitors of other nations who are not restrained from offering
bribes or other inducements to foreign officials. And in many countries of the
world, especially the developing countries, such practices are an accepted way of
life. Although proponents of the law maintain that U.S. superior technology will
win out over payoffs, such superiority is questionable in most industries today.
Particularly hard hit by the act have been makers of heavy electrical equipment,
electrical components, and consumer electronic products and components.[8]

INVITATION TO DISCUSS

A common defense for the practice of offering bribes in certain foreign countries
is: "When in Rome, do as the Romans do!" What is your position on this attitude? Do you think our companies doing business in foreign environments
should face these legal restraints? Why or why not?

THE COMEBACK

Roy A. Anderson was elected chairman and CEO of Lockheed in October
1977. He had been the company's chief financial officer. In contrast to
the "no comment on anything" practice of former chairman Haughton,
Anderson evinced an open-door policy, with frank disclosures. He also
sought to improve public relations in other ways, such as by getting the
company more involved in community affairs at plant locations.

That the company would recover from adversity was fully evident by
1982. Lockheed's earnings had increased substantially, its core business in
particular had strengthened, it had won major new contracts, its capital
structure had greatly improved, and, for the first time in more than a dozen
years, its independent auditors were able to issue an unqualified report as
to the company's financial statements.[9] Table 7.1 shows selected operating
results for 1978–1982.

---

[8]"State Regulators Rush in Where Washington No Longer Treads," *Business Week,* Sep. 19, 1983.
[9]*1982 Annual Report of Lockheed Corporation.*

Table 7.1   Lockheed Operating Results 1978–1982

Dollar figures in millions	1982	1981	1980	1979	1978
Operating Results					
Sales					
Missiles, space, electronics	$2795	$2445	$2080	$1667	$1392
Aircraft and related services	2027	1931	1797	1221	1051
Aerospace support	511	622	447	512	617
Shipbilding and other	280	178	121	132	134
Total sales	5613	5176	4445	3532	3191
Program profits					
Missiles, space, and electronics	170	163	122	97	71
Aircraft and related services	202	216	168	135	119
Aerospace support	61	61	39	68	64
Shipbuilding and other	24	21	14	11	5
Total program profits	457	461	343	311	259
Interest expense	130	186	106	72	49
Earnings from continuing operations	207	155	135	137	117
Loss from discontinued operations,		(467)	(107)	(100)	(52)
net of income tax effect					
Extraordinary items					
Tax benefits		23		20	
Gain on exchange of convertible preferred stock for debentures					
Net earnings (loss)	$ 207	$ (289)	$ 28	$ 57	$ 65

The company was now in the best position it had been in for more than a decade. Lockheed entered 1983 with an order backlog of $7.8 billion. It had increased its research and development substantially. It had also expanded the five-year capital spending program to approximately $3.5 billion.[10] All this was accomplished within the bounds of respectable business conduct.

ANALYSIS

How Guilty Was Lockheed?

Lockheed officials argued that "payments to foreign officials and political organizations are such a necessary part of its business that the U.S. government should not prohibit it from making them in the future."[11] Lockheed President A. Carl Kotchian strongly defended the payments:

> Such disbursements did not violate American Laws. . . . My decision to make such payments stemmed from my judgment that the [contracts] . . . would provide Lockheed workers with jobs and thus rebound to the benefit of their dependents, their communities and stockholders of the corporation. I should like to emphasize that the payments . . . were all requested . . . and were not brought up from my side.[12]

(See the following Issue box about the *acceptability of catering to extortion*.)

Lockheed had a host of supporters who maintained that U.S. firms would lose foreign business without payoffs. In a survey of business leaders, nearly half said they owed it to their companies to make payoffs in countries where such practices were accepted.[13]

Other proponents of payoffs in foreign environments maintained that:

- U.S. firms should not attempt to control foreign counterparts who have different standards and customs.
- Payoffs can prevent delays and expedite action, and are therefore less costly and more effective than not using payoffs. Furthermore, there are no viable alternatives to payoffs in motivating reasonable efficiency in some foreign environments.

---

[10]*Ibid.*

[11]As reported in William A. Schumann, "Lockheed Agrees to End Payouts Abroad," *Aviation Week & Space Technology,* Sept. 1, 1975, p. 19.

[12]A. Carl Kotchian, "The Payoff: Lockheed's 70-Day Mission to Tokyo," *Saturday Review,* July 9, 1977, p. 12.

[13]"The Unfolding of a Torturous Affair," *Fortune,* March 1976, p. 27.

ISSUE: IS CATERING TO EXTORTION AN ACCEPTABLE DEFENSE?

Whereas bribery involves offering something of value in order to influence actions, extortion is the demanding of a fee or payoff. In the first case, the initiative comes from the seller; in the second, from the buyer. Extortion is a type of blackmail.

If a firm wishes to do business in an environment where extortion is prevalent, should it not be excused from any culpability? Is it not the innocent victim? This, of course, was Kotchian's defense for the Japanese payoffs. Kugel and Gruenberg argue that "once the black-bag operation starts, the roles become so enmeshed that it is difficult to determine where bribery ends and extortion begins."[14] And the Foreign Corrupt Practices Act makes no distinction between bribery and extortion in improper payments.

No less an authority than Peter Drucker maintains that we should condemn less strongly the firm that pays a bribe than the person or government that demands it in the first place. "There was very little difference," he concludes, "between Lockheed's paying the Japanese and the pedestrian in New York's Central Park handing his wallet over to a mugger." Yet no one would consider the pedestrian to have acted unethically."[15] Drucker, however, does miss the point that the pedestrian's very life was in danger if he did not hand over his money, whereas Lockheed only stood to lose on the L-1011 contract, important though this might be to the company, its employees, and stockholders.

INVITATION TO DISCUSS:
Discuss the pros and cons of an extortion defense. Which position do you see as the more compelling? Why?

- Without payoffs, U.S. firms will lose foreign business. They will not be able to compete with multinationals of other countries who are not so constrained; and, as a result, the continued viability of U.S. multinationals, and even the U.S. economy, will be jeopardized.

Therefore was Lockheed guilty of the serious charge of bribery and corruption? Despite its supporters, and despite the contentions of its top management at the time, the prevailing judgment was strongly against these practices. Although bribery and corruption may be an accepted way of life in some foreign environments, and although foreign multinationals do not feel compelled to refrain from such practices, they are still anathema to the majority of U.S. citizens. Perhaps a greater factor in judging

---

[14]Kugel and Gruenberg, p. 13.
[15]Peter Drucker, "There Was Very Little Difference," *The Changing World of the Executive* (Truman Talley/Times Books, 1982), p. 237.

Lockheed is the indisputable incontrovertible fact of the sheer extent of Lockheed payoffs: almost ten times the amount of any other U.S. firm. What some might condone in moderation the majority cannot accept in the extreme.

There are those who view payoffs under any circumstances and in any amounts as something to be condemned:

- They decry the lack of moral leadership on the part of top executives who stoop to such means, and they condemn their failure to impose stronger moral standards on their subordinates.
- They feel that payoffs are a sign of moral decay.
- They believe that the social costs of international payoffs outweigh the business benefits. Therefore, morality pays in the long run.

Circumstances Most Conducive to Payoffs

The propensity to fall into a payoff situation follows a certain identifiable pattern. Not all firms are placed in this temptation, nor would payoffs be effective in all situations. When multimillion-dollar products bought by governments rather than private corporations or individuals are involved or when government officials are the negotiators of the sales contracts, the propensity is greater. In oligopolistic markets, where only a few firms compete, international payoffs become a kind of nonprice competition.

A multinational firm with host-country production facilities is better able to resist pressure for payoffs than a firm with only distribution facilities there. The latter firm usually has to rely on foreign sales agents, and as we have seen earlier, such an arrangement has the potential for payoffs under the guise of sales commissions.

WHAT CAN BE LEARNED?

Learning Insight. *Corporations can prevent questionable payments.*

Firms engaged in overseas dealings can take actions to comply with the Foreign Corrupt Practices Act and prevent questionable payments. Admittedly, this is more difficult than with domestic operations simply because of the more distant settings with less direct supervision.

Developing, clarifying, and tightening firm corporate policies concerning questionable dealings, is a starting point. Such policies should be well communicated to employees. Internal auditing can be strengthened in order to monitor employee behavior and assure that policies are being followed. Furthermore, top management must not be allowed to escape responsibility for questionable payments made by subordinates—or for any other unethical and/or illegal acts.

Since foreign agents tend to be a prime source of payoffs, such agents, when used, need to be thoroughly checked out and, of course, well informed of company policies. The use of foreign subsidiaries to export the company's products—especially in Western Europe, where bribery laws are less stringent—permits more flexibility, although the spirit of the law may be in danger of being violated.

Learning Insight. *Payments to expedite normal business transactions in foreign environments are not illegal.*

The law does not prohibit facilitating or "grease" payments that are intended, and needed, to move a transaction to its eventual conclusion where go–no go decisions are not involved. Thus, payments or gifts to a customs officer or a minor governmental official for expediting paperwork and approvals are not in violation. Such payments to relatively low-paid government people are usually small, seldom reaching more than a few hundred dollars. In the local environment, they are considered a means to supplement rather meager salaries.

Issue Insight. *Does a firm have to stoop to the lowest common denominator of ethical conduct simply because "everyone is doing it"?*

If the conclusion is "yes," then the moral conduct of an entire industry can sink to the "pits"; a follow-the-leader attitude prevails, and the firm that does not join the herd sees itself as competitively disadvantaged. This attitude has implications well beyond questionable payments. It includes deception and fraudulent acts of all kinds. In the absence of specific and enforced laws controlling such practices, the herd mentality is all the more evident.

On the other hand, cannot a firm take a stand, assume a moral stance, go against the herd? Such a position may hurt short-term performance but may bring better long-term trusting relationships with customers. But with foreign payoffs, the situation becomes more muted. If U.S. technology and service is far above foreign competitors, a U.S. firm may disdain such payments—despite demands by buyers and competitors' willingness to make such payments— and not be hurt unduly. But is U.S. technology and service so superior to foreign competitors?

Learning Insight. *Surprising though it may be to some, a firm can prosper without payoffs.*

In the years after its payoff revelations, Lockheed, under new operating management and board and with a new moral corporate climate, turned itself around. The early indications of such a turnaround were appearing by late 1977, and by 1982 significant improvements in all aspects of the operation were readily evident. The stock market was quick to recognize this.

Both substantial new business and sustaining business came from U.S. government contracts. But Lockheed also kept making considerable foreign sales.

Does this turnaround mean that foreign payoffs had not been all that effective? Perhaps they were effective at the time, even if some people would argue that they were not truly needed. And perhaps the worldwide publicity given the Lockheed scandals, as well as investigations of other multinationals, brought a more sobering stance toward payoffs by all participants. Still, the Lockheed recovery lends strong support to the view of Foreign Corrupt Practices Act proponents that firms can maintain high ethical standards and still compete and be viable.

FOR THOUGHT AND DISCUSSION

1. Defend Lockheed's position regarding payoffs in the early 1970s as persuasively as you can. Also, plan a rebuttal for the counterarguments.
2. Do you think global standards regarding business practices are likely to be enacted and enforced in the foreseeable future? Why or why not?
3. What factors do you think led Lockheed's top executives down this perilous path of bribery and questionable practices? In your opinion, did such factors excuse these executives from any condemnations for wrongdoing?
4. In this case, unlike some others, the top executives received the major blame, not some lower-level executives. How do you account for top management being so visibly involved in the scandal?

INVITATION TO ROLE PLAY

1. As a special representative of Lockheed, what arguments would you present to Prince Bernhard for accepting the bribe for the use of his influence? What objections would you expect him to raise, and how would you answer them?
2. How would you advise company officials to react to extortion attempts today?

3. As a top executive brought into the company after the serious charges against Lockheed and the resulting negative publicity, how would you attempt to remedy the situation? Make any assumptions you need to, and be as specific as possible.

INVITATION TO RESEARCH

What is the situation with Lockheed today? Is the company still prospering? Have there been any further allegations of misconduct since the mid-1970s?

8

General Dynamics: Fleecing U.S. Taxpayers

Between 1970 and 1986, General Dynamics Corporation became a symbol of corporate irresponsibility and opportunism in the military/industrial sector, fleecing the U.S. taxpayers footing the bills for military hardware. During this time, General Dynamics was investigated by the Defense Department, the Internal Revenue Service, the U.S. Senate, and the Securities and Exchange Commission. A variety of charges were levied, the most serious involving billion-dollar cost overruns incurred on the Los Angeles-class submarine program. Other charges for wide-ranging programs were also levied. America's major defense contractor faced these serious allegations of wrongdoing:

Wild cost overruns

Fraud

Faulty workmanship

Questionable dealings with Washington officials

Bill padding

Mismanagement

Overseas bribery

Tax evasion

These allegations were not unique to General Dynamics. They were symptomatic of the entire defense industry. But, they reached their apogee with General Dynamics.

THE COMPANY

General Dynamics started as the Electric Boat Company, a New Jersey ship and submarine builder founded by John Holland in 1895. During World War II, the Electric Boat Company distinguished itself by producing large numbers of submarines, PT boats, and other ships. At the end of the war, faced with diminishing sales, the company adopted a strong acquisition strategy. In 1952, it merged with Canadair, forming General Dynamics.

By 1984, General Dynamics employed 92,600 people and had nearly $7.8 billion in contracts, with profits of $382 million. The nation's third-largest defense contractor, it produced a wide range of major weapons systems for all branches of the armed forces, including the F-16 Fighter Aircraft, the Tomahawk Cruise Missile, the Stinger Antiaircraft System, the Phalanx Gun System, the Trident and SSN-688 class submarines, the M1 Main Battle Tank, and such defense electronics as the Army's Single Channel Ground and Airborne Radio System.

General Dynamics sold Atlas and Centaur launch vehicles for both government and commercial space launches. Its subsidiary, Cessna Aircraft, was one of the world's top makers of business jets (with 50 percent of the market). Another subsidiary, Material Service Corporation, sold building and highway construction materials, lime, and coal. Upcoming projects included the Navy's A-12 Attack Aircraft (produced with McDonnell Douglas) and the Advanced Tactical Fighter (General Dynamics was one of two contractor teams competing to produce this aircraft). The Electric Boat Division was one of the two ship-builders constructing the new Seawolf class attack submarine for the Navy.

Although General Dynamics' major customer was the U.S. military, it also did business with foreign countries. For example, the F-16 airplane has been ordered by Belgium, Denmark, the Netherlands, Norway, Israel, Egypt, Venezuela, South Korea, Turkey, Greece, Thailand, Singapore, Indonesia, and Bahrain.

EMERGING PROBLEMS

Over the years, General Dynamics had developed a close and symbiotic relationship with the Pentagon. Its products were at the heart of our defense armament during World War II and during the subsequent Cold War. However, allegations of mismanagement, illegal kickbacks, and overcharges had been surfacing for years. To be sure, General Dynamics was not the only object of such charges—the other defense contractors also had their critics—but General Dynamics got most of the spotlight, particularly regarding its Trident and SSN-688 attack submarines.

The story began in 1968. The Navy was under pressure to stay ahead of the growing Soviet submarine threat. This was at the height of the Cold War, with the Berlin Wall completed only a few years earlier (construction on the Wall began on August 13, 1961). The prospects for war brought the decision to seek defense contractors for nuclear submarines. Because of the heavy costs involved, and because this was the first nuclear-powered submarine, the bidding process was limited to what the Navy deemed the two ablest contractors. General Dynamics' Electric Boat Division won the contract and became the first firm to make the Navy's nuclear-powered SSN-688 sub, armed with the most important weapon in the U.S. arsenal, the Trident ballistic missile.

The Navy insisted that the job be done under a fixed-price contract instead of the more common "cost plus" contract. This was exceedingly risky for General Dynamics, since no one knew how much it would cost to build high-speed nuclear submarines. Only years later, when the price ballooned well above the contracted price, did the problems with this arrangement become evident. In 1976, General Dynamics filed a claim for $843 million in cost overruns, this being a $46 million surcharge for each of the 18 subs. General Dynamics claimed the cost increase was due to Navy mismanagement of the contracts, to its constant changing of specifications. On the other hand, the Navy recoiled at paying what they claimed were totally unjustified charges due to gross mismanagement. The low-price bidding practices of the defense industry became vulnerable to intensive critical investigation.

ALLEGATIONS

In 1978, the Navy finally agreed to pay a significant portion of the heavy cost overruns on the submarines. Some people—including Admiral Hyman Rickover, the guiding force behind the nuclear navy, and Senator William Proxmire—were highly critical of the deal. They maintained that the company had falsely attributed the overruns to the thousands of engineering changes ordered by the Navy.[1]

The cost overruns were not limited to the Electric Boat Division. Other projects with major overcharges were the M1 Abrams Tank, the DIVAD Self-Propelled AntiAircraft Gun, and the F-18 Fighter Bomber. For example, the authorized cost per unit of the Abrams Tank was $2 million. But the actual production cost was $2.8 million, a 42.4 percent overcharge.

Although cost overruns received the most attention, they were not the most damaging to General Dynamics. Allegations of fraud were. The Defense

---

[1]Eric Gelman, "A Giant Under Fire: General Dynamics Faces Numerous Charges of Fraud," *Newsweek*, Feb. 11, 1985, pp. 24–25.

Department uncovered evidence that the company illegally gave Admiral Rickover $67,628 in gifts, presumably to gain his influence. Influential he was, supervising billions of dollars of top-secret work at the Electric Boat Shipyard.

The Defense Department discovered other General Dynamics indiscretions, including a history of padding its bills to the Defense Department with dubious overhead charges, such as executives' country-club dues, the costs of lobbying government officials, and, a celebrated example, the cost of boarding a top executive's dog. The company was found to have billed the government for 90 percent of the $22 million in air travel costs for flights from the company's St. Louis headquarters to Albany, Georgia, where General Dynamics Chairman David S. Lewis owned a farm he used as a weekend retreat.[2]

The company was accused of gross mismanagement. Numerous internal documents compiled by congressional investigators revealed the complaints managers at all levels had about the company: poor supervision, low morale, materials not ordered on time, proper records not kept. The documents also suggested that the company had long had a strategy of recouping its losses through false expense claims.[3] Other allegations concerned attempts to manipulate the value of General Dynamics' stock, illegal wiretapping, and improper reporting of income taxes.

In September 1983, more fraud charges arose when P. Takis Veliotis, a Greek shipbuilding executive brought in to straighten out the problems at Electric Boat in 1977, was himself indicted by a federal grand jury for taking kickbacks on contracts he had let while running another General Dynamics shipyard. Veliotis, a dual citizen of the United States and Greece, fled to Athens—out of reach of U.S. law—after the indictment. But, early in 1982, he sought to plea bargain with the Justice Department, providing documents and tapes to help the case against General Dynamics. Veliotis also charged that the company had bribed government officials in South Korea and Egypt in order to sell the F-16 fighter plane.

CONSEQUENCES

In May 1985, as a result of the 1984–1985 investigation, John Lehman, Secretary of the Navy, announced a crackdown on General Dynamics. Some $22.5 million in contracts were canceled, a $676,283 fine was imposed, and a series of housecleaning measures was mandated, including the creation of a rigorous code of ethics for company employees and the settlement of some

---

[2]Tom Morganthau, "Waste, Fraud and Abuse? The Navy Cracks Down on a Major Defense Contractor," *Newsweek*, June 3, 1986, pp. 22–23.

[3]Gelman, pp. 24–25.

$75 million in disputed Navy billings. Lehman decried the "integrity and responsibility" of the corporation.[4]

The next day, General Dynamics' 67 year-old chairman, David S. Lewis, announced his retirement. Also retiring were finance officer Gordon MacDonald, vice president George Sawyer, executive vice president James Beggs, division general manager Ralph Hawes, program director David McPherson, and assistant director James Hansen. Lewis was replaced by Stanley C. Pace, who had a more upright ethical image. (See the information box, on *salvaging a corporate image by a management change*.)

General Dynamics was virtually unpunished, even following convictions of wrongdoing. Although some management changes were made, the value of the cancelled contracts amounted only to .1 percent of the firm's billings the previous year. The partnership with the Pentagon was soon resumed, and the culpable executives received no prison sentences, merely a comfortable retirement.

How could such malpractices be so easily tolerated? Alas, they were endemic to the whole industry, not just limited to General Dynamics.

THE ETHICAL CLIMATE OF THE DEFENSE INDUSTRY

General Dynamics' questionable practices were not unique. They represented flaws "deeply embedded in defense procurement," as *Newsweek* magazine reported. "Some problems, ranging from faulty products to overcharges, seem endemic to defense contractors—especially the giant aerospace, electronics and high-tech companies that make up the bulk of what has long been known as the military-industrial complex."[5]

In the defense industry, major contracts rarely came in under budget. Other abuses were also prevalent. For example, after receiving evidence that thousands of computer chips had not been adequately tested, the Pentagon's inspector general, Joseph Sherick, launched an investigation of 10 semiconductor manufacturers. Several of these were subsequently found guilty of failure to meet government standards. Congressional investigations revealed outrageous overpricing by contractors for commonplace tools and spare parts. As one example, Gould, Inc. charged the Pentagon $436 for a hammer. Subsequent analysis disclosed that the hammer and its packaging cost Gould only $8 to make; the rest was for unspecified overhead and administrative costs.[6]

[4]Morganthau, pp. 22–23.
[5]Susan Dentzer, "How the Pentagon Spends Its Billions," *Newsweek*, February 11, 1985, p. 26.
[6]*Ibid.*, pp. 26–28.

CAN A BELEAGUERED CORPORATE IMAGE BE
SALVAGED BY A MANAGEMENT CHANGE?

Stanley Pace, General Dynamics' new chief executive, supposedly had a strong moral background. After all, he had been long associated with the Boy Scouts of America. Taking over from retiring David Lewis in December 1985, Pace decided his main charge was to improve the company's ethical image. He quickly instituted a series of administrative procedures designed to tone up "executive-level ethics and thwart corruption in the future."[7]

On January 16, 1986, Pace appeared before the National Press Club in Washington to describe the changes he'd made and to try to improve the company's image before the nation's press. The "fixes" he described included tightened procedures for everything from government contract billing to time-card reporting. He said he'd hired a corporate ethics program director "who reports directly to me" and a team of field-based ethics directors who were represented at every General Dynamics site. Also, a 20-page code of ethics handbook was to be distributed to all salaried employees.

Pace was shocked that the reporters did not treat his "fixes" with much respect. They peppered him with skeptical questions, such as: "Aren't you simply *promising* to be honest?" and "Is this what it takes to make a corporation honest?" After trying to defend his actions for half an hour, Pace hurried from the room, pleading another appointment.

The press remained unconvinced that the Pace's announced changes were anything more than cosmetic, that they were symptomatic of a major turnaround in the company's dealings with the government and eventually with taxpayers.

INVITATION TO DISCUSS
Evaluate the importance cosmetic changes can have for a company beset with public image problems. Discuss their necessity and their effectiveness.

As of May 1, 1985, the Defense Department was investigating 45 top defense contractors concerning possible criminal charges. See Table 8.1 for a listing of the 36 companies in open investigation and the allegations against them. General Dynamics was not alone in abusing its position with the government and with the public who pays the bills.

ANALYSIS—ASSESSING BLAME

In analyzing the abuses, identifying the contributory factors, and evaluating the defenses or explanations for what happened, we can categorize these as: (1) those within the organization that reflect directly on management and

---

[7]Janet Fix, "Corruption Thwarter," *Forbes*, Feb. 10, 1986, p. 140.

Table 8.1   Defense Contractors Under Open Investigation by the Defense Department and the Allegations, May 1, 1985

Washington—The Defense Dept. Inspector General's Office is conducting investigations of 45 top defense contractors concerning possible criminal charges, including 36 companies listed as open investigations as of May 1 (AW&ST June 24, p. 15). The list was made public by Rep. John D. Dingell (D.-Mich.), chairman of the House Energy and Commerce oversight and investigations subcommittee.

CONTRACTOR	ALLEGATION
MacDonnell Douglas Corp.	Cost mischarging
Rockwell International Corp.	Cost and labor mischarging
General Dynamics Corp.	Cost mischarging
	Subcontractor kickbacks
	Labor mischarging
	Product substitution
	Security compromise
	Defective pricing
	Cost duplication
	False claims
Lockheed Corp.	Labor mischarging
Boeing Co., Inc.	Cost mischarging
	Supply accountability
	Labor mischarging
General Electric Co.	False claims
	Defective pricing
	Labor cost mischarging
	Product substitution
United Technologies Corp.	Gratuities
	Subcontractor kickbacks
	Cost mischarging
	Bribery
	Defective pricing
Raytheon Co.	Labor mischarging
	Product substitution
Litton Industries, Inc.	Bribery-subcontractors kickbacks
	Labor mischarging
	False claims
	Bid rigging
	Cost mischarging
Grumman Corp.	Cost mischarging
Martin Marietta Corp.	Subcontractor kickback
	Cost mischarging
Westinghouse Electric Corp.	Cost mischarging
Sperry Corp.	Labor mischarging
	Cost mischarging

Table 8.1 (*continued*)

CONTRACTOR	ALLEGATION
Sperry Corp. (continued)	Defective pricing
Honeywell, Inc.	Diversion of government property
	Bid rigging
Ford Motor Co.	Defective pricing-labor mischarging
	Falsification of performance records
Eaton Corp.	Conflict of interest-gratuities
	Cost mischarging
TRW, Inc.	Defective pricing
	Cost mischarging
Texas Instruments	Product substitution
Northrop Corp.	Labor mischarging
	False progress payments
Avco Corp.	Subcontractor kickbacks
	Cost mischarging
Textron, Inc.	Cost mischarging
Allied Corp.	Conflict of interest
Tenneco, Inc.	Cost mischarging
GTE Corp.	Unauthorized acquisition and utilization of classified data
	Labor mischarging
Sanders Associates, Inc.	Unauthorized release of contract information
Motorola, Inc.	Labor mischarging
Congoleum Corp.	Mischarging
	Gratuities/theft
Harris Corp.	Defective pricing
Gould, Inc.	Cost mischarging
Emerson Electric Co.	Cost mischarging
	Gratuities-cost mischarging
John Hopkins University	Civilian health and medical program of the uniformed services fraud
Tracor, Inc.	Product substitution
Lear Siegler, Inc.	Product substitution
Fairchild Industries, Inc.	Gratuities
	Product substitution
	Cost mischarging
	False statements
Dynalectron Corp.	Cost mischarging
Todd Shipyard Corp.	Noncompliances with contract

Source: "Defense Dept. Lists Contractor Investigations," *Aviation Week & Space Technology*, July 15, 1985, p. 89.

workers at General Dynamics, (2) miscellaneous external factors that motivated overruns and other temptations, and (3) the procurement process itself.

Internal Contributing Factors

General Dynamics' management was undoubtedly responsible for a great
number of poor management decisions. Former senior executive, James
Ashton, contended that the problems at the Electric Boat Shipyard during
the 1970s had been caused by mismanagement. He also testified before a
House subcommittee that General Dynamics made such an unrealistic bid
to win the Los Angeles-class contract that it could not afford to hire the
engineers needed to cope with the design revisions. Numerous memos
from managers at every level of the company complained of poor supervision, low morale, ineffective inventories of goods needed, and improper
record-keeping.[8]

Top management cannot be exonerated for the deficiencies of subordinates, of course. In this case, one wonders whether the inability to effectively control their large operation caused upper managers to panic and
attempt to hide mistakes. Top management seemed willingly to embrace
opportunities to recoup losses through false claims. From there, it was but a
short step to ever more serious instances of fraud.

Admittedly, the demands on management and on the entire organization was severe on some of these projects. For example, Newport News
Shipyard, which had received the contract to design the subs, had never
drawn up plans for a nuclear-powered submarine before and was therefore
late getting the blueprints to Electric Boat. The Navy was also late deliver-
ing construction specifications. Meanwhile, General Dynamics' Electric
Boat Division had to grow very rapidly in order to do the mammoth job as
quickly as the Navy demanded. Its shipyard labor force grew from 12,000
workers in 1971 to almost 30,000 by the middle of 1977. The proportion of
skilled workers plummeted from 80 percent of the work force in 1972 to 35
percent four years later.

It quickly became apparent that Electric Boat was in deep trouble. "Its
rapidly hired work force, lacking necessary expertise, wasn't up to the task.
Welders couldn't weld, managers couldn't manage, and quality controllers
couldn't control the quality of materials or workmanship."[9] A Navy inspector reported that 2772 welds had to be repaired. The wrong kind of steel
was used in 126,000 locations in the Trident subs, and much of it had to be

[8]Gelman, pp. 24–25.
[9]O. Kelly, "Inside Story of the Trident Debacle," *U.S. News & World Report*, March 30,
1981, p. 21.

replaced. A faulty turbine was installed in the "Ohio," first of the Trident subs, and had to be taken out piece by piece.[10]

External Contributing Factors

General Dynamics' officials were quick to contend that thousands of design changes initiated by the Navy and Air Force caused, not only delays in the construction of the various defense weapons, but also massive additional expenditures to expedite corrective measures. Undoubtedly, there is merit to this excuse; at least, the blame is not all General Dynamics'.

A major external factor in widespread defense industry fraud and other abuses is the ineptitude of government watchdog agencies:

> [E]vidence is mounting that Justice's Defense Procurement Fraud Unit hasn't lived up to its billing. . . . [C]ritics say most of its prosecutions, which have recovered only $8.2 million, involve penny-ante charges that didn't require much expertise. The unit, they complain, is plagued by inadequate resources and has handled poorly its few major cases.[11]

After a probe into the Sperry Corporation for cost overruns and labor mischarging was called off because of the fraud unit's ineptitude in pursuing the case, Senators William Proxmire of Wisconsin and Charles Grassley of Iowa were shocked, publicly stating: "It is abundantly clear we do not have efficient and effective enforcement against defense fraud."[12]

Such ineffective enforcement resulted in an inability to maintain any accountability of defense contractors. As a consequence, they were allowed to indulge in unchecked spending, wild cost overruns, and fraudulent claims—easy temptations for most firms, large and small, to succumb to.

Another major factor leading to a climate of opportunism and grab-what-you-can is the scarcity of real competition in this industry. These firms are in the cat-bird seat. Defense-sanctioned monopolies that spawn waste, inefficiency, and fraud predominate in the absence of true competition. In other business environments, the customer who is taken advantage of simply shifts to another supplier. But this is not easily done with major defense firms. As Stanley Pace of General Dynamics summed it up:

---

[10]*Ibid.*

[11]Paula Dwyer, "Is Justice Bungling the Defense Fraud Crackdown?" *Business Week*, April 21, 1986, p. 75.

[12]Janice Castro, "Probe Scuttled—A Three-Year Inquiry Ends," *Time*, June 1, 1987, p. 51.

We (GD) have the major heartland programs with each of the armed services. And we have the balance sheet and cash flow to make the investments for the weapons of the future. We are now working both sides of the street.[13]

The Procurement Process

The defense procurement process lends itself to abuses and taxpayer fleecing. To begin with, not all contracts are subject to competitive bidding. General Dynamics holds a monopoly on the building of Trident submarines, the M1 tank, and the F-16 fighter. Undoubtedly, this enabled it to escape serious punishment for all of its problems with the government. With competitive bidding, or even with split-sourcing (having more than one company bid for the contract, the company with the lowest bid receiving 60 percent of the contract, and the losing company receiving the rest), the government's dependence on a single vital supplier would be reduced. The possibility of punitive actions that more closely matched the abuses should act as a deterrent. And price gouging should be tempered.

The number of "layers" in the procurement process promotes inefficiencies. Each of the military branches has its own separate group for acquisitions (Air Force Command, Army Material Command, etc.). At least 165,000 people have been directly employed by the Pentagon for research, development, and logistics; thousands more work for aerospace corporations at the government's expense. Each layer has its own reviews, which call for bureaucratic meetings and paperwork. This adds to the cumbersomeness of the process, the costs, and the fragmentation of control.[14]

Invoice auditing poses another problem. In the mid-1980s, the Defense Contract Audits Agency had a backlog of $70 billion worth of invoices. For years, many of the fraudulent billing claims were allowed to slip through the audits because of a flaw in the process. The auditor's job is tied to the companies audited. If expenditures with a company are reduced, auditing positions are eliminated. This creates a disincentive for auditors to severely scrutinize and follow-up on questionable activities. The solution here would be to evaluate how much waste auditors uncover and eliminate.[15]

Adding to the Defense Department's motivations for continuing questionable programs and hiring questionable contractors is the military career syndrome. Rotations and transfers are so extensive among officers involved with procurement that dozens of people may have been involved

---

[13]Robert Wrubel, "Gunning It," *Financial World*, March 8, 1988, p. 25.
[14]Gregg Easterbrook, "Sack Weinberger, Bankrupt General Dynamics, and Other Procurement Reforms," *The Washington Monthly*, Jan. 1987, pp. 33–46.
[15]*Ibid.*

in purchasing a single system. Such turnover and "new perspectives" often results in ever-changing specifications and add-ons, thus greatly increasing costs. Furthermore, officers advance their careers far more by acquiring weapons systems than by killing projects. Hence, procurement officers often have as much interest in seeing a weapon developed as the manufacturer does:

> Procurement officials and contractors effectively become co-conspirators; both sides may understate the costs of a weapon while its purchase is still being contemplated in an effort to secure the final order.[16]

Add to all this a good dash of politics: "[O]nce politics enters the picture, procurement decisions may not be made on the basis of economics or military decisions, but on the need to satisfy constituents."[17] Woe to the member of Congress who does not protect the major employers in his or her district, no matter how unneeded the output is, or how inefficient or corrupt this large employer may be.

WHAT CAN BE LEARNED?

Issue Insight. *Toward a Balanced View of the Defense Industry.*

There's a temptation to regard General Dynamics' dismal record—and that of the rest of the defense industry—as yet another indictment of a capitalist system fraught with inefficient and self-seeking workers and managers. However, the facts do not totally support this easy, finger-pointing conclusion. Certainly, General Dynamics can be criticized—and perhaps should have received harsher penalties. But the whole system by which the Pentagon procures new weapons systems is flawed.

Every major cost-overrun, scandal, and engineering or production mistake stimulates two powerful political reactions. One, Congress, the media, and the public are quick to look for wrongdoers. Extensive investigations are undertaken, some of which result in grand jury indictments, and the press pounces on any suspicions of corruption and greed. Usually, the charges are eventually dropped for lack of sufficient evidence of criminal intent, or else watered-down plea bargains defuse the public's criticism and blame-seeking. The second powerful reaction is pressure put on the Pentagon to add more checks and balances, more auditors and inspectors—in other words, to

---

[16]Tony Kay, "It's Waste and Fraud As Usual At the Pentagon," *The Nation*, June 15, 1985, pp. 734–738.
[17]Dentzer, p. 27.

burden the procurement process with even more red tape, paperwork, and bureaucracy. For example, the Defense Department, responding to scandal of the $436 hammer, the $600 toilet seat, and the $7,000 coffee makers, "added 7,000 additional staffers to solve such problems."[18]

Neither of these actions are the solution. What is needed is a better recognition of what defense contractors can do well. Crash programs to build whole new fleets (of nuclear submarines, for example) and weapons systems invite trouble. The huge numbers of new workers that the Electric Boat Division needed to build the Trident sub invited trouble: Technicians, managers, workers—none could cope well with the timetable, resulting in poorly built and wildly expensive products. Of course, "the sheer size of the stakes, $100 million or more for a single sub, was enough to excite the greed and test the integrity of even the most well-meaning contractor."[19] The bigger and more complex a project is, the fewer the prime contractors who will be able to bid on it. Relying on a single firm in such a monopoly situation provides a great opportunity for abusive practices, suspicions and distrust by the government, and it lessens the likelihood that there will be sufficient penalties to deter management's darker leanings. (See the Issue box regarding *tolerance of wrongdoings in the framework of national security*.)

ISSUE: HOW TOLERANT CAN WE BE WITH FIRMS VITAL TO OUR NATIONAL SECURITY?

This is a crucial issue, with major implications for how we tolerate discrepancies in cost, quality, and deadlines—not to mention improper and unethical conduct. Theoretically, because national security is at stake, we expect the highest operational and ethical standards. But is this realistic?

Unfortunately, the answer is no. Because of the crucial role such contractors play in national defense, and because of the lack of acceptable alternative contractors, we may have to tolerate conduct that would not be acceptable in other industries. Because of the monopoly position such firms as General Dynamics have, we can hardly refuse to do further business with them, despite their misdeeds. We should not penalize them so severely as to curtail their viability and performance. Beyond publicly decrying their misdeeds and giving them a "slap on the wrist," there is little we can do in the way of punitive measures. So, the firm's risks from overcharging, committing fraud, and currying favoritism are minimal. Even a discredited public image—which could be devastating to firms in other industries—can be disregarded by these firms, since their role is so vital and since the government is their primary customer, not the general public.

---

[18]Jack Robertson, "Currie: Contractors on Tightrope," *Electronic News*, July 1989, p. 35.
[19]Charles P. Alexander, "General Dynamics Under Fire," *Time*, April 1985, p. 57.

So, despite our druthers, these firms' transgressions will continue to be less severely punished—in fact will be tacitly accepted.

Is there any recourse? The major recourse would appear to be monitoring more closely, seeking to develop competitive options, and avoiding the worst of the crash programs that have plagued the military-industrial complex in the past. Perhaps, with the end of the Cold War, our defense contractors, with fewer crash programs, will try to diversify into civilian markets rather than relying totally on government business.

INVITATION TO DISCUSS
Are punitive threats the best way to curb abuses in the defense industry? Discuss, and present any other recommendations.

Learning Insight: *The bureaucratic procurement process invites abuses.*

The relatively few major defense contractors competing for multi-million- and even billion-dollar projects presents an environment fraught with temptations for abuses of all kinds. Influence seeking and peddling can become major factors in procurement decisions and with politicians involved in seeking the fruits of massive governmental contracts for the benefit of their own constituents, the decision-making process can become muddled, and not always objective.

The sheer complexity of these major technological projects defies close control and monitoring, despite government attempts to do so. At the same time, the virtual monopoly position that the winner of a major defense contract assumes tends to deaden the effort to maximize efficiency and keep a tight rein on costs.

So we have mighty cost overruns, quality control problems, the temptation to pad bills and throw in extravagant and irrelevant expenses, as well as other fraudulent practices, even including bribery. While, as we saw in the Lockheed case, the defense industry at one time became notorious for its bribery of foreign governmental officials to win contracts, certainly bribery on a lesser scale was far from unknown domestically. However, it often assumed more subtleties. These might include high-level executive positions for retiring generals and admirals, as well as key procurement officers. They might include lucrative consulting and speaking engagements for politicians and government administrators.

In the normal competitive business environment, such practices and looseness of operations would be little tolerated and would be competitively vulnerable. But in the folds of bureaucracy, and with the cloak of highly complex technologies, the actions of General Dynamics were far from unique, as we have seen.

Is there any solution to this waste in the defense industry? It is questionable if such abusive practices can be completely eliminated, especially during periods of national emergency when defense efforts are intensified. During periods of calm and reduced defense expenditures, closer controls should be possible. Government auditing can be improved, as was discussed in the section on the procurement process. Other constraints would be the encouragement of whistleblowing, and also of investigative reporting.

Learning Insight: *Rationalizing excesses is easy when the burden is spread over millions of taxpayers.*

This situation of millions of taxpayers footing the bill has undoubtedly fueled more excesses than any other single factor. With the burden of extravagance, inefficiency, and bureaucratic expansion spread over the masses, the impact is minor for any individual taxpayer. Hence, the temptation. The great faceless mass is seen as somehow amorphous and hardly to be considered, and certainly unable to exercise restraints, even in election years, when more than 95 percent of incumbents are reelected.

FOR THOUGHT AND DISCUSSION

1. How might the Defense Department bring more competition into the defense industry? Is this feasible?
2. How might government auditing of defense contractors be improved? Would this likely correct most of the misdeeds? Why or why not?
3. On balance, who do you think was more culpable in the defense industry misdeeds: the firms or the government? Why?
4. Compare and contrast General Dynamics and Lockheed as to their relative culpabilities.

INVITATION TO ROLE PLAY

1. You are an assistant to the top executive of the Electric Boat Division. Your division has just received the contract for the Trident sub. This will require a massive buildup of personnel. How would you plan for an orderly assimilation so as to meet the timetable while maintaining reasonable quality? Be as specific as you can, making any needed assumptions.
2. You are a staff assistant to the Secretary of Defense. You are charged with developing a framework for improving the procurement process. What recommendations would you make? What objections would you anticipate?

INVITATION TO RESEARCH

1. Has General Dynamics received any more adverse publicity since Stanley Pace took over as chief executive?
2. Investigate the effects of reduced defense spending on firms such as General Dynamics and on the communities in which they dwell.

CHAPTER 9

The Dalkon Shield: Spurning User Safety

It is February 29, 1984. Three company executives have been summoned to appear in federal district court before Judge Miles Lord in Minneapolis, Minnesota. They are E. Claiborne Robins, Jr., A. H. Robins Company President and CEO; Dr. Carl D. Lunsford, Director of Research; and William A. Forrest, Jr., the company's general counsel. With them in the courtroom is a horde of lawyers.

To the three executives' acute shock, embarrassment, and anger, they hear Judge Lord publicly chastise them and their company for their conduct regarding the marketing of the Dalkon Shield, an intrauterine birth control device.

For some months, Judge Lord had been involved with a combined suit against the company by seven women who had been seriously injured by the Shield. The investigation delved into past Dalkon Shield litigation and the legal tactics employed by Robins for over 10 years. The judge noted in his stinging rebuke:

> And when the time came for these women to make their claims against your company, you attacked their characters. You inquired into their sexual practices and into the identity of their sex partners. You ruined families and reputations and careers in order to intimidate those who would raise their voices against you. You introduced issues that had no relationship to the fact that you had planted in the bodies of these women instruments of death, of mutilation, of disease. . . . Another of your callous legal tactics is to force women of little

means to withstand the onslaughts of your well-financed team of attorneys. You target your worst tactics at the meek and the poor. . . . You have taken the bottom line as your guiding beacon and the low road as your route.[1]

Judge Lord also ordered a search of the company's files. Court-appointed officials found strong evidence that the company had covered up its knowledge of the Dalkon Shield's dangers.

The Robins officials retaliated by bringing a lawsuit against Judge Lord—which they subsequently lost.

Between 1971 and 1975, Robins had sold more than 4 million Dalkon Shield IUDs in 80 countries of the world. In so doing, it had ignored ever-increasing concerns of physicians and others about the Shield's effectiveness and safety. In the United States alone, more than 2 million women were fitted with the inadequately tested contraceptive device by doctors who believed the optimistic claims of the company. As a result, thousands of women suffered serious damage caused by the shield—from pelvic infection to sterility, miscarriage, and even death.

This became one of the biggest business blunders of all time, made so much worse by a firm that at first blinded itself to any danger, then tried to cover it up . . . until finally the dam burst.

How could a respected management, one with the reputation of a multigenerational family firm at stake, have accepted such risks with an untested new product in the crass pursuit of short-term profits? And how could it, in a panic over impending lawsuits, have so deceived itself, as well as the medical profession and the general public, into believing that nothing was wrong, that others—that is, physicians themselves—were to blame?

INTRAUTERINE CONTRACEPTIVES (IUDs) AND THE DALKON SHIELD

Interest in birth control, and in particular IUDs as a form of contraception, goes back to ancient times, although most efforts were perilous and unreliable. Medical reports in the 1920s noted many cases of pelvic infection and inflammation with the crude IUD devices available then, and these devices were generally discredited.

In the early 1960s, interest in birth control greatly increased because of two factors. First, fears had begun to emerge of an overpopulated world. These fears seemed justified, since a billion people had been added to the world's population between 1930 and 1960. Although most of the fears

[1]Miles W. Lord, "A Plea for Corporate Conscience." Speech reprinted in *Harpers,* June 1984, pp. 13–14.

centered on the developing nations of Africa, Asia, and South America, the United States was also experiencing population growth, reaching the psychological milestone of 200 million in the 1960s.

Second, the first oral contraceptive was approved by the Food and Drug Administration in 1960 and was enthusiastically received by both women and the medical profession. However, worries began to surface about the Pill. Some of these concerned its side effects, such as blood clots. Of even more concern was the possibility of long-term risks for women using the powerful birth-control hormones for as many as three decades of childbearing years.

After decades of IUDs being discredited, two developments in the 1960s spurred interest in them. One was the discovery of a new, malleable, inert plastic from which IUDs could be made, and the second was the development of a new molding process. Two new IUDs were patented in 1966: the Lippes Loop and the Saf-T-Coil.

Meantime, Hugh J. Davis, an associate professor of gynecology at Johns Hopkins, and Irwin Lerner, an inventor, came up with an idea for a new IUD—on Christmas Day, 1967. Initial results looked good, and Lerner applied for a patent in 1968. In shape, this new IUD resembled a shield and was a dime-sized, crablike plastic device with a string attached for removal by the physician.

On February 1, 1970, the *American Journal of Obstetrics and Gynecology* published an article by Davis based on his testing at Johns Hopkins Family Planning Clinic of 640 women who had worn the device, named the Dalkon Shield. Davis cited 5 pregnancies, 10 rejections, 9 removals for medical reasons, and 3 removals for personal reasons. He reported a pregnancy rate of 1.1 percent. The article impressed many doctors because of such favorable statistics and because it was tested at the prestigious Johns Hopkins School of Medicine. As a result, many became interested in obtaining the device for their own patients.

Davis and Lerner decided to market the device themselves, and the Dalkon Company was formed in 1969. They worked to refine the product, and by April 1970, they introduced a new, improved device, which made the Shield more flexible and thinner, with barium sulfate to strengthen the plastic, while retaining its flexibility. However, lacking a sales organization, the owners quickly realized that the Shield would have to be distributed by an established corporation.

Schmid Laboratories turned down the idea, but then Upjohn made an offer. However, at a medical meeting in Bedford, Pennsylvania, another company was attracted, A. H. Robins. On June 12, 1970, after three days of negotiating, Robins topped the Upjohn offer and bought ownership rights to the Dalkon Shield for $750,000 plus consulting fees and a royalty of 10 percent on all U.S. and Canadian net sales. (That figure ultimately came to nearly $1.2 million.)

THE A. H. ROBINS COMPANY

The A.H. Robins Company, headquartered in Richmond, Virginia, was a relatively small company ($135 million in sales at the time), but it had subsidiaries in more than a dozen foreign countries. It was best known for such products as Robitussin cough syrup, Chap Stick lip balm, and Sergeant's Flea and Tick collars. It was no fly-by-night company: for more than a century, it had been a solid business citizen.

In 1860, Albert Hanley Robins opened a small apothecary shop in downtown Richmond. In 1878, he expanded into manufacturing: while A. H. Robins handled walk-in business, selling the patent medicines of the day, his son and daughter-in-law had a small pill-rolling operation upstairs.

So the mom-and-pop undertaking continued until 1933, when a grandson, Edwin Claiborne Robins, took over management with dreams of expanding. He stopped selling medicines directly to the public and turned instead to selling prescription drugs to physicians and pharmacists. The first such product was a stomach remedy, Donnatel, which is still a major product. After World War II, the company became a major manufacturer of mass-marketed prescription and nonprescription drugs. In 1963, with net sales of $47 million and profits near $5 million, the firm went public. In the process, E. Claiborne Robins, Sr., turned his family into one of the wealthiest in Virginia. In 1978, E. Claiborne Robins, Jr., became president and CEO.

Since 1965, the company had been interested in the birth-control market and particularly in intrauterine devices, although it had never made or sold a medical device or gynecological product before and had no obstetrician or gynecologist on its staff. It had considered buying the rights for the Lippes Loop, but then the Dalkon Shield opportunity surfaced.

The potential for IUDs as a group seemed attractive. But perhaps the biggest plus for IUDs was that they did not require filing a New-Drug Application (NDA) with the Food and Drug Administration. Since the agency only had jurisdiction over drugs and not over medical devices (which was how IUDs were classified), a manufacturer did not have to file an NDA demonstrating that it had established relative safety with reliable and sufficient clinical and animal testing. Thus, lengthy research safety testing of the Dalkon Shield could be avoided. (On May 28, 1976, the Medical Device Amendments were enacted to bring medical devices under the supervision of the Food and Drug Administration, but these amendments came five years after the Dalkon Shield was first brought to market.)

Robins quickly made plans to bring the Shield to market, and its assembly was assigned to the Chap Stick division. The company saw an urgent need to get into the market before potential competitors could rush in. In January 1971, only six months after Robins acquired the rights, the Dalkon Shield was ready for national distribution. The profitability potential was intriguing: the production cost was only about 25 cents, while the Shield was priced at $4.35. While there were some quality control problems, they were deemed not to be particularly serious.

Promoting the Dalkon Shield

An aggressive marketing strategy was put in place. Several hundred salespeople were trained to contact physicians. The advertising itself was directed at both the medical professionals—physicians as well as agencies and clinics that provided IUDs—and women directly to persuade them to accept the Shield if their physicians should so recommend, and even to request and insist on the device if their physicians were skeptical. Consequently, in addition to medical journals, *Family Circle, Mademoiselle,* and similar magazines carried Dalkon Shield advertising.

Robins wanted to position the Shield as a superior product. In 1970, it was promoted as a modern superior IUD, with the lowest pregnancy rate (1.1 percent), lowest expulsion rate (2.3 percent), and the highest continuation rate (94 percent). Other promotional literature stated that it was the only IUD anatomically engineered for optimal uterine placement, fit, tolerance, and retention.

In the ads in major medical journals, Dr. Davis (the original researcher and coinventor) was shown as an impressive research physician, with citations from the articles he had published. Not disclosed was his financial interest in the product and that he was hardly the objective and unbiased researcher deemed essential to sound medical research.

The Shield proved to be a popular product in the contraceptive market. By 1972, an estimated 12 million IUDs were in use worldwide, with 3 million in the United States. And the Shield was in the forefront: some 1,146,000 were sold in 1971, with an estimated market share of 40 percent. In one month, April 1972, some 88,000 women were fitted with the Shield.

But the physician complaints began to mount. In the early months, many of these complaints focused on the difficulty of inserting the Shield— later, these complaints would assume a more serious nature.

Despite all objections, by August 1973, more than 5 million pieces of promotional literature had been printed. The sales pitch did not change: "No general effects on the body, blood, or brain . . . safe and trouble-free . . . the safest and most satisfactory method of contraception . . . truly

superior."[2] A new, smaller Shield had been brought out, and this was especially directed to women who had never borne children. However, no
safety and effectiveness testing was ever done with this new version.

Storm Clouds

In June 1973, Henry S. Kahn, a researcher working for the Centers for
Disease Control, headed a study to assess the safety of IUDs in general. In a
survey of physicians in the United States and Puerto Rico, some surprising
and troubling things surfaced. There seemed to be a significant correlation
between the Dalkon Shield and the incidence of women hospitalized for a
complicated pregnancy. He suggested that a more detailed investigation
was warranted. At about the same time, Representative L. H. Fountain of
North Carolina was chairing a subcommittee investigating whether medical
devices should be subject to the same kinds of controls as drugs.

In the months that followed, more serious problems came to light,
including some Shield-related deaths. In October 1973, Robins changed its
Shield package label to include the warning, "Severe sepsis with fatal outcome, most often associated with spontaneous abortion following pregnancy with the Dalkon Shield *in situ* has been reported. In view of this,
serious consideration should be given to removing the device when the
diagnosis of pregnancy is made with the Dalkon Shield *in situ*."

Robins convened its own Ob-Gyn advisory panel in February 1974 to
evaluate information on cases of spontaneous septic abortion among women
who became pregnant with the Shield in place. The panel finally concluded
that there was inadequate information to establish a cause-and-effect relationship.

But problems continued to multiply. The Shield had a multifilament
tail, compared with the monofilament tails used in all other IUDs. This tail
was shown in several studies to be an excellent harbor for bacteria. In a letter dated May 8, 1974, Robins informed over 125,000 doctors that the
Dalkon Shield should be removed immediately if a patient became pregnant and, if this was impossible, to perform a therapeutic abortion. The letter did not advise removal of the Shield from nonpregnant women. The
company also stated that it felt the problems shown with the Shield were
common to all IUDs. This letter was reported in the *Wall Street Journal*, and
Robins quickly issued a press release stating that it had no intention of can-
celing production of the Shield.

---

[2]Morton Mintz, *At Any Cost: Corporate Greed, Women, and the Dalkon Shield* (New York:
Pantheon Books, 1985), p. 75.

There were more deaths, and by the end of June 1974, the Food and Drug Administration asked (not ordered) Robins to cease marketing the Shield. Bowing to public pressure, the company announced it would cease marketing the Shield until FDA tests were finalized. However, it still insisted that women who were currently using the Shield were in no danger. Meanwhile, the directors of Planned Parenthood and federally funded family planning programs urged the discontinuance of the Shield.

In October 1974, a preliminary report from the FDA concluded that the Shield was as safe as any other IUD and attributed the problem to the fact that the Shield was the newest IUD on the market and was still undergoing a "shakedown" period. In December 1974, Alexander Schmidt, then commissioner of the FDA, announced that Robins could continue to market the Shield as long as accurate records were kept of all wearers.

The Climax

Robins was never to remarket the device. Where the FDA failed, the judicial system took over. By March 1975, 186 suits had been filed against Robins. Also in March, the first judicial award was made: $10,000 compensatory and $75,000 punitive damages against Robins. In May, a $475,000 judgment was awarded to the estate of a woman who had died while using the Shield. In August 1975, Robins formally announced that it would not remarket the Shield, but it insisted that women who had had it inserted previously were in no danger.

Not until September of 1980, six years after problems with the Shield had begun to surface, did Robins finally send a letter to 200,000 doctors urging them to remove the device from all women who were still using them. The company stated that a "new" study showed that other problems, such as an infection called pelvic actinomycosis, were more likely the longer the device was worn. This move followed a $6.8 million judgment in Colorado in June 1980, in which $600,000 was awarded in compensatory damages and $6.2 million in punitive damages. The punitive award was of serious concern to the company since Robins' liability insurance covered only compensatory damages.

By 1980, 4300 suits were pending against Robins. Some attorneys were spending their entire time suing Robins; this became so popular a cause that a newsletter was published covering IUD litigation, and four-day yearly seminars were held so that more experienced lawyers could instruct on how best to sue Robins.

The Company's 1981 annual report noted that 2300 cases were still pending, whereas 4200 had been settled. Up to now, the company and its insurer (Aetna) had paid out $98 million for Dalkon Shield litigation. Lawsuits continued to multiply, and they became increasingly expensive for the company to deal with. For example, the average settlement in 1976 was $8000; in 1984, the average was in the $400,000 range.

As 1985 approached, Robins's sales continued to climb, reflecting the strength in its other product lines and its international operations. Profits rose more grudgingly because of the heavy legal costs—until 1984. (See Table 9.1 for the trend in sales and profits, as well as a chronology of major events.)

In 1984, hounded by ever-mounting legal costs and judgments and running out of liability insurance coverage from Aetna, Robins took an extraordinary charge of $615 million as a reserve for claims. This resulted in a paper loss of $461.6 million in 1984. In August 1985, Robins filed Chapter 11 bankruptcy. Under Chapter 11 bankruptcy, all litigation against a company is stayed while the company and its creditors attempt to devise a plan to pay

Table 9.1   Trend in Sales and Profits, 1970–84 and Chronology of Major Events

	Sales (000,000)	Profits (000,000)	Profits as Percent of Sales	Major Events
1970	132.6	15.7	11.8	June 12, 1970, Robins buys the Dalkon Shield
1971	151.4	19.1	12.6	January 1971, Robins begins to market it
				April 1972, peak month for number of women fitted with the Shield
1973	189.2	25.4	13.4	October 1973, Robins puts warnings on packages
				June 1974, Robins suspends Shield sales in United States
1975	241.1	26.6	11.0	April 1975, Robins suspends Shield sales in other countries
1977	366.7	26.8	7.2	
1979	386.4	44.7	11.6	June 1980, $6.8 million
1981	450.9	44.2	9.8	judgment against Robins
1983	563.5	58.2	10.3	
1984	631.9	(461.6) loss		February 1984, Judge Miles Lord chastises Robins in Minneapolis court
				October 1984, Robins urges removal of all Shields Robins establishes $615 million reserve for claims in late 1984
				August 21, 1985, Robins files for bankruptcy

the bankrupt company's debts. E. Claiborne Robins, Jr., said the action was necessary to protect the company's economic vitality against those who would destroy it for the benefit of a few. Attorneys for the victims found this action to be fraudulent and in bad faith, an attempt by Robins to escape responsibility for the thousands of injuries the Shield had caused.

Not even Aetna was to escape unscathed. In 1986, a group of former Dalkon Shield users sued Aetna, charging that it had conspired with Robins to keep the alleged health hazards of the IUD from the public. The women claimed that Aetna also participated in intentional destruction of evidence that would have helped the plaintiffs prove the dangers of the device.

A bidding war developed for the troubled Robins Company. Rorer Group, a Pennsylvania pharmaceutical concern, made the first offer. Late in 1987, Sanofi, a French drug maker, made another takeover proposal. A week later, American Home Products Corporation joined the fast-developing bidding war. On January 20, 1988, the bid by American Home Products was accepted. John Stafford, chairman and CEO of American Home Products, was interested in Robins because of the tax advantages and the acquisition of two popular consumer brands: Robitussin and Dimetapp. "Franchises that powerful come along every few decades," he said.[3] And American Home could deduct its funding of Dalkon Shield liabilities from federal taxes.

American Home offered Robins's shareholders $700 million in American Home stock and agreed to pay $2.15 billion in cash to the trust fund of claims. In the final modification, the two top executives of Robins each gave $5 million in exchange for protection against being sued personally over the Shield. This plan, Robins's fourth in its 29 months of bankruptcy proceedings, was the first to receive endorsement from both the company's shareholders and the committee representing the Shield claimants.

POSTMORTEM

Here we see a company in extremis. Its conduct led a well-regarded firm with a 100-year history down the road to bankruptcy, but even worse, the innocent public was brutalized. How could this have happened? After all, these were not deliberately vicious men: they were well intentioned, albeit badly misguided. Perhaps their worst sin was trying to ignore and then cover up their product's increasingly apparent serious health problems, doing this to such an extent that a federal judge castigated them for their company's corporate immorality. How could this situation—in which everyone lost but the lawyers—have been permitted to get so out of hand?

---

[3]Michael Waldholz, "American Home Expects Most of its Price for A. H. Robins Will Be Tax-Deductible," *Wall Street Journal*, Jan. 21, 1988, p. 1.

It began innocently enough, and in accordance with sound business strategy. Robins recognized an emerging opportunity: the birth control market. Although competitors were already in the oral contraceptive market, the IUD sector of this market was virtually untapped yet seemed to offer enormous potential. This sector appeared to be in the early stages of development, with no serious competitors. But the likelihood of strong competitive entry could not be ignored, and Robins thus saw the need to enter this IUD market quickly and secure a major share of it—that is, beat competitors to the punch. Again, we have to recognize that this is textbook business strategy.

In accordance with the desirability of quickly entering the market, many decisions were made with little deliberation. One such decision was to assign production of the Dalkon Shield to the Chap Stick division of the company. Any similarity between the two products was remote at best, but this assignment seemed a matter of expediency and a means of offering lower labor costs. It might be argued that with such a new and unique product, there was not much more compatibility with any other division of the company.

Now we come to the point where Robins deviated from sound business strategy. It was entering a market in which it had no previous experience whatsoever, one in which health dangers ought to have been carefully evaluated. Yet Robins had not a single obstetrician or gynecologist on its staff. The company also neglected to conduct its own testing of the product, relying instead on the limited research that had been done by the Dalkon Shield's inventors. Robins did not question their research and testing, flawed though it soon proved to be. Rather, it rushed the product to market, thankful that the Food and Drug Administration did not have to be involved. Good judgment would have mandated confirmation of the safety of the product by independent parties. But this would have taken time, time that Robins was fearful of spending.

Recognizing an emerging and spectacular strategic opportunity, Robins pursued it with single-minded determination. Unfortunately, such determination ignored prudent and even ethical considerations. For example, much of the product information and advertising that was used was taken from Davis and Lerner's admittedly biased research, and the financial interest that these two "researchers" had in the Dalkon Shield was ignored and certainly never publicly mentioned. Physicians were thereby misled into thinking the research was objective and unbiased.

The impressive research figures cited in the ads were soon to conflict with studies done by others. As one example, Robins's ads originally claimed that the Shield had a low pregnancy rate of 1.1 percent, but later studies showed pregnancy rates varying from 5 to 10 percent. But Robins continued to use the 1.1 percent rate in its advertising until late 1973, when the claimed pregnancy rate was revised upward.

Other advertising claims attested to the safety and superiority of the Dalkon Shield, that "it was generally well tolerated by even the most sensitive women," and that no anesthetic was required. Only after many physicians complained about the difficulty of insertion was the advertising literature changed in November 1971 by removing the statement that no anesthetic was required. The claim of being safe and superior went unchanged.

Robins continued to ignore reports of major problems—such as massive bleeding, pelvic inflammatory diseases, miscarriages, and even deaths—that kept coming in over the years following the introduction of the Shield.

Admittedly, the term "safety" was relative: Was the Shield as safe or safer than the Pill? After all, the Pill was known not to be completely safe—it could cause serious side effects. Still, the evidence was mounting that there were significant dangers associated with the Shield, dangers beyond reasonable risk. Robins opted to ignore these far longer than was prudent and ethical.

Robins maintained that its product was safe—and it proclaimed so publicly. But evidence suggests that the company knew otherwise. Internal memos indicated that the company knew of potential danger less than a month after it acquired rights to the Shield. And more internal company memos were to surface during subsequent litigation: two to three truckloads of incriminating papers.

The basic component of Robins's strategy now became strictly defensive: to cooperate when necessary but to spend most of its time lobbying Congress and defending itself against lawsuits. Major concern was thus with legal and not ethical considerations regarding its past actions.

So, what seemed at first to be an unassailable strategy was found seriously wanting. Was the company guilty of subordinating everything to the profit maximization goal, an end-justifies-the-means perspective? Or did it simply panic, faced with a calamity of extraordinarily severe consequences, and resort to the defense mechanism of denial?

Roger L. Tuttle, a former A. H. Robins attorney, believed the latter.

> I've got to believe that had they known early on what they were dealing with they wouldn't have touched it with a 10-foot pole. It was just that one step led to another, until they had the grenade spinning in the middle of the floor.[4]

Nevertheless, the dire consequences to the company and to its customer-victims represent a classic example of a monumental marketing mistake that should have been handled better. (See the Issue box, which asks *whether management must assume the worst scenario*.)

---

[4]Mintz, *At Any Cost*, pp. 51–52.

ISSUE: MUST MANAGEMENT ASSUME THE WORST SCENARIO?

The Dalkon Shield turned out to be an unmitigated disaster—for the thousands of women victims, and also for the company. Certainly, no company would undertake a business venture that was likely to produce such results. There should be a commonality of interests on the part of consumers and firms to prevent such happenings. Ignoring the issue of a company's culpability for not noticing and then covering up the danger, another question should be asked: Does ignorance of future dire consequences relieve a firm of much of its blame? The contentious segment of the general public—lawyers as well as politicians eager to mollify their constituents—sees a "no mercy" scenario: the corporation is guilty despite ignorance of any wrongdoing, or any danger, at the time. But is this the most equitable viewpoint?

We live in a complex world. And our products are increasingly more complex technologically; some products, such as drugs, asbestos, and cigarettes, may well have long-term consequences far beyond our ability to predict at this time. Was this the case with the Dalkon Shield?

In today's environment, firms are not able to escape the long-term negative consequences of their products. The litigious environment will not permit this, however ignorant the firm may have been. Ethically, the blame has to be more muted for a firm that could not see any dire consequences. But, does the very fact of not knowing really excuse a firm?

Does such "unknowing" absolve Robins with its Dalkon Shield? Hardly. Although knowledge of long-term consequences for any product may be limited, this does not preclude adequate and objective testing to achieve a high level of safety assurance. This Robins did not do. Furthermore, when the first suspicions were raised of possible problems, it ignored them and even concealed them. Here was Robins's great ethical and moral misdeed: it placed short-term company profits above very strong doubts of customer health and safety.

INVITATION TO DISCUSS
Robbins's executives may argue that if they had had any idea of the serious danger of the Shield, they would have jerked it from the market, but they had nothing to confirm this until too late. Therefore, they should be exonerated from any serious wrongdoing. Discuss the pros and cons of this defense.

WHAT CAN BE LEARNED?

The Robbins Company's actions seemed exemplary at first:

1. Identify a business opportunity or strategic window.
2. Find or develop a product to fit this strategic window.
3. Beat competition in being the first to capitalize on this opportunity.

But there was one basic difference from other effective strategies: health and safety were more at stake with this particular product. This should have necessitated a more cautious approach to the window of opportunity to ensure that the product had no risks to customers. Yet, at Robins, health and safety considerations were ignored in a single-minded pursuit of profits. Everything else was secondary to this profit orientation.

Learning Insight. *A firm today must zealously guard against product liability suits.*

Any responsible executive now has to recognize that product liability suits, in today's increasingly litigious environment, can bankrupt a firm. The business arena has become more risky, more fraught with peril for the unwary or the naively unconcerned. Consequently, any firm needs careful and objective testing of any product that can even remotely affect customer health and safety—and this must be undertaken even if product introduction is delayed and competitive entry encouraged.

Learning Insight. *Suspicions and complaints about product safety must be thoroughly investigated.*

We should learn unequivocally from this case that immediate and thorough investigation of any suspicions or complaints must be undertaken—regardless of the confidence management may have in the product and regardless of the glowing recommendations from persons whose objectivity could be suspect. To procrastinate or ignore these warnings poses risks that should be unacceptable.

Learning Insight. *In the worst scenario, go for a salvage strategy.*

Robins faced a crossroads in 1974. Scary reports of problems and lawsuits were flooding in. How should the company react? One course of action was to tough it out, trying to combat the bad press, denying culpability, and resorting to the strongest possible legal defense. This Robins opted to do. At stake was its reputation, its economic life, and the welfare of tens of thousands of women.

The other recourse was what we might call a salvage strategy: recognition and full admission of the problem and removal of the Shield from more than 4 million women amid a full-market withdrawal. Expensive, yes, but far less risky for the viability of the company and certainly for the health of those women involved.

Neither strategy is without major costs. But the first course of action puts major cost consequences in the future, where they may turn out to be vastly greater. The second course of action poses an immediate impact on profitability but may save the company and its reputation and return it to profitability in the future.

Learning Insight. *This is an era of* **caveat vendidor**—*let the seller beware.*

Businesses today have to recognize that this is no longer an age of *caveat emptor*—let the buyer beware. This philosophy ruled the business environment for many decades, but now the pendulum has swung to *caveat vendidor*—let the seller beware. Products or business practices that are perceived as not in the best interest of the public are subject to reprisals—either through customer resentment and public outcry or through lawsuits. Woe to the firm that does not recognize this or underestimates the environmental constraints.

FOR THOUGHT AND DISCUSSION

1. Can a firm guarantee complete product safety? Discuss.
2. Design a strategy for the Dalkon Shield that would have minimized the problems Robins eventually faced. What might be some concerns with such a strategy?
3. After this disaster, do you think Robins could ever have regained a sufficiently respected image to be a viable business under the same management? Why or why not?

INVITATION TO ROLE PLAY

You are the public relations director for Robins in late 1972. Some disquieting information has come to you about far-higher-than-expected physician complaints about the Shield. Top management has so far been unconcerned about such reports, especially because of Food and Drug Administration complacency.

Develop a plan of action for dealing with potential product safety problems that can be persuasively presented to top management.

INVITATION TO RESEARCH

Investigate the performance of American Home Products since it took over Robins in 1988. Was this a wise acquisition?

10

Nestle's Infant Formula: An Unsafe Product in Third World Countries?

When a firm is a huge international conglomerate, with diversification into many product lines, bad publicity and negative public reactions about a single product seemingly should be no particular cause for alarm. The inclination is to ignore such a "minor" problem, assuming it will go away.

But the expectations of Nestle went awry. The attitudes of the general public toward the firm continued to worsen, exacerbated certainly by a negative press and vocal protesters. Far from diminishing over a few weeks and a few months, the situation worsened over years. And far from affecting only the particular product involved—infant formula marketed to underdeveloped countries—other products and other divisions of the company became the object of virulent protests. Nestle had for too long ignored assaults on its public image, and now the road back to public acceptance was slow and rocky.

BACKGROUND

The Trouble Begins

By the early 1970s, there were suspicions that powdered infant formula manufacturers were contributing to the high infant mortality in developing countries by their aggressive marketing efforts directed at people unable to read the instructions or use the product properly. The possible link between infant formulas and mortality through product misuse began to be discussed by medical professionals, industry representatives, and govern-ment officials at a number of international conferences, but public aware-ness of the problem had not yet surfaced.

Then, in 1974, a British charity organization, War on Want, published a 28-page pamphlet, *The Baby Killer*. In it, two multinationals, Nestle of Switzerland and Unigate of Britain, were criticized for engaging in ill-advised marketing efforts in Africa. With the printing of this short publi-cation, the general public became not only aware of the problem but increasingly concerned.

This concern was to intensify less than a year later. The German-based Third World Working Group reissued a German translation of *The Baby Killer* but with a few changes. Whereas the British version criticized the entire infant formula industry, the German activists singled out Nestle for "unethical and immoral behavior" and retitled their version *Nestle Kills Babies*.

The accusation enraged executives at Nestle headquarters, and they sued the activists for defamation. The trial lasted two years and focused worldwide attention on the issue. Though Nestle won the lawsuit, the court advised the firm to review its current marketing practices. "We won the legal case, but it was a public-relations disaster," one Nestle official admit-ted. "The baby-killing accusation was a natural for antiwar groups and others looking for a cause. The company was dealing with the situation on a scientific and nutritional level, but the protesters were dealing on an emo-tional and political level."[1]

The Nestle Company

The Nestle Company, formally known as Nestle Alimentana, S.A., is head-quartered in Vevey, Switzerland. It is a giant worldwide corporation, with sales of $12.5 billion in 1983. It owns or controls extensive interests in numerous companies in the food and cosmetics industries in various parts of the world. Products include instant drinks (coffee and tea), dairy products, cosmetics, frozen foods, chocolate, and pharmaceutical products. In addition, it holds interests in catering services, as well as restaurant and hotel operations such as the Stouffer Corporation, which was acquired in 1973. By 1980, Nestle was marketing its products in Europe, Africa, North America, Latin America, the Caribbean, Asia, and Oceania. Its three top product groups were dairy products, instant drinks, and culinary/sundry products. Infant foods, including the controversial infant formula,

---

[1]"Infant Formula Protest Teaches Nestle a Tactical Lesson," *Marketing News*, June 10, 1983, p. 1.

and dietetic products accounted for less than 10 percent of total conglomerate sales.

Nestle's appetite for acquisitions has continued unabated in recent years. In 1975, it purchased food processor Libby, McNeill & Libby. In 1979, it acquired Beech-Nut, the baby-food producer. Other purchases of note include CooperVision, a contact lens maker; such well-known candy brands as Chunky, Bit-O-Honey, Raisinettes, Oh Henry, Goobers, and Sno Caps; and more recently, Hills Bros. Coffee Company and Carnation.

The Infant Formula Industry

Nestle first developed and marketed a milk food used to nourish premature infants in 1867. This was in response to the urgent need of a premature infant who was unable to take any food. Borden introduced a similar sweetened and condensed milk.

Infant formula foods are somewhat more recent, having been developed in the early 1920s as an alternative to breast milk. Infant formula is a specially prepared food for infants (under six months) and is based on cow's milk. It is scientifically formulated to approximate the most perfect of all infant foods, human breast milk. Today, a number of different artificial milk products are available for infants, and these range in nutritional value from very high (humanized infant formula) to very low (various powdered, evaporated, and sweetened condensed milks).

Sales of infant formula had increased sharply after World War II and hit a peak in 1957, with 4.3 million births in developed countries. After this time, births started a decline that continued into the 1970s. The result was a steep downturn in baby formula sales and profits. Therefore, the industry began searching for new business. This was found in developing countries where the population was still increasing: the less developed countries of Africa, South America, and the Far East.

Total industry sales for infant formula alone, excluding all other commercial milk products, was about $1.5 billion. Of this, an estimated $600 million came from developing countries. Hence, this market segment represented a significant total market potential.

Nestle maintained a strong market share—40 to 50 percent—of the market in developing countries for baby formula. Competitors included three U.S. firms, American Home Products, Bristol Myers, and Abbott Labs, which shared 20 percent of the market. Foreign firms accounted for the remainder. In 1981, the market was estimated to be growing at 15 to 20 percent per year.[2]

---

[2]Kurt Anderson, "The Battle of the Bottle," *Time*, June 1, 1981, p. 26.

THE ISSUE: MISUSE OF THE PRODUCT AND MARKETING PRACTICES

> If your lives were embittered as mine is, by seeing day after day this massacre of the innocents by unsuitable feeding, then I believe you would feel as I do that misguided propaganda on infant feeding should be punished as the most criminal form of sedition, and that these deaths should be regarded as murder.[3]

This lone indictment from a doctor in 1939 evolved from a single cry into a crescendo of protest against the infant formula industry.

Incapability of the Market to Use the Product Correctly

A large number of consumers in developing countries live in poverty, have poor sanitation, receive inadequate health care, and are illiterate. Therefore, the misuse of infant formula would seem inevitable. Water is obtained from polluted rivers or a common well and is brought back in contaminated containers. A refrigerator is considered a luxury item, and fuel is very expensive.

Consequently, powdered formula may be mixed with contaminated water and put into unsterilized bottles and nipples. In addition, the mothers are tempted to dilute the formula with excess water so that it will last longer. An example was cited by one physician at a Jamaican hospital of the malnutrition of two exclusively bottle-fed siblings, 4 months and 18 months old. A can of formula would adequately feed a 4-month-old baby just under three days. However, this mother so diluted the formula as to feed the two infants for 14 days. This mother was poor and illiterate, had no running water or electricity, and had 12 other children.[4]

Studies have given three reasons for the trend to less nursing and more bottle feeding in the developing countries.[5]

First, the sociocultural environment was changing. This consists of urbanization, changing social mores, and increased mobility in employment. Infant formula was seen as representing social mobility, one of the highly regarded modern products, and medical expertise. The smiling

---

[3]As quoted in Cicely D. Williams, "The Marketing of Malnutrition," *Business and Society Review,* Spring 1980–1981, p. 66.

[4]U.S. Congress, Senate, Committee on Human Resources, Subcommittee on Health and Scientific Research, *Marketing and Promotion of Infant Formula in the Developing Nations,* Hearing, 95th Congress, 2nd Session, May 23, 1978 (Washington, D.C.: Government Printing Office, 1978), p. 6.

[5]Prakash Sethi and James E. Post, "Public Consequences of Private Action: The Marketing of Infant Formula in Less Developed Countries," *California Management Review,* Summer 1979, pp. 35–48.

white babies pictured on the fronts of formula tins suggested that rich, white mothers fed their babies this product and that therefore it must be better. The high-income consumers in these less developed countries were the first to use infant formula in imitation of Western practices. Bottle feeding was looked upon as a high-status practice, and the lower-income groups readily followed along.

Second, health care professionals were a factor in the switch to bottle feeding. Many hospitals and clinics endorsed the use of infant formula. A woman's first experience with a hospital may be to deliver a baby. Consequently, any products or gifts she receives there carry medical endorsement. Also, hospital practices are perceived as better and deserving of emulation. Babies are routinely separated from their mothers for 12 to 48 hours and are bottle-fed whether or not the mothers plan to breast-feed.

A third factor was the marketing and promotional practices of infant formula manufacturers, which we will discuss shortly.

In 1951, approximately 80 percent of all 3-month-old babies in Singapore were being breast-fed; by 1971, only 5 percent were. In 1966, 40 percent fewer mothers in Mexico nursed 6-month-old babies than had done so six years earlier. In Chile, in 1973, there were three times as many deaths among infants who were bottle-fed before three months of age than among wholly breast-fed infants. Other statistics of increased illnesses and higher death rates of bottle-fed infants are plentiful.[6]

Quality Control Problems

Nestle had some serious quality control problems in its production of the formula in its far-flung plants:

In April 1977, the Colombian General Hospital encountered an increase in deaths in the premature ward. Bacteria was traced to a Nestle factory, but 25 deaths occurred before the cause was found.

Also in 1977, the Australian Department of Health reported that 134 infants had fallen seriously ill as a result of being fed contaminated infant milk formulas produced by Nestle. Government officials estimated 20 million pounds of contaminated milk had been exported to Southeast Asian counties.

The Australian story started in 1976. The Nestle Tongala plant noticed an increase in bacterial counts in samples of infant milk powder. Inspection revealed cracks in the spray drier used to turn liquid milk into powder form. The bacteria was found to be a variant of salmonella that causes severe gastoenteritis. The State Health Department was not informed, and

---

[6]For more such statistics, see Leah Marguilies, "Bottle Babies: Death and Business Get Their Market," *Business and Society Review*, Spring 1978, pp. 43–49.

Nestle attempted to sterilize the equipment without halting production, but the bacteria continued to be discovered. The drier was kept in operation for a full eight months after the contaminants were found.[7]

Criticisms of Misuse

In fairness to Nestle, the critics who condemned the company and other infant food manufacturers for even attempting to market in the developing countries disregarded any benefits of such products over the alternatives. The problem of water contamination also affects the alternatives to the commercial infant foods, which are various "native" cereal gruels of millet and rice used as weaning foods. The nutritional quality of these gruels tends to be low, and this deficiency is in addition to contamination of the water and containers used to cook the material. Furthermore, the millet or flour often has microbial contamination. Although it is true that infant formula mixed with contaminated water and containers presents dangers, the commercial formulas are more nutritious than local foods and are closer to breast milk than native weaning foods and are therefore easier to digest. A further rebuttal to the critics is that not all people in developing countries face water contamination. Millions can safely mix powdered formula with local water without fear of water contamination.[8] (See the Issue box for a discussion of *good versus evil*.)

Criticisms of Nestle's Marketing Practices

Nestle has undoubtedly been an aggressive marketer in many developing countries. Its promotional efforts have been directed to physicians and other medical personnel as well as consumers. Direct consumer promotion of infant formula has taken many forms. Media have included radio, newspapers, magazines, and billboards—even vans with loudspeakers have been used. Nestle has widely distributed free samples, bottles, nipples, and measuring spoons. In some countries, direct customer contacts have been made through "milk nurses," and these have been the subject of particular criticism.

Nestle employed about 200 women who were registered nurses, nutritionists, or midwives. These professionals were often nicknamed "milk nurses." Critics maintained that these milk nurses were actually sales

---

[7]Reported in Douglas Clement, "Nestle's Latest Killing in Bottle Baby Market," *Business and Society Review,* Summer 1978, pp. 60–64.

[8]John Sparks, *The Nestle Controversy—Anatomy of a Boycott.* Public Policy Education Fund, June 1981.

ISSUE: THE COEXISTENCE OF GOOD AND EVIL— HOW TO RECONCILE?

In some situations, good and evil exist simultaneously; they are inextricably bound. And while the press and vocal critics invariably focus on the evil, the good should not go unnoticed. Such was certainly the case with Nestle and its infant formula.

It could hardly be disputed by even the harshest critics that the formula led to the saving of infants' lives when the mother was not available or the infant could not be breast-fed. Furthermore, the dietary supplement could lead to much healthier babies when used properly. Conversely, when used improperly, it could lead to deaths as mothers mixed the powdered food with contaminated water and their babies died of dysentery.

How can this issue of the good and bad intermixing be resolved? There is no simple solution acceptable to all sides. Emotions, and publicity, tend to run high on issues such as this. Should a firm abandon a product because of some misuse? The implications of such a position can become ludicrous. For example, should cars be banned because of careless use and hundreds of thousands of accidents, injuries, and deaths?

It is but a short step to other raging issues: Should pesticides be banned because they contribute to environmental pollution and possible injury to wildlife and fishes? Should utility plants be closed because they contribute to acid rain? More realistically, should the public be made to pay greatly increased utility rates so that acid rain can be virtually eliminated by the most stringent emissions controls? Should lawn mowers be banned because a few people use them incorrectly? Should all guns be banned because of their escalating misuse?

You can see that there is no solution to such issues that will satisfy all interested parties. The tides of pressure seem to swing from one position to the other: too much environmental influence versus too much "business self-interest." Unfortunately, these issues are highly emotional and easily fanned by press, politicians, and the public relations efforts of special-interest groups.

INVITATION TO DISCUSS
A simple solution to such issues would be to choose the way that offers "the greatest good for the greatest number." Discuss the problems with such a simplistic solution. Can these be reasonably resolved?

personnel in disguise who visited mothers and gave product samples in an attempt to persuade mothers to stop breast feeding. With their uniforms giving them great credibility, the nurses were criticized for being too persuasive for naive consumers.

Promoting these products to physicians and other medical personnel has also been controversial. This type of promotion has generally involved the use of detail people who discuss product quality and characteristics with pediatricians, pediatric nurses, and other related medical personnel. (The use of *detail people, who are a type of missionary sales representative,* is common practice, as we will describe in the accompanying information box.) Materials such as posters, charts, and free samples were made available to physicians, hospitals, and clinics without charge. Physicians and other hospital personnel have also received company-sponsored travel to medical meetings.

Critics felt that the promotion of infant formula had been too aggressive and had contributed to the decline in breast feeding. Despite increased criticisms, however, sales of infant formula in poor countries continued to escalate. It had become the third most advertised product in these countries, after tobacco and soap, and it was generally recognized that new mothers in such countries were most susceptible to advertising. A 1969 study of 120 mothers in Barbados found that 82 percent of those given free samples later purchased the same brand—regardless of whether the samples were received from the hospital or at home.[9]

In summary, the criticisms of promotional practices were that

- Bottle feeding contributes to infant mortality in developing countries.
- Baby booklets ignore or de-emphasize breast feeding.
- Media promotions are misleading in encouraging poor and illiterate mothers to bottle-feed rather than breast-feed their infants.
- Advertising portrays breast feeding as primitive and inconvenient.
- Free gifts and samples are direct inducements to bottle-feed infants.
- Posters and pamphlets in hospitals and milk nurses are viewed as "endorsement by association" or "manipulation by assistance."
- The prices of formulas at the milk banks are still too expensive for many consumers, who are tempted to dilute the formula.

THE SITUATION WORSENS FOR NESTLE

After the publication of the two articles, *The Baby Killer* and *Nestle Kills Babies,* and the subsequent lawsuit by Nestle, which received worldwide publicity, two groups were formed: the Interfaith Center on Corporate Responsibility and the Infant Formula Action Coalition (INFACT). The opposition of these organizations eventually led to a boycott of Nestle products and services.

Since the early 1970s, various agencies had been trying to reduce the promotion and advertising practices of infant formula companies. These

---

[9]Reported in "A Boycott over Infant Formula," *Business Week,* April 23, 1979, pp. 137–140.

THE USE OF MISSIONARY SALESPEOPLE (DETAIL PEOPLE)

Missionary salespeople—these are called *detail people* in the drug industry—are commonly used by many firms to provide specialized services and cultivate customer goodwill. They generally do not try to secure orders.

Missionary salespeople are employed by manufacturers to work with their
dealers. They may put up point-of-purchase displays, train dealer salespeople,
provide better communication between distributor and manufacturer, and in
general try to have their brand more aggressively promoted by the dealer. In the
drug industry the detail people leave samples and explain research information
about new products to the medical professionals so as to encourage prescriptions and recommendations for their brands.

INVITATION TO DISCUSS

Do you think the critics were unfair in condemning the "milk nurses," a type of
missionary salesperson? Do you think Nestle should have bowed to this criticism and discontinued the "milk nurses"?

agencies included the Protein Advisory Group in 1970 and 1973, the World
Health Assembly in 1974, and the World Health Organization (WHO) in
1978.

As a by-product of the growing condemnation of the industry, Nestle
and other firms began to make changes in their promotional practices, at
least on paper. The changes were brought about through the auspices of the
International Council of Infant Food Industries (ICIFI), which was formed
in 1975 by nine infant food manufacturers, including Nestle. The changes
included the following: product information would always recognize breast
milk as best; infant formulas would be advertised as supplementary, and
ads would recommend that professional advice should be sought; nurse
uniforms would be worn only by professional nurses.

But the self-regulation apparently did not work sufficiently to allay the
criticisms. Documentation by the International Baby Food Action Network
confirmed over 1000 violations of the "code" from 1977 to 1981. Some critics scoffed that "asking for self-regulation was like asking Colonel Sanders
to babysit your chickens."[10]

After continued reported violations, a boycott was organized in the
United States in July 1977 and soon spread to nine other countries. It was to
last until January 26, 1982, in the United Sates and Canada, with other
countries ending their boycotts over the next two years.

---

[10]"Killer in a Bottle," *Economist*, May 9, 1981, p. 50; "Nestle's Latest Killing," pp. 60–64.

Nestle was singled out as the sole object of the boycott because of its 50 percent worldwide market share and the fact that it had attracted more adverse publicity than had other firms that were engaged in the same business practices.

The demands of INFACT and the boycotters were:

1. Stop altogether the use of milk nurses.
2. Stop distributing all free samples.
3. Stop promoting infant formula to the health care industry.
4. Stop consumer promotion and advertising of infant formula.

The boycott soon had the support of over 450 local and religious groups across America, and proponents claimed it was the largest non-union boycott in U.S. history. Boycott activity was strongest in Boston, Baltimore, and Chicago, where INFACT established an office with five full-time staffers. Thousands of signatures were gathered on various petitions urging removal of Nestle products from supermarket shelves. Some grocers acquiesced, agreeing to remove such products as Taster's Choice. The boycott also hit college campuses. With the slogan "Crunch Nestle," boycotts were encouraged on products ranging from milk chocolate to tea, coffee, and hot chocolate. The college boycott reportedly began at Wellesley College and soon spread to others, such as Colgate, Yale, and the University of Minnesota.

This boycott was undoubtedly effective, not only directly in causing lost business and profits for the company but also indirectly in crystallizing public opinion against the company and in invoking governmental response. For example:

The government of New Guinea enacted stringent laws to curb the artificial feeding of babies in the summer of 1979. Bottles and nipples now could only be obtained by prescription. Other countries also began introducing legislation to reduce the marketing and advertising of breast-milk substitutes.

The World Health Organization (WHO), in May 1981, adopted a restrictive ad code that applied only to the infant food industry. A portion of Article 5 of the code states: "There shall be no advertising or other forms of promotion to the general public of products within the scope of this code."[11] The products covered were infant food formulas and other weaning foods.

---

[11]"World Health Organization Drafts Restrictive Ad Code," *Editor & Publisher*, April 11, 1981, p. 8.

The European Parliament in France voted overwhelmingly for strict enforcement of the WHO code throughout the 10-nation European Community. The European Parliament also placed responsibility on firms of member nations for the actions of their subsidiaries abroad in observing the WHO code.

Nestle Fights Back

Nestle's first efforts to combat vituperative accusations resulted in more harm than good, as we have seen. As its public image continued to worsen, the worldwide boycott finally surfaced in 1977. Now Nestle could no longer ignore the protests and hope they would go away. Obviously they were not going to go away. Initial strategy at this point was to treat the boycott and widespread protests as a public-relations problem. The public-relations department of the firm was upgraded into the Office of Corporate Responsibility. The world's largest public-relations firm, Hill & Knowlton, was hired to assist. Over 300,000 packets of information were mailed by Nestle to U.S. clergymen, informing them that they were wrong in their denunciations of Nestle. Finally, Daniel J. Edelmon, a renowned public-relations specialist, was hired. He advised the company to keep a low profile and try to get third-party endorsement of its actions.

Finally, in 1981, after failing to improve its image and mute the critical cries against it, Nestle dismissed its two public-relations firms and took upon itself the task of reestablishing its reputation. Ignoring the situation had not helped; public outcries, rather than lessening, had increased. And efforts to angrily denounce the critics had only exacerbated the situation. Now the firm was ready to try a new tack in efforts to establish its credibility as a humane and responsible corporate citizen.

One of the first steps was to endorse the World Health Organization's Code of Marketing for Breast Milk Substitutes—a step that three other U.S. manufacturers did not make until two years later. Compliance with the code was voluntary. It banned advertising to the general public, as well as distribution of samples to mothers.

Next, Nestle sought an ethical group to vouch for its compliance with the code and settled on the Methodist Task Force on Infant Formula.

Nestle's relations with the press had been abysmal. For example, in the first six months of 1981, the *Washington Post* published 91 articles critical of Nestle. In the company's multifaceted attempt to rebuild its image, the policy for dealing with the media was changed to an "open-door, candid approach."[12]

---

[12]"Fighting a Boycott," *Industry Week*, Jan. 23, 1984, p. 54.

The most effective restorative strategy finally adopted was the establishment of a 10-member panel of medical experts, clergy, civic leaders, and experts in international policy to publicly monitor Nestle's compliance with the WHO code and to investigate complaints against its marketing practices. This Nestle Infant Formula Audit Commission (NIFAC) gained credibility with the acceptance of the chairmanship by Edmund S. Muskie, former secretary of state, vice presidential candidate, and Democratic senator from Maine. The commission was established in May 1982.

This so-called Muskie Commission worked with representatives of WHO, the International Nestle Boycott Committee (INBC), and UNICEF to resolve conflicts in four areas of the WHO code. Points of contention were: educational materials, labels, gifts to medical and health professionals, and free or subsidized supplies to hospitals. These were resolved, and Nestle agreed that, on educational material it distributed, the social and health aspects of formula versus breast feeding would be addressed. Its infant formula labels would clearly state the dangers of using contaminated water and the superiority of mother's milk. Personal gifts to health officials (which smacked of bribery and seeking preferential treatment) were banned. Finally, free samples of formula distributed to hospitals were to be limited to supplies that go to mothers incapable of breastfeeding their children.

At last, after years of Nestle's adversarial posture, which had only resulted in a growing crescendo of criticisms and boycotts and bitter accusations that the company was causing the deaths of millions of babies in developing countries because of its marketing practices, the situation was improving. "We have all learned a lesson, . . ." said Rafael D. Pagan, Jr., president of the Nestle Coordination Center for Nutrition. "Companies should be sensitive and listen carefully to what consumers and members of the general public are saying. When problems surface, they should seek a dialogue with responsible leaders and try to work out the problems together."[13]

After a decade of confrontation with protesters and seven years of boycotting, early in 1984 most groups agreed to a suspension of their boycott. While some diehards refused to accept the conciliatory efforts of Nestle, several large groups—for example, the American Federation of Teachers, the American Federation of Churches, the Federation of Nurses & Health Professionals, the United Methodist Church, and the Church of the Brethren—had either withdrawn from the boycott or decided not to join it.

---

[13]"Nestle Gains Formula Accord: Product Boycott Is Suspended," *Marketing News*, Feb. 17, 1984, p. 5.

Nestle admitted, however, that perhaps 20 obdurate boycott leaders and 50,000 followers in the United States may never stop ostracizing the company no matter what Nestle does.[14]

The results in lost business for Nestle are difficult to pinpoint. Company estimates ranged up to $40 million in lost profits as a direct result of the boycotts. However, lost business was probably far greater than this, with some coming in the years before the boycotts began as consumers turned to alternative brands from firms with better reputations. Even during the years of boycotts, not all consumers were militant protesters, but they could certainly take their business elsewhere, as a silent protest. Admittedly, infant food business accounted for only 3 percent of total Nestle sales worldwide, but other Nestle products were blackened to an unknown degree by the destroyed public image of this one minor part of the total business. One of the most obvious negative consequences of the boycotts was the loss of meetings and convention business at Stouffer facilities, with some planners choosing to schedule at other locations as a means of avoiding any association with negative publicity.

Table 10.1 shows the sales and profits for the Nestle conglomerate during 1974–1983. It shows profits declining in some years, perhaps as a result of the protests. We really cannot measure how much is the direct effect of the confrontation. We can only guess at the extent of unrealized potential.

Table 10.1   Nestle Sales and Profits, 1974–1983 (in thousands of Swiss Francs)

Years	Sales	Profits
1974	16,624,000	742,000
1975	18,286,000	799,000
1976	19,063,000	872,000
1977	20,095,000	830,000
1978	20,266,000	739,000
1979	21,639,000	816,000
1980	24,479,000	638,000
1981	27,734,000	964,000
1982	27,664,000	1,098,000
1983	27,943,000	1,261,000

Source: Company annual reports.

[14]"Fighting a Boycott," p. 55.

WHAT CAN BE LEARNED?

The Nestle debacle should be sobering for many firms. It should raise some real concerns about the possibility of damage to the public image—damage that can be difficult to rebuild. Specifically, the following are major lessons to be learned from this experience.

Learning Insight. *The public image is especially at risk for large firms.*

A reputable image, or at least one that is neutral and not negative, can be quickly besmirched. A firm should not underestimate the power of social awareness and activist groups. Furthermore, the large firm is more vulnerable—even if other firms in the industry are engaged in the same practices—and is the most desirable target for activist groups. Large size brings with it greater visibility and public recognition than is the case with smaller competitors. This makes a large firm the target of choice: the goal is to bring down the giant. And public sentiment, be it on the athletic field, in business, or wherever, is not on the side of the big and powerful.

Learning Insight. *Beware of the power of a hostile press.*

A bad press can both arouse and intensify negative public opinion. It can fan the flames. A firm cannot rely on the press to be objective and unbiased in such reporting. The press tends to be eager to find a "fault object," and when this is a large and rather impersonal firm, the likelihood is all the greater that bad actions or the negatives of a particular situation will be emphasized far more than the positive and helpful side of the issue. Although infant formulas had many benefits and were a positive health influence in many situations, publicity focused almost exclusively on alleged abuses.

Learning Insight. *A besmirched reputation is not easily overcome.*

Nestle's expectations that the controversy would die out were certainly quashed by the duration and increasing virulence of the protest movement. Without constructive efforts by Nestle in the early 1980s, the gathering strength of the protest movement probably would have resulted in ever-greater boycotting and most likely in restrictive legislation by many countries. Thus, a tarnished reputation is not suddenly going to become bright and shiny just because of the passage of time. Strong positive efforts must be made by the firm to try to restore its image, or it will not be improved.

Learning Insight. *Public relations efforts by themselves will seldom improve a negative public image.*

Public relations is not the answer when certain aspects of a firm's operation are the focal points of criticism. The act must be cleaned up first. The public-relations efforts of Nestle were notoriously impotent, despite hiring two of the largest and most expensive public-relations firms in the world. Without improving the operations under question, no amount of public-relations statements—even mailing some 300,000 pamphlets to clergy promoting Nestle's position—could produce positive and lasting results.

Learning Insight. *Marketing efforts tend to have the strongest impact on public image.*

Many of Nestle's problems emanated from its marketing efforts in developing countries. Normally, such efforts would be viewed as effective; under different circumstances, they could even have been lauded as models for introducing a new and improved product. Here, however, they were seen as far too effective in swaying a naive population in not wholly desirable directions. A firm's marketing efforts are the most visible aspects of its operation. This visibility can sometimes be a curse, as it was with Nestle.

Suggested Responses to a Darkening Public Image

The Nestle example gives us helpful insights as to how best to respond to smears and protests. Ignoring the problem seems ill-advised if the protests are severe enough and the issue is inflammatory. And certainly, alleged culpable loss of life—whether from chemical dumps or spills or from the ill-advised use of infant formula—is inflammatory enough.

Direct confrontation and an adversarial stand is seldom effective either. As Nestle found out the hard way, a court case, even if you win, only increases the negative publicity and fuels the protestations. Even if the weight of evidence is on the firm's side, the propaganda and one-sided criticisms of the opposition will likely win over the general public.

So it seems more prudent for the firm that falls into the snare of public-image problems regarding its social role to approach the situation with a spirit of cooperation and constructive participation with opposing groups, despite some diehard activists who may refuse all efforts at conciliation. We cannot fault the efforts of Nestle in 1981–1983 in working with the more reasonable critics. But we can severely fault the company for waiting so long to take such constructive actions.

Many firms need a greater sensitivity to potential problem areas involving corporate social performance. They need to try to anticipate potential problems and nip them quickly. Failing this, an organization should strive to resolve as many of the objections as it can, even if this means assuming the burden of an inequitable compromise position. The consequence otherwise may be a gradually deteriorating image, despite the fact that negative public perceptions are not fully based on facts.

A firm doing business in sensitive areas needs to prove that it is a responsible corporate citizen and not an insensitive giant organization. More attention to the public image may well prevent the type of image problems that bedeviled Nestle for years.

FOR THOUGHT AND DISCUSSION

1. Faced with activist protesters, do you think a firm has any recourse but to yield to their complete demands? Is there any room for an aggressive stance?
2. Could the public-relations efforts of Nestle have been used more effectively?
3. Do you think Nestle was unfairly picked on? Why or why not?

INVITATION TO ROLE PLAY

1. As the staff assistant to the CEO of Nestle, you have been asked to develop a position paper as to the desirability of withdrawing infant formula from the market in developing countries. Discuss the pros and cons of such a move, and then make your recommendations and support them as persuasively as you can.
2. You are the manager of a Stouffer hotel. A delegation of clergy and lay people has approached you with the threat of boycotting your premises. Be as persuasive as you can in trying to dissuade them from doing so.

INVITATION TO RESEARCH

Has infant formula been withdrawn from developing countries? If not, have the critics been satisfied?

TWO

CONTEMPORARY ETHICAL CONTROVERSIES

CHAPTER 11

Union Carbide's Bhopal Catastrophe

On the night of December 3, 1984, a Union Carbide chemical plant located near the congested streets of Old Bhopal, a low-income area north of Bhopal, India, was involved in a disaster of monumental proportions. Dwarfing Union Carbide's earlier air-pollution problems in the Ohio Valley, the Bhopal disaster resulted in the loss of life, which made it perhaps the worst industrial disaster until that time. (Less than two years later, on April 26, 1986, a much worse disaster occurred in the Russian Ukraine when the Chernobyl nuclear plant spewed radioactive material over thousands of square miles of Europe.) Union Carbide was far more caring and responsive after the Bhopal disaster than it had been during the Ohio Valley controversy. Still, the disaster occurred. How culpable was the company? How might the loss of human life have been avoided?

THE DIMENSIONS OF THE DISASTER

Some time after 11:00 P.M., a worker in the plant noticed that the temperature of tank 610, which stored MIC (methyl isocyanate, a toxic chemical used in the production of pesticides), was growing dangerously high. Sometime after midnight, after attempts to bring the tank's temperature under control failed, the concrete over the tank began cracking. A runaway chemical chain reaction was taking place. Suddenly, 40 tons of MIC escaped, forming a dense fog of toxic gas that began to drift toward Bhopal.

The night air was cool, around 60°F, and the wind was calm. These conditions added to the disaster, preventing the fog from dissipating. Slowly, the fog made its way through the railroad station, into homes, shops, temples, up and down streets and alleyways. It left behind bodies, both human and animal, and panic.

An estimated 2500 deaths would occur, with upwards of 300,000 people injured. "Even more horrifying than the number of dead was the appalling nature of their dying—crowds of men, women, and children scurrying madly in the dark, twitching and writhing like the insects for whom the poison was intended."[1] Thousands struggled to hospitals and clinics for relief from burning eyes and searing lungs, resulting in a medical chaos that made record-keeping well-nigh impossible. Severe environmental damage also occurred to the land and livestock, with an estimated 20,000 cattle killed.

Long-term repercussions awaited. Thousands were no longer able to put in a full day's work. Children suffered from breathing problems and memory lapses. Some experienced months of severe vomiting. Among pregnant women, nearly a fourth of whom were in their first trimester at the time of the disaster either miscarried or had premature or disfigured babies. Psychological problems—depression and anxiety— were common.

Beyond the physical were the economic consequences. In the year following the leak, the Indian government spent about $40 million on the victims. This included food, medical attention, new hospitals, research projects, and individual payments of $835 to the 1,500 families who lost members to the disaster and $125 to the 12,000 families with incomes below $40 a month.[2] Training was offered to women who had lost their providers, but little was done to find jobs for the thousands of men who could no longer spend long hours at manual labor: many of them were doomed to be permanent welfare dependents. The economy of Bhopal was devastated. As people lost their source of income, merchants faced greatly decreased per capita spending.

BACKGROUND

Bhopal is located 360 miles south of New Delhi. It is the capital of the Indian state of Madhya Pradesh, one of the poorest and least developed

---

[1]Richard I. Kirkland, Jr., "Union Carbide: Coping with Catastrophe," *Fortune* 111, Jan. 7, 1985, p. 50.

[2]Judith H. Dobrzynski et al., "Bhopal, A Year Later: Union Carbide Takes a Tougher Line," *Business Week*, Nov. 25, 1985, p. 96.

states. Bhopal's population of more than 700,000 people is basically divided into two areas: New Bhopal, where the city's rich live amid spacious residences, and Old Bhopal, the congested, low-income district.

After the accident, questions were raised as to why such a dangerous plant was located so close to a densely populated area. However, at the time the location was selected, more than 17 years before the accident, the area was not densely populated. In India, the people looking for jobs and economic gain tend to gravitate toward areas that contain manufacturing facilities. Over the years, housing spread until it reached the very fences that surrounded the plant. The population of Bhopal had tripled since the plant was opened.

The chemical plant is operated by Union Carbide of India, Ltd. It is 50.9 percent owned by Union Carbide and 49.1 percent by Indians. Management links between the Indian subsidiary and Carbide's corporate headquarters in Danbury, Connecticut, were few. Though Carbide was the majority owner, the plant was essentially an Indian operation. Most of the other investors, as well as all the managers and workers, were Indian.

Union Carbide is not a newcomer to India, having had facilities there since 1905. By 1983, its Indian subsidiary was one of India's largest industrial concerns, with 14 plants scattered throughout the country. In 1985, this subsidiary had sales of $202 million and profits of $8.8 million.

Union Carbide was the third-largest U.S. chemical company. It is a true multinational firm, operating plants in 38 countries and manufacturing a wide range of products, from industrial chemicals and powerful pesticides to such consumer goods as Glad Trash bags and Prestone automotive products. Of Carbide's 1984 sales of $9.5 billion, over 14 percent came from international operations, which contributed 21.6 percent of total profits.

Carbide was the only U.S. manufacturer of MIC. MIC was first manufactured commercially in the United States in the mid-1960s. It is a highly volatile, highly flammable, toxic chemical that is stored in liquid form in refrigerated stainless steel tanks. Refrigeration is necessary since MIC vaporizes into a gas at 100° Fahrenheit. As a gas, the pressure begins to build, and a relief valve is essential to vent the gas in order to prevent the tanks from rupturing.

A number of U.S. pesticide manufacturers buy MIC from Carbide as an intermediate to make pesticides. United States consumption of MIC reached 23–28 million pounds in 1982, with production capacity believed to be close to 50 million pounds.[3] Carbide also produces MIC at its plant in Institute, West Virginia, a facility nearly identical to the one in Bhopal.

---

[3]"Carbide's Search for Answers," *Chemical Week*, 135, Dec. 19, 1984, p. 34.

WHY DID THE ACCIDENT OCCUR?

The exact details of how the disaster occurred are to this day a matter of great controversy. Carbide and the Indian government do agree that the cause of the accident was the entry of 1000–2000 gallons of water into the MIC storage tank resulting in a runaway reaction. The resulting rapid rise in pressure caused a relief valve to open, releasing the poisonous gas for about two hours. During the release, pressure probably averaged 180 psig (pounds per square inch gauge), and maximum temperature probably exceeded 200° Celsius. MIC is normally stored at 0°C at a pressure of between 2 and 25 psig. The relief valve opens at 40 psig to avoid excessive pressure buildup.[4] Further investigation revealed that the following problems existed and presumably were not known by corporate headquarters:

1. The MIC unit's refrigeration system had been shut down for more than five months. As a result, the MIC temperature in the tank was 15–20°C instead of 0°C, a temperature that would have retarded reaction rates.

2. The tank temperature alarm had not been reset when the refrigeration unit was shut down. When the water reacted with the MIC, temperature and pressure rose, but there was no alarm to signal the change.

3. The unit's vent gas scrubber was on standby for over a month and had to be restarted manually after the release was discovered. The scrubber releases caustic material meant to destroy the escaping gas automatically as it is sensed entering the containment area.

4. The flare tower, which is intended to incinerate any of the highly flammable gas that escapes past the scrubber, was out of service.

The possibility of sabotage became a major controversy between Union Carbide and the Indian government. The company maintained that the cause of the disaster was a "deliberate act" by a disgruntled plant worker. Water was introduced directly into the MIC tank with the intention, said Carbide, "not to create a hideous disaster, but to ruin the batch of MIC as an act of mischief."[5] The Indian government disagreed, stating that the disaster was brought about by the plant's dangerous location, the unsafe production and storage of MIC, inadequate safety systems, operating mistakes, and preventable employee problems.

---

[4]"Bhopal Disaster: Union Carbide Explains Gas Leak," *Chemical & Engineering News*, 63, March 25, 1985, p. 4.

[5]Wil Lepkowski, "Union Carbide Presses Bhopal Sabotage Theory," *Chemical & Engineering News*, July 4, 1988, p. 8.

COMPANY REACTION

With such an overwhelming disaster, Carbide's management had to decide how best to aid the victims, how to be sure that whatever happened at Bhopal could not happen again somewhere else, how to help employees keep up morale, how to assure investors and creditors that the company was financially stable, and, last but by no means least, how to protect the company from expensive, legal liability that endanger the survival of their firm.

On the day of the disaster, Carbide halted production of MIC in its plant at Institute, West Virginia. To prevent any further problems at the Bhopal plant, it went back into production there to neutralize the remaining 15,000 tons of MIC. Until the exact cause of the disaster was determined, Carbide stopped all shipments to customers. Operations were not resumed at the Institute MIC plant until the spring of 1985.

Initially, Carbide's management was skeptical about the accuracy of the burgeoning estimates of dead and injured, which seemed beyond the limits of possibility. Help was quickly sent to India: medical supplies, respirators and similar equipment, and a doctor with extensive knowledge of the effects of the chemical. Still, the company was operating with imperfect information. Shortly, a team of technical experts was sent to examine the plant.

On the evening of December 4, with the death toll still mounting, Warren Anderson, the chairman of Union Carbide, took the company jet and followed the technical team. Unfortunately, his journey accomplished nothing. Indian officials, still stunned by the disaster, arrested Anderson upon his arrival. They held him briefly before releasing him on $2500 bail, then sent him to New Delhi, the capital of India. There, officials told Anderson to leave the country for his own good. Government officials refused his offer of $1 million in immediate aid and the use of the company's guesthouse in the hills above Bhopal to orphans of the victims.

Anderson's dash to India was dismissed by some as an empty gesture. Still, the trip showed Carbide's concern in a way no other action could. That it accomplished nothing during a time of crisis and wild emotionalism does not detract from the top executive's good intentions.

The team Anderson took with him was denied access to the Bhopal plant, and the Indian government seized all of the plant's records and arrested the plant supervisors. As a result, facts were hard to come by, and rumors were rampant. With only two phone lines to Bhopal and the plant supervisors there under arrest, Carbide was reduced to relying on Indian news reports relayed by phone from employees at its subsidiary in Bombay.

Carbide's attempts to administer financial and medical aid were initially rejected by government officials. Anderson believed that "if we try to do something with our name on it, the Indian government turns it down. They're worried that if they take anything it would have negative implications on the lawsuit."[6]

CONSEQUENCES

Image Problems

On Wall Street, nervous investors, scrambling to unload their stock, drove the price down by more than 11 points to about $37 a share, a total loss in market value of nearly $900 million. This plunge in Carbide stock led the company to begin stressing its financial soundness in press releases and briefings. However, these actions had the unwanted side-effect of making the company seem bottom-line oriented rather than compassionate.

According to a Harris poll taken a few weeks after the event, 44 percent of Americans who had heard of the accident believed that Carbide had done only a "fair" or "poor" job of telling the truth about what happened, as opposed to 36 percent who judged it to have done an "excellent" or "good" job. Of those surveyed, 31 percent declared that they would be "less likely" to buy Carbide products if it turned out that either company or employee negligence was responsible. Normally, only about 20 percent of the public can identify a company of Carbide's size; yet, 47 percent of those polled, without prompting, were able to name Carbide as the company involved in the accident.[7] These results caused Carbide concern: Bhopal might be the only thing many people knew about Carbide. Its image appeared to be in the pits.

Impact on Sales and Profits

Table 11.1 shows Union Carbide sales and net income during the 1980s. We see that Carbide's business was very cyclical, the two years preceding Bhopal not nearly as good as 1980 and 1981. The huge deficit of 1985 directly reflects the impact of Bhopal, with write-offs and reserves set aside for future settlements. The much lower sales figures in the latter part of the decade reflect company streamlining and divestiture of certain operations. In the process, earnings again reached toward the peak years of 1980 and 1981.

[6]Dobrzynski et al., p. 97.
[7]Stuart Jackson, "Union Carbide's Good Name Takes a Beating," *Business Week*, Dec. 31, 1984, p. 40.

Table 11–1 Union Carbide's Sales and Profits, 1980–1989

	Sales	Net Income
	(millions of $s)	
1980	9,994	673
1981	10,168	649
1982	9,061	310
1983	9,001	79
1984	9,508	341
1985	9,003	599 deficit
1986	6,343	130
1987	6,914	232
1988	8,324	662
1989	8,744	573

Source: Company annual reports.

The company has bounced back from its Bhopal adversity. As we will see in the next section, the litigation essentially favored Carbide, and the viability of the company was fully preserved.

Legal Effects

Like hungry vultures, U.S. lawyers flocked to India. They saw representing the victims as an excellent opportunity for financial gain. Some felt that each individual victim should be represented separately; others saw a class-action lawsuit against Union Carbide as the best strategy for their clients and themselves. A famous and flamboyant San Francisco attorney, Melvin Belli, along with four other lawyers, filed a $15 billion suit on charges of negligence and defects in the company's design and construction of the Bhopal MIC storage facility. The complaint also alleged that Carbide failed to warn the citizens of Bhopal and the Indian government about the dangerous nature of MIC and MIC storage. Further, the Belli complaint stated that Carbide did these things "knowingly, willfully, and wantonly, or with utter disregard for the safety of the residents of Bhopal, India."[8]

The American lawyers thought the trial should be held in the United States because the victims could win more money. Carbide held that since the accident occurred in India and the victims and witnesses were Indians, the trial should be held there. Some of the Indian attorneys also maintained that the case should be tried in their country. The stakes were huge on this particular issue: the viability of Union Carbide was even at stake, given the multibillion dollar awards U.S. juries were likely to dispense.

[8]"Bhopal: The Endless Aftershocks, "*Chemical Week,*" Dec. 19, 1984, p. 42.

A major ruling was made in May 1986, a year and a half after the actual accident. All claims in U.S. federal courts against Union Carbide were dismissed, and the trial was to be kept in India. This effectively put an end to the involvement of American lawyers, and preserved Union Carbide. In February 1989, the company paid $425 million to settle all litigation arising from the 1984 leak. Union Carbide of India Ltd. also paid a rupees equivalent of $45 million. Now the company was finally freed from its legal encumbrances.

UPDATE

As a result of the Bhopal disaster, enforceable international standards that define the best practices for designing and operating hazardous facilities are in the developmental stage. The National Academy of Sciences is focusing on extensive testing for new and old chemical products, while belatedly noting that of 65,000 chemicals in common use, we currently know very little about 90 percent of these.[9]

Overall, the lax regulation of occupational safety and environmental laws was of great embarrassment to India when the accident occurred. As a result, the laxity in developing countries is starting to reverse. Brazil, for example, has tightened its safety regulations considerably since Bhopal.

ANALYSIS

Due to the backward state of the Indian economy, much of the technology of the Bhopal plant was imported. Union Carbide of India paid a technical service fee to the parent for its technology, patents, and training. Consequently, Union Carbide of India was dependent on the parent to provide the information necessary to use this technology effectively. But the question can be raised: Was the technology too complex for an undeveloped country?

The employees' low educational and technical level, coupled with a lack of "safety mentality," may have greatly contributed to the accident. Insufficient technical competence among both managers and workers is by no means unique to India. It is a problem many multinational firms face as they export advanced technologies to less developed countries. (See the Issue box concerning ultimate *responsibility for worker competence*.)

A major incentive for building manufacturing facilities in underdeveloped countries is the high rate of return on investment, higher than often

---

[9]Ward Morehouse and M. Arum Subramanian, *The Bhopal Tragedy* (Council of International and Public Affairs, 1986), p. 112.

ISSUE: RESPONSIBILITY FOR WORKER COMPETENCE IN THIRD WORLD COUNTRIES

Manager and worker incompetence at Bhopal showed up both in the build-up to the disaster and in the mishandling of the crisis itself. Their training and monitoring by the parent company left something to be desired. But a major issue is raised for multinationals as they extend their operations to less-developed countries:

Are these people trainable to acceptable standards of technical knowledge, work ethics, and careful adherence to safety and quality?

Some would argue that the multinationals should be able to train and develop native workers to acceptable standards, and if they do not, the blame is solely on the big corporation. But it can also be argued that the governments of such countries are at least partially to blame in not providing sufficient education to their people so that they are fully trainable in modern technology.

The two positions sound very much like passing the buck—"blame the other guy." But both arguments have merit. For the multinational corporation, however, the Bhopal experience should raise concern about exporting advanced technology to developing countries, especially when health and safety are involved, without very careful and continuous monitoring and the tightest controls.

INVITATION TO DISCUSS

Take a position on either side of this issue. Collect as many arguments as you can to support your position. Be sure and cover difficulties in implementation. What would your compromise position be?

---

can be achieved in more advanced economies. Labor costs, of course, are typically lower. But another irresistible incentive is avoiding costly, safety-related measures—especially in the absence of government-prescribed safety standards. (See the Issue box for an additional discussion of these *flawed incentives.*) Instituting the same safety standards prescribed in the United States would make such foreign investments far less attractive.

As underdeveloped countries understandably increase their safety standards, they will also have to create more incentives to attract firms that will now find the costs of doing business in these countries just as high as in more developed countries—but with the higher risks that come from less-educated workers. Perhaps this situation will place a new responsibility on the governments of these countries to bring their local laborers and managers to a higher level of technical and workplace competence. This is a new challenge for education in such environments.

ISSUE: FLAWED INCENTIVES FOR BUILDING PLANTS IN LESS-DEVELOPED COUNTRIES?

It is common practice for multinational firms to locate plants within developing countries, such as India. Labor costs are lower. Usually industrial safety standards are lower than those in the United States. Often these governments, eager for the economic benefits of such plants, provide incentives, including development costs and natural resources. Thus profits can be greater than with domestic operations. For a company with an altruistic bent, the prospect of raising living standards in another country is a nice rationale.

But in the production of hazardous substances, the dangers at these plants are extremely high. Although Union Carbide and other multinational firms contend that the plants they build abroad are identical to those built in the United States, the operations may be far more lax and imprudent. As Peter Thacher, former deputy executive director of the United Nations Environmental Program, noted: "You have to assume that in a developing country, people will not be as careful in terms of inspection, quality control, and maintenance. And you must assume that if a problem occurs, it will be more difficult to cope with."[10]

So, the multinational, in its quest for higher profits and fewer restrictions on worker safety and environmental protection, faces the risk of accidents occurring—unless it exercises extreme care and close monitoring. But these add to costs.

INVITATION TO DISCUSS
In the absence of adequate safety and environmental-protection standards in many developing countries, how might a multinational lessen risks of accidents? Argue the case for not doing so. Which position do you think is the most persuasive, from the firm's viewpoint?

India did receive substantial benefits from the Bhopal plant. Pesticides are estimated to have saved 10 percent of the Indian food crop, enough to feed 70 million people. The Green Revolution, started in India under the Ford Foundation in the early 1960s, increased the life expectancy of the average Indian citizen from 30 to 50 years, prevented many deaths from starvation, and alleviated much malnutrition.[11]

So, how culpable was Union Carbide? Was there a blatant disregard of human consequences? Was the company calloused and uncaring? Was it criminally negligent?

---

[10]Peter Thacher, "the Lesson of Bhopal: The Lure of Foreign Capital Is Stronger Than Environmental Worries," *Atlantic,* March 1987, pp. 30–33.

[11]Larry Everest, *Behind the Poison Cloud* (Chicago: Banner Press, 1985), pp. 107–117.

A terrible accident happened. With the benefit of hindsight, it need not have happened. The company did not deliberately disregard safety measures. But it did not exercise the close controls needed for a dangerous product in a distant and less technically proficient land. Management should have known better. But, of course, no one expected a catastrophe of such magnitude—and yet it happened. Then, company officials, particularly the chief executive, Warren Anderson, acted with compassion and deep concern. At the same time, he had to protect the company from a multitude of lawsuits—no matter how much compassion he felt for the suffering victims and their families.

Anderson summed the situation up in this way in a January 1985 interview by *Chemical & Engineering News:*

> Union Carbide had a good reputation for health, safety and the environment; we're a company that has resources; and we can cope with an issue like this one. Maybe out of this will come a whole new approach to this issue of health, safety and environment. Not only in developing countries, but in the United States as well. If it had happened to a company that didn't have Carbide's capabilities, maybe not as much would have been learned. So we have a commitment and an obligation to lead the way if we can. The world's going to be a better place. It's a hard way to learn a lesson, but if we went through a disaster like this and didn't learn anything, that would be the worst.[12]

WHAT CAN BE LEARNED?

Learning Insight. *Expect and prepare for a worst-case scenario.*

There are those who preach the desirability of positive thinking, of confidence and optimism—whether it be in personal lives, athletics or business practices. But expecting and preparing for the worst has much to commend it, since a person or a firm is then better able to cope with adversity, not be overwhelmed, and therefore make prudent decisions. Certain industrial activities carry with them a potential risk so large as to threaten the organization's very survival. With such high potential risk, managers, employees, and community residents need to be coached on safety procedures in the event of an accident. Local governmental bodies and hospitals should be well prepared to treat any local industrial accident victims and should stock appropriate drugs and equipment—just in case of the worst scenario. Mock accident drills could be conducted from time to time.

---

[12]"Carbide's Anderson Explains Post-Bhopal Strategy," *Chemical & Engineering News,* Jan. 21, 1985, p. 15.

A side benefit of such active accident awareness might well be that people might not be so eager to live near such dangerous plants, thus minimizing the potential for massive injuries and deaths.

Issue Insight. *Should multinationals follow U.S. safety standards worldwide?*

The risk of a catastrophe on the scale of Bhopal is remote; accidents on a smaller scale involving workers and perhaps some environmental degradation are more likely. But the consequences of a Bhopal-like disaster are almost as life-threatening to the corporation as to the population, with litigation becoming ever more costly in defense and in settlement. Prudent companies dealing with hazardous products or processes can no longer afford to tolerate less-stringent safety standards than those in the United States. Indeed, the argument can be raised that standards ought to be even more strict because of the caliber of the workforce. It is myopic thinking to do otherwise, rather akin to Russian roulette.

Learning Insight. *Cost-cutting must not have the highest priority.*

The Bhopal plant design focused on cost-cutting measures that would enhance profitability. For example, the storage tanks. Other manufacturers of MIC use many smaller storage tanks instead of a few large ones: Bayer's West German facility, for example, had tanks with a 10-ton capacity, in contrast to the 100-ton capacity of Bhopal's tanks.

Many of the safety systems at Bhopal were manual. The only computers were those used for accounts payable and payroll applications. None were used in instrumentation and controls. Any leaks were investigated when workers noticed odors or when their eyes became irritated.[13]

Admittedly, it will be more costly to shift toward safer methods of processing, storing, and manufacturing hazardous substances. But Bhopal should be an object lesson on the dangers of cost-cutting with such products and processes.

Learning Insight. *A laissez-faire decentralization is not appropriate in underdeveloped countries when safety and environmental degradation are at stake.*

Complete "hands-off" decentralization of subsidiary operations in foreign countries (leaving only financial and capital expenditures directly con-

---

[13]Everest, pp. 33–40.

trolled by corporate management) is far from adequate when hazardous products are involved. Clear, ongoing lines of communication are vital to such operations. The corporate headquarters can no longer act as an "ivory tower," performing only high administrative functions. The same social-responsibility criteria must be used for home-country and foreign-country decisions. Corporate officials need to more closely monitor foreign operations and react to inefficiencies as they would if the problem had occurred in their home country. Unfortunately for Union Carbide, this lesson was a costly one.

FOR THOUGHT AND DISCUSSION

1. Do you agree with the decision to legally try the case in Indian courts rather than U.S. ones—thereby saving Union Carbide billions in settlement costs? Why or why not?
2. Debate the issue: Union Carbide is guilty of such a terrible crime against humanity that it should be dissolved and no longer be permitted to exist as a complete entity.
3. Should Warren Anderson and other high-level corporate executives have been prosecuted and even jailed? Discuss the issue.
4. Could the company be blamed for the population growth around its plant's perimeter? How might this have been prevented?
5. Do you think the public image of Union Carbide was heavily damaged in the United States? Why or why not?

INVITATION TO ROLE PLAY

1. Place yourself in the position of Warren Anderson, CEO of Union Carbide at the time of the disaster. You are determined to fly to Bhopal. What agenda do you propose having? What would you hope to accomplish?
2. You are a worker at the Bhopal plant. Several months before the accident, you notice that your eyes are burning around tank 610. What, if anything, would you do? Assess the possible consequences.

INVITATION TO RESEARCH

Is the Bhopal plant operating today? If so, is it still producing MIC? Did the local managers receive prison sentences?

CHAPTER 12

Beech-Nut: Adulterated Apple Juice—For Babies

On February 17, 1988, two former top executives of Beech-Nut Nutrition Corporation were found guilty of violating federal laws by intentionally marketing phony apple juice intended for babies.

The previous November, the company itself pleaded guilty to 215 felony counts and admitted to willful violation of the food and drug laws by selling adulterated apple products from 1981 to 1983. Although the apple juice, Beech-Nut's best-selling product, was labeled "100% fruit juice," it was actually a blend of synthetic ingredients, a "100% fraudulent chemical cocktail," as one investigator testified.[1]

Beech-Nut was the second largest U.S. baby food manufacturer. Founded in 1891, it had always stressed purity, high quality, and natural ingredients in its marketing programs and company philosophy.

How could such a reputable concern have strayed so far from its reputation and, indeed, its heritage?

BACKGROUND

Beech-Nut was founded as a meat-packing company and expanded into a large, diversified food concern, eventually including Life Savers, Table Talk

[1]Chris Welles, "What Led Beech-Nut Down the Road to Disgrace?" *Business Week*, Feb. 22, 1988, p. 124.

pies, Tetley tea, Martinson's coffee, chewing gum, and baby food. In 1969, the Squibb Corporation took over Beech-Nut, and four years later, in 1973, a remnant of the original company was taken private by a group led by a lawyer, Frank Nicholas. By now, the company had divested and sold only baby food.

Unfortunately for Beech-Nut, the Nicholas group had acquired the company entirely with borrowed funding. They were forced to run the company on a bare-bones budget. They neglected the 80-year-old Canajoharie, New York, plant. And with a 15 percent market share, the new owners could not begin to match the marketing outlays of Gerber Products Company, which had 70 percent of the market. Losses mounted, and millions of dollars were owed to suppliers. A new buyer was desperately needed, and one was finally found. In 1979, Nestle bought out Nicholas for $35 million. Nestle then invested another $60 million, hiking marketing budgets and boosting sales. But the pressure to turn a profit intensified. The Beech-Nut president, Neils Hoyvald, would testify in 1981 that

> he had grandiosely promised Nestle that Beech-Nut would earn $700,000 the following year [1982], though there would be a negative cash flow of $1.7 million. The answer shot back from Switzerland: the cash flow for Beech-Nut, as for all other Nestle subsidiaries, would have to be zero or better. The pressure, [Hoyvald] conceded, was on.[2]

But the company had been trying to pare costs for some years. In 1977, it had abandoned its long-time supplier of apple-juice concentrate for a less-expensive version from a Bronx-based supplier, Interjuice Trading Corporation, and its distribution arm, Universal Juice. While the new concentrate was less expensive, its quality was not questioned by Beech-Nut. Eventually, the price of Universal's concentrate fell to 25 percent below the market price. Should this have alerted Beech-Nut to the possibility that the concentrate was adulterated?

It did. In initial testing, Beech-Nut chemists found indications of impurities, and John Lavery, vice president of operations, sent two employees to inspect Interjuice's concentrate source. They were shown a storage area, but they were denied access to the processing facility.

Jerome LiCari, director of research and development at Beech-Nut, was one of the few questioning Universal's credibility. Acting on his suspicions, he sent samples of the concentrate to an outside laboratory for testing. Results indicated that the juice was adulterated, probably with corn syrup, and Lavery was so informed. LiCari dispatched samples of the concentrate

[2]James Traub, "Into the Mouths of Babes," *New York Times Magazine*, July 24, 1988, p. 37.

to another laboratory in April and July 1979. April's tests showed adulteration, but July's showed no signs of tampering. He concluded that the supplier had switched from corn syrup to beet sugar, an adulterant that current technology could not detect. Again LiCari informed Lavery of the results, and this time Lavery ordered the concentrate to be blended into mixed juices, where the adulteration would be more difficult to detect.

By spring 1981, LiCari was devoting most of his time to improving adulteration testing. But he was finding it difficult to convince his superiors to end Beech-Nut's dealings with Universal. On August 5, 1981, LiCari sent a memo to a number of executives, including Lavery, urging a high-level meeting to discuss his most recent findings in what he and his fellow scientists believed was an irrefutable case against Universal. But his concerns were ignored. Lavery criticized him for not being a team player and threatened him with termination.

LiCari then met with the president of Beech-Nut, Neils Hoyvald, at Beech-Nut headquarters in Philadelphia. Although the president appeared shocked and surprised at LiCari's report, months passed with no apparent action. LiCari resigned in January 1982, convinced that the company was bent on breaking the law. (See the Issue box for a discussion of a *manager's options when caught in an ethical dilemma* similar to LiCari's.)

MOUNTING PRESSURE

In spring 1982, the Food and Drug Administration (FDA), in a routine analysis, collected samples of apple juice from grocer warehouses. The juice from two New York state producers was found to be adulterated, and one of the firms used juice from Universal. Later, the FDA learned that Beech-Nut was also a customer of Universal Juice.[3] An inspection of Beech-Nut quickly followed. The company was advised of the FDA's negative findings in July 1982; officials responded that they had stopped using concentrate from Universal earlier in 1982. The FDA raised concern about the product already in distribution channels, at which point Lavery told the FDA that the company did not plan any recall because the juice posed no health hazard.

Concurrently and independently, a trade association, the Processed Apples Institute (PAI) started its own investigation of Universal Juice. PAI hired a private investigator, Andrew Rosenzweig, a former New York City narcotics detective. He diligently investigated Universal and its Food Complex division. He questioned employees, he searched dumpsters in the middle of

---

[3]Vern Modeland, "Juiceless Baby Juice Leads to Full-Strength Justice," *FDA Consumer*, June 1988, p. 16.

ISSUE: A MIDDLE MANAGER'S OPTIONS IN AN ETHICAL DILEMMA

What, if anything, should a less-senior manager do when confronted with an obdurate top management in an unethical setting? That was the situation Jerome LiCari faced. He had investigated the situation thoroughly, was convinced of the truth of his suspicions, and then contacted his superiors, including the president of the firm. But nothing happened. For his persistence, he was threatened with dismissal and criticized for not being a team player. He resigned in protest. Did he do the right thing?

In such a situation, a person generally has three alternatives: (1) accept the situation and acquiesce to the less-than-ethical climate fostered by top management, (2) resign, or (3) be a whistleblower and seek public attention (we discussed whistleblowing in Chapter 2). The easiest course of action—the one most people follow—is the first: accept what you are not likely to change without jeopardizing your career. The other courses of action are for those more dedicated to high moral principles, those who are more courageous.

INVITATION TO DISCUSS
What would you do if you were in LiCari's situation? Would your decision differ if you had family responsibilities and heavy debts? Are there any options other than the three mentioned?

---

the night; he observed chemicals and beet sugar, but no apples, going into the Food Complex plant. And, on June 25, 1982, he followed a tanker truck of concentrate from Food Complex to Beech-Nut. Offering conclusive proof of the bogus concentrate, Rosenzweig asked Beech-Nut to join other juice makers in a lawsuit against the supplier. Beech-Nut refused, but the company did stop purchasing concentrate from Universal. However, it continued to sell products containing the phony concentrate for almost another year.

Thinking that government seizure action was imminent, Beech-Nut, on the night of August 12, 1982, began removing the tainted juice from New York state jurisdiction. Nine tractor-trailer loads of product were taken to a warehouse in Secaucus, New Jersey. In other efforts to unload the $3.5 million inventory, quantities were shipped out of the country.

Through time-buying tactics, Beech-Nut's lawyers also tried to keep federal and state agencies from seizing the product. All the while, the company continued to ship and sell the phony juice. Finally, FDA Administrator Taylor Quinn, threatening to seize the juice, wrung from the company a pledge to begin a nationwide recall. However, the recall covered only straight apple juice. Mixed juices made from the bogus concentrate continued to be sold until March 1983, months after the recall. President Hoyvald boasted of his triumphs in a management report to Nestle:

It is our feeling that we can report safely now that the apple juice recall has been completed. If the recall had been effectuated in early June, over 700,000 cases in inventory could have been affected. Due to our many delays, we were faced with having to destroy approximately 20,000 cases. We received adverse publicity in only one magazine.[4]

RETRIBUTION

Beech-Nut's delaying tactics, in order to try to preserve its $3.5 million inventory, proved disastrous. Had the company recalled its inventory in June 1982, it would have been able to successfully portray itself as a victim of unscrupulous suppliers.[5] An attorney close to the case thought Beech-Nut had committed a "grave tactical error":

They could have nipped this in the bud, owned up, paid a fine, and it would have been a pimple for them. But they stonewalled, and the stonewalling became the issue, and the case changed from civil to criminal, and it became a nightmare.[6]

The FDA recommended that the Justice Department bring criminal charges against Beech-Nut and its top executives; in June 1985, a criminal investigation was begun. By November of 1986, both Hoyvald and Lavery had been indicted by a U.S. grand jury and granted leaves of absence from Beech-Nut to prepare their defenses. At this time, Nestle said that "it was standing by its executives and would fight the charges."[7] Beech-Nut itself paid a $2 million fine as part of a guilty plea to 215 criminal counts stemming from the sales of millions of bottles of phony apple juice. This fine was by far the largest penalty ever paid in the 50-year history of the Food, Drug, and Cosmetic Act. The company also settled a class-action suit in a Philadelphia court for $7.5 million, admitting guilt rather than engage in a long trial.

However, Hoyvald and Lavery pleaded innocent in their trial. The evidence against them seemed overwhelming. Their first attorney even suggested that Lavery plead guilty instead of standing trial. But the defendants both maintained that they were guilty of nothing worse than committing an error of judgment. LiCari proved a strong prosecution witness.

Lavery was found guilty of 448 criminal counts of conspiracy, mail fraud, and violations of the federal Food, Drug, and Cosmetic Act. Hoyvald

---

[4]Traub, p. 52.
[5]"Stonewalling at Beech-Nut," *Business Week*, Feb. 22, 1988, p. 174.
[6]Welles, p. 26.
[7]William Dullforce, "Indicted Chief of Beech-Nut Goes on Leave," *Financial Times*, Nov. 8, 1986, p. 2.

was convicted of 351 felony counts of violating the food act. Both men were fined $100,000 and sentenced to a year and a day in prison. The Brooklyn U.S. Attorney's office maintained that the two executives deserved stiff sentences for what it called one of the greatest consumer frauds in U.S. history. The government contended that Lavery knew of the phony concentrate as early as 1978 and Hoyvald knew of its use in January 1981. Hoyvald's lawyer, Brendan Sullivan pleaded for leniency. He argued that Hoyvald had lost position and prestige and that the product was harmless: ". . . there was never a word of concern uttered that the product would endanger a single child or make a child sick."[8] Sullivan asked for a sentence of community service and probation, and proposed that Hoyvald give ethics lectures at business schools—which shocked many professors of business ethics, who saw the evils of the business world being rewarded. Eventually, Lavery served time in prison and Hoyvald did six months of community service.[9] (See the Issue box for a discussion of *punishment for white-collar crime.*)

ISSUE: IS WHITE-COLLAR CRIME SUFFICIENTLY PUNISHED?

Eventually, the two executives involved in the apple-juice fraud received light sentences: the president of Beech-Nut got only six months of community service. But a pickpocket, a shoplifter, or other petty thief often goes to prison. Is it just and equitable that white-collar crime, which can reap monumental payoffs, should go relatively unpunished?

Supporters of leniency for the executive would argue that bodily harm was not in question, whereas a pickpocket or other petty thief could become violent. Supporters would also argue that the public destruction of a prominent person's reputation is far greater punishment than any jail sentence. But is it? Or does this issue really revolve around social class and racial considerations? Are the downtrodden punished out of proportion to their crimes? Or is it that the rich can afford expensive lawyers to find legal loopholes? Many would say that our judicial system favors the rich, the "members of the establishment." But is this fair?

INVITATION TO DISCUSS
What are your thoughts on this issue? How do you see the destruction of a reputation as a substitute for the jail time a common criminal serves?

---

[8]"Former Beech-Nut Executives Get Prison Terms," *Reuter Business Report*, June 16, 1988 (no page numbers available).

[9]James Benson, "FDA Enforcement Activities Protect Public," *FDA Consumer* Jan./Feb. 1991, p. 7.

FINAL CONSEQUENCES

The lawsuit and scandal cost Beech-Nut an estimated $25 million in fines, legal costs, and slumping sales. Negative publicity led to the company's market share dropping by about 20 percent in 1987, resulting in new record losses.

Fortunately for Nestle, most of the bad publicity focused on Beech-Nut, not on Nestle, the parent company. None of the legal action involved Nestle or Nestle executives. But, of course, the profit problems of a subsidiary impact on the parent. And Nestle executives must have feared that its involvement with adulterated apple juice could have been connected in the public's eye to Nestle's infant formula scandal.

ANALYSIS

We need to determine just what led responsible executives to blatantly disregard ethical and even legal considerations. Were they honorable men? There is no evidence that as private citizens, they were not. We are forced to conclude that unethical and illegal acts can be undertaken by essentially honest and well-respected individuals. This defies our darker musings, but it is true. Here we have a company in serious financial straits. The opportunity is presented to save millions of dollars through adulterated ingredients that would not easily be detected. What a temptation! Health and consumer safety apparently were not major considerations here: the adulterated ingredients were hardly life-threatening. So, we have a little cheating. How bad is this, really? Maybe that's what the executives involved asked themselves. (See the Issue box for a discussion of the classic issue: *Does the end justify the means?*)

In situations like this, it is easy to rationalize. Another rationalization was that there was no good, solid proof that the concentrate was not authentic. Lacking this, why should the executives suspect the worst? But the clues were there for any objective observer:

- 20 percent lower cost than any alternatives—how could this be without something being amiss?
- The lack of full disclosure by the supplier.
- The almost certain proof of adulteration as seen by the Beech-Nut research and development department.

The defense maintained that there wasn't positive proof that the concentrate was bogus. But shouldn't grave suspicion lead to further investigation? When top management adopts a laissez-faire or hands-off policy about a serious charge—especially when millions of dollars of inventory are involved, suggesting a conflict of interest—it can hardly be condoned.

ISSUE: DOES THE END JUSTIFY THE MEANS?

This age-old issue, which encompasses the widest scope of activities, provokes perhaps the greatest controversies and the most fanaticism of any moral issue. The issue boils down to this: does a desirable result (the end) justify less than desirable practices (the means) to accomplish it? Some maintain that the end, no matter how desirable it might be, never justifies abusive or unscrupulous means to achieve it. Others believe that some bad consequences may be acceptable if the good to be achieved outweighs the bad, and if no other reasonable alternatives to achieve those desired ends are available.

Essentially, to subscribe to a means/end ethic is to believe in moral compromise. We compromise our morals for the greater good. That's the rationale extremists use. They will stop at nothing to further their cause, whether through bombings, kidnappings, airplane and ship hijackings, even war.

Does saving a company justify some moral transgressions? That was at least the implicit rationale for the Beech-Nut executives to drag their feet in the investigation and recall of the adulterated apple juice. In an earlier case, we showed the ITT Corporation belief that protecting some of its property in a developing country justified trying to interfere and even overthrow the country's president. Where do we draw the line?

INVITATION TO DISCUSS

In general, how do you feel regarding this means/end issue? Where would you draw the line between what is acceptable conduct and what is totally unacceptable under any circumstances? How about the survival of a country? Does this justify the most extreme measures?

So, a company's public image can be vulnerable—and should be vulnerable—when it commits unethical practices, whether those practices impinge on public health and welfare, as Nestle's infant formula did (Chapter 10), or whether they involve "merely" a misrepresentation of what the product is made of.

WHAT CAN BE LEARNED?

Learning Insight. *Unethical and illegal actions do not go undetected forever.*

It may take months, it may take years, but a firm's dark side will eventually be revealed. Its reputation may then be besmirched, its competitive position eroded—or worse. In Beech-Nut's case, heavy fines were levied on the corporation and punishment was meted out to two responsible executives, one of them the president of the firm. It could have been worse, as we saw in the earlier case of the Dalkon Shield.

To expect deceptive and fraudulent practices to go undetected forever is hardly realistic thinking. The eventual disclosure may come from a zealous employee or a disgruntled employee. It may be uncovered by an alert regulatory body or by an investigative reporter. Eventually, the deviation is uncovered, and retribution follows. Such a scenario should be—but is not always—enough to constrain those individuals tempted to commit unethical and illegal actions.

Learning Insight. *Top managers are no longer assured of escaping blame and prosecution for corporate misdeeds.*

In the past, top managers usually escaped direct culpability for corporate misdeeds under the guise that they knew nothing about such misdeeds, that subordinates acting on their own were to blame. (We saw this in the General Motors' case, and we will encounter it again.) But in the Beech-Nut case and in the Dalkon Shield case, top managers were not protected. The business environment has shifted today. Top executives can no longer expect to be insulated; nor should they be, for responsibility cannot be abdicated by top executives, not matter how much delegation is done to subordinates.

Learning Insight. *Beware the offer that is "too good."*

Both executives and consumers should beware of too low a price, too attractive an offer. Fraud and deception frequently hide behind unusually attractive price quotes. The low-priced "apple" concentrate that Beech-Nut bought from Universal was too good a price to be genuine. Company executives should have been alerted to the fact something was not right. They may well have had their doubts about the quality of a product priced so much below the competition, but they chose to ignore their doubts in the interest of keeping costs down.

Learning Insight. *Suspicions of malpractice should be promptly, thoroughly, and objectively investigated.*

The Beech-Nut organization was not amiss in investigating the "apple" concentrate. LiCari and his staff were zealous in pursuing their suspicions and substantiated them. The problem was that higher management would not accept LiCari's denunciations: even more, they discouraged him from investigating further, and, essentially, whitewashed any criticism of their supplier—until outside pressure became overwhelming. As Carbide's handling of the Bhopal disaster showed, naively ignoring suspicious situations can be as dangerous to a firm as intentionally attempting to cover up.

Learning Insight. *Trying to cover up usually exacerbates the situation. Moral: quick admission of guilt is less consequential than prolonged attempts at covering up.*

We have seen this scenario in several other cases, and we will see it in later cases. It seems to be a human impulse to cover up failings or misdeeds as long as possible, not realizing that cover-ups usually make the situation worse. If Beech-Nut had publicly admitted its mistake early, it would have received little criticism. Indeed, the brunt of the criticism would have focused on Universal, the supplier. By covering up as long as possible, and by attempting to profitably dispose of the products with bogus ingredients, Beech-Nut made the situation far worse, to the point where the company and certain of its executives could not escape culpability. The temptation to evade public condemnation and punitive action as long as possible—with the misguided belief that such evasion will never be caught—seems to be an overwhelming one for many executives. Yet, it could hardly be more misguided.

FOR THOUGHT AND DISCUSSION

1. Do you think the bogus apple juice situation was blown out of proportion? After all, health and safety were not an issue.
2. Beech-Nut was in serious straits. Does this situation justify taking some shortcuts? Discuss, considering as many dimensions as you can.
3. Do you think Beech-Nut should have recalled all of its apple-based baby food after the first charges by LiCari? Why or why not?

INVITATION TO ROLE PLAY

1. You are the president of Beech-Nut, Neils Hoyvald. You are under strong pressure from Nestle to show a profit; your job is at stake. Would you have acted differently? (Explain why) Discuss, considering the various implications.
2. You are an assistant to Jerome LiCari, director of research and development, the man who brought overwhelming evidence that the apple juice was bogus. Your boss has just resigned in frustration over his inability to persuade top management to recall the adulterated apple juice. What do you see yourself doing at this point? Discuss your rationale.

INVITATION TO RESEARCH

What is the situation with Beech-Nut today?

13

Burroughs Wellcome: Price Gouging by Pharmaceutical Firms

The pharmaceutical industry periodically comes under governmental scrutiny for the pricing practices of individual firms. Critics maintain that the high prices for some drugs are unjustified, even unconscionable. The drug companies stoutly maintain that high prices relative to the drug's production costs are justified, even essential, to support the high research and development expenditures, and to compensate the companies for the particularly high risks associated with new drug introductions. What makes the issue especially troublesome is the fact that drugs are so essential to our lives. Unlike most products, where there are alternative brands available, where the purchase decision is entirely discretionary, some drugs have few or no substitutes. The consumer—often someone elderly with limited resources—may have no option, short of jeopardizing health, but to pay whatever the drug firm demands.

In the last few years, the issue has received renewed attention. A new drug (AZT) to help AIDS patients was developed. It initially cost $10,000 for a year's supply. Critics asked how any firm could place such a price tag on a life-saving drug. Are the drug companies unscrupulous bandits, oblivious to any human context in their quest for maximized profits? Can their actions be defended? How much profit should a manufacturer of a product essential for life and welfare be permitted to earn? Indeed, should government really exercise any constraints over price-setting? These are some of the issues we will confront in this case.

The issue of price gouging of drugs will again be encountered in Chapter 21. There we have Johnson & Johnson, a company renowned for its responsible conduct toward customers during the Tylenol scare when some of its capsules were poisoned. However, in 1992, J&J was accused of pricing a drug effective for colon cancer 100 times higher than essentially the same drug when used by veterinarians for decades in treating sheep for parasites.

THE PHARMACEUTICAL INDUSTRY

The pharmaceutical industry comprises three sectors: the medicinal chemicals industry, producers of bulk active ingredients; the biological products industry; and the pharmaceutical preparations industry, which includes firms that manufacture and distribute dosage-form drug products. This latter sector has attracted most of the critical attention.

The pharmaceutical preparations industry is further broken down into proprietary drugs and ethical drugs. The former are the common household drugs promoted directly to consumers, with no prescription needed. Ethical drugs are marketed to medical professionals. Ethical drugs are further classified as prescription drug products, such as tranquilizers, antibiotics, and sedatives, and over-the-counter drug products, which may be sold without a prescription but are usually recommended by a doctor and are therefore marketed directly to medical professionals. Although the distinction between these products is often blurred, a more meaningful categorization is between prescription and nonprescription drugs. The pricing of prescription drugs has sometimes led to charges of price gouging and excessive profits at the expense of a helpless public.

The development of the sulfa drugs—known as "wonder drugs"—in the 1930s, and the introduction of penicillin during World War II, led to major scientific and economic changes in the drug industry. During this time, some of the industry's chemical suppliers found that they could increase revenues and profits by turning their bulk materials into finished products themselves. Meanwhile, the old-line prescription drug firms, former bulk-sales customers of chemical suppliers, started to produce some of the needed ingredients themselves. Many nonprescription drug firms also began diversifying into prescription drug products.

Increased competition brought more systematic research and development; it also brought more aggressive marketing practices. Physicians began to be deluged with intense promotions. And prescription drugs lent themselves to aggressive marketing simply because promotion could be narrowly focused on a small, homogenous target group of about 300,000 practicing physicians, even fewer if the marketing was directed to specialists.

This industry presents a marketing situation that is virtually unparalleled in any other industry:

> The physician who selects and orders a drug product is not the customer who pays for it, and the customer usually has no voice in the selection of the drug.

Moreover, once the producing company has established the quality of its product and the company's integrity in the doctor's mind, adoption of future products is facilitated.

The influence of government programs—regulatory and Medicare-type programs—has greatly affected the industry since the 1960s. Approval of new products is more difficult and time-consuming, with rigorous testing required. This, coupled with the increasing costs of research and development, has increased the stakes in this industry.

Pricing in the Pharmaceutical Industry

Demand for most prescription drugs is inelastic, which means that it is unresponsive to changes in price. The consumer who cannot pay for medications and therefore goes without is definitely in the minority. Other purchases may have to be sacrificed, but medicine must be maintained. The industry therefore is unresponsive to price reductions, as the president of Schering Corporation testified before a congressional committee:

> Unlike consumer marketing, Schering cannot expand its market by lowering prices. Cortisone proved this. After all, we cannot put two bottles of Schering medicine in every medicine chest where only one is needed, or two people in every hospital where only one is sick. Marketing medicine is a far cry from marketing soft drinks or automobiles.[1]

When demand is elastic, prices that are set high can cause a significant reduction in sales. In the ethical drug industry, with its inelastic demand, this constraint on price policies is not a factor.

Monopoly power is inherent in this industry, and this causes high markups. Companies achieve monopoly power through their patents, through heavy advertising and sales promotion, and by persuading doctors to write prescriptions in terms of brand names rather than generic names.

---

[1]Hearings on Administered Prices in the Drug Industry before the Antitrust and Monopoly Subcommittee, 86th Cong., pt. 14, p. 7856.

Governmental Scrutiny and Regulation

The United Sates did not regulate drugs before 1906. Upton Sinclair's novel, *The Jungle*, aroused public concern about unsanitary working conditions in meat-packing plants. This resulted in the Pure Food and Drug Act of 1906. In 1938, the federal Food, Drug and Cosmetic Act was enacted to control interstate sales of pharmaceuticals. Drugs not proven safe were prohibited from being sold across state lines. The Food and Drug Administration (FDA) was vested with the responsibility for evaluating the safety of new compounds.

These regulations were still inadequate. In the 1950s, a drug called thalidomide was given to pregnant women. It was soon discovered that this drug caused serious deformities in their children. In response, the Drug Amendments of 1962, also known as the Kefauver-Harris Amendments, required that all new drugs developed after 1962 must demonstrate safety as well as effectiveness. The amendments required that all adverse drug reactions be reported to the FDA, and that full risk/benefits profiles be provided to physicians on each product.

In the early 1960s, Senator Estes Kefauver, chairman of the Senate Sub-Committee on the Pharmaceutical Industry, launched hearings on drug pricing and promotion. These received heavy media attention. Similarly, in the mid-1970s, Senator Edward Kennedy conducted a round of hearings that questioned drug pricing and promotion. Worldwide attention was becoming focused on the marketing of drugs, particularly on the appropriateness of their pricing practices.

We will examine two cases of controversial drug pricing, one very recent, the other several decades ago.

BURROUGHS WELLCOME

Researchers at the pharmaceutical firm Burroughs Wellcome expected to be heroes. Only three years after scientists had learned what caused AIDS, the company won government approval for AZT, the first drug authorized by the Food and Drug Administration for use against the disease. A little-known firm had triumphed over the major drug makers and would soon become famous—and infamous.

In a classic case of miscalculation, the company priced the drug so that it would cost users $10,000 a year, thereby making it one of the most expensive drug treatments in history. Amid the fears of a fatal epidemic, Burroughs' pricing decision for this seemingly "savior" drug brought widespread condemnation, once again rousing the public's scorn over the pharmaceutical industry's pricing practices. The researchers' great accomplishment was ignored. And the issue was cast: How could any firm be justified in charging such a price for a drug so essential to life itself?

Within days of the price announcement, an aroused Congress summoned company officers to answer charges of price gouging. Demonstrators acted out their condemnations on the evening news. The company was further accused of stealing credit for the discovery of the drug, conducting unethical clinical trials, and even letting children die of AIDS without treatment.

Background

Was the company an uncaring monster interested only in profiteering at the expense of hapless victims? The facts hardly support this contention, although the price decision was ill advised, given the violent emotions aroused by the AIDS epidemic.

Burroughs has a history of research in obscure diseases, leaving the more common ones to other firms. Of the eight Noble Prizes for medicine, Burroughs' scientists have won four, an incredible achievement. Given the direction of the research, much has resulted in marginally profitable drugs for tropical diseases. In 1984, after other researchers had found that an unusual virus caused AIDS, the company became fully committed to finding a treatment.

Sam Broder was the senior researcher at the National Cancer Institute (NCI). He aggressively urged drug companies to send him promising drugs for testing. Burroughs sent about 50 compounds. In February 1985, Broder's staff reported that one, AZT, was by far the most effective. Therein lies a controversy: that Broder's involvement cut months or years off the time required to develop the drug, thus minimizing Burroughs' research costs.

Early testing of AZT in humans was impressive: 15 out of 19 people dying of AIDS showed improvement and weight gain. The next step was to expand the testing to hundreds of people. Now a serious dilemma ensued. Dying AIDS victims clamored for the drug. The usual procedure for medical research is to give half the patients a placebo—that is, a useless pill. Thereby, effectiveness can readily be compared. In view of the early promise of AZT, the company was pressured to drop the placebo step, thereby saving lives. But Burroughs stoutly maintained the placebo trials in 1986, despite AIDS activists' accusations that the company was being callous with human lives.

The company did not reckon with the power of the gay activist groups. Indeed, in its entire history, Burroughs had maintained a careful and noncontroversial relationship with doctors, relying on them, instead of advertising, to push its products. Now, suddenly, a vastly larger and highly vocal and contentious group—gay doctors, scientists, journalists, congressional aides, and others—demanded accountability.

The clinical trials for AZT were highly successful. Of the 137 patients who got placebos, 19 died; of the 145 receiving AZT, only one died. The FDA (Food and Drug Administration) approved the drug for sale to seriously ill patients in March 1987. Now the marketing could begin. But the key decision was how much to charge. The company placed a high ante on the drug.

Rationale for the Pricing Decision

At the time, the high price seemed entirely reasonable to Burroughs' top executives. As they would explain in Congressional hearings, their rationale was as follows: the early market for AZT was small—less than 50,000 seriously ill patients. Not until March 1990 did the FDA broaden the approval of the drug to those carrying the virus but not showing symptoms. The company did not yet know how much it would cost to produce the drug on a large scale, but it expected to spend tens of millions of dollars on raw materials, plant, and equipment. Furthermore, the company fully expected the AZT's market dominance to be short-lived: other drug companies already had compounds in trial. AZT was certainly vulnerable to competition, because of its severe side effects and the fact that it did not actually cure AIDS.

Not the least of Burroughs' pricing considerations was its need to recover its R & D (research and development) costs as quickly and completely as possible, not only for AZT but for other unsuccessful compounds, and for future R & D projects. In the five years before AZT was put on market, Burroughs had spent $726 million in fruitless research efforts.

Such explanations hardly satisfied the critics. And company officials refused to open the company's books to explain their costs.

Consequences

In December 1987, nine months after the Congressional hearings, Burroughs cut the price 20 percent, explaining that manufacturing costs had dropped. But this hardly appeased the critics.

Burroughs had made other enemies as well. The company gave little credit to government and university researchers who worked with them, some of whom became vocal critics.

Burroughs cut the price 20 percent a second time in September 1989. But researchers had found that the drug was just as effective at half the original dosage. By 1992, the cost of a year of AIDS treatment declined to $3,000.

AZT had a positive, though not a huge, effect on Burroughs' sales and profits. See Table 13.1 for sales and profits.

Table 13.1 Burroughs-Wellcome–Sales and Profits, 1987-1990

	1987	*1990*	*% increase*
	(millions of dollars)		
Total company revenues	1,748.4	2,473.3	41.5
AZT revenues	24.7	290.0	1,074.0
Other revenues	1,723.7	2,183.3	26.7
Total net profit	145.8	350.7	140.5

Despite the revenue and profit gains, Burroughs' return on equity of under 25 percent put the company at the low end for drug firms, well below Merck, with 40 percent, and American Home Products, maker of Anacin, with 60 percent.[2]

HOFFMAN-LA ROCHE

In 1975, Swiss-based Hoffman-La Roche was the world's largest ethical drug manufacturer. Its sales were $1.9 billion, up from $1.4 billion the year before. Earnings were $205 million, compared with $170 million the previous year. Also in 1975, Merck & Co., the biggest U.S.-based ethical drug company, earned $210.5 million on sales of $1.3 billion.

The company manufactured about 100 prescription drugs, aromatics, and flavorings, and also was involved with bioelectronics equipment used in clinical testing and diagnosis. In addition, La Roche was the world's largest manufacturer of synthesized vitamins, used in both animal feeds and by humans. The company was truly a worldwide enterprise. With plants in 40 countries, it marketed to 100 countries and employed 37,000 people worldwide, 9,500 of these in the United States. Two of its most successful products were the tranquilizers Valium and Librium. Together, these contributed half of the company's worldwide profits and 25 percent of its total sales. In the United States, the two drugs accounted for 90 percent of all tranquilizer sales. Indeed, according to the Justice Department's Drug Enforcement Administration (DEA), Valium was far and away the most frequently prescribed drug in the United States, accounting for 4 percent of all prescriptions written, with no other drug accounting for as much as 1 percent. In 1974, three billion tablets of 5-milligrams (mg) of Valium were sold in the United States at an estimated retail value of $550 million. The same year, one billion Librium capsules were sold at a retail value of $120 million.[3]

---

[2]"The Inside Story of the AIDS Drug," *Fortune*, Nov. 5, 1990, pp. 113–129.
[3]"A Drug Giant's Pricing Under International Attack," *Business Week*, June 16, 1975, p. 51.

The company had a strong research emphasis: 1300 of its 37,000 employees were involved in research. In 1975, the program was budgeted at $300 million, all of this paid out of profits: the company had no long term debt.

Despite its profitability and dominant position, La Roche was finding itself under attack, not by competitors, but by governmental bodies in Europe and the United States. Investigations were being made into its research, production, and distribution costs. The charge: that the company was greatly overpricing it products.

In April 1973, La Roche lost a crucial battle with British antitrust authorities. Because of the alleged excessive profits on Valium and Librium, the company was ordered to make price cuts of 75 percent and 60 percent respectively. La Roche went to the courts in an attempt to reverse this order. In so doing, it was forced to release sales and profit information, which would have dire consequences.

According to the British Monopolies Commission report, the active ingredients in Valium cost La Roche less than $50 a kilo. These ingredients were sold to the British subsidiary for the equivalent of $23,000 a kilo, and the manufactured drug was then sold to the retailers for the equivalent of $50,000 a kilo. Still, the markups in Britain were the lowest prices in the world, by far. Table 13.2 shows comparative wholesale prices of Librium and Valium in various countries, as of March 1, 1975.

Such revelations triggered reactions around the world. Late in 1974, West Germany ordered La Roche to cut the price of Valium by 40 percent and Librium by 35 percent. In Holland, where drug prices were the highest in Europe, La Roche agreed to a 7 percent price cut. Other European countries, and the Common Market itself, started investigations. So did Australia, South Africa, New Zealand, Japan, and Canada. In the United States, Senator Kennedy, chairman of the Health Subcommittee of the Labor and Public Welfare Committee, opened hearings on drug pricing in the summer of 1975.

The British Monopolies Commission report also revealed the *transfer pricing* techniques used by La Roche and other drug companies in order to

Table 13.2 Prices of Librium and Valium to Subsidiaries, 1975[a]

	Librium	*Valium*
Britain	$ 0.14	$ 0.11
West Germany	4.38	5.35
Switzerland	4.75	5.44
United States	5.80	6.89

Source: Data from Hoffmann-La Roche.
[a]Librium prices are for one hundred 10 mg capsules; Valium for one hundred 5 mg tablets. Prices as of March 1, 1975.

take advantage of tax havens in countries with minimal corporate taxes. (See the information box for additional discussion of *transfer pricing*.)

IN DEFENSE OF THE DRUG COMPANIES

Are the drug companies—or at least some of them—conscienceless price gougers, victimizing their hapless customers and adding greatly to burgeoning health costs? The answer is not clear-cut, despite the emotional reactions to Burroughs-Wellcome's AIDS drug or the massive markups of Librium and Valium in the 1970s.

La Roche maintained that high profits were necessary to pay for $300 million a year in research expenditures (comprising 3.5 percent of total employees). Most drug companies rely on a relatively few big-selling drugs to support the research necessary to remain competitive.

La Roche further defended its pricing by pointing out some comparisons:

> In England, the actual price for a daily dosage of Valium costs less than a single cigarette. In Switzerland, the daily dosage costs less than a glass of beer.[4]

TRANSFER PRICING

A transfer price is the price a firm charges its various units or subsidiaries for ingredients or products that will be further manufactured or marketed. Instead of charging subsidiaries the cost plus a nominal markup, multinational companies can use transfer pricing to avoid taxes. For example, some American companies sell their U.S.-manufactured, patented drugs cheaply to their subsidiaries in Bermuda, which is a tax haven. Subsidiaries resell the drugs at high markups to the company's subsidiaries in other countries, thus confining the bulk of the profits to the Bermuda operation.

La Roche did much of its manufacturing for its European markets in Switzerland, which is also a tax haven. The company's profits came from the hefty markups charged to its other foreign subsidiaries. In La Roche's case, however, the discrepancy in the prices it charged to its subsidiaries in various countries, as we saw in Table 13.2, aroused harsh scrutiny and resentment.

INVITATION TO DISCUSS
Do you see any ethical problems in charging different subsidiaries different prices for the same ingredients or products? Why or why not?

---

[4]"A Drug Giant's Pricing," p. 56.

While the relative cost of Valium or Librium is modest, even with giant markups, the same could certainly not be said for AZT, Burroughs-Wellcome's AIDS drug. Burroughs wanted to both cover the cost of developing the drug and recoup losses on other research that had failed to produce profitable products—not unlike what all pharmaceutical companies strive to do. Unfortunately for the company, it picked on a patient group that, with its supporters, was clamorous in its public denunciations.

The gay activist groups' power came as a shock to Burroughs. In retrospect, the company should have included this in its pricing decision. But management felt that the risks and the costs of developing AZT were so high—including an uncertain demand—that a high price was justified.

As noted before, AZT had serious limitations. It has severe side effects, and it is not a cure. It does not rid a patient of the virus, it only slows its growth. For example, without AZT, a person may live 12 months fighting AIDS-related pneumonia; with the drug, the life expectancy might be 21 months. Other drug companies were researching in this area. No one could expect AZT to remain the dominant drug for very long.

AZT's manufacturing costs were also unclearly defined and therefore worrisome. Although the drug cost under $50 million to develop, large-scale production would cost tens of millions more—this for a product with uncertain demand and life expectancy.

Burroughs sought both a reasonable return on its research efforts for AZT and other compounds and enough money to fund future research. The president of Burroughs, Philip Tracey, noted: "You don't price on a drug-by-drug basis. Our business is R & D. You have to look at your incomes from all your products."[5]

But the fact remained that Burroughs priced a drug—at that time the only legal drug treatment available to AIDS patients—at a price that most would view extraordinarily high.

ANALYSIS

The main issue in this case is how high a price can a firm ethically charge? But, before resolving this question, we need to consider the issue of profit: how high a profit margin is ethically acceptable? Is there any limit to an acceptable profit margin?

There are those who maintain that a firm should be permitted to charge as high a price, and make as much profit, as it possibly can. This is

[5]"The Inside Story of the AIDS Drug," p. 124.

simply the rewards of the free enterprise system, so say the classical econo-mists. Profit fuels research, innovation, and risk-taking. And since no one reimburses a company for its failures, shouldn't it be entitled to the fullest possible reward for its successes? Other firms, sensing opportunities, may then choose to enter the industry.

Such reasoning is easier to accept for nonessential products, such as shampoo and perfume. It may be a little less acceptable for non-essential products that are part of a monopoly situation, such as the hot dogs, soft drinks, and beer sold by vendors at the ballpark on a hot afternoon.

With a product that's important to health, even life, does a company's unlimited pricing discretion change? Should Hoffman-La Roche and Burroughs and the other drug companies be content with more "reason-able" prices and profits? Should a firm's products be priced so high as to subsidize the rest of its operation? (See the Issue box for a discussion of *product-line pricing*.)

ISSUE: PRODUCT-LINE PRICING AND THE ROBIN HOOD PHILOSOPHY

Should certain products be priced high so that less-profitable products in the company's line can be maintained? Or other company operations, such as research and development? This is the Robin Hood philosophy: Take from the rich to support the poor.

Roche and Burroughs cite the need to sustain their other products, as well as fund heavy R & D expenditures, as the rationale for high profit margins on a few winning products. Is this philosophy justified? Is it ethical?

As with many ethical issues, the answer is clouded and controversial. It is partly a matter of degree. Some products typically carry higher profit margins than other products in the same product line: luxury "top of the line" items usu-ally bring more profit than the "economy" models. This reflects the basic strat-egy of *product-line pricing*. But how far should we go in milking a winner? What are acceptable profit margins under such circumstances? Here, we have wide-ranging disagreement. But when health, and even life itself, is involved, there is less tolerance for extreme profit margins.

INVITATION TO DISCUSS

Many universities charge a high enough price for their MBA programs to support other programs, such as the sciences, that cannot support themselves. Does this situation cause you any ethical concern?

WHAT CAN BE LEARNED?

Learning Insight. *The Robin Hood philosophy is only acceptable by society in moderation.*

For products deemed essential for health and welfare, the Robin Hood philosophy appears to be vulnerable in the extreme, despite the fact that it's a common practice by pharmaceutical firms. Today, with investigative reporting and a skeptical general public—and their governmental representatives—such a strategy, when practiced in the extreme, makes individual drug firms, even the entire industry, vulnerable to escalating public protests and governmental intervention. Even for nonessential products, a militant society may no longer accept price opportunism.

Learning Insight. *The confidentiality of profit margins is vulnerable today, especially for products having to do with health and life essentials.*

As we saw in both of these cases, attempts to keep cost and profit margins a secret failed. Governmental investigators demanded that the companies' books be opened. Firms in sensitive industries can no longer depend on secrecy to protect activities likely to be embarrassing, but that can lead to far worse consequences for the corporation. Disclosure ultimately prevails, even over those persons and organizations who perpetuate fraud and laundering money from illegal activities through creative accounting and various cover-up procedures.

Learning Insight. *A militant society may no longer accept price/profit opportunism.*

Although economists and executives may view very-high profit margins—when these are possible in a competitive environment—as fully acceptable in a market economy, the general public is less accepting. Publicity about high profit margins only fuels the critics' fire, reinforcing the perception many people have of business being entirely self-serving and seeking high profits at all costs.

Learning Insight. *The power of special interest groups in a pluralistic society is greatly magnified by media publicity.*

Special interest groups in our society abound, and they are becoming more militant and vocal. An organization must tread very carefully to avoid cries of racism or discrimination. Pro-choice or Pro-life groups, environmentalists, gay groups, and many others can be quick to attack business. Executives can be sure that charges against them will receive wide publicity. Litigation is always lurking in the wings. Burroughs was dismayed by the pressures raised by gay groups. In retrospect, they should not have been surprised. And they should have considered such probabilities in their strategic planning.

Learning Insight. *The pharmaceutical industry has a history of bad public relations: it needs to tread with caution.*

Over the past half a century, few industries have incurred as much suspicion and skepticism as the drug makers. And yet, no industry has contributed more to human welfare. Although there have been some instances of insufficient drug testing—now largely corrected by watchdog governmental agencies—most of the critical scrutiny has concerned pricing. As described earlier in this chapter, this industry's unique marketing situation—the customer who pays for the drug but has no voice in the selection of products—stimulates abuses that would not be possible under more directly competitive conditions.

Regardless of the legitimacy of the suspicions about the drug industry, Senate committees and their chairpersons, thanks to widespread publicity, have gained the images of consumer "watchdogs." The drug industry's public-relations efforts have traditionally been noteworthy for their ineffectiveness.

It is high time this important industry woke up to the importance of its public image.

Learning Insight. *R & D expenditures should represent "sunk costs." They should not burden future projects and pricing.*

Sunk costs are outlays that have already been made; they cannot be revoked or canceled. The most common example of a sunk cost is a research and development expenditure aimed at new products or product improvement. Sometimes, such an expenditure results in valuable discoveries, sometimes not. Usually, costs already "sunk" should be ignored in making price decisions. And most firms in a competitive environment cannot afford to consider sunk costs in making their pricing decisions. But the pharmaceutical industry, with its unique marketing situation and its near-monopoly environment, has a predilection for pricing to recover R & D sunk costs. This is the major rationale for certain drugs' spectacular profit margins.

FOR THOUGHT AND DISCUSSION

1. Is Hoffman-La Roche's argument that a daily dose of Valium costs less than a cigarette or a glass of beer acceptable to you? Do you think the price-gouging criticism is less compelling in the case of low-priced drugs? Does this justify the pricing strategy?
2. How can a firm support lower-profit products if not by the Robin Hood philosophy?
3. Do you think the Burroughs' pricing rationale for AZT was justified? Why or why not?
4. What would you consider a reasonable profit margin for drugs? Does your opinion differ for nondrug products?

INVITATION TO ROLE PLAY

1. Place yourself in the position of Adolph Jann, the president of Hoffman-La Roche, at the time the publicity broke about the profit margins on Valium and Librium. How do you think this public controversy should have been handled?
2. Place yourself in the role of the president of Burroughs at the time of the AZT controversy.
   (a) How should the pricing decision have been handled in the beginning?
   (b) Given the decision that was made, how could the controversy have been better handled?

INVITATION TO RESEARCH

1. What is the situation regarding AZT today?

14

The Savings & Loan Disaster: Repudiating Management's Trusteeship Responsibility

In the 1980s, a financial disaster of monumental proportions suddenly intruded on the public consciousness. That it involved the savings of ordinary people, and that the long-term consequences would be borne by all taxpayers, made it all the more consequential. That it involved huge losses from management incompetence and violation of depositor and shareholder trust through excessive spending and lending brought widespread media attention.

Our savings and loan (S & L) industry, the source of home ownership for millions of Americans, was on the verge of total collapse; indeed, hundreds of institutions would go bankrupt. But the savings of the depositors were protected by the federal government, and were not at risk, though the government bailout would be the costliest in history.

How could this have happened? What can we learn from it? What management mistakes were made that other managers (in other times and places), can avoid? And what were the keys to the success of the S & Ls that survived and prospered during this time?

A SAMPLING OF FIASCOS

Sunbelt Savings

Edwin T. McBirney III was 29 years old when he began his run to a vast fortune in the savings and loan business. The year was 1981. While still in college, he had shown unusual business acumen, starting his own business of leasing refrigerators to college students. Upon graduating, he turned to real estate, becoming a broker and investor in the booming Dallas market.

In December 1981, he formed an investment group that began buying small S & Ls. One of these was Sunbelt Savings, an obscure S & L in Stephenville, Texas. McBirney was to merge these holdings into one large S & L, which he named Sunbelt Savings Association. In less than four years, Sunbelt became the nucleus of a $3.2 billion financial empire. Its growth came mostly from commercial real estate loans that were so risky that Sunbelt gained the nickname "Gunbelt" for its shoot-from-the-hip lending policies. As one example, Sunbelt lent $125 million (secured only by raw land) to an inexperienced Dallas developer in his twenties, who went on to lose $80 million.[1] In its heyday, Sunbelt owned mortgage and development-service companies, had a commercial-banking division, and made real estate loans to developers from California to Florida.

McBirney and his executives soon were covering Texas in the company's fleet of seven aircraft. McBirney liked to throw sumptuous parties. He would serve lion and antelope to hundreds of guests at his palatial Dallas home. In 1984 and 1985, Sunbelt footed $1.3 million for Halloween and Christmas galas including a $32,000 fee to his wife for organizing the parties. No end seemed to be in sight for these Texas big spenders. But it was there, just around the corner.

In 1984, the Empire Savings and Loan of Mesquite, Texas, collapsed after funding massive high-risk investments. Its demise raised troubling questions about the entire industry. Edwin Gray, chairman of the Federal Home Loan Bank Board, a regulator of S & Ls, became fearful of a disaster and slammed on the brakes. He forced reappraisals based on current market values, he increased capital requirements, he limited direct appraisals, and he hired hundreds of new examiners and supervisory agents. Appraisers found that the collateral backing billions of dollars of loans had been overvalued by up to 30 percent. Many thrift organizations had to lower the book value of their loans, thereby reducing their already weak capital positions. And then real estate values plummeted as Texas's economy began collapsing, led by declining oil prices. The domino effect took over as a rash of loan delinquencies led to one foreclosure after another.

Now the excesses of McBirney's heyday came home to roost. Hundreds of examiners descended on the Dallas home-loan office in the spring of 1986, and most of the Sunbelt S & Ls were declared insolvent. While Sunbelt was spared temporarily, McBirney was forced to resign as chairman

---

[1]Howard Rudnitsky and John R. Hayes, "Gunbelt S & L," *Forbes*, Sept. 19, 1988, p. 120.

by June. Of the foreclosed real estate on Sunbelt's books, only a few million out of its $6 billion portfolio of troubled assets could be sold off. By late 1988, the Federal Home Loan Bank Board estimated that it would cost as much as $5.5 billion just to keep Sunbelt alive over the next 10 years.[2]

To add to the insult, a lawsuit filed against McBirney and other insider shareholders charged that nearly $13 million in common and preferred dividends had been taken out in 1985 and 1986, this at a time when Sunbelt's capital was rapidly evaporating because of wild expenditures and devaluation of assets.

Shamrock Federal Savings Bank

In Shamrock, Texas, the little savings and loan on the corner went belly-up. The collapse of the Shamrock Federal Savings Bank left a bitter pill for this town of 3000 in the Texas Panhandle. It was a common story for many Texas communities: a small-town thrift taken over by an outsider; fast growth followed by sudden insolvency; a trail of incompetent management and soured high-risk ventures in places far beyond the town limits. "We made a mistake selling it. We should have kept it under local control, making loans in our community," declared one of the original directors of the town's only savings and loan.

Back in 1977, Phil Cates, a state representative and head of the local Chamber of Commerce, had a vision of a financial institution that would serve Shamrock and other small towns near the Oklahoma line. He started pushing townsfolk to start their own savings and loan association in view of the oil and gas boom that was bringing hundreds of people into the town. Shamrock's two family-owned banks shunned long-term home mortgages and refused to pay competitive interest rates. Cates sold the idea of a local S & L to hundreds of local residents. When the Red River Savings and Loan Association opened in 1979, it had more than 350 stockholders in a town of 2834. Community pride ran high.

These were the days of S & L deregulation, and small-town thrifts like Red River were hot properties, targets for promoters and speculators. One such was Jerry D. Lane. He offered $21 a share, more than double the original price, and the townspeople jumped at the opportunity.

The name was changed to Shamrock Savings Association, and in three years deposits rocketed from $11.6 million to $111.3 million. This was mainly accomplished by shifting the thrift's focus far beyond the small town of Shamrock, with offices opened as far away as Amarillo, Texas and

---

[2]For more detail, see "Why Our S & Ls Are in Trouble," *Reader's Digest*, July 1989, pp. 70–74.

Colorado Springs, Colorado. Lane also began buying other thrifts' outstanding loans.

Disaster struck in 1987 when the Federal Savings and Loan Insurance Corporation filed a $150 million racketeering suit against Lane and others after the 1985 failure of State Savings of Lubbock, Texas, where Lane had been chief executive officer. Federal regulators had found a pattern common to the S & L industry, and they would soon find it at Shamrock: making fraudulent loans to developers, concentrating an "unsafe" amount of credit with one client, basing loans on inflated property appraisals, and making them without proper credit documentation. "Loans were made over lunch with a handshake."

Shamrock was closed by federal regulators in November 1987; it owed $16.6 million more than it was worth. But its betrayal of the local communities occurred before that. It had been conceived to make loans locally for homes and other projects that could help the community. But with its buyout and the shift of emphasis far beyond the local community, it had little interest in providing less lucrative but less risky local loans.

Shamrock was characteristic of a large segment of S & Ls, especially in the heady days of the oil boom when Texas and other southwestern states thought there was no stopping the runaway building boom built on the belief that oil prices could only go up. But prices dropped to $14 a barrel in the early 1980s, knocking the cash supports out from under commercial real estate projects all across the Southwest.[3]

Lincoln Savings and Loan: Political Scandal

Charles Keating is the former owner of California's Lincoln Savings and Loan. He purchased Lincoln in 1984 and switched it from investing in safe single-family mortgages to speculating in raw land, junk bonds, and huge development projects like the $900-a-night Phoenician Resort in Scottsdale, Arizona.

Keating was a heavy campaign contributor, giving to five prominent U.S. senators: Glenn, Cranston, McCain, Riegle, and De Concini. In total, these influential politicians received $1.3 million. When his failing S & L came under the scrutiny of the Federal Home Loan Bank Board, which found enough bad loans and shaky business practices to shut it down, he sought help from these senators. Action was delayed for two years because of their intervention. During this time, the federally guaranteed cost of

[3]Adapted from "Small Town's Dreams Vanish," *Cleveland Plain Dealer,* Aug. 13, 1989, p. 3C.

paying back Lincoln's depositors increased by $1.3 billion to $2.5 billion, making this one of the costliest thrift failures.[4]

Keating has since been convicted of racketeering, fraud, and conspiracy in using the institution's funds. And the senators' complicity has been scrutinized.

So we see in this sampling of S & L blunders a repudiation of any systematic planning, with megabuck deals made on the spur of the moment, without investigation, and heedless of risks and probable consequences. (The information box summarizes the desired *strategic planning process* for coping with long-range environmental changes and opportunities.)

THE FULL FLAVOR OF THE S & L DEBACLE

By 1988, of the nation's 3178 so-called thrift institutions, 503 were insolvent. Another 629 had less capital on their books than regulators usually require. In 1987, 630 thrifts had lost an estimated $7.5 billion, half again as much as the earnings of all the rest combined.[5] Most of the "terminal" S & Ls got into trouble making risky loans. But fraud also contributed to the failures of nearly 50.[6] More than half the troubled thrifts were to be found in Texas. But other thrifts were also crashing. Beverly Hills Savings & Loan in California, which had much of its $2.9 billion in assets invested in dicey real estate ventures and junk bonds, closed in 1985. Sunrise Savings & Loan of Florida, with $1.5 billion in assets, was liquidated in 1986. In Arkansas, First South Federal Savings & Loan was closed in 1986 after 64 percent of its $1.4 billion in loans were found to be speculative. (See Table 14.1 for a sampling of Sunbelt S & Ls on the "deathwatch" as of September 30, 1988.) Still, the worst excesses occurred in Texas. And there were suspicions that some of the insolvent Texas S & Ls were shuffling bum loans from one to another to stay a step ahead of the bank examiners.

Undeniably, part of the motivation for taking wild risks with deposits was that individual accounts were insured up to $100,000 by the Federal Savings and Loan Insurance Corporation (FSLIC). But even the resources of this government agency would have been insufficient to cope with the problem without congressional appropriations in the billions of dollars.

The lurking danger, of course, was that depositor panic would create a devastating run on the nation's $932 billion in thrift deposits, bringing down scores of S & Ls, threatening the $14 billion of capital in the 12 regional

---

[4]Margaret Carlson, "$1 Billion Worth of Influence," *Time*, Nov. 6, 1989, pp. 27–28.
[5]John Paul Newport, Jr., "Why We Should Save the S & Ls," *Fortune*, Apr. 11, 1988, p. 81.
[6]Robert E. Norton, "Deep In the Hole in Texas," *Fortune*, May 11, 1987, p. 61.

THE STRATEGIC PLANNING PROCESS

Strategic planning is the managerial process of figuring out how to cope with an ever-changing environment over the long run. Strategic planning is very much forward-looking. One manager described it as "an eager seizing of opportunities." This type of planning should permeate an organization, not be limited to top executive suites and ivory towers.

Strategic planning begins with determining the company's fundamental mission. Usually, this involves deciding "What business should we be in?" The answer may or may not be the same as that of "What business are we currently in?"

After the mission has been determined, objectives or performance goals are established. Firms may have multiple goals, although in many, especially smaller, firms, these may be implicit or ill-defined. Goals may be stated too vaguely or have the flavor of public relations. Nevertheless, there are important benefits to stating goals and objectives in explicit language and in order of priority, because some goals may conflict. Goals that are well communicated and understood by all units of the organization can provide criteria for making policy decisions, thus introducing consistency into planning and decision making.

The final step of the strategic planning process is to assess environmental opportunities or potential—this is often called *environmental scanning*. This assessment should be guided by the firm's more generally stated objectives and goals. The firm's present business is the starting point for this assessment, commonly called a *portfolio analysis*. Then the firm considers other potential customers, chosen perhaps as a result of previous business relations with them, the similarity of these customers' operations to those of the firm's present customers, intriguing growth possibilities these customers might offer or simply because they are not well served by our firm's competitors.

In this assessment of environmental opportunities or potential, a risk/reward ratio should be carefully considered. That is, are the risks of seeking the new business opportunities sufficiently modest compared with the possible gains? Are these risks manageable? As many savings and loans learned to their profound dismay, the risks in new endeavors can sometimes far outweigh the short-term gains.

INVITATION TO DISCUSS
Describe how the risks of new business opportunities may be assessed. Do you see any problems?

Federal Home Loan Banks (which would have to supply emergency funds to the thrifts) and potentially swamping the FSLIC. The simplest solution would be to write off the insolvent thrifts and pay off their depositors. But this would exceed the FSLIC's original resources and could cost more than $100 billion. Taxpayers will eventually have to foot the bill.

HISTORY OF THE SAVINGS AND LOAN INDUSTRY

At first they were called building and loans, and they filled a real need. Before the Great Depression, many commercial banks would not lend on middle-class residential property. Working-class people were eventually forced to band together to form cooperative associations to take their deposits and lend those funds out as home mortgages. The Depression saw the failure of thousands of banks and building and loans, and the Roosevelt administration created the two deposit-insurance funds we know today, the FSLIC for S & Ls, and the Federal Deposit Insurance Corporation (FDIC), which insures commercial bank deposits.

In the late 1960s, the S & Ls began experiencing some troubles. By law, the federally regulated S & Ls were required to lend long with home mortgages, but they borrowed short, with most of their lendable funds coming from passbook savings accounts. This situation of long-term loans and short-term lendable resources posed no problem at first—until inflation started rising. When this happened, the value of the S & L portfolios fell, like that of all fixed-rate long-term debt. In 1971, the S & L industry had a negative net worth of $17 billion. But the inflation rate in the 1970s worsened, and the industry faced ever larger losses on its loan portfolios.

The environment was changing in other ways as well. In particular, money-market mutual funds came on the scene, aided by computer technology. These money-market funds accumulated high-yielding financial instruments, such as jumbo certificates of deposit (CDs), commercial paper, and government notes, and then allowed the small investor to own a piece

Table 14.1   S&Ls on the "Deathwatch" as of September 30, 1988[a]

State	Thrift	Negative Net Worth (millions)
Texas	Gill Savings, Hondo	($542.7)
	Meridian Savings, Arlington	($387.7)
New Mexico	Sandia Federal, Albuquerque	($482.6)
Arizona	Security S & L, Scottsdale	($351.6)
Arkansas	Savers Federal, Little Rock	($286.5)
California	Westwood S & L, Los Angeles	($222.7)
	Pacific Savings, Costa Mesa	($206.6)
Florida	Freedom S & L, Tampa	($231.6)

Sources: SNL Securities, Inc., and *Fortune,* Jan. 30, 1989, p. 9.
[a]This is only a sampling.

of the high-yielding package. Technology enabled customers to write checks on these money funds, while still receiving high interest. Computers made possible the extremely complex bookkeeping for such transactions.

The effect on banks and S & Ls was, of course, substantial. Money flowed out of them and into money-market funds by the hundreds of billions of dollars. This, combined with the double-digit inflation of the late 1970s, brought the S & L industry, with its long-term loans at low interest rates, seemingly to the point of disaster. By 1981, 80 percent of the thrifts were losing money and 20 percent were below the minimum capital requirements set by regulators.[7] (See Table 14.2 for a summary of the worsening S & L situation during the 1980s.)

In order to save the thrift industry from a potentially devastating outflow of funds, Congress passed the Depository Institutions Deregulation and Monetary Control Act in 1980, which gradually phased out interest rate ceilings on deposits and allowed S & Ls to make various kinds of consumer

---

Table 14.2 Summary of the Worsening S & L Situation During the 1980s

1980–1982: Congress begins phasing out interest rate limits. Banks and S & Ls are allowed to offer new savings accounts that compete with market interest rates. Federal deposit insurance is boosted from $40,000 to $100,000 per account. Money that flowed out of S & Ls in 1980, when deposit rates were capped at 5.5%, begins flowing back. But the new deposits cost more than S & Ls can earn on the old fixed-rate mortgages made in the 1960s and 1970s at rates as low as 6% and even lower. Now, S & Ls are losing billions of dollars, and hundreds fail. The Garn–St. Germain bill is passed in 1982, allowing S & Ls new lending and investment freedom.

Mid-1980s: A lending spree develops, with billions of dollars loaned for apartments, office buildings, and other projects, especially in the booming Southwest. Many S & Ls are seeking high-profit investments to make up for the low rates on old mortgages. In a climate of drastically loosened controls, wild speculation and outright fraud characterize the operations of hundreds of thrifts.

1986: Oil prices plunge, the Texas economy collapses, and the overbuilding comes home to roost as developer loans are defaulted and the properties foreclosed are worth only fractions of building costs. More S & Ls are brought to insolvency. The Federal Savings and Loan Insurance Corporation finds its capital depleted by earlier S & L failures and needs massive infusions of capital. Prospective acquirers are attracted to take over the dead and dying thrifts under most favorable terms.

1988–1989: A massive government bailout is prepared and enacted.

---

[7]John J. Curran, "Does Deregulation Make Sense?" *Fortune,* June 5, 1989, pp. 184, 188, and 194.

loans. The FSLIC's insurance coverage was also raised from $40,000 to $100,000—essentially, the government deregulated the industry. But then a rate war developed among the thrifts, with some paying depositors double-digit interest rates.

Congress acted again to "remedy" the situation, only the remedy led to worse abuses. In 1982, the Garn–St. Germain Act was passed. This further loosened the restraints on S & Ls, now giving them lending powers to make acquisition, development, and construction loans, form development subsidiaries, and make direct investments. If properly handled, the new freedom should have enabled S & Ls to better match assets and liabilities and find a sounder footing. They could begin lessening their dependence on mortgage lending and instead seek higher yielding investments. Figure 14.1 shows the decline in mortgage lending by S & Ls over the last 18 years.

By now, with the constraints of regulation mostly unraveled and a new business environment in place, S & Ls needed to give careful attention to their strategic planning. Most important, they needed *to reevaluate their company mission*. (See the information box on *company mission*.)

The deregulatory "solution" to S & L problems did not reckon with the unbridled greed that was soon to accompany this greater freedom. It was particularly inviting for schemers and eager speculators in Texas. Previously, Texas regulations had limited the lending power of S & Ls to the lesser of the purchase price or the appraised value of any project. But the new federal regulations overrode this requirement, permitting S & Ls to lend 100 percent of appraised value, even if the actual purchase price was much lower. And it was not difficult to find appraisers who would greatly inflate the value of property.

At this point, using federal deposit insurance, developers got low-rate debt to put into their housing and shopping center developments. If the

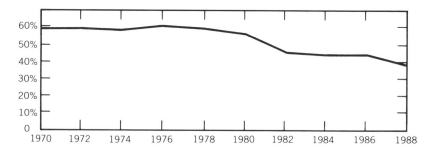

Percent of mortgage debt for 1–4 family homes held by savings and loans, excluding mortgage securities.

Figure 14.1. Decline in mortgage lending by S & Ls over 18 years.
Source: Federal Reserve.

WHAT SHOULD OUR MISSION BE?

As we noted in an earlier box, strategic planning should begin with an assessment of the company's current mission and whether this fundamental mission should be changed in light of changing circumstances. Usually, this involves deciding "What business should we now seek to be in?" A mission determination should involve the following factors:

1. Assessing the environment and how it is changing or is expected to change.
2. Appraising competitive factors and how these may be changing.
3. Weighing the particular strengths and weaknesses of the company—what it does best and where it has been deficient.

Mission statements can be too broad—for example, "to make a profit"—or too narrow, focusing on a particular product or service that may become obsolete as technology and customer requirements change. Narrow definitions restrict perspectives and the grasping of different opportunities, just as too broad a definition is useless as a guide for definitive action. An example of a definitive and useful mission statement of a manufacturer is the following:

> The mission is to serve the industry and government with quality instruments used for the primary measurement, analysis, and local control of fluid flow, level, pressure, temperature, and fluid properties. . . . Markets served include instrumentation for oil and gas production, gas transportation, chemical and petro-chemical processing, cryogenics, power generation, aerospace, Government and marine, as well as other instrument and equipment manufacturers.[8]

But a company's mission, whether formally stated or merely resting in the top executive's mind, can be distorted to a reckless abandonment of former successful and durable practices. It can repudiate the community's best interest and trust, as we saw with Shamrock and with Sunbelt. Government regulation in the early 1980s provided S & Ls with a vastly expanded arena for doing business. Far too many of them saw their mission now as one of wild growth, unrestrained by cost considerations and risk potential.

INVITATION TO DISCUSS
Critique these mission statements:

- to improve our customer service
- to be No. 1 in our industry
- to be a good corporate citizen

[8]John A. Pearce II, "The Company Mission as a Strategic Tool," *Sloan Management Review,* Spring 1982, p. 17.

projects were successful, fortunes were made. If unsuccessful, the Federal Home Loan Bank Board and the FSLIC absorbed the loss. As Art Soter, a bank analyst at the Morgan Stanley investment banking firm, noted: "What regulators failed to see is that the current system of deposit insurance increases the propensity to take risks."[9]

A further error of deregulation occurred: equity capital standards were lowered. For years, thrifts had to have capital equal to at least 6 percent of their deposits. Then, as industrywide losses caused capital to deteriorate (in only two years, between 1980 and 1982, the value of capital in the industry fell from $32 billion to less than $21 billion) thrifts were allowed to expand by taking as many deposits as they could.

Soon, brokered deposits moved in. These are funds collected by stock-brokers and sent in large amounts to the highest yielding thrifts. With such brokered deposits, there was nothing to slow the growth of the reckless S & L operations. Phenomenal growth was possible, as described in the following example:

> American Diversified Savings was a small thrift in a rural town, Lodi, California. In June 1983, it had $11 million in assets. In only 18 months its assets totaled $792 million, mostly from brokered deposits attracted by its high yielding certificates of deposit. The owner, Ranhir Sahni, a former commercial pilot, put the money into his favorite projects: geothermal plants, wind-driven electric generators, as well as a venture to supply local manure to a fertilizer business. In 1988, the government had to find $1.1 billion to pay off the depositors and liquidate the thrift.[10]

So the seeds for disaster were laid. Washington aggravated the problem and the potential for disaster by failing to hire adequate regulatory staff or replenish the reserves of the Bank Board or FSLIC. All this time, S & Ls in the Southwest continued to slide into bankruptcy.

THE GOVERNMENT BAILOUT

Thus, there were thrifts with billions of dollars of losses while the governmental agencies responsible for them had not nearly enough resources to bail out the insolvents. In August 1989, a costly bailout measure was enacted by Congress and signed by the president. Upward of $166 billion was expected to have to be spent to close or sell hundreds of insolvent S & Ls over the next decade.

One obvious solution was to attract would-be acquirers to take over the dead and dying thrifts and rejuvenate them. So Congress allowed acquirers to use the great bulk of the accumulated tax losses of the previous

[9]Curran, p. 188.
[10]*Ibid.*

owners. Thereby, federal income and other taxes would be greatly reduced, while taxpayers absorbed the losses through a larger deficit, reduced government services, and new taxes. The Federal Home Loan Bank Board made the deal even better. Not only would it guarantee the losses on the nonperforming portfolios, but is also guaranteed the performing portfolios against losses. For example, should interest rates move adversely and lower the value of the performing assets (i.e., those assets still viable and paying interest), the Bank Board would make up the loss if the S & L later found itself illiquid. This was an El Dorado for acquirers. As *Barron's* noted:

> From the moment an acquirer signed the papers, he would be able to deduct already acquired losses of, say, $1 billion. Against a combined corporate tax rate of about 40%, he would be saving about $400 million in year one. For his out-of-pocket outlay of $50 million, he would have made a return of eight times.[11]

In December 1988, Robert Bass, a 40 year-old Texas billionaire, took over the crippled American Savings and Loan of Stockton, California. This represents perhaps the consummate gilt-edged deal to one of America's richest men.

American Savings was once the largest thrift in the United States, but it got into the same trouble as many others, with brokered deposits and high-risk loans. The Bank Board seized American in 1984 and installed fresh management. But the new team gambled and failed, and the Bank Board eventually granted exclusive bargaining rights to Bass.

In the deal, American Savings was split into two entities: a healthy S & L with $15.4 billion of good assets and a "bad" one that would liquidate $14.4 billion in sour loans. For a total investment of only $500 million, the Bass Group got 70 percent ownership of the good thrift, a huge, healthy S & L with 186 branches. As another sure thing, more than half of this thrift's assets consisted of a $7.8 billion loan to the "bad" S & L that was fully guaranteed by FSLIC to pay a handsome 2 percent more than the cost of the funds. Also as part of the deal, Bass was rewarded with some $300 million in tax benefits.

Taking all this into account, Bass stood to make $400 to $500 million in straight profits over the next four years, which was roughly equal to his original investment of $500 million.[12]

DID THE S & Ls FACE AN IMPOSSIBLE ENVIRONMENT IN THE 1980s?

More than one-third of the nation's S & Ls were either insolvent or on the verge of insolvency by 1988. In 1987, losses were so high for 730 thrifts—

---

[11]Described in Benjamin J. Stein, "Steal of the Century?" *Barron's*, Feb. 20, 1989, p. 7.
[12]Described in S.C. Gwynne, "Help Your Country and Help Yourself," *Time,* Feb. 20, 1989, p. 72.

$7.5 billion—that these were half again as much as the meager earnings of the other 2500.

In such a catastrophic environment, can we find any success stories, any S & Ls that effectively bucked the trend? Yes we can! Their keys to viability and success? Careful growth without wild speculation; staying with traditional products and services; austerity in facilities and operations; good and better customer service—in essence, a controlled growth through sound marketing and management.

Suncoast Savings and Loan Association

Suncoast of Hollywood, Florida, is one of the largest originators and servicers of mortgages in the Southeast. Its strategy has been to reduce the interest-rate risk inherent in rate fluctuations. As we have seen before, many of the devastated S & Ls blamed their demise on rising interest rates in which the costs of funds increased while the return remained low because of long-term mortgage commitments.

How did Suncoast reduce such risks? By the purchase and resale of mortgages complemented by its loan servicing capability. Suncoast and its subsidiaries purchase and originate mortgage loans for resale into the secondary market. In the process of reselling, however, Suncoast retains servicing rights on these mortgages, and these fees make up a major part of its income. These two activities—purchase and resale of mortgages, and its loan servicing capability—are complementary. For example, when interest rates are declining, mortgage lending increases, because more people buy property during such favorable conditions. But when interest rates rise and loan volume decreases, loan servicing increases in importance as more borrowers hold on to their existing mortgages.

Suncoast gains further risk reduction by contracts in which major Wall Street investment banks purchase mortgage-backed securities on specific dates at agreed-on interest rates and discounts. While this conservative approach is costly, the risk protection from higher interest rates is deemed worth it. The conservative operating strategy resulted in the company's assets more than doubling between 1987 and 1988, while net income rose from 60 cents per share in fiscal 1987 to 98 cents a share one year later. By December 31, 1988, $2.7 billion was serviced in mortgage loans, versus $1.1 billion a year earlier. And the return on equity was 14 percent in 1988.[13]

The Boston Bancorp

Boston Bancorp's management consciously decided not to pursue diversification into nontraditional activities. It reasoned that the historical focus on

---

[13]Robert Chaut, "The Well-Managed Thrift: Five Success Stories," *The Bankers Magazine*, July-August 1989, pp. 35 and 38.

retail deposit accounts and home mortgages could be profitable if costs were kept low.

And this Boston Bancorp did. It limited investment in "brick and mortar," having only four branches serving middle-income communities in metropolitan Boston. A long-established bank-by-mail program eliminated the need for an extensive branch system. Use of funds primarily was in single-family mortgages, commercial mortgages in apartment buildings, and high-quality government obligations and corporate stock—conservative and far from risky. With this approach, Boston Bancorp's return-on-equity exceeded 18 percent, and it grew to $1.4 billion in assets.[14]

Austerity also paid off for other S & Ls—for example, TCF Banking and Savings. New management took over during the turbulent mid-1980s. The first thing to go was a luxurious suite of executive offices, as well as 35 of the association's top brass.[15]

USA Today, in a 1989 feature story, described a number of thrifts that bucked the trend and were success stories during a time of turmoil in the industry. The common denominators for all of these was *careful growth*, dedicated commitment to pursuing home mortgages rather than commercial deals and brokeraged deposits, and a creativity in bettering customer service.[16]

CONCLUSIONS

The S & L industry in the 1980s represented the greatest industry debacle since the Great Depression of the 1930s. The disaster engulfed hundreds of savings and loans in all types of communities, from the very small rural communities to the largest cities, from areas of depressed growth to those with the greatest growth. The taxpayers' bill to salvage what can be salvaged will be in the hundreds of billions of dollars.

How could this have happened? Could it have been avoided? What, if anything, can we learn from all this that might be transferable to other situations and other times, that in effect may lessen the probability of such happenings occurring again?

Some have attributed the blame for the S & L crisis to external circumstances that S & L executives had no control over. They were simply victims, so these "experts" would lead us to believe. Government has received much of the blame. In its desire to help the industry during a time of high and increasing interest rates, it promoted a dangerous deregulation by permitting

---

[14]*Ibid.*

[15]Harlan Byrne, "Practicing Thrift, Austerity Pays Off for a Midwestern S & L," *Barron's*, Sept. 21, 1987, p. 15.

[16]David Elbert and Harriet Johnson Brackey, "Slow Growth Was the Key to Survival," *USA Today*, Feb. 15, 1989, pp. B1 and B2.

S & Ls wide latitude to invest their funds far beyond the traditional home mortgage lending, as well as by relaxing equity restraints. No one could foresee that the wild boom in oil prices and land values would so abruptly deflate.

Yet, such "excuses" for the debacle rest on unsubstantial foundations. Although hundreds of S & Ls failed, more hundreds maintained viability and even showed strength and growth. The common denominator of uncontrollable environmental factors does not hold the valid answer of who or what to blame and how disaster could have been avoided. Furthermore, it was the height of imprudence to expect boom conditions to be everlasting.

Where then lies the blame? As with most mistakes, management cannot escape primary responsibility. In this case, the fault lies with a management that violated the integrity of the planning function. (See the information box on *discipline in planning and decision making*). The violation occurred in two respects: (1) injudicious failure to rein in expenses during a time when the profitable spread of traditional mortgage business was narrowing and (2) a wild spree to highly risky undertakings and investments once governmental regulation was loosened. To this one must add a good dash of outright fraud, asset-stripping, corruption—white-collar crimes. (Of course, the inability of government inspectors to monitor closely enough permitted some of the worst excesses. But we are concerned here with management mistakes, *not* government mistakes.)

THE FINE ART OF DISCIPLINE IN PLANNING AND DECISION MAKING

Planning and decision making are vulnerable to abuses—abuses in overreaching, in not prudently assessing rewards versus risks in proposals, in operating beyond reasonable means, in simply not keeping a tight rein on costs. Such abuses are especially tempting in times of wild optimism, such as were occurring in the Southwest during the oil and land boom.

Discipline needs to be imposed when the inclination is to run amok. Discipline implies controlled behavior, careful evaluation of actions and opportunities, not growing beyond resources and management capabilities. In the quest for the fine line between disciplined and undisciplined growth, the executive faces the dual risk of being too conservative or too aggressive. The first risk may present the decision maker with missed opportunities and permit competitors to gain an advantage; the second risk may jeopardize the viability of the company. In walking this thin line, the continued viability of the company should receive priority.

INVITATION TO DISCUSS
How would you attempt to walk the "thin line" between being too conservative and too aggressive in important marketing decisions?

WHAT CAN BE LEARNED?

We can draw significant insights from the blunders of the sick and dying thrifts, and the comparison with the prospering ones.

Learning Insight. *Adversity creates opportunities.*

We are left with the growing recognition that adversity—in this case, a supposedly inhospitable environment—can also create opportunities for those who would adjust, adapt, and plan creatively in this environment, even embrace it with gusto—but without reckless abandon. The S & L situation created great opportunities for firms and individuals who had the resources and skill to "rescue" the troubled thrifts, with substantial government largess. And for the healthy competitors, new growth opportunities were also created, albeit the bad image of the failures cast all S & Ls in suspicious light.

Learning Insight. *The fallacy of aggressive and conservative extremes.*

Many of the failed thrifts were victims of their own aggressiveness, carried to the extreme of recklessness. If real estate prices and a building boom had continued into the foreseeable future in the high-growth areas of the South and West, then some of the reckless speculations would have brought above-average payoffs. Unfortunately, a wild house-of-cards philosophy eventually succumbs, with the whole structure collapsing. Excesses can only be tolerated so long in the normal course of events, as has been proved time and again over many centuries. The dangers of a speculative frenzy date back at least to 1634 in Holland, when individual tulip bulbs were bid up to fantastic prices in a wild but doomed speculation.

The extremes of conservatism have dangers, too. As we examine in the next Learning Insight, the environment is in flux; it is constantly changing. To stand pat, to not even take minor risks, regardless of potential opportunities, to not make needed adjustments to a changing business clime—these can hardly be praised. The extreme example here is the buggy whip manufacturer unwilling to adapt to the new environment of horseless carriages. Ultraconservatism simply invites competitors to gain advantage.

In general, a middle ground between extreme aggressive risk-taking and ultraconservatism usually will lead to the most durable success.

Learning Insight. *How much adaptability to change?*

A useful perspective about reactions to a changing environment can be gained by considering a continuum of behavior to change such as:

Degree of Responsiveness to Environmental Change

Inflexible *Unchanging*	*Adaptive*	*Innovative*

Thus, a firm can be viewed as occupying a certain point along this continuum: the more conservative and rigid firm toward the left, the more progressive firm that is constantly developing new ideas toward the right.

The two terms, adaptive and innovative, are somewhat different, although related. We will consider them as different degrees of responsive behavior on the same dimension. Innovative may be defined as originating significant changes, implying improvement. Adaptive implies a better coping with changing circumstances but a response somewhat less significant than an innovative reaction.

In a sense, the failed thrifts were adaptive to a changed environment, that of greater deregulation. They adapted by forsaking any plans of judicious expansion in favor of a freewheeling strategy of high risks and opportunism. Then they found themselves unable to cope with the suddenly menacing environment of drastically falling real estate prices and a newly concerned regulatory climate.

Learning Insight. *Austerity wins out over high living.*

Nowhere is the contrast between high living and a lack of cost constraints, on the one hand, and relative austerity on the other, more evident than here. Reckless spending is a trap. Admittedly, when things are going well, when prospects seem boundless, the temptation is to open the spending floodgates both at the corporate level as well as for personal aggrandizement.

On the one hand, many of the failed thrifts were guilty of wild spending. Conspicuous examples of this were lavish entertainment, grand facilities, fleets of airplanes, even expensive art collections.[17]

On the other hand, we have examples of firms that owe their viability to their austerity. They kept themselves lean, controlled costs, and were able to survive and prosper and even be in position to take over their extravagant competitors.

---

[17]For example, see Martha Brannigan and Alexandra Peers, "S & L's Art Collection, Ordered to be Sold, Faces Skeptical Market," *Wall Street Journal*, Oct. 18, 1989, pp. 1, A12.

Whereas some would argue that lavish spending created a public image of great success and prosperity, thus winning new business, a more sober appraisal would be one of foolish waste. Lack of cost restraints is incompatible with effective management, and should not be tolerated by shareholders or creditors.

Learning Insight. *A government "crutch" is a destructive delusion.*

The knowledge that depositors' accounts were insured up to $100,000 by the Federal Savings and Loan Insurance Corporation undoubtedly motivated some of the reckless investments and other dealings of the failed thrifts. That the government would foot the cost of any speculations that turned sour and bail out depositors, seemed a siren call for some executives. But those who felt entirely shielded by this governmental crutch were to learn to their dismay that while depositors were protected—at great cost to the government and taxpayers—they, the management, faced ouster and even the possibility of legal prosecution.

The shifting tides of politics bring the threat of being "blind sided" to those who rely too much on government support and protection. The government has no great history of sound legislation: witness the S & L legislation of the early 1980s, designed to save the S & Ls but which in reality presented a temptation for doom that many found impossible to resist.

Issue Insight. *What is the responsibility of management?*

Managers are well paid. Isn't responsibility for protecting assets a condition for management? Even if these assets are somewhat protected by the government? Is there not also a responsibility to the enterprise, that it not be liquidated or merged into extinction? Are not managers custodians of shareholders' trust?

These are some of the troubling questions that arise when management has been completely oblivious to the greater good of the corporation and its shareholders (and depositors). Ancillary questions also arise: Can selfish greed be tolerated in managers who should have our trust and who can hardly afford to abdicate their responsibility? Can recklessness be tolerated? What should be the penalties for fraud?

USA Today opened a "hot line" for the public's responses to the S & L mess. Here is a sampling of responses.[18]

I don't see how they could have squandered this money and not get prosecuted.

---

[18]Denise Kalette, "Callers Want S & L Cheats Punished," *USA Today*, Feb. 15, 1989, p. B1.

> When I mishandle my money, I have nobody to go bail me out. If [S & Ls] are incapable of handling the trust that was placed in them, maybe they should go belly-up.
>
> The guilty parties to this fraud should be paying off these banks. If a guy owns a $2 million home, it should be auctioned off, and he should be put in jail.
>
> Every bank that approved big loans over $100,000, when they knew they were shaky, they should be made to pay them back, even if it causes executive hardship.
>
> They've got to take responsibility for their actions. This makes Watergate look real simple compared to what they've done our country.

In this case, then, we see mistakes on a grand scale. Perhaps managers guilty of gross misconduct in connection with the public trust should face stronger penalties than simply ouster from a well-paying job, with most of their assets intact. What do you think?

FOR THOUGHT AND DISCUSSION

1. Would you have recommended changing an S & L's mission during the early 1980s, when most government restraints were relaxed? If so, what should the mission have been changed to?
2. How would you respond to an S & L executive who carefully points out to you that if land and oil prices had not collapsed without warning, his portfolio of high-interest loans would have brought great profitability to the firm?
3. "S & Ls no longer serve a useful purpose, and they should be phased out." Evaluate this statement from the position of an executive in a solvent S & L.

INVITATION TO ROLE PLAY

You are the controller of a medium-size S & L in the mid-1980s. Your CEO is a flamboyant individual who has just announced his intention of building a new home office on a rather lavish scale. He claims this is necessary to convey the desired image of the firm. Develop a systematic analysis to disprove this recommendation.

INVITATION TO RESEARCH

1. What is the S & L situation? Has it improved or worsened?
2. Look for other S & L success stories. What are the keys to their bucking the trend?

15

Raiders: Raping American Corporations

The 1980s was a time of frenzied takeovers and leveraged buyouts (LBOs). Sometimes, the buyers were friendly; more often, they were hostile raiders, making their powerful challenges with heavily borrowed funds, usually so-called junk bonds. Junk bonds provided lenders with higher interest than many other investments, but at the expense of a greater risk of default.

Robert Campeau, a French Canadian real-estate developer, was a major player in the latter 1980s. In May 1988, Campeau scored a major victory over R. H. Macy & Co. in a bitter battle for the Federated Department Store Corporation and its prestigious division, Bloomingdale's. Less than two years earlier, Campeau had acquired another major department store corporation, Allied Stores. Campeau was amassing a retailing empire.

He was soon to find these acquisitions too big to swallow. But, while suffering from indigestion, he traumatized these prestigious retailing organizations and their employees. Through no fault of their own, these companies were thrust into Chapter 11 bankruptcy.

Another major player in the 1980s was England's Sir James Goldsmith. Goldsmith had already earned the dubious reputation of being an "asset stripper" when he set his sights on Goodyear Tire and Rubber Company of Akron, Ohio, the world's leading tiremaker and the most effectively managed. Akron and the state of Ohio rallied around Goodyear. Goldsmith was fought off, but the company, left heavily burdened with debt, was forced into deep layoffs. And Goldsmith? He consented to being bought off by Goodyear and left the scene pocketing $93.75 million in "greenmail."

Here we have two examples of the negative consequences that result from corporate raiders' extreme machinations. Did the raiders serve the public interest in any way, or were they entirely self-seeking—white-collar blackmailers?

ROBERT CAMPEAU

Campeau's life is an intriguing "rags to riches" story. The eighth of 13 children, he grew up in a devout Catholic family in the mining town of Sudbury, Ontario. His father was an auto mechanic. Robert left school at 14 to help support the family. He swept garage floors at a local mining company.

By 1949, at the age of 25, he was a factory supervisor. During his free time, he built a house in Ottawa for his wife and young child. However, instead of moving them in, he sold the place for a $3000 profit, doubling his money. Encouraged, he built 40 more houses that year. This was the beginning of his climb to great wealth.

In the 1950s and 1960s, Campeau gained both a fortune and a reputation as a master builder. He put up 20,000 houses around Ottawa; he was the first to build on Toronto's lakefront, now one of the city's priciest areas; and he became one of the Canadian government's major builders. He and his good friend Pierre Trudeau, the Prime Minister of Canada, frequently went on ski trips together.

Still ambitious, Campeau attempted several corporate takeovers in Canada, including that of Royal Trustco Ltd., one of Canada's oldest and richest trust companies. When these attempts failed, he blamed it on the British-descent financiers' prejudice against a French-Canadian. So he turned his sights south, and with great initial success.

With the acquisition of the Federated Department Store Corporation, Campeau had an empire consisting of 382 department stores. But his personal life was in shambles. He was suing his eldest son in a corporate power struggle. He divorced his wife to marry his mistress, with whom he had already sired two children that his first family did not even know about.

What kind of boss was Robert Campeau? He has been widely characterized as eccentric, emotional, ego-driven—some call his temperament "mercurial"—hardly an easy man to work for. One talented executive, Robert H. Morsky, former vice chairman of the successful Limited Stores, could only stand Campeau for two months before leaving after a clash of egos. Campeau has been known to call employees at 3 A.M. He berated executives publicly, even shrieking at them. He has even been accused by former associates of cheating them at golf. One former executive who worked briefly for Campeau characterized him as having an "Ivan the Terrible management style."[1]

Naturally, in such a managerial climate, Campeau had trouble keeping executives.

THE ACQUISITION BINGE

After failing in his takeover attempts in Canada, Campeau turned his attention to the United States in 1986, with a vengeance. He found an expensive takeover expert and investment banker in Bruce Wasserstein and First Boston Corporation. Allen Finkelson, a partner of a New York law firm, was another key player. They found Campeau eager to take risks with little concern for debt accumulation or liquidity constraints.

Although he knew nothing about retailing, Campeau bought Allied Stores Corporation, an operator of such department stores as Jordan Marsh, for $3.4 billion in December 1986. Then, in May 1988, he won the highly publicized 10-week bidding war with Macy's to acquire Federated and its upscale department stores, Bloomingdale's, paying a premium price of $6.6 billion to do so. In the process, he incurred hefty expenses: $167 million in golden parachutes and other stock buyouts for former Federated executives; over $200 million in investment banking, legal, and other fees; and $150.5 million for bridge-loan fees and interest to First Boston Corp. and two other investment bankers.

The classic strategy used by raiders who are willing to incur mountainous debt to gain the takeover has been to sell off some of the assets—some of the divisions they acquire—to pay off a portion of the debt. Thereby, they supposedly are able to handle the interest payments on the remainder of the debt. Campeau's strategy was no different.

By late 1988, he had cut over $6 billion from his debt load by selling certain divisions of Allied and Federated. He raised $1.2 billion by selling Allied's Brooks Brothers and Ann Taylor divisions, and Federated's Gold Circle, Main Street, and Children's Place Stores. He wanted to keep the Jordan Marsh and Maas Brothers chains that had produced almost two-thirds of Allied's profits in 1986 before he bought it. Table 15.1 shows his "empire" after his initial pruning of assets. Campeau wanted to retain some of Federated's best stores: Bloomingdale's, Lazarus, Abraham & Straus, Burdines, and Rich's/Goldsmith's. He slashed expenses by $125 million a year at Allied and $250 million at Federated—mostly by eliminating employees. For example, 5000 jobs were eliminated at Federated alone. By early 1989, further sales of Federated's specialty and discount stores were

[1]Kate Ballen, "Campeau Is on a Shopper's High," *Fortune*, Aug. 15, 1988, pp. 70–74.

expected to bring total debt down to $5.6 billion. It appeared that Allied and Federated's combined cash flow would amount to about twice the $600 million needed for interest payments, a comfortable margin.

Campeau had other plans. He believed that both Allied and Federated could be streamlined by consolidating their backroom operations and by motivating executives through stock options. And he saw the possibility of a real *synergy* of real estate and retailing. (See the following information box.)

In capitalizing on the possible synergy of real estate and retailing, Campeau planned to open three to five shopping centers annually, in partnership with Edward DeBartolo, the shopping center czar, who had loaned Campeau $480 million previously. With Campeau's prestigious stores anchoring such shopping malls, there would be no difficulty attracting other retail tenants. Campeau also planned to expand the Bloomingdale's chain by 17 stores over the coming five years.

TROUBLE!

Just 18 months after Campeau scored the major victory over Macy's by obtaining Federated, his dream became a nightmare. In September 1989, Campeau needed cash, a lot of it, and quickly. By now, the company was carrying almost $11 billion in short- and long-term debt, and the annual interest burden was more than $1 billion. By December 1, 1989, $401 million in notes were due First Boston Corporation.

The first inklings of trouble occurred the year before, in November 1988—the Christmas season, with its heavy short-term borrowing needs.

Table 15.1   Campeau's Holdings, Summer 1989, after Initial Asset Sales

Allied Stores:
> Jordan Marsh, 26 stores—Connecticut, Maine, Massachusetts, New Hampshire, New York, Rhode Island
> Maas Brothers-Jordan Marsh, 28—Florida, Georgia
> Stern's, 24—Pennsylvania, New Jersey, New York
> The Bon, 39—Idaho, Montana, Oregon, Utah, Washington, Wyoming

Federated Department Stores:
> Abraham & Straus, 15—New Jersey, New York
> Bloomingdale's, 17—Connecticut, Florida, Massachusetts, Maryland, New Jersey, New York, Pennsylvania, Texas, Virginia
> Burdines, 30—Florida
> Lazarus, 43—Indiana, Kentucky, Michigan, Ohio, West Virginia
> Ralphs Supermarkets, 132—California
> Rich's/Goldsmith's, 26—Alabama, Georgia, South Carolina, Tennessee

SYNERGY

Synergy is the creation of a whole that is greater than the sum of its parts. Thus, the whole can accomplish more than the total of the individual contributions. In an acquisition, synergy occurs if the two or more entities, when combined, are more efficient, productive, and profitable than they were as individual operations before the merger.

How can such synergy occur? If duplication of efforts can be eliminated, if operations can be streamlined, if economies of scale are possible, if specialization can be enhanced, if greater financial and managerial resources can be tapped—then a synergistic situation is likely to occur. Such an expanded operation, then, should be stronger than anything that was before.

In theory, synergism provides a mighty stimulus for acquisitions and for the investors who make them possible. But instead of synergy, sometimes the reverse happens: negative synergy, where the combined effort is worse than the sum of individual efforts. If friction arises between the entities, if there is an incompatibility of organizational missions, if an organizational climate is fostered that is fearful, resentful, and frustrated, then synergy is not likely to be achieved. And if greater managerial and financial resources are not realized—if, indeed, financial resources are depleted because of the credit demands stemming from the acquisition—then synergy becomes negative. The whole, then, is less than the sum of its parts. Until such a situation can be corrected, an organizational blunder on a grand scale has been accomplished. Unfortunately, this would prove to be the case with Campeau.

INVITATION TO DISCUSS:

1. Would you expect synergy to be more likely with friendly takeovers than hostile ones? Why or why not?
2. How might synergy have been better realized in the Campeau acquisitions?

Campeau's ability to tap previous lenders was petering out. Underwriters at First Boston had failed to sell a $1.5 billion offering of junk bonds for the Federated unit. They scaled back the offering to $750 million but still could not find sufficient investors and had to acquire a large portion of the bonds themselves. And First Boston got "burned" as Federated bonds soon dropped 20 percent and Allied Stores bonds declined 45 percent. Other financing by bonds fell through as well, with the public becoming skittish about junk bonds.

Working capital was rapidly depleting at both Allied and Federated stores, but costs were not dropping significantly, despite Campeau's efforts to reduce overhead. Although Campeau was able to weather the Christmas 1988 borrowing needs, now another Christmas season was looming, with most of this merchandise payable in October. And the situation was critical if his stores were to have merchandise to sell during the peak selling season. With apparently nowhere else to turn, Campeau finally approached Olympia & York, owned by the wealthy Reichmann family of Toronto, with whom he had already borrowed substantially in his acquisition drives.

THE CLIMAX

On September 11, 1989, *USA Today* reported in a cover story that Bloomingdale's, the "jewel" of Campeau's "retail empire," was on the block, up for sale.[2] Indeed, only Bloomingdale's, with its high-fashion image, returned, in one shot, the kind of cash Campeau needed to meet his interest payment deadlines. Analysts estimated Bloomingdale's would sell for $1 to $1.5 billion. None of the other divisions would bring in nearly as much. Bloomingdale's, of all Campeau's acquisitions, was the one he was most proud of, had the highest expectations for.

By the end of the week, the headlines trumpeted that Campeau had saved his retail kingdom, that he had convinced the Reichmanns to give him a crucial $250 million loan to keep the corporation afloat. However, to do this he had to give up control of the company. An Olympia & York executive, Lionel G. Dodd, was named chairman of a four-man committee formed to oversee the restructuring, and Campeau was conspicuously left off the panel.

By early 1990, the Campeau Corporation was on the verge of bankruptcy. Expectations were widespread that several more divisions, in addition to Bloomingdale's, would be put up for sale. Reputations and fortunes were being wrecked. Robert Campeau was removed from active participation, relegated to working only on the company's real-estate operations. He had lost wealth that it took him a lifetime to accumulate: nearly $500 million. Most of this represented the paper losses on some 27.7 million shares of rapidly depreciating company stock. A good part of this had already been seized by creditors for nonpayment of loans. Perhaps as bad as his financial losses was the humiliation of falling from stardom.

The troubles also enveloped the wealthy Reichmanns, who had badly misjudged the extent of the Campeau problems. Altogether, they were estimated to have invested more than $700 million in Campeau. Their stake was largely depreciated.

First Boston Corporation, which masterminded both of Campeau's takeovers and lent him its own money to help complete the deals, now

---

[2]Patricia Gallagher, "Bloomie's On Block in Bid to Buy Time," *USA Today*, Sept. 11, 1989, pp. 1B and 2B.

found itself with a soured reputation for imprudence—as well as hundreds of millions in losses, so much so that its debt rating was downgraded by Moody's. Bruce Wasserstein, one of the guiding lights of Campeau's efforts, was also hurt. Finally, not the least of the losers were the thousands of employees who lost their jobs and the prestigious retail stores whose images were besmirched.

On January 15, 1990, the Campeau Corporation filed for Chapter 11 bankruptcy protection from its creditors.

ANALYSIS

While precariously extended, Campeau had expected to meet his financial obligations. What went wrong? Part of the trouble was that cash flow from these big retailers was considerably less than Campeau had expected. Part of the trouble was sagging apparel sales nationally. But the day-to-day operations of the stores were also faltering. The layoffs may have cut into muscle as well as fat. Perhaps the pruning of thousands of jobs in order to cut overhead had severely strained management and staff operations. Such upheavals would demoralize any organization: instead of tending to business, the employees would naturally be worrying about when and on whom the ax would fall next. Résumés would be readied and other job opportunities explored. But above all, the cost-reduction plans were up to $200 million too optimistic.

Campeau paid far too much for Federated. A *Wall Street Journal* article claimed that he paid $500 million too much, and that this was key to the financial problems.[3] Actually, Campeau initially offered $4.2 billion for Federated but finally won at $6.6 billion.

The first asset sales went smoothly. In the spring and summer of 1988, Bullock's, I. Magnin, Foley's, and Filene's were sold for $2.75 billion, and Ralphs was spun off and refinanced to generate $800 million in cash. But the remaining asset sales fell far short of expectations. Campeau expected to sell Gold Circle, MainStreet, The Children's Place, and assorted real estate for $727 million; instead, these brought only $562 million.

With inadequate asset sales, incomplete cost-cutting, and a grim look for apparel sales, this was a bad time to bring out Federated's $1.5 billion issue of junk bonds. Only $750 million of these were sold at exorbitant costs and interest rates. The stage was set for disaster. Obviously, imprudent borrowing was at the heart of Campeau's troubles. But times were

---

[3]Jeffrey A. Trachtenberg, Robert Meinbardis and David B. Hilder, "An Extra $500 Million Paid for Federated Got Campeau in Trouble," *Wall Street Journal*, Dec. 11, 1990, pp. A1, A6.

turning against all corporate raiders who had amassed vast fortunes earlier in the 1980s. Many of these acquired businesses were deeply in the red, and their huge debt payments contributed to defaults that were beginning to play havoc on the junk bond market, the major source of marauder financing. The raider strategy of "using somebody else's money to leverage and strip a company to get rich . . . the days of the free ride" were nearing an end.[4]

Retailing presents a rather unique situation for working capital requirements, which makes highly leveraged operations more risky. The Christmas season accounts for one-third of the year's sales and about one-half of the year's profits. But to achieve this, a heavy inventory buildup is needed, and this requires substantial short-term funds. In addition, Federated and Allied divisions needed money for a number of longer-term projects, such as developing private-label goods (which carry a higher profit margin) and normal remodeling and refurbishing of stores. The heavy leverage used left little cushion for such financial needs. Earlier in 1989, Bonwit Teller and B. Altman department stores which had been previously taken over by Australia's Hooker Corporation had already gone into Chapter 11 bankruptcy.

The problems of Campeau and other raiders raise questions about the *transferability of management skills*, as the following information box elaborates.

GOLDSMITH AND GREENMAIL

"I like to think of myself as a revolutionary," Sir James Goldsmith has said.[5] Even though he is one of the world's richest men, Goldsmith despises big business. He moves in on companies he believes are undervalued and then sells off less-profitable divisions, earning him the reputation of being an "assets stripper." The Crown Zellerbach Corporation was Goldsmith's most widely known conquest. He took over this giant forest and paper products firm, sold off certain assets, and came away with millions in profits. Similarly, he acquired Diamond International Corporation, divesting all the assets except for 1.7 million acres of forests, leaving him with an estimated $500 million in potential profits.[6]

In Goodyear Tire and Rubber Company, Goldsmith saw yet another opportunity.

---

[4]John Greenwald, "The Big Comeuppance," *Time*, Dec. 11, 1989. pp. 74–76.
[5]John Rossant, "The Two Worlds of Jimmy Goldsmith," *Business Week*, Dec. 1, 1986, p. 98.
[6]Thomas Gerdel, "Goldsmith Called Assets Stripper," *Cleveland Plain Dealer*, Nov. 5, 1986, p. 1B.

TRANSFERABILITY OF MANAGEMENT SKILLS

Are management skills transferable to other companies and other industries? The common belief is that they are, that the successful manager or administrator in one situation will be able to effectively use these skills and talents in other endeavors, even those completely unrelated to the particular industry experience. Perhaps.

But we see a paradox with Campeau. A highly successful real estate magnate and developer, he acted more like a babe in the woods in his retail empire building. He vastly overestimated his sales and cash flow projections, he greatly underestimated his ability to pare expenses and sell off assets. He completely miscalculated the substantial financial needs of major retail stores in their buildup of inventories for the peak Christmas selling season. And he practically destroyed a smooth-functioning organization and its morale.

Can it be that there is a limit to the transferability of management skills? Could it be that, at least with retailing, the outsider has a considerable period of adjustment and learning before being able to effectively take the reins? Or could it be that skill as a raider and as a financial manipulator does not prepare one for operational management? Although we can hardly generalize to all individuals and all situations, the Campeau debacle casts some doubts on the cherished notion of complete and easy transferability of managerial skills. And other raiders, such as T. Boone Pickens and Carl Icahn, have not proven notably successful in operating their conquests.

INVITATION TO DISCUSS

1. Why does it seem difficult to transfer financial management skills to operations management?
2. Are entrepreneurial skills easily transferable?
3. Are technological and engineering skills transferable?

Goodyear

Goodyear Tire and Rubber Company, headquartered in Akron, Ohio, had been the world's leading tire manufacturer, for 80 years. With 100 plants around the world, it had about a 23 percent share of the global tire market, assets of $4.6 billion, and sales in excess of $10 billion a year. It was the 35th largest company in the United States.

During the 1980s, neither the company's size nor management's proficiency brought immunity to a hostile takeover. Financial analysts began touting Goodyear as a possible takeover target for several reasons: it was the most efficient tiremaker in the United States, it had very competent management, and it had an extremely undervalued share price. Investment bankers at Merrill Lynch, viewing the company as a desirable takeover target, accumulated $1.9 billion to help finance whoever sought their assistance in acquiring Goodyear. Sir James Goldsmith was quick to take advantage of this financing opportunity.

It was not until Goldsmith was forced to file a disclosure statement with the Securities and Exchange Commission that Goodyear knew for certain that it was to be the defendant in a hostile takeover attempt. Securities laws in the United States require buyers to disclose their holdings in a company when those holdings reach 5 percent or more. However, the buyer has 10 days in which to do so. Those 10 days allowed Goldsmith to accumulate an additional 6.5 percent stake in the company, or 12.5 million shares, before making his disclosure to the SEC.

Goodyear and its chairman, Robert Mercer, decided to fight the Goldsmith takeover attempt. In so doing, Mercer had to reluctantly abandon his efforts to diversify the company. Although revenues from the tire business contributed 80 percent of the firm's total revenues, Mercer had envisioned a long-term strategy in which the energy and aerospace subsidiaries would each contribute up to 25 percent of total revenues. But now, with the takeover pending, Mercer was forced to reverse his course. Consolidation and restructuring became the new objectives. Efforts were concentrated on short-term profit maximization rather than long-term goals.

Immediately, Goodyear's subsidiaries, Celeron Corporation and Goodyear Aerospace, were put up for sale. Analysts estimated that Goodyear could get nearly $2 billion from these sales, which could be used to buy back 30 to 40 million shares of the company's own stock. This would increase Goodyear's earnings per share and thus raise its stock price, which would increase the amount Goldsmith would have to offer per share in order to gain control of the company.

Many people questioned Goldsmith's reasons for wanting to take over Goodyear. "Management is doing all the right things," analysts said. "[They've] put their long-run future ahead of their short-term financial gains to improve productivity and world market position."[7]

It could be argued that the only reason Goldsmith was attempting to take over Goodyear was to drive up the stock price so he could reap a huge profit—either by selling the stock or by accepting greenmail. (Greenmail is the term used to describe the corporate raider's practice of acquiring a block of a company's stock, threatening takeover, and then agreeing to sell back the stock to the company at a premium price.)[8] But Goldsmith insisted:

---

[7]Thomas Gerdel, "Takeover is Threatened for All the Wrong Reasons," *Cleveland Plain Dealer,* October 30, 1986, p. 2F.

[8]George A. Steiner and John F. Steiner, *Business, Government, and Society,* 5th ed. (New York: Random House, 1988), p. 666.

"Anybody who thinks greenmail is the purpose totally misunderstands the marketplace, totally misunderstands Goodyear, and most importantly, totally misunderstands me.... I'm prepared to be a tiremaker.... Goodyear's diversifications have taken it out of focus."[9]

The strengths of the company were unassailable. This was not a weak company managed by incompetents. In 1986, Goodyear held an estimated one-third of the domestic tire market, up from 20 percent in 1980. Its 23 percent of the global market was up from 19 percent in 1980. Expenditures for R & D (research and development) totalled $1.5 billion in the 10 years prior to 1986. In the 25 years prior to the takeover attempt, Goodyear had higher returns on investment equity than the industry average. In the first half of the 1980s, the company had made capital expenditures for plants and equipment of approximately $1.3 billion. By continually investing heavily in plants and research—approximately $250 million in 1986—Goodyear was keeping its competitive edge in the industry. As one financial analyst stated: "These investments would help Goodyear remain the low-cost producer and gain market share from its rivals. If Goldsmith succeeds in his takeover attempt and slashes research and capital spending to increase profits, Goodyear's tire rivals could benefit.... I can't believe Sir James is interested in running a tire business in the long term."[10]

Goodyear's Defense

Goodyear was not able to prevent Goldsmith from making a tender offer of $49 a share for the remaining Goodyear stock. What Goldsmith did not count on, however, was the plethora of stockholders who took up the battle in support of Goodyear.

In Akron, Ohio, where Goodyear employed 10 percent of the city's work force and paid 16 percent of the city's income taxes, residents rallied around Goodyear. At University of Akron football games, cheerleaders helped 50,000 people to sign petitions declaring their support and concern for the company's employees and the future of Akron. The petitions were given to Representative John Seiberling to submit to the House subcommittee hearings on the takeover.[11] This support was matched in many other cities across the country that had a stake in Goodyear's future.

---

[9]Zachary Schiller and John Rossant, "Trying to Beat Sir Jimmy to the Punch," *Business Week*, Nov. 17, 1986, pp. 64–65.

[10]Thomas Gerdel, "Goldsmith's Aim Questioned," *Cleveland Plain Dealer*, Nov. 8, 1986, p. 6B.

[11]Zachary Schiller, "In Akron, Jimmy Goldsmith's Name is Mud," *Business Week*, Nov. 25, 1986, p. 40.

During the House Judiciary subcommittee hearings on the takeover, Seiberling, whose grandfather had founded Goodyear, listened to Goldsmith continually berating Goodyear's management and then acidly responded, "My question is, who the hell are you?"[12]

In Columbus, Ohio, the Ohio Senate responded by amending Ohio corporate law specifically to help Goodyear fight off Goldsmith. Three separate anti-takeover measures made the acquisition much more difficult and expensive but not quite impossible.

The mounting opposition finally seemed to convince Goldsmith to give up his takeover attempt. He "graciously" consented to let Goodyear buy back his stock holdings, which cost Goodyear over $620 million and brought Goldsmith and his partners more than $93 million in profits. The whole Goodyear takeover effort was over barely three weeks after it had begun, but it left Goodyear reeling.

CONSEQUENCES TO THE COMPANY

The damage had been done: the successful defense left the company badly weakened. It had incurred a hefty $2.6 billion of debt in the share buyout program. Subsidiary businesses that had been expected to give the company vitality and new directions in future years had to be sold. A cost-reduction program was necessary to meet debt payments: about $250 million a year was saved through job reductions, and capital expenditures were slashed by 75 percent.

In 1990, Goodyear sustained a $38.3 million loss, its first annual loss since 1932. It lost its position as the world's largest tire maker, a position it had held since 1916. See Table 15.1 for Goodyear's operating statistics from 1981 to 1990. Note in particular the heavy increase in long-term debt that occurred in 1986, as manifested in debt as a percentage of capital.

In a speech, a bitter Robert Mercer described the negative effects raiders have on our society:

> The raiders' product is not goods and services as we know them. Their interest is not in preserving and strengthening America's industrial base and providing jobs. No, their product is simply "deals," and that is not a product which a country—any country—can base a future on. The only real benefactors are those in on the deals.... [n]o responsible American businessman should stand mutely on the sidelines while the very future of our industry and our economy is threatened by "Terrorists in Three-Piece Suits."[13]

---

[12]Tom Diener, "Mind Your Own Business," *Cleveland Plain Dealer*, Nov. 19, 1986, p. 6D.

[13]Robert E. Mercer, "Terrorists in Three-Piece Suits," *Vital Speeches of the Day*, Vol. 53, May 1, 1987, pp. 422–423.

Table 15.1   Goodyear Operating Statistics, 1981–1990

Year	Sales (000)	Net Income (000)	Percent Long-term Debt to Capital
1981	$ 9,152,905	$243,895	30.4%
1982	8,688,700	247,600	27.6
1983	9,735,800	270,400	16.0
1984	10,240,800	411,000	15.1
1985	9,588,100	412,400	19.8
1986	9,103,100	124,000	40.5
1987	9,905,200	770,900	55.8
1988	10,810,400	350,100	53.2
1989	10,869,300	189,400	50.3
1990	11,272,500	38,300 (deficit)	53.7

Source: Company public records.

ANALYSIS OF HOSTILE TAKEOVERS—A BALANCED VIEW

Robert Mercer delivered a harsh indictment of corporate raiders. Of course, his criticisms were hardly coming from an objective perspective. Another strong critic was Fred Hartley, Chairman of Unocal, the parent of Union Oil Company of California, itself a takeover target of another raider, T. Boone Pickens, Jr. Hartley also conducted a successful defense, although Unocal incurred some $4.16 billion in new debt. Hartley raged:

> I call these people [corporate raiders] "financial barbarians" because they attack successful companies, hoping to loot them of their equity, then gallop off into the sunset, their pockets stuffed with profits. They don't give a damn about long-term growth or the competitive strength of the industry.[14]

On the other hand, the raider, Pickens, criticized managers who fight off tender offers: "The main reason they're [the managers] upset is because they're vulnerable, and they're vulnerable precisely because they've done a lousy job for the shareholders."[15]

Who Benefits from Hostile Takeovers?

Do stockholders benefit from hostile takeovers? They do at first, when the market price of their stock is bid up. But, they often have to be nimble (i.e.,

---

[14]Fred L. Hartley, "Oil Company Takeover and the Future of the Petroleum Industry." Speech before the Joint Annual Conference of the National Association of Petroleum Investment Analysts and the Petroleum Investor Relations Association, Colorado Springs, Colorado, Sept. 20, 1985.
[15]T. Boone Pickens, Jr., "Takeovers and Mergers: A Function of the Free Market," *The Diary of Alpha Kappa Psi*, September 1986.

sell while the stock price is up), since prices can fall after the takeover attempt, especially if it is unsuccessful. How do other investors fare? Here, we are talking primarily about the junk bond holders involved in the financing of the deal. As we saw with Campeau's investors, the collapse of the junk bond market in such highly leveraged situations can bring drastic losses to such investors. Of course, the investors in Goldsmith's greenmail reaped huge rewards.

Do employees, suppliers, customers, and communities benefit? Usually, heavy cost-cutting is involved, careers are damaged, families uprooted. Communities may be abandoned, pensions may be jeopardized, and long-standing relationships with suppliers and customers may be disrupted.

When companies that are not being run efficiently are taken over, the effect can be entirely positive. Consider the following example.

Contrast: A & W—A Highly Leveraged Buyout that Succeeded

Lest we conclude that all takeovers involving heavy borrowing are ill-advised, reckless, and imprudent, let us look at a positive example. A & W root beer is part of America's motorized culture; its roadside stands date back to 1919. The draft beer was not sold by the bottle until 1971, when it quickly became the top-selling root beer in the country, surpassing brands such as Hires and Dad's. Still, root beer was not nearly as popular as cola in the competition for shelf space.

In 1983, A & W's root beer syrup business was sold to a group of investors. Along with the syrup business, the new owners also got Lou Lowenkron, who had come to A & W in 1980 with some 25 years in the soft-drink industry. Lowenkron quickly found that the new owners did not bring money for expansion. He thought a golden opportunity was being wasted by not capitalizing on the potentially powerful A & W name.

In 1986, Lowenkron engineered a leveraged buyout for $74 million, with $35 million in junk bonds. The buyout raised A & W's long-term debt to a dangerous 90 percent. But Lowenkron at last had full control of the company. Unlike Campeau, Goldsmith, and most of the other raiders, he had an intimate knowledge both of the company and of the industry. He quickly made some major moves. First, he introduced a cream soda, A & W's first line expansion in 70 years. A & W soon held half of the $350 million U.S. cream soda market. Then Lowenkron bought the rights to three other brands: Squirt, a grapefruit soda; Country Time Lemonade; and Vernors, a spicy ginger drink. By 1989, these three brands together accounted for more than one-third of A & W's revenues and about 40 percent of operating profit. A & W emerged as the clear leader in niche soft drinks. By 1989, the company's sales surpassed $110 million, more than triple what they were before the buyout; profits reached $10 million, compared to a small loss in 1986.[16]

What was the difference between Lowenkron and most other raiders? We see at least three major differences:

1. The leader of the A & W buyout was highly experienced in that particular industry.
2. Lowenkron had a personal interest and had developed a real commitment to overcoming the deficiencies of the present operation and ownership.
3. Lowenkron brought innovation and fresh growth to a staid and conservative organization.

So, we must conclude, as with most controversies, that the issue is not black or white, but gray. Sometimes, takeovers are constructive; other times, destructive. Although highly leveraged buyouts are risky because of the heavy debt burden, they can offer the means for good management to replace ineffective or highly conservative management. However, too many times, the beneficiaries are the dealmakers and their lawyers and bankers instead of the consumers, the firm, the employees, the stockholders, and society in general.

WHAT CAN BE LEARNED?

The Campeau and Goldsmith scenarios are by no means unique. They illustrate the great infatuation raiders and investors had with leveraged buyouts and the ready acceptance of junk bond financing that made the buyouts possible.

By 1989, when junk bond financing had soured dramatically—hastened in large part by Campeau's highly publicized excess—the collapse of high-risk financing seemed to come sooner than even the most pessimistic experts predicted.

Learning Insight. *Highly leveraged situations are extremely vulnerable, and this vulnerability does not need worsening economic conditions.*

During most of the 1980s, many managers, and not just raiders like Campeau, pursued a strategy of debt financing in contrast to equity (stock ownership) financing. Funds for such borrowing were usually readily

---

[16]Edward Giltenan, "Root Beer Gloat," *Forbes*, Dec. 11, 1989, pp. 156–160.

available, heavy debt had income tax advantages, and profits could be distributed among fewer shares so that return on equity was enhanced. During this time, a few voices decried the overleveraged situations of many companies. They predicted that when the eventual economic downturn came, many such firms would find themselves unable to meet the heavy interest burdens. Most lenders paid little heed to such lonesome voices and encouraged greater borrowing.

Campeau's widely publicized problems, and the earlier problems of Hooker and other raiders, suddenly changed the expansionist lending atmosphere. The hard reality dawned that some of the buyouts were fragile indeed, especially when they rested on optimistic projections for asset sales, for revenues, for cost savings (otherwise the interest payments could not be met). An economic slowdown proved unnecessary to bring some of these ill-advised speculators to their knees.

We have to conclude that, in deciding to commit heavily to borrowed funds, a company must adopt a worst-case scenario in estimating cash-flow sufficiency. Commitments that depend on optimistic projections and allow no room for more sobering developments should be shunned.

Learning Insight. *The synergy of mergers and acquisitions is suspect.*

As we discussed in an information box earlier in this chapter, the concept of synergy is that a new whole is better than the sum of its parts, since operations can be streamlined, greater management and staff competence can be brought to bear, and greater financial and other resources can be tapped. Yet, we saw no synergy in Campeau's case and none in Hooker's acquisitions; synergy is not readily apparent in many other acquisitions either. More often, such concentrations incur severe digestive problems— problems with people, systems, and procedures—that take time to resolve. Furthermore, greater size does not always beget economies of scale. The opposite may in fact result in an unwieldy organization, slow to act and vulnerable to more aggressive, innovative, and agile smaller competitors. The siren call of synergy is often an illusion.

Learning Insight. *Retailing presents unique working capital problems.*

As noted earlier, because of the great seasonality and the substantial buildup of inventory necessary for the Christmas season, working capital requirements in the retail industry, even for ordinary operations, present serious problems to highly leveraged situations. Campeau carelessly overlooked this.

Further adding to the problems, vendors become reluctant to ship needed goods at the first hints that they might not get paid. Any publicity about financial problems can play havoc with getting sufficient merchandise to meet Christmas selling needs—this was true even for the prestigious Allied and Federated stores. Despite the cash transfusion from the Reichmann brothers, vendors were still concerned about Christmas shipments. A Dun & Bradstreet cautionary note, reported in the December 7, 1989 *Wall Street Journal*, exacerbated the problem. And a week later, one of the largest factoring companies in the country, Heller Financial, told its clients to stop shipping merchandise to Campeau's retailing operations.[17]

Learning Insight. *The concept of organizational restructuring for acquisitions is becoming a myth.*

The idea of restructuring generally means "downsizing," in raider parlance, that is. Some assets or corporate divisions consequently are sold off, and the remaining organization is streamlined, which usually means layoffs. Thereby, the raider can pay off some of the huge debt burden and generate more cash flow to cover the remaining interest payments. The assumption is that the parts are worth more if sold than the corporation as a whole is valued by investors, as reflected in stock prices. The other assumption is that the organization has gotten fat and inefficient, that people and operations can readily be pruned.

For some years, this strategy of restructuring or downsizing seemed to work fairly well, as eager investors bid up the prices of spun-off assets. But the investment mood changed, with disillusionment setting in. Campeau did not anticipate this change, and could not sell some of his divisions for the expected prices. Another raider, L. J. Hooker Corp., was not even able to sell its B. Altman department-store chain, and had to liquidate it.[18] By late 1989, many raiders in addition to Campeau were mired in debt, saddled with bankrupt companies, and finding that they could not run companies as efficiently as the bosses they had ousted. Such well-known corporate raiders as Merv Griffin and T. Boone Pickens were among those having rude awakenings.[19]

Not the least of the emerging problems coming from the organizational restructuring of the LBOs was the demoralization of the organizations involved. Massive layoffs and forced retirements, complete reassigning of

---

[17]Jeffrey A. Trachtenberg, "Campeau Assails Dun & Bradstreet's Advice to Clients Not to Ship It Goods," *Wall Street Journal*, Dec. 7, 1989, p. A4; Jeffrey A. Trachtenberg, "Heller Financial Tells Clients to Halt Shipping Their Goods to Campeau Units," *Wall Street Journal*, Dec. 15, 1989, p. A3.

[18] Barbara Rudolph, "Debacle on 34th Street," *Time*, Dec. 11, 1989, p. 77.

[19] Greenwald, "The Big Comeuppance," p. 75.

people, traumatic personnel and policy changes, destruction of accustomed lines of communication and authority—these were hardly the inputs needed to preserve stability and motivation. Worse, in many instances, the raiders, such as Campeau, in their rush to try to free up working capital to meet hefty interest charges, began their restructuring and streamlining without sufficient assessment and preparation. The operational deficiencies of Federated stores after the Campeau takeover illustrate the negative consequences of hasty major "restructuring."

Learning Insight. *Successful and constructive takeovers require good operating executives.*

A variety of factors beset corporate raiders in the late 1980s, dulling their luster. At least in some instances, the key factor was that they could not manage. It became increasingly apparent that many firms in such takeovers were not improved, but diminished.

The raiders were able to amass the financial strength for their acquisitions, but they could not handle the operational consequences. Staying power is the name of the game for true success. The comet that flares through the sky and dies brilliantly is hardly the material of success. Yet, this describes many corporate buccaneers during the 1980s—a colorful bunch of mighty egos who frightened many boardrooms. A mighty *ego* can be a strength but also a crucial weakness, as discussed in the following information box.

THE ROLE OF EGO

Reporters in the national press were quick to declare that an inflated ego was behind Campeau's reckless expansion binge. Perhaps they were right. Coming from humble beginnings, Campeau—like many other highly successful people—felt an overwhelming drive to be successful. Ego drive, or profound ambition, can be a good thing. It can be the major fuel for hard work, personal advancement, and entrepreneurship. But ego needs to be harnessed. The drive can exceed the bounds of what is prudent (just as we saw with some of the S & L excesses). When ego gets out of hand, it can lead to excessive spending. At this point, ego is no longer a positive factor, but a negative and even destructive one. As with so many things, moderation is the key to success, much more desirable than either extreme.

INVITATION TO DISCUSS
Do you think Goldsmith was also on an ego trip? If so, how might Mercer have deflated any Goldsmith's ego trip?

FOR THOUGHT AND DISCUSSION

1. Campeau bought good—even the best—properties. How could he have gone so wrong?
2. Why did the concept of synergy not appear to work for Campeau's acquisitions?
3. Are management skills transferable to retailing institutions? Discuss.
4. Do you see any ethical problems with greenmail? Why or why not?

INVITATION TO ROLE PLAY

1. You are a management consultant. How would you advise Campeau on organizational restructuring after his initial acquisitions of Allied and Federated? Do you think these moves would have made any difference?
2. You are a confidant to Robert Mercer. Would you advise him to buy out Goldsmith for the $93 million profit? What other options, if any, might he consider?

INVITATION TO RESEARCH

1. What is the status of Federated and Allied stores today? Have they overcome the Campeau-induced debacle? What conclusions can you draw from this?
2. Update Campeau's situation. Has he been able to come back?
3. What is Sir James Goldsmith doing these days?
4. How prevalent are hostile takeovers in the 1990s? How do you account for the differences from the situation in the 1980s?

16

The Alaskan Oil Spill: How Much Corporate Responsibility?

At 12:04 A.M., in the darkness of the cold Alaskan night of March 24, 1989, a huge oil tanker, the Exxon Valdez, came to an unexpected and abrupt halt. At that moment, the worst maritime oil spill in U.S. history commenced. The damage to the pristine waters, fish, and wildlife of Prince William Sound, and to the people who depended on it, was feared to be profound. Exxon, the giant petroleum firm, would show ambivalent behavior about the oil spill: responsiveness and concern, then reluctance and blame shifting, finally the grudging continuation of cleanup efforts. And so, despite the $2.5 billion the company eventually spent for cleanup efforts, its image of callousness toward the environment was not dispelled. Of course, Exxon was not alone to blame for the disaster.

THE CAPTAIN

The captain of the Exxon Valdez was Joseph Hazelwood, a 20-year Exxon veteran who had commanded the Valdez for 20 months. At age 42, he was pretty young to be captaining such a vessel, but he was regarded as a talented seaman. An honors graduate from New York Maritime College, Hazelwood was only 32 when he received his Masters License. At home on the sea, he had displayed coolheadedness, courage, and skill, qualities that helped his rapid rise. But he had a dark side as well: he was rumored to be a drinker, with a reputation for alcohol abuse.

It was never proven that Hazelwood was drunk when he captained the Exxon Valdez on March 24. Nine hours after the collision, his blood-alcohol level was .06, which is higher than the .04 considered acceptable for captains by the Coast Guard. Assuming a normal metabolism rate, this would put the level at .19 at the time of the accident, almost double the amount at which most states consider a person to be legally drunk. However, Hazelwood maintained that he had consumed a low-alcohol beverage in his cabin after the accident, the ship having been stabilized.

Fueling the suspicions about Hazelwood was the fact that he had twice been convicted of drunk driving in the preceding five years and had had his driver's license revoked three times. At the time of the accident, though he retained his license to command a super tanker, he was not permitted to drive a car. In 1985, Exxon had sent him to an alcohol rehabilitation program, but after the accident the company claimed it was not aware that his alcoholism had persisted.

After the accident, Exxon fired Hazelwood. Contrary to general belief, he was not fired for drunkeness on duty—a charge difficult to prove—but for not being on the bridge of the ship as company regulations require. Having been convicted of negligent discharge of oil, Hazelwood was sentenced, a year after the accident, to 1000 hours of community service helping clean up the oil spill. A jury had acquitted him of three more serious charges: criminal mischief, reckless endangerment, and operating a vessel while intoxicated.

THE ACCIDENT

Only two years, old the Exxon Valdez was the newest and best-equipped vessel in Exxon's fleet. It had such advanced technology as collision avoidance radar, satellite navigational aids, and depth finders.[1] Some 987 feet long, it drew 33 feet of water when loaded. It made regular trips from the Port of Valdez to the terminal at Long Beach, California, a five-day trip. On this particular trip, it was loaded with 52 million gallons of crude oil. Because of its sheer size and mass (211,000 tons) this loaded ship required a full minute to respond to any steering changes.

Still, there was no reason to expect any trouble as the Valdez left port at 9:12 P.M. on March 23, under the guidance of harbor pilot Ed Murphy. After all, 8548 tankers had made the rather routine and boring trip before this, without a serious accident. When the local pilot left the tanker at 11:24 P.M., Captain Hazelwood took command. Inexplicably, he left the bridge

[1]William C. Rempel, "Disaster at Valdez: Promises Unkept," *Los Angeles Times*, April 2, 1989, p. I-20.

and went below to his cabin, thus violating company policy that a captain stay on the bridge until the ship reaches open water. But the Valdez was still passing through the narrow waters of the Valdez Arm of Prince William Sound. Third Mate Gregory Cousins, who was not licensed to steer a vessel through the coastal waters of Alaska, was left in charge.

A short time later, the tanker radioed the Coast Guard for permission to steer a course down the empty incoming ship lane to avoid icebergs in the outgoing lane. Permission was granted, and the Valdez altered course. The Coast Guard lost radar contact with the tanker soon afterwards. The Exxon Valdez had run aground on Bligh Reef in Prince William Sound, with Hazelwood still in his cabin.

By 5:40 A.M. the Valdez had lost more than 8.8 million gallons of oil. By 7:27 A.M. the oil slick was 100 feet wide, five miles long, and spreading. Eventually, 10.1 million gallons would be spilled, threatening the year's $100 million seafood harvest, Alaska's lucrative tourism business, $750 million a year in commercial fishing, and the entire aquatic ecosystem.

The oil slick continued to spread, soon covering more than 1000 square miles (an area larger than the state of Rhode Island) and contaminating hundreds of miles of beaches. The slick eventually moved 100 miles out into the Gulf of Alaska.

BACKGROUND

Alaskan Oil

Oil and natural gas were discovered in January 1968 on the frozen north slope of Alaska's Prudhoe Bay. Tests indicated that at least 10 billion barrels of oil and 26 trillion cubic feet of natural gas were lurking below the surface. But, for years, debate raged whether this reserve should be used and how it would be transported to processing plants. Intense lobbying by Alaska and a tie-breaking vote by Vice President Spiro Agnew cleared the way for the Trans Alaska Pipe Line and Tanker Route. An oil industry pledge that the environment would be protected at all costs was a key to congressional approval of the pipeline. Alaska agreed to create a Department of Environmental Conservation (DEC) to regulate and monitor the oil industry. In 1973, construction started on the pipeline. In 1977, the four-foot diameter, 800-mile-long pipeline and ship-loading terminal were completed. Oil started flowing.

More than two million barrels a day move through this pipeline, about 25 percent of America's oil needs. Alaska has benefitted greatly. Valdez, where the ship-loading terminal is located, gets 94 percent of its tax revenues from oil. Oil-related money has made state income taxes unnecessary; the state even paid an annual oil dividend to each resident amounting to at least $800 per person. Other economic developments—jobs, roads, schools, libraries, and cultural activities—resulted from this oil prosperity. As one resident stated after the accident: "For 12 years we enjoyed the prosperity of our state's oil wealth without having to face its trade-offs—until the wreck of the Exxon Valdez."[2]

Exxon

Exxon Corporation is America's second-largest corporation and the world's third-largest oil company. In 1989, the year of the oil spill, Exxon sales were over $86 billion dollars, with profits close to $3 billion. However, dividends decreased when Exxon put aside funds to finance the cleanup and pay the legal and punitive costs for the spill. Table 16.1 shows Exxon operating statistics from 1986 to 1990.

Exxon has diversified beyond oil, but oil remains its major emphasis. With Exxon's worldwide organization and purchasing power, it was in a position to mobilize experts, equipment, planes, materials, and an army of manpower to combat the oil spill. It is unlikely that any other environmental or government agency could have done this. Yet, somehow, relief efforts were flawed.

Aleyeska

Aleyeska was born with the creation of the Trans Alaska oil project. It is a consortium of the seven oil companies that invested in the Alaskan oil venture: Exxon, British Petroleum, Mobil, Atlantic-Richfield, Amerada Hess,

Table 16.1   Exxon Operating Statistics, 1986–1990

Year	Revenues (millions)	Earnings (millions)	Dividends (dollars per share)
1986	$69,888	$5,360	$7.42
1987	76,416	4,840	3.43
1988	79,557	5,260	3.95
1989	86,656	2,975	2.32
1990	115,794	5,010	3.96

Source: Company public records.

---

[2]Art Davidson, *In the Wake of the Exxon Valdez* (San Francisco: Sierra Club Books, 1990), p. xiv.

Unocal, and Phillips Petroleum. Each company has a partial interest in Aleyeska, with Exxon having a 20 percent interest. Aleyeska brought unified efforts to the design, construction, planning, operation, safety, and personnel for the oil transportation from Prudhoe Bay to Valdez. The biggest part of this operation was in the city of Valdez, and Aleyeska played a big role in that city's affairs.

Aleyeska was also entrusted with preventing any adverse environmental effects that might be caused by this massive drilling and transportation operation. The consortium was heavily involved in the preliminaries, submitting plans for operations, safety, environmental impact, emergency response procedures, and readiness programs to the newly created Department of Environmental Conservation (DEC). The construction of the pipeline was even delayed until all plans were approved.

Unfortunately, when the accident occurred, Aleyeska failed miserably. Although charged with safeguarding against such an accident, and with providing the initial response if one should happen, Aleyeska proved unable to cope. It left the major part of the cleanup efforts to Exxon.

Other Participants

The DEC had the role of watchdog. It was empowered to enforce the environmental laws and regulations created for the Alaskan oil transportation system. However, the agency seemed more motivated to make sure oil flow was not interrupted than concerned with environmental safeguards.

Fishermen were the most adversely affected by the oil spill. Protecting fish hatcheries became a top priority for them. Unable to get enough oil containment booms, they made their own with logs, chains, and plastic. With financial backing from Exxon, these homemade booms helped to preserve the future of the industry.

Almost overnight, Valdez became a boomtown, with people pouring in to help in the cleanup. All the chaos and opportunism of any boomtown became the lot of Valdez.

CLEANUP EFFORTS

For a spill of this size, the cleanup technology is woefully inadequate. Add human carelessness and incompetence to the enormity of the oil spill, and a problem of monumental proportions was created. The timing of the disaster could hardly have been worse. Millions of fish were headed toward Prince William Sound for spawning and millions of birds were migrating north. All this fueled the cry for action.

The Technology

Basically, oil spills can be controlled in four ways: containment, collection, dispersion, and burn-off. The first priority should be containment. If the slick is prevented from spreading over a wide area, it is obviously easier to collect. But containment efforts failed here. Containment booms that can be used to surround the oil at the very earliest stages of a leak were not aboard the Exxon Valdez; the nearest booms were in the town of Valdez. Preparedness plans called for a response within two and a half hours. However, the barge used for transporting the booms was damaged and in dry dock for repairs. It took 14 hours for the first booms to arrive at the site, and by that time the slick was out of control, beyond the capability of containment.

Once an oil spill is contained, various methods can be used to collect the oil. In a skimmer operation, ships travel through a slick and "skim" off the thicker, lighter oil on the water surface and place it into larger storage barges. The problem with an oil slick of this magnitude is finding enough storage barges to hold the collected oil so that the skimming can be resumed.

Chemical dispersants are another possibility. These react with the oil much like dish soap does with grease. However, these chemicals do not actually remove the oil, and they are themselves toxic. There is disagreement as to which of the two evils is worse.

Finally, the oil can be set on fire, which has obvious drawbacks: controlling the fire, air pollution, and ash fallout. This alternative also requires calm waters. But although the weather cooperated at first during the Exxon oil spill, bureaucratic bungling and disagreement impeded early burn-off efforts. Then the weather worsened.

Operational Problems

A number of organizations were involved in cleaning up the spill. They all had the same objective, but they disagreed wildly on how best to cope with the problem. Besides Aleyeska, Exxon, and the DEC, other groups involved were the Department of Fish and Game, the U.S. Coast Guard, the Environmental Protection Agency, fishermen, and various conservation groups. Their vastly different viewpoints created major impediments.

Exxon assumed immediate responsibility and control. The president of the subsidiary Exxon Shipping, Frank Iarossi, was assigned the cleanup task. Because the mechanical means to contain the spill and collect it from the water were either not available or not in working order, and because of the size of the slick, Iarossi's solution was to use dispersants, fire or both. But this met with strong disapproval by local groups and government agencies. Debate raged for four days, while the problem escalated. By the time permission was granted to use dispersants and a permit was issued for burning, the calm weather conditions had turned into gale-force winds, a blizzard, and 20-foot waves. Planes scheduled to spray the chemicals were grounded; boats to be used for sea operations could not leave their safe harbors. The monster spill was unchecked. Before long, virtually every island in Prince William Sound was surrounded by oil, and over 800 miles of beaches were covered. The battle plan now changed from recovering the oil to protecting the fish hatcheries and cleaning up the beaches. Dissension, confusion, and a lack of unified and decisive action had allowed the monster to spread.

There was one aspect of the operation that Exxon *could* control: the lightering of the ship. Lightering was the process by which the ship's remaining 11 million gallons of oil were off-loaded to another tanker. Exxon feared that the ship might split, thus releasing even more oil and geometrically worsening the situation. But even lightering the ship was criticized as self-serving, since it enabled Exxon to profit by sending the oil on to Long Beach.

CONSEQUENCES

After a 16-month investigation into the accident, the National Transportation Safety Board issued a report on July 31, 1990. The report cited the failures of the ship's captain, its third mate, Exxon Shipping Company, the U.S. Coast Guard, and Alaskan authorities in the disaster.

The report concluded that Captain Hazelwood was not able to supervise the tanker at the time of the accident because he was impaired from alcohol, that Third Mate Cousins, the man in charge at the moment the tanker ran into the reef, was unable to avoid the accident because of fatigue and overwork. Exxon was blamed for failing to provide a fit Master and a rested and sufficient crew and failing to monitor Hazelwood's drinking problems. The U.S. Coast Guard was criticized for inadequately tracking ships and icebergs in the area. And the state of Alaska was criticized for not having a pilot aboard past the dangerous reef.[3]

On October 8, 1991, a federal judge in Anchorage, Alaska, approved a settlement reached between Exxon, the Alaskan government, and the U.S. Justice Department over criminal charges arising from the accident. The judge's approval effectively ended all state and federal lawsuits resulting from the spill. Exxon agreed to pay a total of $1.025 billion in fines and restitution payments through the year 2001. The settlement guaranteed,

[3]*Facts on File*, Oct. 10, 1991, p. 602.

however, the rights of native Alaskans and other private litigants to continue to bring separate lawsuits against Exxon.

The spill's immediate destruction of fish, wildlife, and unspoiled beaches shocked the nation. Pictures of oil-covered birds and animals, of beaches covered with a gooey layer of crude oil, became commonplace in the media.

However, after the initial confusion and delay, Exxon employed thousands of temporary workers in a massive cleanup operation. Unfortunately, these cleanup operations were not without their downside. Beaches were left sterilized, unable to support life. Thousands of people came to collect the $16.67 an hour Exxon paid for clean-up labor, but unsanitary conditions, crime, and garbage were byproducts of these efforts.

By early May, 1989, Exxon had revised its cleanup plan, leaving some of the cleanup work to wave action and nature. By the end of the summer, much of the surface pollution had been eradicated, though there was the question of how much had sunk to the ocean floor as thick black gunk. Efforts continued in the following summers, with the company spending over $2 billion in cleanup efforts.

The massive cleanup seemed to pay off. By the fall of 1990, little evidence of the oil remained on beaches, although below the surface it still was a problem. By November 1990, about 85 percent of the shoreline had been adequately cleaned.

Environmentalists' worst fears were apparently not realized. Cold weather did not prevent the oil slick from disintegrating. Even the predicted destruction of fish and wildlife did not occur. Estimates were that up to 2000 otters and some 33,000 birds may have died. More worrisome was what the long-term effects might be, especially the effects of the oil deposits that sunk to the ocean floor. Could these release harmful hydrocarbons for several years, contaminating the food chain and ruining the catches of shrimp, salmon, herring, and crabs?

The impact of the Exxon Valdez oil spill could have been much worse: about 10.1 million gallons were released from the accident, but the tanker was loaded with 52 million gallons. One wonders at the environmental impact if five times the volume of oil had escaped.

Exxon's Public-Image Problems

Exxon's reaction to the spill, its crisis management and handling of the publicity, did not cast it in good light. The media and the public remained hostile to the company. Environmentalists, including Ralph Nader, castigated the company. Customers were urged to boycott Exxon and cut up their credit cards. Some 40,000 cards were destroyed, but this was out of 7 million cards outstanding.

Even some business executives were critical. Responding to a survey, 200 Americans and Canadian executives said that Exxon was slow to react, attempted to shift blame on others, ducked its responsibility, failed to manage the local political scene, lacked preparation, seemed arrogant, was negligent, lost control of information processes, and ignored opportunities to build public support.[4]

Perhaps Exxon's apology was late. But it did take full-page ads in newspapers nationwide a week after the accident with a statement from its CEO, Lawrence Rawl, that the company was sorry and that it would meet all of its obligations. Rawl was criticized for not personally appearing at the site of the spill. From a public relations standpoint, this perhaps was a mistake. He defended his lack of presence in a later interview:

> The tanker went on the rocks, and visually it was perfect for TV and not too bad for pictures of oily birds in the printed media. How would those environmentalists ever let that go? If I just went up there and said I was sorry? I went on TV and said I was sorry. I said a dozen times that we're going to clean it up. . . . [I]t wouldn't have made any difference if I showed up and made a speech in the town forum. I wasn't going to spend the summer there; I had other things to do, obviously.[5]

Certainly, Exxon spent money: besides the $2 billion it spent on the cleanup itself, it reimbursed the city of Valdez, the state of Alaska, and the federal government for direct expenses, wildlife rescue, and rehabilitation. It also gave Alaskan fishermen $200 million for their merely having a fishing license and the previous year's tax return.

What it failed to do was immediate containment and cleanup. Perhaps most important, it failed to convey a public image of sufficient concern, openness, and repentance. In an accident of this magnitude, surely the CEO, as the company's figurehead, should be the company's spokesperson.[6] Lawrence Rawl's defensive mindset was perhaps best expressed by his own statements just a year later:

> There were 30 million birds that went through the sound last summer, and only 30,000 carcasses have been recovered. Just look at how many ducks are killed in the Mississippi Delta in one hunting day in December! People . . . said,

---

[4]James E. Lukaszewski, "How Vulnerable Are You? The Lessons from Valdez," *Public Relations Quarterly* 34, Fall 1989, pp. 5–6.

[5]Richard Behar, "Exxon Strikes Back," *Time*, March 26, 1990, p. 62.

[6]William J. Small, "Exxon Valdez: How to Spend Billions and Still Get a Black Eye," *Public Relations Review* 17, Spring 1991, p. 9.

"This is worse than Bhopal." I say, "Hell, Bhopal killed more than 3,000 people and injured 200,000 others!" Then they say, "Well, if you leave the people out, it was worse than Bhopal."[7]

ANALYSIS

Who Can We Blame?

The Exxon Valdez accident was not as simple as a drunken sailor steering a tanker onto rocks. Many events led to the shipwreck and to the disastrous handling of the situation that followed. We know how Exxon handled the situation. Would some other oil firm—British Petroleum for example—have handled it better? Or worse? Business, government, and society all contributed to the disaster. The finger of blame cannot realistically point to just one person or one organization.

The common denominator was complacency. For 12 years, oil flowed through the pipeline and waterways without serious mishap. The few minor mishaps that happened were handled without trouble: "A decade with few major mishaps lulled oil companies and regulatory agencies into complacency, driving down demand for cleanup crews and expertise."[8]

For example, at Traffic Valdez, the Coast Guard commander requested that the tracking system be updated to add another radar station at Bligh Island. Instead, as a result of budget cuts, the existing 100,000-watt radar unit was replaced with a 50,000-watt unit. With such weakened radar, controllers were often unable to track ships well before they reached Bligh Island and the wider waters of Prince William Sound.

Budget cuts at Aleyeska also affected disaster readiness. When the pipeline system was new, equipment, procedures, and trained personnel were organized and ready. Scheduled periodic drills were conducted at considerable cost. By 1989, when the accident occurred, drills had been discontinued, equipment was in disrepair, and trained personnel had been reassigned.

The Alaskan people also grew complacent. Each year, when they received their $800 windfall checks, they took oil's presence a little more for granted; any criticisms or worries were muted.

Even the Reagan administration can be faulted for creating a climate of less regulation and more reliance on businesses to govern themselves. Yet, when left to govern themselves, businesses find it difficult to balance short-run profit objectives against long-term environmental "might happens." (See the Issue box for a discussion of *the ethics of accidents*.)

---

[7]Behar, p. 63.

[8]Kenneth R. Sheets, "Would You Believe $16.67 an Hour to Scrub Rocks?" *U.S. News & World Report*, April 17, 1989, p. 48.

ISSUE: THE ETHICS OF ACCIDENTS

When an accident occurs, does it automatically mean the person or organization involved has acted unethically? The issue is often murky. Less murky is the issue of legal responsibility. Damage suits on behalf of victims abound, regardless of how culpable the deep-pocketed defendant is. Ethics and legality are not always synonymous.

The ethics issue hinges on carelessness, negligence, or bad judgment,—perhaps in product or plant design or in maintenance (e.g., placing victims in a risky situation). But what about acts of God or terrorists which cannot reasonably be foreseen—the unexpected wind shear that destroys a plane, the terrorists' bomb? Hardliners will argue that these should be foreseen and avoided. But is this expecting too much, even of a prudent person?

The issue becomes more complicated when several parties are negligent, as was true in the Exxon Valdez situation. It can be argued that, with adequate radar, the Coast Guard could have warned the ship in time, or, that if better disaster planning and training had been in place, the spill could have been contained with far less environmental damage. If Exxon was guilty of unethical practices because of carelessness or negligence, so was the Coast Guard, Aleyeska, the state of Alaska, the Environmental Protection Agency, and others. Of course, Exxon was the organization with the "deep pockets."

INVITATION TO DISCUSS

1. If a person uses a product in a dangerous manner for which it was not intended—such as using a power lawn mower to trim a hedge—is the seller guilty of unethical behavior? Is the seller vulnerable to a damage suit?

2. If Captain Hazelwood had been completely sober and in his correct station on the ship and a severe and unexpected storm had forced the Valdez onto the rocks, would Exxon have been guilty of unethical behavior? How about legal vulnerability? Do you think Exxon should foot the major responsibility for the cleanup in this scenario?

Can This Happen Again?

For more than 10 years, no serious mishaps had occurred, despite thousands of trips and millions of tanker miles. Yet, somehow, the right combination of circumstances came together. Could this happen again? Hopefully, all the involved parties have learned from this experience. Better safeguards have been established, controls have been tightened, and more resources have been committed to radar and prevention training. We hope any future accidents will be less serious and more quickly controlled. Yet, it is naive to think that we have seen the last oil spill.

Safeguards Needed

After every serious accident, recriminations rage (which is not always constructive); preventative measures are proposed (which should be constructive, if followed up on). Such is certainly the case with the Exxon Valdez episode: what measures should be taken to minimize the chances of any future occurrence?

Obvious measures are better radar and closer monitoring of potential problems, improved and rigorously maintained disaster training, continued efforts at improving technology for coping with oil spills, well-planned and rehearsed procedures for handling any future mishaps—and, perhaps, such imposed safeguards as *double-hulled tankers*. (For a discussion of these controversial vessels, see the following Issue box.)

Whether these ambitious safeguards could be maintained during a decade or more with no major disasters is doubtful, human nature being what it is. A further motivation to allow high-levels of preparedness to slip is the fact that no human lives were lost in this worst scenario, only a few birds and animals, as the nonenvironmentalists, including Exxon Chairman Lawrence Rawl, would hasten to point out.

ISSUE: SHOULD DOUBLE-HULLED TANKERS BE REQUIRED?

None of the tankers using the Valdez terminal at the time of the spill were double-hulled. Double hulled tankers had been proposed as a safeguard against spills in the initial planning of the pipeline in the 1970s, but they were not adopted.

There are some tradeoffs. Although double-hulled tankers would lower the probability of oil leakages occurring from a mishap, they cost up to 8 percent more to build, and they have only 60 percent of the capacity of a single-hulled tanker. This latter factor is the more serious limitation. To maintain the same daily flow of oil, two additional tankers would be needed for every five single-hull ships, meaning much more traffic and more docking facilities.

So, although we may have safer ships, the possibility for human error would be increased. And human error is usually responsible for such mishaps, not the ships. Drug and alcohol testing and tougher personnel rules and training have been proposed for minimizing the probability of human error. But can human error ever be eliminated?

INVITATION TO DISCUSS
Do you think employees should be tested for drug and alcohol abuse? Would this eliminate human error?

WHAT CAN BE LEARNED?

Learning Insight. *The environmental lobby is powerful today and growing stronger. Moral: business beware.*

It should come as no surprise to business executives that public sentiment is moving strongly toward protecting the environment, at almost any cost. Many see this as a welcome—and needed—change from the old frontier attitude that the environment must be conquered. But the new attitudes pose new constraints on business; they lead to less tolerance, public decrying, and strong pressure on governmental bodies to take punitive and restrictive measures.

This is the third case in this book in which the environment was an issue. (The other cases were Union Carbide's polluting of the Ohio Valley and its catastrophe in Bhopal.) Exxon's management may have been surprised at the public outcry over an accident that "only killed a few birds and animals." "After all, the company did not deliberately set out to wreak havoc on the environment," and "no human lives were lost," as the company would maintain. But these attempts to defend the company were lost on a general public unwilling to accept excuses, quick to blame "insensitive corporations," and readily supported by the media and by politicians eager to gain publicity as "defenders of the environment."

In this milieu, the prudent business firm does not try to buck the tide, but instead exerts extraordinary precautions to prevent anything that smacks of environmental degradation.

Learning Insight. *Many environmental problems lend themselves to graphic portrayal by the media. This exacerbates the condemnation of the business firm involved.*

The polluting smokestack, the contaminated pond or stream, oil-covered birds and animals—these are easily caught on camera and transmitted to a concerned and indignant public, thus fanning cries for punishment and preventative governmental action. No other questionable business dealings lend themselves to so much graphic portrayal.

This is all the more reason for business firms to tread carefully in such matters, to seek the image of an environmental defender.

Learning Insight. *In grave public concerns, the top corporate executive must assume an active role, lest the company gain the reputation of being uncaring and arrogant.*

One of the harshest criticisms levied at Exxon was that it was uncaring and arrogant. Although Chairman Rawl defended his actions for not personally taking charge, this did not mollify the critics. No amount of company institutional advertising (i.e., nonproduct advertising aimed at public relations) achieved what might have been gained by Rawl's prompt and concerned presence.

Learning Insight. *An accident saddles the firm with major public-image challenges, the response to which can either enhance or denigrate the firm's reputation.*

Although a serious environmental or product-safety accident is about the worst scenario any corporate executive can envision, what is usually overlooked is that such scenarios present an opportunity to enhance the firm's reputation as a caring and concerned presence.

To convert catastrophe into some gain is very difficult to accomplish. (In Chapter 21, we encounter a firm that did this to an exemplary degree.) It usually requires an out-of-the-ordinary sacrifice of short-term profits, a real unselfish commitment to correcting the situation and helping the victims regardless of cost, and an attitude of openness and caring in all public actions and statements. Even then, of course, the efforts may be misunderstood and condemned, as were the efforts of Warren Anderson, the chairman of Union Carbide during the Bhopal disaster. But there is far greater risk of a destroyed reputation when such a spirit of openness and concern is not publicly conveyed.

Learning Insight. *Firms need to plan for worst-case scenarios.*

We have encountered this insight before. In many of these ethical blunders, the worst-case possibilities are not considered, not planned for, not even given any thought. Yet the lesson is clear: the worst-case scenario, by some happenstance or human error or whatever, is always a possibility, even though the probability seems remote. Therefore, plan for the worst scenario, and all other mishaps should be more easily handled.

But such planning requires commitment. It is often difficult to get this, because costs are involved, and short-run profits may be somewhat curbed. But catastrophes occur just frequently enough that such contingency planning has merit. Many parties could have benefited from contingency planning before the great oil spill: Exxon, Aleyeska, Alaska's Department of Environmental Conservation, the U.S. Coast Guard, etc. Easier said than done, but our worst-case disaster would be curbed—or at least quickly and effectively reacted to—with such foresight.

FOR THOUGHT AND DISCUSSION

1. Do you think the federal government should have taken over the cleanup operation rather than leaving it primarily up to Exxon, with

superficial help from various other bodies such as Aleyeska? Why or why not?

2. How can an organization guard against culpable human error like Captain Hazelwood's? An airline pilot's errors, a bus driver's, a railroad engineer's? Are your suggested measures an unacceptable invasion of privacy? Discuss.

3. Do you think Hazelwood was unfairly treated? Why or why not?

4. Do you think Chairman Rawl of Exxon should have been publicly chastised and forced to resign? Why or why not?

5. In your opinion, was too much fuss made over the loss of a few thousand birds and animals (out of millions)? Please discuss.

INVITATION TO ROLE PLAY:

1. You are the staff adviser to Lawrence Rawl, the CEO of Exxon, at the time of the Alaskan spill. How would you advise him to handle this situation? Be as specific as you can.

2. You are Captain Hazelwood, confronted with the reality of the worst oil spill in U.S. history. You were resting in your cabin when the crash occurred. You rush up on deck and survey the disaster. What do you do now? How do you defend your conduct? Can you possibly salvage your highly successful career?

INVITATION TO RESEARCH

1. What happened to Hazelwood after this catastrophe?

2. Is Lawrence Rawl still actively managing Exxon?

3. What safety regulations have been enacted to prevent a similar disaster from occurring?

CHAPTER 17

Dow Corning and Silicone Breast Implants: Another Dalkon Shield?

On February 10, 1992, Dow Corning Corporation replaced its top executive, John S. Ludington. The same day, it released hundreds of internal memos and other documents that revealed the company had received complaints for decades of medical problems associated with its silicone breast implants.

Was the released data so incriminating that it would bring down the company as the Dalkon Shield brought down A.H. Robins? Should silicone implants have been taken off the market years before? Was the company guilty of deception, fraud, cover-up, and not caring for human life and welfare? Was it a despicable corporate citizen? Judge for yourself as the picture unfolds.

ATTEMPTING TO STEM THE EVER-MOUNTING CRISIS

The man selected to replace Ludington on February 10 was Keith R. McKennon, 58 years old, executive vice president responsible for research and development, manufacturing and engineering at Dow Chemical.

McKennon had a reputation as a negotiator and peacemaker, and this, the *Wall Street Journal* speculated, might signal a more conciliatory attitude by the company. The fact that McKennon had struggled with lymph cancer seven years before might give him special rapport with implant patients who were concerned about their health. In the past, McKennon had dealt effectively and diplomatically with a major safety issue: Dow Chemical's Agent Orange defoliant, which was used during the Vietnam War. He had also handled another crisis situation effectively, this one concerning Dow's drug for morning sickness during pregnancy, Bendectin. The drug was the subject of numerous health and safety lawsuits. McKennon's experience in dealing publicly and internally with these problems uniquely qualified him, so the company thought, in coping with one of its biggest crises: the silicone breast implant.

To his credit, McKennon took several quick actions, as well as actions costly to the firm. These included paying the medical costs of women who wanted to have their breast implants surgically removed but could not afford to do so. (The price for removing breast implants typically ranges from $4500 to $6500.) He also proposed sitting down with the Food and Drug Administration (FDA), its advisory panel, the physicians on both sides of the controversy, and the women involved, all toward seeking a consensus about new research that needed to be done (at company expense).[1]

PRELUDE

On January 6, 1992, Food & Drug Administration Commissioner Dr. David A. Kessler, ordered a 45-day moratorium on the sale and use of silicone gel implants. He urged manufacturers to stop marketing the devices and surgeons to stop inserting them in women. Other countries, such as Spain and Australia, quickly followed; whereas Canada, Britain, and France reviewed their policies.

A horde of lawyers eagerly waited in the wings. An estimated 1 to 2 million women in the United States alone had received breast implants over the last 30 years. If the implants could be proven sufficiently dangerous, the potential liability suits could run in the billions of dollars.

Instances of medical problems with the implants had been surfacing, as listed above, and lawsuits were increasing. For example:

Soon after Karen Reid felt something pop in one of her implanted breasts, she developed immunological problems and noticed nodules popping up on her arms and legs. Convinced that the source of her problems was silicone that had leaked from a ruptured breast implant, she sued for millions in damages from the manufacturer, Dow Corning Corporation.[2]

Kali Korn was diagnosed with scleroderma a decade after she had silicone implants inserted for cosmetic reasons. In scleroderma the skin thickens and stiffens and there is a buildup of fibrous tissue in the lungs and other organs. Doctors removed the implants and her condition improved.[3]

---

[1]Thomas M. Burton and Joan E. Rigdon, "Management Shake-Up at Dow Corning Signals a More Conciliatory Attitude," *Wall Street Journal*, Feb. 12, 1992, p. A3.
[2]Example from John Carey, "I'm Frightened for My Life," *Business Week*, Jan. 20, 1992, p. 32.
[3]Example from "A Strike Against Silicone," *Time*, Jan. 20, 1992, p. 40.

Mariann Hopkins claimed that her 1976 implants ruptured and damaged her immune system. The trial resulted in a $7.34 million jury award against Dow Corning.[4] Internal company documents that were rather incriminating surfaced during the Hopkins trial.

Acting on pressures resulting from these cases, as well as from revelations of internal company memos expressing early concern about the implants, the FDA imposed the moratorium until further evaluation of the possible link between silicone gel and immune system diseases could be made.

HISTORY OF BREAST IMPLANTS

In the early 1960s, Dow Corning and several other firms began marketing silicone-filled breast implants. Although most women opted for this operation for cosmetic purposes, about 20 percent did so after the travail of a mastectomy. Such implants became the third most popular form of cosmetic surgery, after nose and liposuction operations.

Breast implants were not regulated by the FDA until 1976. They were already on the market when Congress for the first time empowered the agency to regulate medical devices, which included implants. This was largely due to the Dalkon Shield catastrophe, which motivated the May 28, 1976 Medical Device Amendments.

Concerns about the safety of such implants began increasing by 1990, triggered, as we have seen, by a series of lawsuits and some multimillion-dollar awards for women claiming that the implants deteriorated and the silicone leached throughout their bodies, causing serious health problems. Thus, uneasiness had been surfacing before the January 1992 moratorium.

In April 1991, the FDA told implant manufacturers to prove scientifically that their products were safe. In November 1991, the FDA advisory panel judged that the data the manufacturers submitted were insufficient to demonstrate safety, but decided to leave the implants on the market because of what it called a "public health need" for the devices. This permission, of course, was revoked with the moratorium, which called for a review of new information that had come to light in the recent product-liability suits against Dow Corning.

An investigation by *Business Week* some months earlier had uncovered evidence that the industry had been aware for at least a decade of animal studies linking implants to cancer and other illnesses.[5] But these studies,

---

[4]Example from Tim Smart, "This Man Sounded the Silicone Alarm—in 1976," *Business Week*, Jan. 27, 1992, p. 34.

[5]Tim Smart, "Breast Implants: What Did the Industry Know, and When" *Business Week*, June 10, 1991, p. 94.

which suggested some risks for humans, were not publicized until the more recent court cases.

A Whistleblower

Thomas D. Talcott had been a Dow Corning materials engineer for 24 years. In 1976, he quit his job in a dispute over the safety of the implants. He had helped develop the silicone gel that the company earlier used to fill implants. When Dow switched to a more liquid gel designed to make the implants softer, Talcott believed the thinner gel could migrate through the body, causing harm, and he wanted no part of that. After leaving Dow Corning, he worked for two other implant makers, then started his own materials-consulting business.

Talcott's warnings were unheeded and his quitting Dow Corning in protest went ignored—until 1991. Then he testified as an expert witness in the California lawsuit brought by Mariann Hopkins, and was instrumental in her $7.34 million jury award against Dow Corning. "The manufacturers and surgeons have been performing experimental surgery on humans," he told a congressional panel in December 1991.[6] He obtained a list of confidential documents, which he circulated to the head of the FDA 's advisory panel, top FDA officials, and Congress. This was a factor in the FDA's decision to impose a 45-day moratorium on the sale of implants.

Dow Corning attempted to refute Talcott's allegations in a January 13th press conference. Company officials restated their contention that breast implants were safe, and they dismissed the memos as part of the normal give-and-take of scientific debate. The next day, however, the company halted implant production.

Company officials further questioned Talcott's objectivity and integrity, noting that he earned $400 an hour for his expert testimony. He "left as a disgruntled employee. You've got to question to some degree his motive," said Dan Hayes, president of Dow Corning's breast-implant subsidiary.[7]

The Company, Dow Corning

Dow Corning was incorporated in Michigan in 1943 by Corning Glass Works and Dow Chemical Company. It is owned equally by these two major corporations. Dow Corning is principally engaged in the development, production, and sale of silicone and related products. Corporate offices and principal R & D facilities are in Midland, Michigan.

[6]Smart, "Breast Implants," p. 94.
[7]Tim Smart, "This Man Sounded the Silicone Alarm," p. 34.

Although far smaller than its parents, Dow Corning is still of considerable size. Sales in 1990 were $1.7 billion, with a net income of $171 million. As of December 31, 1990, there were approximately 8000 employees. Although the company was a leading manufacturer of implants, this business represented less than 1 percent of the company's product line and had had five years of financial losses. Robert Rylee, Dow Corning's health care general manager, said that the company had been staying in the implant business because the medical profession and "millions of women" have been "counting on us."[8]

The Role of Lawsuits

Although the FDA vacillated on declaring a moratorium on implants until January 1992, earlier lawsuits were critical and damaging to the company. In 1984, a San Francisco federal court jury concluded that the company had committed fraud in marketing its implants as safe, and awarded Maria Stern $1.5 million in punitive damages. United States District Judge Marilyn Hall Patel wrote that the company's own studies "cast considerable doubt on the safety of the product," doubt which was not disclosed to patients, and she said that the jury could conclude that Dow's actions "were highly reprehensible."[9]

In 1985, after the Stern case, Dow Corning included a package insert with the product, warning of the possibility of immune-system sensitivity and other medical problems should the implant rupture. This was apparently intended to blunt subsequent legal contentions that the company had not adequately disclosed potential risks.

But in 1987, Dow Corning discounted the immune-system problem, maintaining that silicone of improved purity was now being used.

Following the settlement of the Hopkins case in 1991 (in which whistle-blower Talcott was the key plaintiff witness), hundreds of women began filing suits, alleging that their implants had deteriorated and caused serious medical problems. Some lawyers began comparing the legal possibilities to the multibillion-dollar litigation over the Dalkon Shield.

Dow Corning and the other implant makers still downplayed the legal dangers, pointing out that the awarded damages were not very high in the majority of cases, since health problems were relatively modest. But Ralph Nader's Public Citizens Health Research Group now joined the battle, and trial lawyers began organizing to coordinate attacks. Pressure was mount-

[8]"Dow Corning Makes Changes in Top Posts," *Wall Street Journal*, Feb. 11, 1992, p. A4.
[9]Smart, "Breast Implants," p. 98.

ing for full disclosure of all documents relating to the silicone implants, and Dow Corning capitulated on February 10, 1992.

Although the newly-released company documents did not disclose cancer and immune-system problems, they did show a long history of complaints, leaky implants, production problems, and concern for public relations. Listing the complaints received required nearly 20 pages of computer printouts. Most complaints involved rupture of the implant, but there were also reports of leakage, discoloration, bubbles, sterilization, infection, optical nerve atrophy, and tumors.

SHIFTING FDA POSITION

Although the early Dow Corning studies with rats showed the presence of malignant tumors in up to 80 percent of the test animals, the figures were so high that the review panel considered the research suspect and inconclusive. Another Dow study 10 years later found that tumors could be induced in rats when foreign agents, such as silicone, were put in them. But FDA officials, who again reviewed the research concluded that the rat studies provided no proof that humans would be similarly affected.

The FDA also vacillated on banning the sale of an implant made by Bristol-Myers. A link was apparently found between the foam used to coat the device and a cancer-causing agent, 2-toluene diamine (TDA). The foam was primarily used in automobile air and oil filters, and one could question its use in breast implants. Indeed, in the 1970s, the FDA banned TDA's use in hair dyes because of increased risk of birth defects. Bristol-Myers withdrew its implant following FDA disapproval. But on April 17, 1991, the FDA seemed to reverse itself, playing down the cancer risk in public pronouncements.

Many, including lawmakers were wondering why the FDA had not acted more forcefully regarding an apparently unsafe product. On April 26, 1991, Representative Ted Weiss (D-N.Y.), chairman of a subcommittee studying the implant issue, criticized the agency for moving so slowly: "FDA documents indicate that for more than 10 years, FDA scientists have expressed concerns about the safety of silicone breast implants that were frequently ignored by FDA officials."[10] The agency offered the excuse of having higher priority matters to deal with.

Now, with pressure mounting steadily for action by the FDA, the moratorium was issued.

---

[10] *Ibid*, p. 95.

Explanation for FDA Vacillation

Several factors appear to have contributed to the FDA's foot-dragging:

1. The health dangers were not as well defined and severe as those in such cases as the Dalkon Shield. One could wonder whether the still rather few cases where problems arose (one out of several million operations) were not blown out of proportion by trial lawyers and some activists.

2. The FDA's advisory panels—medical experts upon which the FDA relies—may not have been completely unbiased and objective. For example, two years after the 1976 law gave the FDA jurisdiction over medical devices, its advisory panel recommended that implants be so classified that manufacturers could sell them without having to prove they were safe. This advisory panel was heavily staffed with plastic surgeons. And plastic surgeons are the medical specialty most heavily involved in implant surgery, to the tune of some $450 million a year in medical fees.

3. The FDA does not have the personnel or the budget to do all the research needed for approval of a new drug or medical device. Therefore, although it scrutinizes the results of industry research, it has to trust the accuracy, objectivity, and full disclosure of the pharmaceutical manufacturers.

The Power of the FDA

A curious and unhappy anomaly exists with respect to the FDA: it is entrusted with assuring the safety of all medical drugs and devices in the United States, but it is rather a toothless watchdog. Unlike most other federal agencies, it lacks the legal clout to subpoena a company's internal records if a problem is suspected. Nor has it been able to use emergency powers to pull a dangerous drug from the market.

Pressure is building to increase the FDA's scrutiny of medical drugs and devices. In particular, some are advocating postapproval monitoring. Such surveillance would expand the evaluation from a few hundred or thousand clinical trials over a relatively short period of time to many thousands and even millions over a lengthy time period. Thus, long-term side effects and risks could be uncovered that never could be under normal procedures.

Damned If You Do and Damned If You Don't

The implant controversy accentuates a familiar dilemma for the FDA. On the one hand, the FDA is pressured by lawyers, aggrieved victims, activists, and some legislators to ban a drug or a medical device for being unsafe and putting users at risk. On the other hand, sizable numbers of people are willing to accept some risk in the quest for improved health, longevity, or simply for cosmetic beauty reasons, such as a bigger bust. Who do you please? The answer is that you cannot please everyone, you cannot avoid criticism, you can always be second-guessed, and, even worse, have your objectivity questioned. Such is the unenviable position of Dr. Kessler and the FDA.

On February 7, 1992, the *Wall Street Journal* reported that a group of concerned women and doctors together sued the FDA, alleging that its moratorium on silicone breast implants was illegal and unconstitutional.[11] "The FDA has torn loose from its legal moorings and spread fear and panic among women, with no scientific basis," Stanley Brand, an attorney for the group, asserted at a news conference. Pulling silicone implants off the market would "constitute a major tragedy for hundreds of thousands of women who would benefit from them," said one of the plaintiffs, John Woods, a plastic surgeon at the Mayo Clinic. The suit also argued that silicone is widely used in testicular implants, pacemakers, heart valves, needles and syringes, none of which had been banned by the FDA.

Further criticism was levelled that a senior aide to Dr. Kessler was biased against implants because her husband was a senior attorney for the Public Citizen Litigation Group and its director, Sidney Wolfe, a leading critic of silicone implants.

IN DEFENSE OF THE INDUSTRY

Were Dow Corning and the other implant makers guilty of deception, greed, and callousness to product safety and public health? (An article in *Time* broadened the scope of the question: "Can Drug Firms be Trusted?")[12] Is the trusting relationship between the medical-products industry and the FDA being violated?

Dr. Kenneth Kaitin of the Center for the Study of Drug Development at Tufts University, observed: "If a drug has to be pulled from the market, it's very bad for public relations, financially and in every possible way. It just doesn't make sense that they [manufacturers] would intentionally conceal real problems."[13]

With the controversy heating up, Dow Corning initially released 90 corporate documents requested by the FDA. Robert Rylee, expressed his

---

[11]Bruce Ingersoll, "FDA's Moratorium on Breast Implants Prompts a Lawsuit," *Wall Street Journal*, Feb. 7,. 1992, p. B5A.

[12]Christine Gorman, "Can Drug Firms Be Trusted?" *Time*, Feb. 10, 1992, pp. 42–46.

[13]Gorman, p. 43.

concerns about such publicity: "In fact we are doing nothing more than fanning the flames created by contingency-fee lawyers who base their cases against manufacturers not on what the scientific evidence shows, but on 15-year-old memos that state one person's opinion about what research should have been done."[14] (See the following Issue box concerning possible excesses of *litigation*.)

Other Proponents of Breast Implants

Through early 1992, about 3500 women had complained to the FDA that their implants caused pain, infection, and hardness. Many of these women said that migrating gel from ruptured implants had caused autoimmune diseases, arthritis and scleroderma, a skin-tightening disease. Implants can also delay detection of breast cancer. But the proportion of women having problems with their implants was still relatively small.

Not the least of the voices raised in favor of silicone implants were those of many women. On the night of February 7, 1992, the prime-time TV program 20/20 questioned a number of models about their use of implants. Overwhelmingly, they responded that such breast enhancers were not only desirable but necessary to earn a living. The general consensus was that the implants resulted in increased assignments, with income tripling or quadrupling. Without hesitation, these women stated that they would accept any slight risk in order to meet the modern standards of beauty and thereby safeguard their economic livelihood. They said that if such implants were banned in this country they would have no choice but to go to Mexico or other foreign countries to have the operation performed.

Virginia Postrel, editor of *Reason* magazine, has argued that many products in common use by women carry some health risks—for example, both the Pill and tampons (which, unlike breast implants, have been definitely linked with fatalities caused by Toxic Shock Syndrome). Postrel condemned the notion that "political appointees in Washington will decree what's necessary and what's better, with help from puritanical pressure groups."[15]

As the debate heated up, a powerful media and lobbying campaign surfaced in late 1991. The nation's plastic surgeons and implant makers flooded Congress and the media with their side of the story: women's satisfaction with their implants. In October 1991, 400 women, accompanied by their plastic surgeons, flew to Washington to lobby members of Congress. A massive letter-writing campaign resulted in thousands of letters to

[14]"Fanning the Flames," *Forbes*, Feb. 17, 1992, p. 30.
[15]Virginia I. Postrel, "Is This An FDA Right?" *Cleveland Plain Dealer*, Feb. 1, 1992, p. 5C.

ISSUE: IS LITIGATION GETTING OUT OF HAND?

The publicity about the dangers of silicone implants represented a bonanza for many trial lawyers. As of February 1992, more than 1000 lawsuits had already had been filed on behalf of women who claimed they were harmed by the devices. With the February 10 release of more Dow Corning documents, it became obvious that many more suits would be filed. In what seemed on the verge of becoming a feeding frenzy, some lawyers had:

- Set up toll-free telephone numbers to encourage more litigation.
- Advertised in newspapers, on billboards, and on TV with the themes, "We can help" and "Learn the facts and your rights about breast implants."[16]
- Held conventions to discuss strategies in breast-implant suits.

In its February 17, 1992, issue, *Forbes* magazine reported on the skyrocketing cost of tort suits in the United States.[17] The rewards for lawyers can be huge in such suits. Lawyers usually work on contingency fees for such damage suits, whereby no fee is charged if the suits fail but 30 percent or more of any proceeds (which may run into the millions) are charged if the actions are successful.

On the other hand, legal action and its threat can be a powerful deterrent to · reckless or uncaring corporate actions. For the person who has been harmed, it provides a needed recourse. Sometimes deficiencies of regulatory agencies can be uncovered and corrected.

The problem seems one of degree—that is, too many lawyers promoting as much business as they can. Abusive practices can creep in such as frivolous lawsuits; the use of expert witnesses, sometimes called "hired guns," who do not always have the right qualifications but are experienced in impressing jurors and ignoring the benefits of drugs and medical devices while attacking problems in what may be a small percentage of cases.

Vice President Dan Quayle has pushed for tort reform. Among his proposals are banning contingency fees for expert witnesses, curbing punitive damages (whereby the defendant is assessed a "punishment" beyond the amount of the plaintiff's injury and suffering), and adopting the English Rule, whereby losers pay the winners' court costs, thus discouraging frivolous suits.

INVITATION TO DISCUSS

1. On balance, what do you see as the arguments pro and con for contingency suits? Do you think they should be banned?
2. Do you think Quayle's proposed reforms are likely to pass? What implications do you see in your prediction?

---

[16]Michael D. Lemonick, "Lawyers to the Rescue," *Time*, Feb. 1992, p. 46.
[17]Leslie Spencer, "The Tort Tax," *Forbes*, Feb. 17, 1992, pp. 40–42.

Representative Ted Weiss (D-NY), who had pushed to have implants investigated, and Senator Edward Kennedy, chairman of the Senate Labor and Human Resources Committee. The FDA received an unprecedented 20,000 letters in support of implants.

To encourage the organized protest, the plastic surgeons' society (The American Society of Plastic and Reconstructive Surgeons) accumulated a $1.3 million fund for lobbying. At stake were hundreds of millions of dollars a year that its members charged for implant surgery.

So we have the two sides arrayed in strong opposition: women, supported by trial lawyers and professional activists, versus women, allied their plastic surgeons and implant makers. Women may have justification for siding with either position (if they have had complications, they are against implants; if they have not, they tend to be strongly positive), but their supporters can hardly be cast as objective and unbiased. (See the following Issue box for a discussion of the issue of *right of choice*.)

LATER DEVELOPMENTS

Late in February 1992, the FDA's advisory panel, after a three-day marathon of hearings, voted unanimously *not* to ban implants. Dr. Elizabeth Connell, an Emory University professor and chairman of the panel, explained: "We don't feel a clear cause and effect relationship has been established."[18] At the same time, in a confusing obfuscation, the panel recommended sharply limiting breast implants while conducting far-reaching clinical trials. Women with mastectomies would get preference, but all women receiving implants from now on would essentially be guinea pigs, with their results closely monitored. Presumably, the bureaucracy would determine how many women would get future implants, and under what circumstances they would get them—not a very satisfactory resolution of this issue.

Although women were left in a position of great uncertainty regarding the risks of future implants, manufacturers were in a worse quandary. The advisory panel had said there was no proven risk, but manufacturers knew they faced millions of dollars in litigation suits. There were rumors that Dow Corning was earnestly seeking to get out of the implant business.

As of March 1992, despite 30 years of use, knowledge about breast implant safety was still shockingly sparse. No one knew for sure how many women had had implants: estimates ranged from 1 to 2 million. There were no statistics on how many implants had ruptured, or how many were leak-

---

[18]"FDA Does and Doesn't," *Wall Street Journal*, Feb. 24, 1992, p. A14.

ISSUE: SHOULD GOVERNMENT TAKE AWAY A PERSON'S RIGHT OF CHOICE?

In this case, we have seen women vehemently taking both sides of the issue of risk-versus-choice. How far should a government agency go in dictating whether or not we can use a certain product? How much must we be protected from our darker leanings, without infringing on our right of choice?

With the Dalkon Shield, there was no question about the appropriateness of banning a notoriously unsafe product. Such was not the case with Nestle's infant formula: the product had substantial benefits, but not if used improperly. And such is not the case with silicone implants. These have significant benefits, some of them merely cosmetic, but verging on the essential for those needing reconstructive surgery. The use of implants for cosmetic reasons can provide powerful psychological benefits. So we have a gray area indeed.

An extension of this controversy concerns the right of government to dictate how we should protect ourselves. Safety helmets for cyclists have been made mandatory in many states; so have seat belts and children's car seats. Are such statutes intruding on our right of choice? How about government going a step further and banning dangerous sports, such as bungee jumping, hang gliding, mountain climbing, even sandlot football? There is the massive issue of abortion and a woman's right of choice. How much do we need to be protected from the more reckless aspects of our nature, or what some would see as a violation of the natural law?

Like so many issues, the judgment is rather one of degree. We need protection from some extreme risk-embracing—for example, dueling, Russian roulette, playing "chicken" on the highway. These can hardly be tolerated. But should not women have a choice to have a breast enhancement operation, as long as they know the risks involved and are willing to accept them?

INVITATION TO DISCUSS

How do you feel about the government taking away some of your freedom of choice? How far do you think the hand of government should extend to protect us from ourselves?

---

ing, or even what the health significance was of stray silicone in the body. Confusion prevailed.

In early March 1992, responding to the heat arising from its hesitant stance regarding the breast implants, the FDA announced that, under the provisions of the 1976 Medical Device Amendments, it would begin scrutinizing more than 100 untested medical devices that were put into use before 1976. Included were implants for the testes, shoulders, and knees; electrical brain stimulators; balloons that open arteries; and lens implants for the eye. Signaling a new stance, agency officials noted that while these devices had been in use for 15 years or more, reports about adverse reactions had been sparse, and thus health problems might have gone unreported and unstudied heretofore.[19]

On March 19, 1992, Dow Corning announced that it was pulling out of the implant business, and would give women up to $1,200 each to help pay for having its implants surgically removed.

ANALYSIS

Was Dow Corning a villain? You have seen the evidence.

This issue is still evolving as we go to press, and we cannot assess it as thoroughly as we would like with the benefit of hindsight. Still, certain reasoned judgments are possible.

As with many issues and controversies, the matter is not clearcut, but some shade of gray. The villain is not entirely a villain, but has some redeeming qualities. Other protagonists are right in some respects, but not in others.

Dow Corning was reluctant to reveal memorandums and other documents of questionable or recriminating nature. It undoubtedly suppressed information from the general public and the press, although it appears that the FDA was apprised of some of this data, if not of all the internal memos.

Dow Corning wanted to convey the best image for the implants as possible. Accordingly, it did not release the full scope of complaints. Many people would not see this as the actions of a responsive firm. And yet, the problems did not seem to be serious or widespread (as was the case with the Dalkon Shield). Although Dow Corning executives were concerned, they reasoned that the implants resulted in far more good than harm.

Dow Corning was certainly concerned with its public image, the negative impact that full revelations of certain product leakages and harmful consequences would have brought. It had hoped to prevent public relations problems—but was eventually unable to—by not disclosing the full extent of the complaints of physicians and their patients. This can hardly be condoned. The company was guilty of withholding incriminating evidence. But the company was earnestly striving to correct the problem, which seemed to emanate from quality control lapses. Is Dow Corning therefore a monster?

Perhaps the main issue rests on the judgment of whether the problems outweighed the benefits—in other words, the risk/reward ratio. For many thousands of women, the ratio would seem favorable. For those suffering the severe trauma of mastectomies, the breast implants represented a return

---

[19]Philip V. Hilts, "FDA Wants Safety Data from All Implant Makers," *Cleveland Plain Dealer*, March 5, 1992, p. 11F.

to a normal life-style; for other women, breast enhancements could provide a psychological boost; for models, actresses, and others in the public lime-light, they could provide strong economic and professional advantages—despite the risk of some medical problems.

So, does the good outweigh the bad? You be the judge. Although Dow Corning was guilty of some cover-up—and will certainly pay for this in damage suits—was it calloused and uncaring? At least under the new regime of Keith McKennon, company policies seem to have shifted to a more conciliatory and responsive attitude.

WHAT CAN BE LEARNED?

Learning Insight. *Regulatory agencies often have operational problems.*

We have seen in this case that the FDA was a rather toothless entity. It could not even demand pertinent company documents and research-related memos. It could not pull a drug or medical device, once approved, off the market. It did not have the budget to do independent auditing of manufacturer research tests. It had to rely on a trusting relationship with the pharmaceutical industry, a relationship subject to abuse.

One can question whether the public is well served by such a toothless agency. Making the matter more grave is that not some merely frivolous product claim is involved, but serious claims, with health and even life itself at stake.

All regulatory agencies tend to be poorly funded. They can hardly monitor the full scope of the marketplace. Hence, efforts tend to be concentrated or prioritized: what are the most important concerns and the most visible culprits? A further deficiency of the FDA and many other regulatory agencies is a lack of complete objectivity, that is, their reliance on advisors with special interests, which usually means some involvement with the industry itself. In the case of the FDA and the silicone breast implants, the advisory boards were primarily staffed with plastic surgeons, who were intimately involved with implant operations and depended on them for a substantial part of their income. At the least, the objectivity of such special-interest groups is suspect.

What is the answer? Bigger budgets, in a time of budget cutting? Relying on outsiders for review boards instead of the experts? The solution is hardly simple or uncontroversial. For the foreseeable future, neither consumers nor industry executives can expect monumental changes in the effectiveness of our regulatory agencies.

Learning Insight. *Drugs and medical devices present long-term safety risks—for both people and firms.*

Long-term dangerous side effects of drugs and medical devices can seldom be predicted with absolute certainty. Initial tests prior to approval for distribution may guarantee minimal short-term risks, but research of a few years only cannot possibly assure there will be no long-term problems. Hence, the manufacturer faces risks of unknown degree. With throngs of eager trial lawyers ready in the wings, the unexpected risks can be monumental. In 1991 alone, we have seen Upjohn's sleeping pill, Halcion, linked with paranoia and agitation, Eli Lilly's antidepressant, Prozac, linked with extreme agitation, and Hoffmann-La Roche's liquid anesthetic, Versed, linked with deaths due to breathing and heart problems. Further, Pfizer's Bjork-Shiley heart valve was blamed for more than 300 deaths due to valve fractures and weak welds, and Bolar's Dyazide high-blood-pressure pill was found to be defective.

Certainly, the users of these drugs and medical devices are also at long-term risk. Sometimes, the drugs are used unwisely, either through the fault of the patient or the doctor; other times, a small proportion of patients may be affected adversely while the great majority have no ill effects.

Can we as a society expect no risks? Probably not. But we should be able to expect the risks to be minimal and to occur in a very low percentage of total usage. Otherwise, the testing and approval process is seriously flawed. For the firm, the risk/reward ratio should favor putting the product on the market. If longer or more intensive testing is needed to improve the risk/reward ratio, then this should be undertaken. It is misguided indeed to rush a product to market to reap a large payoff, only to find later that there are serious health and safety problems, which lead to burgeoning lawsuits as well as a denigrated reputation.

Learning Insight. *The pharmaceutical industry needs to improve its public image.*

Drug firms have reputations, despite recent advances in medicines, that are in the pits. They are seen as uncaring, profit-mongering makers of unsafe and defective products—not to be trusted. This negative image receives widespread press coverage. The litigation suits consequently yield awards out of proportion to actual injuries in many cases. On top of this, the pricing practices of some drug firms—discussed in another case—engender their own harsh criticisms. This industry truly needs to be concerned about its public image and take strong measures to improve it.

Learning Insight. *Unbiased judgment and objectivity are hard to find in issues involving business firms, special-interest groups, lawyers, and regulatory bodies.*

Despite the desirability of evaluating issues soberly and objectively, this is often not done. In this case, we saw the lines being drawn between manufacturers, tort lawyers, and certain activist groups, with women themselves strongly divided on the issue.

And the hapless FDA was in the middle, pressured by both sides. Not to be overlooked among the players is a press eager to sensationalize, quick to criticize, and often just as nonobjective as the other players.

In such a stew of conflicting and competing interests, how are justice and fair decisions ever to come about? Alas, that is the great challenge of our socio-ethical framework. Executives should recognize the reality of unfair and biased confrontation.

Learning Insight. *Strong support by some users for a product may not be enough in the presence of strong opposition by other factions to the same product.*

Dow Corning faced such a controversy with its silicone implants, and eventually fled the field. Charges and countercharges between the company and opposing groups can damage a company's reputation with negative publicity. Although the product may have considerable support, this may not be sufficient to save it. Such a hostile environment for doing business is uncomfortable at best, and fraught with legal peril at worst. Often the easier course of action is to withdraw the product.

If a courageous management attempts to ride out the storm and combat the detractors while embracing the supporters, then public relations must be well honed. In particular, the company should seek good rapport with reporters and other media representative through honesty and full disclosure. Executives who may be interviewed on camera should be well trained and coached in this important role of company spokespersons.

Learning Insight. *A coverup of negative research findings will seldom remain unrevealed.*

Why are firms so reluctant to hide negatives about their product(s), especially when such involve health and safety? The common rationale is that the limitations or dangers have not be proven to the company's satisfaction, and they therefore think it's reasonably safe. But we have seen in several cases that company documents came to light in legal proceedings which branded the firm as calloused and deceptive. Would it not be better for all concerned—the company, its customers, and physicians alike—if any possible health risks were readily revealed, objectively and dispassionately?

FOR THOUGHT AND DISCUSSION

1. Do you think the FDA's January 6, 1992, moratorium on implants should have been imposed? Should it have been imposed sooner? If so, when?
2. Do you think the whistleblower, Thomas Talcott, was justified in his actions? Why or why not?
3. Should Dow Corning be banned from producing any more implants as a punishment for its lack of candor and full disclosure of implant problems? Defend you position.
4. From the perspective of trial lawyers and plastic surgeons, what are the arguments pro and con for banning implants. Which side's position is the more compelling?

INVITATION TO ROLE-PLAY

1. You are the public relations director of Dow Corning in early 1980. Information has been surfacing about continued problems with your implants. What would you advise the CEO? Be as specific as you can and defend your recommendations.
2. Defend as persuasively as possible Dow Corning's decision to withhold most of the incriminating data for years. Also defend the company's decision to continue manufacturing silicone breast implants.
3. Taking the position of David Kessler, the FDA commissioner, defend your long procrastination in banning these breast implants?

INVITATION TO RESEARCH

What is the current situation regarding implants?

18

PowerMaster Beer: Targeting the Ghetto

AN EFFECTIVE MARKETING STRATEGY

In 1991, the beer industry experienced a 2.1 percent decline in sales from the previous year. But one sector of the industry was able to achieve a sensational growth of 10.4 percent: the malt liquor category. Malt liquor is the high-potency end of the brewing industry. Whereas regular beers contain 3.5 to 4 percent alcohol content, malt beverages typically contain between 4.5 and 6 percent.

Leading the pack were smaller brands such as St. Ides from the San Francisco-based McKenzie River Corporation and Midnight Dragon from Brooklyn's United Beers, brands that registered a growth rate of between 25 percent and 30 percent.[1]

Aggressive marketing practices played a major role in this surge. Unfortunately, some of these practices involved questionable ethical conduct. Heretofore, the largest demographic group of consumers had been older blue collar workers. Now, marketing efforts were turning aggressively to inner-city African-Americans and Hispanics. To do this, promotions used popular rap musicians, some of whom were notorious for their gang culture ties. The rap artists afforded a psychological appeal to young urban poor by casting the products with an element of danger and machismo.

[1]Alan Wolf, "Malt Liquors Gain Popularity, Notoriety," *Beverage World*, March 31, 1992, p. 8.

Other brewers joined the trend. Pabst Brewing Company pitched its Olde English 800 with the theme "Its the Power," referring to its higher alcohol content.

G. Heileman Brewing Company became the focal point for black outrage about the industry's aggressive targeting of ghetto youth. Heileman had long made one of the top-selling malt liquors in its Colt 45. Now it released an even stronger malt called PowerMaster. This was one of the very strongest malt liquors, with a 5.9 percent alcohol content compared with Colt 45's 4.5 percent alcohol, and regular beer's 3.5 percent.

OUTRAGE

Criticisms of PowerMaster focused both on the strength in alcoholic content as well as the evocative name. Black activists were the first to lash out, seeing a danger to the social structure of their fragile communities. Foremost among these was the Reverend Calvin O. Butts III, pastor of Abyssinian Baptist Church in Harlem.

Rev. Calvin Butts

Since 1989, Rev. Butts has been pastor of the most famous black church in America. As such, he has become one of the most visible new leaders in New York City. He preaches to standing-room-only crowds every Sunday.

Abyssinian Baptist Church has a distinguished history within the black community. It was once led by the flamboyant Adam Clayton Powell, Jr., who used the church as a base to catapult himself to office in the U.S. House of Representatives. The church has long been a center of hope and social action for black New Yorkers.

Butts was born in New York City in 1950. His father was a chef and his mother a supervisor in the city's welfare system. He attended Morehouse College, one of the nation's most prestigious black colleges, where he was a student activist. He came to Abyssinian in 1972 as a junior minister and quickly found himself in the spotlight. Now, as leader of the church, he is sought out by politicians and is generally viewed as an emerging force for social change. The *New York Times* calls Butts a strong influence both in an "Establishment" mode, through managing construction of low-income housing and building coalitions, and as a "Protest Leader."[2] And protest Calvin Butts has done, leading well-publicized campaigns to paint over billboards in Harlem that advertise liquor and tobacco.

---

[2]J. Dreyfuss, "Harlem's Ardent Voice," *New York Times Magazine*, January 20, 1991, p. 18.

On a Sunday morning in April, 1991, Rev. Butts spoke to his congregation. The object of his concern was beer, a strong beer, a malt liquor, with a provocative name, PowerMaster, and advertising targeted with little subtlety to young black males of the ghetto.

Rev. Butts thundered from the pulpit, "Wine is a mocker, strong drink is raging; and whosoever is deceived thereby is not wise" (Proverbs, 20:1). He went on to compare Heileman, the maker of PowerMaster, and its black-owned advertising agency to crack dealers on the street. Moreover, he charged, "We all know that power does not come from a can. It comes from the beer of the Lord!"[3] He assailed the "insidious and diabolical marketing methods of PowerMaster . . . sold to primarily low-income powerless people so you get a feeling of euphoria and that you are powerful and masterful when in fact things that make you powerful and masterful you are not doing—you're drinking malt liquor."[4]

Other reactions

Surgeon General Antonia Novello joined in the criticism of PowerMaster, charging that Heileman was aiming its product at "a group with a level of cirrhosis of the liver more prevalent than others": young black males.[5] Two Chicago priests, the Reverends Michael Pfleger and George Clements, assailed PowerMaster as "a slave master in the inner cities of our country."[6] They announced their call for a picket and boycott of any inner-city store that stocked PowerMaster. The priests made a "pilgrimage" to La Crosse, Wisconsin, the company's headquarters, to present their protests to company chairman Thomas Rattigan. After being denied a meeting with company officials, they refused to leave and were arrested for trespassing. But the mayor of La Crosse intervened and arranged a meeting with Rattigan.

Pressure continued to mount against Heileman to drop the brand. ABC's "Nightline," as well as CNN's "Crossfire," devoted full programs to PowerMaster. Newspaper headlines ranged from "New Brew Sparks Black Rage" in a feature article in the *New York Post*, to a *New York Times* editorial, "The Threat of PowerMaster." The salient point in the *Times* was that ". . . a responsible company wouldn't just can the name. It would stop targeting a population already devastated by alcohol and drug problems."[7]

---

[3]Frank Rose, "If It Feels Good, It Must be Bad," *Fortune*, October 21, 1991, p. 95.

[4]"BATF Orders Heileman to Discontinue 'PowerMaster' Label for Malt Liquor Product," *Alcoholism Report*, Vol. 19, June-July 1991, p. 11.

[5]"Barrage of Criticism Hits New Brew Aimed at Blacks," *Alcoholism & Drug Abuse Week*, July 3, 1991.

[6]*Ibid.*

[7]*Ibid*, p. 3.

A supporter of Heileman was James Sanders, president of the Beer Institute. He told reporters that the campaign against PowerMaster was "patronizing" to black and Hispanic customers, and noted that "people can make up their own minds about what product they prefer."[8]

Responding to the crescendo of criticisms, the federal Bureau of Alcohol, Tobacco, and Firearms (BATF) informed Heileman that it could no longer use the name PowerMaster because it illegally promoted high alcohol content. Then BATF ordered the firm to stop marketing the malt liquor altogether. The company was allowed to sell its remaining stock, estimated in early July 1991 as four weeks' worth. So, the brand was discontinued shortly after it was introduced.

The issue was not to die so readily, however. Negative attention began to focus on the marketing practices of the entire malt liquor industry, which had long made use of macho messages, some subtle and others far from subtle. (See the following information box for a discussion of the generally effective strategy of *target marketing* or *segmentation*.)

St. Ides Beer

PowerMaster died a quick death. But St. Ides, another malt liquor, from the San Francisco-based McKenzie River Corporation, became the focus of critical attention. (It is interesting to note that while McKenzie markets St. Ides, it contracts out for the brewing, rather than doing it by itself. And who do you suppose its brewer is? Our old acquaintance, Heileman.) Using recording artists such as Ice Cube and King Tee, St. Ides was promoting a 40-ounce container as a single serving, with lyrics like "I grab me a 40 when I want to act a fool . . ." Aphrodisiac benefits were suggested: "Get your girl in the mood quicker." Ice Cube even appeared in posters touting the product with a hand gesture having street gang symbolism.

The high-octane malt liquor was singled out by New York State Commissioner of Consumer Affairs Richard Kessler for "obscene" and "illegal" ads that infer that the product will "put hair on your chest" and "make her talk about the birds and the bees."[9] The Oregon Liquor Control Commission also banned St. Ides commercials featuring Ice Cube because the agency believed the ads fostered gang violence.

The controversy continued to flare as 3000 Korean grocers boycotted the malt liquor because of St. Ides' TV and radio ads featuring Ice Cube. The complaints were directed at the rapper, who apparently had advocated the burning of Korean stores in black neighborhoods as expressed on the "Black

---

[8]"Barrage of Criticism Hits New Brew Aimed at Blacks," p. 2.
[9]"St. Ides Blues," *Beverage World*, Dec. 1991, p. 10.

THE POTENT STRATEGY OF TARGET MARKETING OR SEGMENTATION

Most firms find it impossible to target their offerings to the entire buying population because few products can satisfy everyone's taste. It is usually better for a firm to identify and select smaller target markets (often called market segments) in which it can best adapt its products and marketing efforts to satisfying customer wants.

The following criteria are useful in selecting a target market:

1. The market should be of sufficient size to be worth the effort to tap it; furthermore, the trend of its size should not be downward.
2. It should be accessible through available communication and distribution sources.
3. It should be compatible with the firm's experience and resources.

It also helps if the segment is not being well-served by existing competitors.

Black males represented an attractive target market for PowerMaster. The size of the market was sufficient, and it was readily accessible by various broadcast media using rock stars. The experience of Heileman with malt liquor production and promotion was more than adequate. And while other brands as well as distilled liquors were competitors, Heileman saw opportunity in aggressively promoting a stronger beer with a provocative name.

Alas, it did not reckon on the controversy its seemingly sound target marketing strategy would engender.

INVITATION TO DISCUSS:

1. Should not the Heileman executives have foreseen the controversy PowerMaster was likely to arouse?
2. How could such militant agitation have been anticipated? What research or investigation would likely have aroused concerns?

Korea" track of the Priority album "Death Certificate." The boycott ended on November 20, 1991, when McKenzie River pulled the advertising spots.

However, McKenzie River Corporation continued to use other hardcore rappers in its advertising, including the Geto Boys, Compton's Most Wanted, and Rakim.

ANALYSIS OF THE CONTROVERSY

Were certain sectors of the brewing industry far out of line in promoting strong beer? Are activists out of line in trying to decree what disadvantaged people should eat, drink, and smoke? Where does ethical behavior end and abusive practices begin?

Is the PowerMaster Name Offensive and Unethical?

Critics condemned the PowerMaster name as overly suggestive to many young black males. They saw such a name as highly suggestive that the use of the product would enable them to be masterful and powerful with women as well as with society in general. The name is alleged to cater blatantly to a macho image. But are such criticisms justified? Is this name so negatively provocative and suggestive?

It is hard to deny that the name is somewhat suggestive to the impressionable. But is it so much so as to warrant banning? In the spillover of the criticisms of malt liquors, other brands with more innocuous names—Colt 45, St. Ides, Olde English 800—were also the targets of critics. (See the following information box, which describes how Heileman capitulated to protests about the PowerMaster name.)

Is the Method of Advertising Unethical?

Some would see the use of certain hard rock stars and their uncensored gestures or rebelliousness and sexual innuendos to be unacceptable and unethical—and certainly in poor taste. Yet for the target market of young males, their use was an effective promotional strategy. The rock musicians were popular celebrities for this group and ones whose association with a brand would carry great weight.

So, is it unethical to use the most effective strategy to reach your target market if such is distasteful to many persons? If the strategy simply caters to the interests of a particular target group, probably not. However, in this instance, the advertising could be seen as fanning rebellious and anti-social inclinations that could lead to consequences most of society would condemn. In this sense, then, may we contest the undesirability of such advertising, even though it may imply some limiting of the advertiser's free speech?

Is it Unethical to Sell Strong Beer?

Such an assertion disregards the fact that even strong beer has many times less alcoholic content than gin, vodka, whiskey, or even wine. Whereas malt liquor admittedly is stronger than regular beer, it is still weak compared to the alternatives.

Implied in this criticism is that selling strong beer is particularly bad in the ghetto, that ghetto youth are being victimized by their exposure to powerful promotional efforts for such undesirable products. Critics charge that young urban black males are being corrupted by unscrupulous marketers, of strong brews that are "slavemasters of blacks." (The implication is that urban youth and other nonghetto consumers have more willpower, so that the products are not so bad for them.)

MOST RECENT ACTIVITIES REGARDING POWERMASTER: A NEW NAME

Less than a year after removing PowerMaster from the market amid a crescendo of protests, G. Heileman Brewing Company changed its strategy. Not admitting defeat, it quietly reintroduced the product with a different brand. The product, according to governmental regulators and rival firms, is the same: a high-alcoholic malt beverage in the same black can emblazoned with a red horse. Only the name has been changed to Colt 45 Premium.

This change was acceptable to the Bureau of Alcohol, Tobacco, and Firearms. Yet, the slogan "Be a Premium Player" has inner-city connotations of power and sexual success. For example, "Player" is the scrawled graffiti sign-off of a gang in south central Los Angeles.

Heileman's vice president of marketing, Charles Powell, denies any allegation of conscious targeting to blacks. "It is aimed at the same people we target all the time—men, generally."

Heileman introduced the new product with caution, trying only Detroit and Philadelphia to begin with. Success there will induce further expansion. And Heileman needs a winner as it struggles under a huge debt load, which resulted in its filing for protection from creditors in bankruptcy court in 1991.

Black leaders, however, were not fooled by the change in name. The Reverend Jesse Brown, a militant Philadelphia minister, vowed: "We certainly won't play dead on this one. It's sad that Heileman disrespects us so badly that it believes it can come back a second time with the same product and the community wouldn't respond."

Source: Alix M. Freedman, "Heileman Tries a New Name for Strong Malt," *Wall Street Journal,* May 11, 1992, p. B1.

INVITATION TO DISCUSS

1. Was the Heileman response to the PowerMaster controversy (quietly changing the name) a justifiable strategic reaction? Why or why not?
2. Given the emerging agitation about the new brand, how would you handle this situation if you were the decision maker for Heileman?

Another aspect of this argument contends that teenagers below the legal drinking age are being induced to take up drinking by the abundance of "lifestyle" advertisements that depict drinking taking place in all kinds of pleasurable contexts. Such critics would seek to ban all beer commercials just as other alcoholic beverages have been banned from TV and radio.

Traditional Defenses of the Beer and Liquor Industries

Defenders of beer and liquor marketing decry the confused paternalism in government: telling people what they should and should not consume.

Although full disclosure of any risks is not the issue, the alcoholic beverage industry has pleaded for full and unbiased information so that an informed public can weigh the possible dangers against the pleasures. But full disclosure is not possible in the beer industry. Since 1935, it has been illegal for beers to advertise their alcoholic strength in commercials or on containers. The reasoning was that beers would then be unable to compete on the basis of strength. But this hardly leads to an informed public.

Whereas critics rightly focus attention on drunken drivers and on the abuses of alcohol, defenders quickly point out that only a small proportion of drinkers are alcoholics, and that they would probably be little deterred by banning advertising and making the products more difficult and more expensive to obtain. Abuses of alcohol are by no means limited to the ghetto, even though such extreme abuses may grease the slide to impoverishment for the unfortunate few.

The brewing and liquor industries are quick to point out their constructive public relations efforts. For example, the Miller Brewing Company is the founder of the Marshall Fund, established to honor Thurgood Marshall, a retired black Supreme Court Justice, to help black colleges. Hundreds of thousands of dollars have been given by the industry to the American Medical Association to publicize alcohol-related problems. Commercials to discourage drinking and driving have been used for some years but have intensified in recent years as the beer and liquor industries have come under increased criticism. Such name stars as Gloria Estefan have been enlisted for commercials advocating the responsible use of these products. The National Beer Wholesalers Association signed up Cindi Lamb, a stalwart of Mothers Against Drunk Driving, to help promote responsible drinking and also to assist in policy. The industry has also strenuously promoted the theme "Know When to Say When" as well as its new non-alcoholic malt beverages. But critics still castigated the industry for insincerity and hypocrisy in such endeavors.

WHAT CAN BE LEARNED?

Learning Insight. *Marketing efforts need to be socially responsible in ALL market segments.*

Businesses cannot adopt different standards of conduct with different segments of society. This is no longer acceptable by a concerned public.

As we have seen with the PowerMaster and St. Ides confrontations, the use of questionable marketing techniques directed toward such minority markets as African-American and Hispanic neighborhoods are likely to be no more tolerated there than in the most affluent white neighborhoods. They may even be less tolerated and accepted. (In a somewhat similar instance, not many years ago, brewers sought to expand sales in the college market through "beer busts" and "get bombed" campaigns that included free beer. Criticisms also forced the curtailment of such efforts.) But a firm today cannot have one standard for certain segments, and a different standard for others.

Does this mean that a firm should not try to target minorities, and particularly, minority youth? Not at all. But if it does not use socially accepted practices, similar to what it uses with other groups, then very likely it exposes itself to bitter opposition.

Learning Insight. *Strong public criticisms of products and practices can seldom be effectively combatted without bowing to the demands.*

We have seen the reality of this insight in several other cases, particularly Nestle and to a lesser extent Dow Corning. Aggressive critics will seldom fade away. Their cause often attracts strong supporters, and eventually, government involvement. Public relations efforts, increased advertising, counter-offensives attacking the credibility and objectivity of the critics— these will seldom be effective. The most prudent course of action for a firm finding itself in such a predicament is simply to back away, even to the point of abandoning the product or project, and to do this as graciously as possible. As the old adage says, "Don't continue to beat a dead horse."

Learning Insight. *When a new product or a planned marketing strategy may be suspect, objective evaluation is essential before proceeding.*

When there is a question about the possibility of criticism and public concern, a firm should appraise the situation most carefully. This may involve getting outside opinions, even from members of the target market, especially if this is a minority market. Perhaps certain changes should be made before introducing the product and the strategy in order to make them both more acceptable. It might even be best to immediately abandon the project in some cases before the company's public image is tarnished. (See the following information box, which discusses an interesting analytical tool for assessing risk/reward, a *qualitative* or *nonquantitative cost/benefit analysis.*)

HOW GOOD IS A QUALITATIVE COST/BENEFIT ANALYSIS?

An analytical tool for assessing courses of action that bear some degree of risk is the cost/benefit analysis described in an earlier case. The problem in many of these situations is numerical data so vague and conjectural that any helpfulness in decision making is tenuous. However, the absence of tangible numerical inputs need not negate the analyses.

Let us take the example of how a qualitative cost/benefit analysis might have been used by Heileman in its planned strategy of targeting young ghetto males with PowerMaster.

The benefits in increased sales revenue might be forecast with the usual degree of confidence that any forecast of success for a new brand or product might warrant. Still, we have some tangibility here; sales predictions can be improved, of course, if a test market is conducted by introducing a new brand in one or a few representative markets and extrapolating the sales results.

However, we run into serious problems in trying to quantify the costs in such a situation. For example, the costs of such a controversial product as PowerMaster would include:

Hassles—Confrontational preaching, even community boycotts, are possible. .

Bad publicity—The media, as we know, are quick to pounce on anything negative, especially in regard to business dealings.

Governmental scrutiny—Emanating from the adverse publicity and from the inclination of political aspirants to maximize an opportunity, governmental scrutiny, and even regulatory action, may be forthcoming.

Legal intervention—Finally, the courts may be involved in lawsuits against the alleged perpetrator of misdeeds.

INVITATION TO DISCUSS
Do you see such a qualitative cost/benefit analysis as having any practical use-fulness for decision making? Might it have helped Heileman executives in their initial strategy planning for PowerMaster?

FOR THOUGHT AND DISCUSSION

1. Do you think people should have a right to make a buying choice freely, or should they be protected from their darker instincts by a "big brother" of the government or some social organization? Explain your position.

2. In your opinion, is the PowerMaster name really all that bad? Why or why not? Is it any worse than the accepted Colt 45 name?

3. Do you think Heileman, as well as McKenzie, were acting unethically in targeting the ghetto?

4. The threat of boycotting a product, and even other products of the offending firm, is often used by activist protestors. How big a threat, really, does this seem to you? Should a company discontinue an effective marketing strategy because of a few such threats by militant leaders? Discuss.

INVITATION TO ROLE PLAY

1. You are a politician facing a difficult reelection campaign. Discuss how you would use the malt liquor controversy to further your reelection chances. Be as specific and as creative as possible.
2. How would you mount a public relations campaign to offset the negative allegations about your company's PowerMaster beer? Would your campaign strategy differ if your product was St. Ides?

INVITATION TO RESEARCH

What is the most current situation regarding malt liquor? Is the St. Ides brand still marketed, and is it successful?

19

Recent Cigarette Controversies

Cigarettes are among the world's most profitable consumer products. A cigarette "costs a penny to make, sell it for a dollar, it's addictive, and there's fantastic brand loyalty,"—so said takeover specialist Warren Buffett as he unsuccessfully sought to take over RJR Nabisco, the tobacco conglomerate.[1] Perhaps because of its profitability the morality of the business has long been suspect.

EARLY SOCIAL PRESSURES AGAINST CIGARETTES

Almost from the beginning, tobacco has faced social disfavor from certain sectors of the population, notably medical and religious groups, as well as others who espoused particular moral beliefs. Cigarettes were being referred to as "coffin nails" even before the Civil War. A group consisting of educators, doctors, and the famous showman P. T. Barnum formed an alliance to fight the nicotine habit. Later, Horace Greeley, publisher of *The New York Tribune*, condemned tobacco. School children were exhorted to join the Anti-Cigarette League with a pledge to abstain. Some businesses refused to hire men and boys who smoked.

Antismoking legislation was also passed by some states. Some banned the use of cigarettes by any person under 16 years of age. Some legislation

[1]"The Tobacco Trade: The Search for El Dorado," *Economist*, May 16, 1992, p. 21.

prohibited the use of coupons in cigarette packages; a 1901 New Hampshire law even went to the extreme of declaring it illegal to make or sell any form of cigarette. In New York, women were absolutely forbidden to smoke in public. By 1910, only in Wyoming and Louisiana had no antismoking legislation passed either by state or local bodies.

World War I brought a major change in attitudes toward smoking. The cigarette fitted perfectly the needs of fighting men for an easy-to-carry and easy-to-use short reprieve from the rigors of military life. The public was encouraged by no less than John J. Pershing, commanding general of the armies, to send cigarettes to soldiers, most of whom were ardent cigarette smokers when they returned home.

Further, the increased tempo of life that came with the congestion and strains of urban life favored the short smoke of cigarettes over the more leisurely smokes of cigars and pipes. This trend was further accentuated by the shift of population from rural to urban. The voices of the social reformers were drowned out by the stampede to cigarette smoking in the late 1920s by all sectors of society. The development of mass communication advertising media—at first radio, then TV—expanded the love affair for cigarettes by most elements of society. The Second World War provided even more impetus for a societal addiction.

Later Societal Pressures

By the 1960s, negative publicity was again surfacing about cigarettes. The Surgeon General issued a report on January 11, 1964, stating that cigarette smoking was injurious to health and shortened life. Subsequent studies began to provide overwhelming evidence of the dangers of cigarette smoking, despite contrary claims by the tobacco industry. On June 22, 1964, the Federal Trade Commission issued a trade regulation order that all cigarette labeling and advertising must carry a health warning. That same year, Congress passed the Federal Cigarette Labeling and Advertising Act reaffirming the regulation of the FTC and the required statement: "Warning: The Surgeon General Has Determined That Cigarette Smoking Is Dangerous to Your Health."

Then, as of January 2, 1971, cigarette commercials were banned from TV and radio. At that time, it was thought that the $250 million spent annually by the industry for TV and radio commercials could never be completely rechanneled, with the result that tobacco usage would decline without such potent advertising stimulation.

This hope was quickly dispelled. Advertising expenditures for 1971, the first year of the ban, had practically all been rechanneled into other media.[2]

---

[2]"Where the Cigarette Men Go After the TV Ban," *Business Week*, November 21, 1970, pp. 64–69; "Cigarette Makers Do Great Without TV," *Business Week*, May 29, 1971, pp. 56–57;

Gradually over the next two decades, growing publicity about the health consequences of cigarette smoking coincided with an emerging social concern with health and fitness. As a result, cigarette consumption in the United States dropped substantially, and smoking was banned from domestic air flights and many buildings as even second-hand smoke was considered harmful by medical experts.

CONTROVERSIAL STRATEGIES IN TODAY'S SHRINKING MARKET

Faced with a steadily declining market in the United States, the tobacco industry has responded with a proliferation of brands: more than 300 brands were created, boasting of such features as being longer, slimmer, cheaper, flavored, microfiltered, pastel colored and even striped. One of these was an R. J. Reynolds brand called Uptown.

The Controversy over Uptown

Uptown was packaged in a showy black-and-gold box and was a menthol blend. R. J. Reynolds designed the product to appeal to a particular market segment, much as the other new brands had been designed for.

Because cigarette consumption had fallen in the United States, tobacco companies were increasingly directing their efforts to specific groups, such as women, Hispanics, and African-Americans. The last group, in particular seemed a fruitful target market: 39 percent of black males smoke, while 30.5 percent of white males do.[3] Using careful research and design, everything about Uptown—even the name—was tailored to the tastes of black consumers. It was, indeed, the first cigarette aimed specifically at African-American smokers. Alas, this was the rub.

A storm of protests quickly ensued. Critics maintained that the marketing of Uptown represented a cold-blooded targeting of blacks, who already suffered a lung cancer rate 58 percent higher than whites. The protests even reached the office of Louis Sullivan, the Secretary of Health and Human Services. He quickly sided with the critics: "Uptown's message is more disease, more suffering and more death for a group already bearing more than its share of smoking-related illness and mortality."[4] He called for an "all-out effort to resist the attempts of tobacco merchants to earn profits at the expense of the health and well-being of our poor and minority citizens."[5]

---

and "Where Cigarette Makers Spend Ad Dollars Now," *Business Week*, December 25, 1971, pp. 56–57.

[3]Michael Quinn, "Don't Aim That Pack at Us," *Time*, Jan. 29, 1990, p. 60.

[4]*Ibid.*

[5]Ben Wildavasky, "Tilting at Billboards," *New Republic*, August 20, 1990, p. 19.

Given the virulence of the protests, R. J. Reynolds abandoned its plans to test market the cigarettes in Philadelphia. It decried the negative attention being focused on the brand by a few zealots and angrily compared the acceptability of a retailer designing a line of clothing for blacks with the outcry accompanying the same marketing strategy for a cigarette.

On March 16, 1990, the *Chicago Tribune* announced that R. J. Reynolds Tobacco Company had stated it was not likely to pursue the controversial marketing of Uptown. But the company defended its marketing efforts.[6] The critics had won.

A Similar Controversy: Dakota. Another new cigarette brand, also targeted to a specific group, found itself beset with controversy. This was Dakota, aimed at "virile females."[7] Critics of tobacco's relationship with lung cancer and heart disease were quick to attack this as a blatant appeal to women.

Another group was especially upset. In some Native American languages, Dakota means friend. Yet, to a group that already had high rates of smoking addiction, such a brand name seemed a betrayal.

Controversies over Tobacco Company Sponsorships

As a result of the 1971 ban on the use of TV and radio cigarette commercials, the tobacco companies desperately sought other media in which to place their hundreds of millions of advertising dollars. They were fairly successful in doing so, but by the early 1990s serious questions were being raised about their use of certain of these media.

We have already seen the great criticisms and aggressive actions taken against billboards promoting cigarettes and alcohol in black communities. Advertising support of black media by tobacco companies was also coming under fire. Yet, such support for many years existed in a vacuum, with few other major firms and industries supporting advertising in black media.

Now, tobacco company support for minority organizations also began to be questioned. The National Association of Black Journalists turned down a $40,000 Philip Morris donation: ". . . we couldn't take money from an organization deliberately targeting minority populations with a substance that clearly causes cancer," said the group's president, Thomas

---

[6]Janet Cawley, "Target Marketing Lights Smoky Fire," *Chicago Tribune*, March 16, 1990, p. 1.
[7]Paul Cotton, "Tobacco Foes Attack Ads that Target Women, Minorities, Teens and the Poor," *Journal of the American Medical Association*, Sept. 26, 1990, p. 1505.

Morgan. "We simply became more aggressive in our fund-raising so we could do without it."[8] But for many small minority publications, such was not an option: they would have simply folded without the advertising dollars furnished by tobacco companies.

Women's organizations also are beholden to support from the tobacco industry, which has liberally provided money to such groups at a time when other sources were virtually nonexistent. As a major example of such support, Virginia Slims brought women's tennis into prominence at a time when no one else would. And this raises another major controversy, discussed in the following Issue box.

ISSUE: TOBACCO COMPANY SPONSORSHIP OF ATHLETIC EVENTS

Is it right to allow tobacco companies to sponsor certain athletic events? What seems like a simple and uncontroversial question becomes far more complex when we consider the sponsorship of tennis tournaments such as Virginia Slims. There is no longer any doubt that cigarette smoking causes serious damage to the heart and lungs. Yet, tennis requires top physical fitness and aerobic capacity.

Although the sponsorship of such athletic events came about as the industry sought alternative media after being banned from TV and radio, their sponsorship has particular advantages from the industry's perspective. It creates the false association of cigarette smoking with vitality and good health, and it directly targets women. Essentially, the company is taking advantage of the inadequate funding of women's sports by making itself a strong presence in this sector.

So we have an unhealthy product—as almost all experts but the tobacco industry stoutly maintain—sponsoring a prestigious athletic event for women that would probably never be able to exist without such funding. Do we refuse to accept this sponsorship? Do we ban all cigarette promotions that appear to have some tie-in with health and fitness? Does the evil outweigh the good?

INVITATION TO DISCUSS

You are a feminist leader with strong convictions that women's athletic events should be promoted more strongly. The major source of funding for tennis and golf tournaments has been the tobacco industry, with no alternative sponsors likely in the near future. Discuss your position regarding the acceptability of tobacco company sponsorships. What is your position on this controversy? Present your rationale as persuasively as you can.

---

[8]Paul Cotton, "Tobacco Foes Attack Ads," p. 1506.

The Old Joe Camel controversy

In 1988, R. J. Reynolds Tobacco Company stumbled upon a promotional theme for its slumping Camel brand. Using a sunglass-clad, bulbous-nosed cartoon camel that it called Joe, a $75 million-a-year advertising campaign was instituted. The company featured Joe in an array of macho gear, and targeted the campaign to appeal to younger male smokers who had been deserting the Camel brand in droves.

The campaign was an outstanding success. In only three years, Camel's share of sales among the 18- to 24-year age group almost doubled, from 4.4 percent to 7.9 percent.

But the appeal of Old Joe went far beyond the target age group. It was too potent. It was found to be highly effective in reaching young people, especially children under 13. Children were enamored with the camel character. Six-year olds in the United States even recognized Joe Camel at a rate nearly equal to their recognition of Mickey Mouse.[9]

According to a study published in the *Journal of the American Medical Association*, teenagers are far better able than adults to identify the Camel logo. Children as young as three could even identify the cartoon character with cigarettes. Of even more concern, Camel's share of the market of underage children who smoke is nearly 33 percent, up from less than a percentage point before the Old Joe campaign. See Table 19-1 for the results of the survey.

THE PROTESTS EXPAND

Uptown

Critics of Uptown initially focused attention on its billboard advertising in ghetto neighborhoods. They soon expanded their protests beyond a single cigarette brand to cigarettes in general and to alcohol as well and began whitewashing offending billboards. Their only recourse, they argued, was to use civil disobedience to attract attention to their cause. Although maintaining that they had nothing against billboards in general, protestors demanded more educational themes as well as such wholesome products as orange juice for these billboards in ghetto neighborhoods.

Dr. Harold Freeman, director of surgery at Harlem Hospital, is co-author of a study that found that men in Harlem have a lower life expectancy than men in Bangladesh, at least partly because of alcohol and tobacco use. Speaking to an audience at Harlem's Abyssinian Baptist

[9]Judann Dagnoli, "'JAMA' Lights New Fire Under Camel's Ads," *Advertising Age*, December 16, 1991, pp. 3, 32.

Table 19-1   Survey Results of Knowledge and Attitudes Regarding Camel's Old Joe Advertisements

	Students	*Adults*
Have seen Old Joe	97.7%	72.2%
Know the product	97.5	67.0
Think ads look cool	58.0	39.9
Like Joe as friend	35.0	14.4
Smokers who identify Camel as favorite brand	33.0	8.7

Source: Data from the *Journal of the American Medical Assn.*, as presented in Walecia Konrad, "I'd Toddle a Mile for a Camel," *Business Week*, December 23, 1991, p. 34. The results are based on a survey of 1055 students, ages 12 to 19 years, and 345 adults, aged 21 to 87 years.

Church, Dr. Freeman asked, "Is it ethical, is it moral, to sell cigarettes and alcohol specifically to a community that is dying at a much higher rate than others?"[10] And with this, the church's pastor, Rev. Calvin O. Butts III, led his flock out of the church and throughout the city, painting signs with black paint to denote their Afrocentric perspective. (In similar fashion to the crusade against strong beer, described in the last chapter, the protesters turned their indignation to billboards promoting tobacco products.)

The agitation against billboards was by no means limited to Harlem. For example, in Dallas, County Commissioner John Wiley Price led a group that whitewashed 25 billboards, resulting in arrests and misdemeanor charges. And Chicago priest Michael Pfleger was also arrested for allegedly painting billboards and throwing paint at a billboard company employee.

Antismoking and antibillboard activists were having a field day. California launched a $28.6 million antismoking campaign using money from cigarette taxes. Similarly, the Office of Substance Abuse Policy began a nationwide 7000-billboard campaign targeting drug and alcohol abuse.

Business began heeding the mounting pressure. In June 1990, the Outdoor Advertising Association of America, representing 80 percent of billboard companies, announced a new policy encouraging its members to keep billboard ads for products that are illegal for minors at least 500 feet from schools, as well as from places of worship and hospitals. The association also recommended voluntary limits on the number of billboards that advertise cigarettes and alcohol in any given area, such as minority neighborhoods. Gannet Outdoor, the largest billboard company in North America, began putting decals on billboards near schools and churches indicating that no alcohol or tobacco ads were to be posted there.

[10]*Ibid.*

Assessment of the Controversy of Targeting Minorities. Was R. J. Reynolds Company the ogre that some critics depicted it as? Or were the critics self-seeking extremists more interested in publicity and crying wolf when the wolf was really rather toothless?

Without question, inner-city blacks have shown higher rates of tobacco and alcohol use than their suburban contemporaries; along with this, they have higher incidences of the accompanying health problems. And despite a few weak company disclaimers, there can be little doubt that tobacco firms thought they had developed a new and effective market targeting strategy. The dispute hinges on this:

> Are certain minority groups—such as blacks and women—particularly susceptible to marketing blandishments so that they need to be protected from potentially unsafe products?

While the proponents of controls argue that certain groups, such as young blacks, need such protection, others see that as indicative of paternalism. Even some black leaders decry the billboard whitewashing and the contentious preachings of certain ministers. To Adolph Hauntz, president of the Dallas Merchants and Concessionaires Association, whitewashing signs "treats blacks as if we are a stupid bunch of people that are overly influenced by billboards." And NAACP Executive Director Benjamin Hooks makes the same point, condemning billboard whitewashing for "saying that white people have enough sense to read the signs and disregard them and black people don't."[11] Certainly, tempting people is hardly the same as oppressing them. After all, no one has to buy cigarettes and alcohol.

Butts, Sullivan, and others countered that comments such as those of Hooks simply reflected the tobacco and alcohol industries' success in muting criticisms of their minority targeting policies by their large donations to such groups as the NAACP, the United Negro College Fund, and the National Urban League.

Regardless of the pro and con arguments concerning the susceptibility of inner-city youth to advertisements for unhealthy products, there is more validity to the contentions of susceptibility when we consider the vulnerability of children to the attractive and sophisticated models found in most of these commercials.

Finally, if local, state, or federal legislation is enacted to ban certain products from being promoted on billboards, as was done with radio and TV advertising two decades ago, where should the line be drawn? Should

---

[11]Wildavsky, "Tilting at Billboards," p. 20.

promotions in ghetto neighborhoods be banned for products that are economically extravagant, such as expensive athletic shoes? Or should promotions be banned for high-cholesterol foods that might cause high blood pressure? Or for high-powered "muscle" cars?

Joe Camel

Not surprisingly, a storm of criticism ensued after the American Medical Association's disclosure of the study that found that Joe Camel appealed far more to children than to adults. Health advocates demanded that the Federal Trade Commission ban the ads. Surgeon General Antonia Novella took the unprecedented step of asking RJR to cancel its campaign voluntarily. Even *Advertising Age* published an editorial entitled "Old Joe Must Go."[12] The basis for the concern, of course, was that the popular ads might encourage underage children to start smoking.

RJR refused to yield. It denied that the ads are effective with children: "Just because children can identify our logo doesn't mean they will use the product."[13] Defensively, Reynolds moved to counter the bad press. It distributed pamphlets and bumper stickers and put up billboards discouraging kids from smoking. And it stoutly maintained its right to freedom of speech.

Assessment of the Old Joe Controversy. Some advertising people believed RJR's stubbornness was badly misguided: "RJR . . . is taking a huge chance. By placing Old Joe as a freedom-of-speech issue instead of an unintentional marketing overshoot, the conglomerate risks goading Congress into bans and restrictions on all tobacco advertising. Lawmakers might, for instance, look more favorably on legislation just introduced . . . which would shift responsibility for tobacco products to the Food and Drug Administration [which] could regulate the tobacco industry into oblivion."[14]

Old Joe was a marketing success beyond all management expectation. But in a time of increasingly critical attention by society, should any firm in a sensitive industry hold itself aloof from a groundswell of denunciations? Are some bumper stickers and billboards with messages to discourage kids from smoking likely to be more than token and impotent efforts, given the popularity of a cartoon character that commands virtually as much recognition and affection as Mickey Mouse?

---

[12]"Old Joe Must Go," *Advertising Age*, January 13, 1992.
[13]*Ibid.*
[14]Craig Stoltz, "RJR Appears Intent on Sticking with Old Joe to the Bitter End," *Adweek Eastern Edition*, March 23, 1992, p. 18.

Then this thought may be raised (while we hesitate to denigrate any firm): could it be that targeting the young is seen as a long-range strategy for gaining future smokers? Perish the thought! See the following Issue box for identification of more *cigarette issues*.

TARGETING FOREIGN MARKETS

With increasing restraints on cigarette advertising in the United States and the steadily diminishing per capita consumption of cigarettes, it is not surprising that the industry began focusing greater attention on foreign markets. Unfortunately for cigarette makers, criticisms and restraints did not long remain subdued in these markets, either.

At least as early as 1984, the Royal College of Physicians in the United Kingdom harshly denounced tobacco usage, stating that smoking killed 100,000 people a year in the United Kingdom and resulted in 50 million lost working days a year.[15] But the Royal College particularly condemned the lack of availability of low-tar cigarettes, "which are practically unknown in the Third World. The incidence of lung cancer among men in the Natal Bantustan in South Africa has increased 600 percent in the last 11 years. Developed countries bear a heavy responsibility for the worldwide epidemic of smoking."[16]

By 1990, the *New York Times* was reporting strong criticisms by women's groups and health organizations in India over attempts to promote Ms, a new cigarette brand aimed at upwardly mobile Indian women. Billboards and print ads for the products showed strong, happy Indian women in Western-style clothes and affluent settings. Opposition groups condemned the "evil message that cigarette smoking is part of a healthy and logical way of feminine life."[17]

Despite intense lobbying by the tobacco industry, two European Community directives on tobacco advertising were proposed by the European Commission in 1989. The first, barring television advertisements, was readily accepted by EC governments and went into effect in October 1991. The second directive would ban press and poster advertising, and was backed by the European Parliament. The second measure awaiting passage would ban tobacco advertising in "any form of communication, printed, written, oral, by radio and television broadcast and cinema." Even

---

[15]"Developing Countries: Governments Should Take Action Against Cigarettes Before Too Many People Acquire the Potentially Lethal Habit," *New Scientist*, December 1, 1983, p. 42.

[16]*Ibid.*

[17]"Women in Delhi Angered by Smoking Pitch," *New York Times* (National Edition), March 18, 1990, p. 11.

ISSUE: REGARDING CIGARETTES AND SMOKING

The controversies concerning cigarettes go beyond those detailed in this chapter. For example: ·

- Should smoking be restricted in the workplace? In restaurants? In airplanes?
- What about some firms not allowing employees to smoke even when they are not at work?
- Should the tobacco industry pay for employee suits concerning their "right to smoke"?
- Should nonsmokers be protected against passive smoke?
- In general, are the rights of smokers being violated?

INVITATION TO DISCUSS
You may want to discuss, and even debate, these and any another smoking issues you and your students may come up with.

---

logos on cigarette lighters and matches would be forbidden. The tobacco industry, which claimed there was no link between tobacco publicity and the 430,000 deaths a year in Europe from smoking-related diseases, not surprisingly was frantic at this possible outcome.[18] But John Major, Prime Minister of Great Britain, was against the measure, and a minority of countries were likely to block it temporarily. (However, bans on print ads for tobacco are already in force in such EC countries as France, Italy, and Portugal.)

With Western Europe's mounting inhospitality to the industry, U. S. tobacco firms today are eagerly pushing into Asia, Africa, Eastern Europe, and the former Soviet Union. These markets are big—$90 billion a year— and the local cigarette makers appear highly vulnerable to the slick and aggressive efforts of U. S. firms. For example, Marlboro's cowboy is even more widely known in most of Asia than in the United States. As a result, Philip Morris can get its message across simply by playing the brand's theme song or flashing a single image of the cowboy.[19]

For years, Western companies were kept out of these lucrative markets by governments eager to preserve state tobacco monopolies or anticapitalist ideologies. But these barriers have crumbled, especially in Eastern Europe.

---

[18]"EP Backs Ban on Tobacco Advertising," *Europe 2000*, March 1992, p. R41.

[19]Mike Levin, "U.S. Tobacco Firms Push Eagerly into Asian Market," *Marketing News*, Jan. 21, 1991, p. 2.

Tobacco companies have been invited into enormous new markets such as the former Soviet Union, where "cigarette famines" have long existed. Now Philip Morris is shipping billions of cigarettes to Russia.

Countries in the expanding sales area have few marketing or health-labelling controls. In Hungary, for example, Marlboro cigarettes are even handed out to young fans at pop music concerts.[20]

In Asia, protectionist tariffs and import bans had to be cracked before these markets could be entered by foreign tobacco firms. The United States was successful in using Section 301 of its 1974 Trade Act to threaten retaliatory tariffs on the exports of such countries as Japan, South Korea, Taiwan, and Thailand if their markets were not opened to U. S. tobacco firms. Tobacco-state representatives in Congress have been strong influences in such pressures, and they were successful in opening up these markets. By 1992, cigarette advertising on television in Japan—it is not allowed in the United States—had soared from fortieth to second place in air time since 1987 and even appears during children's shows. Smoking has greatly increased among women, who were largely ignored before the Western firms arrived but are now prime targets. Tobacco companies found good market potential among women in such Asian areas as Hong Kong, where fewer than 5 percent of women smoke. Philip Morris is tapping this market with its Virginia Slims, a feminine brand famous for its slogan, "You've come a long way, baby."[21]

Assessment of the Overseas Push by U.S. Tobacco Firms. A firm seems entitled to make all the profit it can make. If certain markets are drying up or are being severely constrained, should not a firm have the right to seek other markets aggressively? This is what the tobacco companies are doing.

The issue is clouded because cigarette smoking is generally conceded to be hazardous to health. But not immediately so, and by no means certainly so. As long as many people are willing to take the risk, how can the tobacco makers and growers and advertisers and retailers be so negatively judged?

When sophisticated and aggressive promotional efforts are directed at the developing countries where consumers are more easily swayed and far more vulnerable to promotional blandishments, does our perception of what is ethical and what is undesirable conduct change? Should it?

---

[20]"The Tobacco Trade: The Search for El Dorado," *Economist*, May 16, 1992, p. 23.
[21]*Ibid.*, p. 24.

WHAT CAN BE LEARNED?

Learning Insight. *Public perception of unethical conduct seems to be ever expanding.*

Formerly, deceptive practices or unsafe products were the most commonly condemned examples of misconduct. But as we have seen in these last few cases, such no longer holds true. The ethical arena for a firm is no longer finite and predictable. It is a lurking quicksand for the unwary or the unconcerned. Consequently, the need for vigilance is greater, and more attention and sensitivity must be accorded a diverse and changing environment.

Learning Insight. *Effective marketing strategies may need to be reconsidered in today's changing social milieu.*

Strategies honed in the past may no longer be appropriate; they may be vulnerable to public protests, boycotts, negative publicity, even governmental pressure and regulation. How is a firm to cope with this changing environment?

The answer would seem to lie in increased sensitivity, especially concerning relations with minorities, whether of race, sex, or age. A new brand or a new marketing strategy should be carefully assessed for its acceptability and freedom from potential criticism before widespread introduction. Even then, surprises may come. And stoutly maintaining a strategy in the face of mounting opposition may well not be the best course of action, for the firm or its industry. Sometimes this assessment may necessitate scraping a successful product or brand or advertising campaign.

Learning Insight. *Unacceptable actions in one environment may no longer be transferred to another without risk.*

Cigarette firms, finding the U.S. market hostile to aggressive promotions, naturally turned their efforts to more hospitable market segments and countries. Not many years ago, such efforts would have been not only effective but would have activated very little critical attention or publicity. Now, a firm may find only a short-term advantage in targeting another market for products and practices criticized at home. Criticism tends to become contagious, even though oceans may separate. A firm may no longer be insulated from adverse publicity and possible punitive regulations when it attempts to move aggressively into minority segments and foreign markets.

Issue Insight. *Does a vocal minority in its aggressive efforts to promote its own self-interest represent acceptable behavior?*

In a pluralistic society, many minorities are openly encouraged to present their positions. The issue becomes one of degree: what level of critical behavior is acceptable? Is whitewashing or destroying billboards acceptable behavior? Is firebombing the stores of opportunistic shopowners of different ethnic origins acceptable? Where do we draw the line? Unfortunately, there is no common ground for society's approval; inconsistencies abound. For example, society generally views burning stores to be unacceptable. But whitewashing offending billboards seems to be acceptable. Where should the line be drawn, and who is to be the judge: a firebrand preacher, a government agency, the police department, the courts . . . ?

Issue Insight. *Is it ethically right for a firm to vigorously promote a product that is seen by almost everyone except its own industry as unsafe and even deadly?*

This issue gets to the heart of the whole matter of tobacco production and marketing. Generally considered by all health experts as dangerous and in the long term, life threatening, tobacco is still protected by powerful governmental interests, even if the industry is no longer pampered.

The tobacco industry stubbornly refuses to admit the health charges, citing its own research to the contrary. And the industry is huge, with many stakeholders: tobacco growers, processors, retailers, tax collectors . . . as well as influential people in the halls of government.

Not the least of the proponents for the industry are the users themselves, even though this is a declining number every year in this country. The health dangers can be discounted as being both far in the future and affecting only a minority of users. "And never me!"

The morality? It is easy for the stakeholders to rationalize that any bad consequences are uncertain at best, that the good outweighs any bad possibilities. But somehow, some of us are left with the sneaky feeling that maybe, just maybe, the profit motive is deemed stronger than any possible dire consequences to society.

FOR THOUGHT AND DISCUSSION

1. Do you have any problems with the idea of activist ministers leading their flock to whitewash offensive billboards? If not, is tearing down such billboards acceptable? Please discuss as objectively as possible.

2. Do you consider the proof adequate that cigarettes pose a substantial health threat and should be banned or tightly constrained? If you accept this position, should tobacco growers be allowed to continue growing such "unsafe" harvests?
3. Is there really any difference in the targeting of minority markets by brewers and the liquor industry and the obvious targeting by certain tobacco brands?
4. Playing the devil's advocate (one who argues an opposing point for the sake of argument), what arguments would you put forth that the cigarette manufacturers should be permitted complete freedom in targeting developing countries?
5. How do you assess the relative merits of the tangible financial contributions that the tobacco industry has made to various minority groups and media, and the negative health consequences of smoking?

INVITATION TO ROLE PLAY

1. You are the public relations spokesperson for a major cigarette maker. How would you defend your company's aggressive marketing practices in Third World countries?
2. You are a young black woman who uses Uptown cigarettes and likes them. At a church outing your minister denounces Uptown and the company that makes them. Describe how you might respond to such a tirade against your favorite brand.

INVITATION TO RESEARCH

1. Has the hubbub over minority targeting by cigarette companies subsided as of today?
2. What is the most current situation regarding overseas incursions by U.S. tobacco companies?
3. Has the hubbub about Joe Camel subsided? Did RJR pull this advertising campaign?

20

Potpourri of Abusive Practices Toward Customers

In this chapter, we examine abusive practices toward customers as found, more often than we would like, in three industries: health clubs, small consumer loans, and auto repairs. Whereas violations of the public trust are not limited to these three areas, they provide at least their fair share of abusive practices. These industries also typify the range of unethical practices directed to consumers, who may not be naive and unsophisticated but certainly have less technical knowledge and are consequently at the mercy of unscrupulous sellers, calloused sellers, or both. As we will see, some of these firms are not fly-by-night undertakings but are major corporations in our society. Although many reputable firms follow forthright and fully ethical practices, there are those that do not.

HEALTH CLUB ABUSES

Over the last few decades, more and more Americans have turned to the pursuit of physical fitness, which is promoted as a means to a more attractive and satisfactory lifestyle, and also as an assurance of healthy longevity. Many people have joined health clubs for the equipment and expertise to pursue such healthy lifestyles, and for the social encouragement that they need to persevere in these efforts. Alas, some health clubs have failed their dedicated fitness seekers. Some have evinced outright fraud in their solicitation of memberships; most have shown the extremes of high-pressure selling; others have been built on flimsy financial structures and have closed, taking the money of members who have paid advance fees or leaving them no alternative memberships.

Health Club Closings

Some health clubs have fraudulently solicited memberships with the intention to fold their tents and slink away when sufficient funds are gained, leaving their erstwhile patrons with little recourse while the promoters count their gains. But it is a thin line between such scams and the enterprise that is poorly funded, poorly planned, and cannot survive and thus presents its patrons with the same consequences, even though the intent may not have been quite so evil.

Business Atlanta pointed out such problems in the Atlanta area where health clubs folded and left their members stranded. For example, the two largest facilities in the area, Richard Simmons Anatomy Asylum and Mademoiselle Spa Figure and Fitness, together generated 1,500 complaints to the state Office of Consumer Affairs. Four smaller clubs also went under for a total of 57 clubs that closed out of 122 listed in the Yellow Pages.

People complaining about useless health club contracts say their spas showed no hint of impending disaster. For example, Nancy George got little use out of her $500 Richard Simmons membership before that center folded. She said to reporters, "I was cheated out of a lot of money, and it just closed down on me with no warning. I was worried, too, because one of the other clubs had been in trouble, so I asked the managers who ran my club about it. They assured me it would not close."[1] But close it did, with no warning.

Barry Reid, administrator of the governor's Office of Consumer Affairs, noted that a major problem was that spas asked for large amounts of money in advance. While they operated under the guise of legitimacy, there were clubs set up from the beginning as a scam.[2]

In many instances of failed and/or closed health clubs, the members still owed money on their contracts. It would seem an easy solution for members simply to refuse to make any further payments. Alas, this solution was not that simple. Invariably, the health clubs had sold the contracts to a third party, a loan company, now supposedly an innocent *holder in due course* that was entitled to full recompense. Customers were threatened with the loss of their credit ratings if they did not continue paying for

---

[1]Maxine Rock, "Health Club Hijinks," *Business Atlanta*, October 1988, p. 104.
[2]*Ibid.*

THE HOLDER IN DUE COURSE CONTROVERSY

Traditional legal doctrine prescribes that when a seller sells a note or credit contract to a third party such as a bank or loan company, this new owner is the innocent holder in due course; the purchaser must pay the full amount of the obligation to this third party *regardless* of his or her satisfaction with the purchase, whether it is even usable or, in the case of health club memberships, even in business. Thus, the rights of the third party are fully protected, whereas the purchaser's rights are no longer protected once the credit obligation has been sold to a third party.

You can see the inequity this system can impose on the innocent purchaser. Not to pay the full amount of the contract can bring legal action and destroy a credit rating. No wonder the purchasers of memberships in health clubs that went under feared to stop their payments. The injustice for the consumer of holder in due course obligations has come under public scrutiny and some states have moved to modify the full ramifications of this law of long standing.

For example, in 1984 laws regulating health clubs in Georgia were enacted requiring reimbursement of members on defunct spa contracts through posting by the club of a bond or a letter of credit with the state. The law also stated that consumers have the right to refuse payment to a finance company holding the contract under certain circumstances, even under the holder in due course rule. Consumers must notify the finance company in writing of their intention to cease monthly payments and explain why they are doing so. But many persons were unclear about the law and feared consequent actions by finance companies for nonpayment.

INVITATION TO DISCUSS

Either to enforce the holder in due course rule or to rescind it poses inequities. The innocent third party is protected with the rule; the innocent consumer is better protected if it is rescinded. As a state legislator considering the issue of rescinding, how would you try to resolve the issue? How would you balance off the competing claims? Which position would you expect to carry the most weight, and why?

the defunct membership. (See the information box above for a discussion of the traditional rights of the *holder in due course* and the consequences for the consumer.)

Defenders of the larger health club chains pointed out that they were operating completely within the law. Existing corporate rules permit a chain to set up many stores, each as an individual entity, so the potential failure of one does not drag down the others. Therefore, the other units of a chain are insulated from the incompetencies and inefficiencies of some outlets.

High-Pressure Selling

Surprisingly, high-pressure sales efforts have prevailed with many health clubs despite the fact that most potential customers are neither poor nor unsophisticated but are young professionals and executives who should be more resistant and turned off by high pressure.

The larger organizations appear to have been more successful in this type of selling. Because of greater resources than smaller health spas, they are able to use the media more effectively to bring potential clients to their premises. They can afford more impressive equipment. And they can hire people who are experienced in hard sell and whose own compensation and even jobs depend on how many contracts they can write.

Potential customers, even though they may be well educated and with good jobs, seem particularly vulnerable to appeals to health, beauty, and social attractiveness. Such emotional appeals, when coupled with the right atmosphere of attractive customers and employees, can be powerfully persuasive. Strenuous efforts to induce the potential customer, often called a "target," to make a commitment on the spot often succeed.

With employees themselves under pressure to make the sale—in some cases under surveillance through monitoring devices and one-way mirrors—the unscrupulous health spa has reasonable assurance that only the most sales-resistant potential customers will be "allowed" to escape.

State Efforts to Curb Abusive Practices

A number of states have attempted to regulate health clubs more closely. For example, Pennsylvania Attorney General LeRoy S. Zimmerman testified before the state legislature in support of a bill for a health club act that was drafted by the state House Consumer Affairs Committee.

The attorney general displayed boxes filled with consumer complaints. He told the committee that in only five months his office had received more than 2,500 complaints regarding health clubs.

In particular, the proposed legislation would require health clubs to post bonds or letter of credit to ensure that money would be available to reimburse clients if the facility closed. The bill would also remedy another frequent source of complaints, the decision by a health club with two or more locations to close one of these locations. Usually, such clubs refuse to give refunds to members who used the closed location, reasoning that those members can use one of the remaining locations. "This sounds reasonable, and may be acceptable to members when the other location is just down the street," Zimmerman noted. "But it is neither reasonable nor acceptable when, as happened recently, a club closed [one facility], and told members to use a related facility . . . more than 50 miles away."[3]

Other provisions needed to protect consumers would allow for cancellation of membership and a refund if the member dies, is disabled, or moves out of the area. And an important protection against high pressure to finalize the sale on the spot is a three-day waiting period after signing the contract, during which it can be canceled without penalty.

SMALL LOAN COMPANY ABUSES

Most people in the financial straits of needing personal loans are not financially sophisticated. California Attorney General John Van de Kamp noted that most of the victims of an alleged scam were poor people who were easy prey. "These are people who are often desperate," he said. "They're borrowing money for food for their children."[4]

The vulnerability of many such customers is increased by their youth (they lack experience) or advanced age (they may become easily confused and hesitant to ask for explanations or clarifications). Furthermore, many of these customers are in precarious financial situations and have few alternatives to doing business with a small loan company.

So we have a situation that can motivate loan companies to take less than scrupulously honest actions. While abuses are by no means limited to the following example, this particular large company epitomizes the type of questionable practices that can occur in this industry. Interestingly, our example of consumer personal loan abuses concerns the same large corporation we encountered in an earlier case when its nefarious activities involved interference with a foreign government.

ITT Consumer Financial Corporation

ITT Consumer Financial Corporation is a unit of ITT (formerly called IT&T), a multinational firm diversified into such areas as communications, information and financial services, manufacturing, and hotels. ITT Consumer specializes in small consumer loans, and its practices have come to the critical attention of attorneys general in a number of states. The complaints have centered mostly on high-pressure selling techniques, inadequate or

---

[3]"Pennsylvania Attorney General Speaks in Favor of H.B. 819, the "Health Club Act," *PR Newswire*, May 21, 1987, p. 8.

[4]Charles McCoy, "ITT Unit Settles Fraud Charges in California," *Wall Street Journal*, September 22, 1989, p. A3.

nonexistent disclosure that certain add-ons were optional and cost more, and uselessness of some of these add-ons. Added to these specific allegations against ITT were the more pervasive charges against most small loan firms in general: exorbitant interest rates and aggressive and abusive collection techniques.

The attorneys general were particularly concerned with "packing," a lucrative practice in which the lender adds payments for "optional" insurance and other products to the amount of the loan without the customer's requesting them, sometimes without the customer's knowledge either that they have been added or that they could have been refused. For example, take the case of Katherine Snow.

Needing money for Christmas, she sought out Wisconsin's biggest consumer-loan company, a division of ITT. It agreed to lend her $126.72. But she was also induced to borrow $14.74 for credit life insurance, $73.44 for property insurance, and $202 for term life insurance. Not satisfied with this, the lender also pressured her to become a member of the ITT Consumer Thrift Club, entitling her to discounts on consumer products. All of these add-ons were financed at interest rates above 22 percent.[5]

Although the company maintained in defense that its policies were to emphasize to customers that all these additional purchases were voluntary, internal company memorandums suggested otherwise—that branch managers were ordered to sell certain amounts of add-ons in connection with loans, or face disciplinary action.

The profitability in selling insurance with consumer loans has not gone unnoticed by other lenders. Banks, auto dealers, and other consumer-loan companies have also moved to tap this fertile field. But ITT's proficiency was unsurpassed, with the result that a number of states either took or threatened legal action against ITT. An out-of-court settlement was reached with the Wisconsin attorney general whereby ITT agreed to return as much as $12 million to Wisconsin policyholders. A similar settlement was reached with the Iowa attorney general and class action suits alleging insurance packing were pending against ITT in Wisconsin, Alabama, and Arizona. Minnesota and Colorado were also investigating the company's lending practices.

But the biggest case and decision occurred in California. In one of the largest settlements ever in a consumer fraud case, ITT Consumer Financial Corporation agreed to pay restitution, fines, and other penalties that could eventually total $100 million. The California Attorney General's Office had alleged that ITT defrauded thousands of California consumers by promising them preapproved credit, inducing them to take out loans that some-

---

[5]Walt Bogdanish, "Irate Borrowers Accuse ITT's Loan Companies of Deceptive Practices," *Wall Street Journal,* February 26, 1985, p. 1.

BAIT AND SWITCH—WHEN IS IT ETHICAL?

In bait and switch, the customer is enticed into a store because of very low prices, only to find that such goods are "no longer available," and is then switched to more expensive items. This can be deceptive and abusive. The abuse is most prevalent in ghetto stores: an appliance or a set of furniture may be advertised at an unreasonably low price; the objective is to entice customers into the store. But when they attempt to purchase the "sale" item they find it, in the parlance of retailing, "nailed to the floor." In other words, it is not available; the only piece at that price may be broken, shopworn, have missing parts, or carry a "sold" tag. The customer is then traded up to a more expensive and more profitable product.

But this is the extreme. It is commonplace for reputable retailers to advertise their most attractively priced items and then attempt to sell a customer something else. Some retailers even offer items below cost (so-called loss leaders) to generate customer traffic, expecting that regular-price items will be bought as well. Some weekly grocery ads are of this type. The difference between such bait-and-switch advertising and the deceptive kind is that the sale item is available; customers can buy it if they so desire (and some, indeed, may buy nothing else but loss leaders).

INVITATION TO DISCUSS

Bait and switch, where the product or the price advertised is not available or the interest rate stated over the phone is incorrect, is illegal as well as unethical. Yet, it is still practiced. What accounts for the pervasiveness of the practice, despite its illegality?

times carried rates as high at 35 percent and then illegally charging them for insurance, club memberships, and other services that the customers did not request and frequently had no idea they were receiving and paying for.[6]

In addition to complaints about packing, other complaints focused on bait and switch (see the above information box), exorbitant interest, and harassment. For example:[7]

Interest rates quoted over phone were 18.5 percent, raised to 28.5 percent when papers were signed.

My loan was for $1200. When they finished in the end I was to pay back $3500.

They harassed me at home and on my job and I was only a day late.

---

[6]Charles McCoy, "ITT Unit Settles Fraud Charges in California," *Wall Street Journal,* September 22, 1989, p. A3.

[7]A sample of an unpublished survey of small loan customers in Cleveland, Ohio, 1990.

ABUSES IN AUTO REPAIRS

Few business interfaces with consumers are susceptible to more abuses than the repair industry. Although we focus our attention here on some specifics of the auto repair sector, abuses are wide ranging, from small appliance repairs to those for larger home appliances such as TVs and kitchen appliances, to plumbing and electrical repairs, and on and on. But the auto repair sector epitomizes the questionable practices of this entire industry capitalizing on consumers' need for repairs.

The well-publicized example of Sears provides the focus for this exposé. However, we need to recognize that these wrongdoings are by no means unique to Sears and seem to be endemic in this industry. The repair industry is one in which the consumer is absolutely at the mercy of the repair professional, whose expert judgment can hardly be questioned by any but the most skillful consumer. Not only are typical consumers unable to gauge what is needed in any repairs, but they also have little basis for judging the time spent on any repairs or, indeed, even the seriousness of the problem. The temptation for the repair worker then, is to replace more than is really needed and to pad the time spent on the repairs—in other words, to beef up the cost of the repairs 30, 40, 60, 100 percent and more. And who is to judge the reasonableness of the charges, outside of hiring another "expert" to appraise the problem and results? Except for investigative reporters hoping to uncover a scam, this kind of follow-up is almost never done. Appliance repairers will often price their estimates slightly below the costs of a replacement appliance, thus putting the consumer in the position of deciding whether to have the old appliance repaired or to dash out and buy a new one.

In mid-1992, wide publicity emanated from disclosures of auto repair abuses by a large and reputable retailer. Sears was embarrassed, and sales of its auto division dropped. The company offered a public explanation and apology and promised certain wide-ranging changes to correct the worst of these abuses. But, again, they only typified practices that are all too common in much of the repair industry.

Accusations of Fraud at Sears Auto Centers

On June 12, 1992, national publications reported that the California-Department of Consumer Affairs had accused Sears of systematically overcharging auto-repair customers. The agency even went so far as to propose revoking the company's license to operate its automotive centers in the state.

The year-long undercover investigation had been prompted by a growing number of consumer complaints. For example:

> Ruth Hernandez of Stockton, California went to Sears to buy new tires for her 1986 Honda Accord. The Sears mechanic insisted that she also needed new struts at a cost of $419.95. Shocked, she sought a second opinion, and another auto-repair store told her the struts were fine. Hernandez was livid and she returned to Sears where a sheepish mechanic admitted his diagnosis was wrong. "I keep thinking," Hernandez reflected, "how many other people this has happened to."[8]

The Department of Consumer Affairs found that its agents were overcharged at Sears Centers nearly 90 percent of the time by an average of $233. The department said that repairmen were pressured to overcharge by Sears's setting punitive sales quotas. "This is a flagrant breach of the trust and confidence the people of California have placed in Sears for generations," said Jim Conran, director of the department. "Sears has used trust as a marketing tool, and we don't believe they've lived up to that trust."[9]

The Sears case may be the biggest fraud action ever against an auto-repair firm. Although the investigation was conducted in California, the findings probably represent a much more widespread problem, perhaps involving Sears's 850 auto-repair centers nationwide.

At first, Sears vigorously contested the allegations. It called the accusations by California regulators politically motivated and denied any fraud. It accused regulators of trying to gain support at a time when they were threatened by severe budget cuts. Sears used its lawyers to hold to that position for several days. But the crisis intensified, especially a few days later when New Jersey regulators said that they, too, had found overcharges common in Sears shops.

Sears soon adopted a more conciliatory stance. Full-page ads were taken out in major newspapers in the form of a letter from Edward A. Brennan, the company's chairman, expressing deep concern about the problem and pledging that Sears would satisfy all its customers: "With over two million automotive customers serviced last year in California alone, mistakes may have occurred. However, Sears wants you to know that we would never intentionally violate the trust customers have shown in our company for 105 years." But auto-service sales dropped 15 percent in little

---

[8]Example taken from Keven Kelly, "How Did Sears Blow This Gasket?" *Business Week*, June 29, 1992, p. 38.

[9]Tung Yin, "Sears is Accused of Billing Fraud at Auto Centers," *Wall Street Journal*, June 12, 1992, pp. B1, B6.

more than a week. And this was a division that produced 9 percent of Sears's merchandising group's revenue, which totaled $19.4 billion in 1991, and had been one of the fastest growing and most profitable business units in recent years, servicing 20 million vehicles in 1991.[10]

Sears's Belated Response to the Allegations

Nearly two weeks after the initial charges by California investigators, Sears moved aggressively to combat the charges and to attempt to stem its business erosion. Chairman Brennan accepted personal responsibility for the troubles and announced that Sears was discontinuing the employee compensation policies that led to the problems.

By now, Florida had joined New Jersey and California in investigating practices at Sears's auto-service centers. To stem further state actions, Sears sent a copy of its new auto-repair policies to the attorneys general of every state.

Although Brennan continued to deny the regulators' charges, he announced that Sears would:

- For those who diagnose car problems, change the pay system from a commission system, which regulators claimed encouraged phony diagnoses, to a straight pay system.
- End a system of sales goals for specific products.
- Hire an independent group to conduct undercover "shopping audits" of its auto centers.
- Expand its current internal monitoring.
- Encourage state attorneys general to determine whether Sears meets their states' standards.
- Help organize and pay for an effort involving the industry, government regulators, and consumer groups to recommend uniform standards governing the auto-repair field.

"The clear objective of the actions announced today is to safeguard against such allegations arising again," Brennan said. "We have talked to enough people over the last 12 days to believe that the policies for compensation and goal setting, created by management for our service advisers in the auto centers, were mistakes."[11] (See the following Issue box about the *desirability of commission compensation in retailing*.)

---

[10]Gregory A. Patterson, "Sears's Brennan Accepts Blame for Auto Flap," *Wall Street Journal*, June 23, 1992, pp. B1, B12.

[11]"Allegations Prompt Change in Sears Auto-Repair Policies," *Cleveland Plain Dealer*, June 23, 1992, p. 8-H.

ISSUE: IS COMMISSION COMPENSATION
UNDESIRABLE IN RETAILING?

The blame for the abusive practices in Sears's auto-service centers was placed on the commission structure of the centers' employees, who were motivated to recommend unnecessary repairs to customers. The issue then became one of motivating employees without making them too pushy.

Many retailers in recent years have followed the lead of the highly successful Nordstrom department store chain, whose sales force works almost entirely on commission. Whereas in 1981, 21 percent of all retail sales people earned just a salary and no commission, by 1990 only 7 percent earned just a salary, according to Dartnell Corporation, a sales-compensation firm.

Now, in the wake of Sears's bad publicity, as well as their own customer complaints and alienated customers, such major retailers as Dayton Hudson are starting to scale back their aggressive commission plans. Even a few automobile dealers—in particular, those of General Motors' new Saturn car division—are starting to pay their salespeople salaries instead of commissions in order to improve customer service and teamwork among the sales force.

Still, opinions differ whether the benefits of substantial commissions for motivation and greater attentiveness to customers outweigh the drawbacks of high pressure and aggressiveness and sales people who resent any non-selling activities that may lessen their sales opportunities.

INVITATION TO DISCUSS
Discuss the pros and cons of having auto dealer salespeople work on straight salary rather than straight commission. Are there any other compensation options?

Source: For greater detail, see Gregory A. Patterson, "Distressed Shoppers, Disaffected Workers Prompt Stores to Alter Sales Commissions," *Wall Street Journal,* July 1, 1992, pp. B1 and B5.

ANALYSIS

In this chapter we have seen three sectors involving consumers where less-than-ethical practices prevailed. This is hardly symptomatic of the entire business community interface with consumers. These are the exceptions to forthright conduct. But we have to recognize from these examples that in at least three arenas consumers are vulnerable to abuse:

1. Where advance payments are required for services to be rendered later.
2. Where consumers are in financial straits and are desperate for relief through loans.

3. Whenever repairs are involved—be these with automobiles, appliances, home repairs, or whatever—the consumer is helpless before the expertise of the repair person in assessing the validity of charges and parts replacements.

These situations create serious temptations for sellers to take advantage of naive and helpless consumers. Where no repeat business is likely, at least in the short run, and where customer loyalty is not a major consideration, temptations to overcharge even to the point of fraud are ever present.

It is evident today that large firms are the focus of regulatory attention and attorney general purview. They are the visible players in their respective industries. As we saw with the ITT small loan investigations and the more recent allegations against Sears's automotive servicing and repairs, the social and legal environment today makes any large firm particularly vulnerable to public scrutiny and worse if its practices are not scrupulously honest. A small firm may be far more guilty of abuses, but generally will escape most public condemnation.

Was Sears's Reaction to the Public Charges Praiseworthy?

In Chapter 21, we describe a firm faced with a catastrophe of mean proportions; through no fault of the company, Johnson & Johnson, some people died because of criminal tampering with some of its Tylenol capsules. Johnson & Johnson reacted in what almost all analysts consider to be a most exemplary and responsive fashion. As a result, the company is frequently cited as the epitome of positive customer concern and a model for the unselfish assumption of corrective and protective measures for its customers, regardless of the impact on profits. Could Sears be viewed in a similar fashion, upon reflective assessment?

Certain conditions obviously are not the same. Johnson & Johnson had no culpability; Sears did. But perhaps Sears's culpability was not as serious as might seem at first. The abuses were long-standing accepted practices. Indeed, such practices are more common than not in the repair industry. Sears's present management cannot escape responsibility for practices that have persisted for decades even though they probably were little aware of all such. Creating incentives for padding repair bills can hardly be condoned; still, close contact by top management with all aspects of a behemoth organization may not be possible despite their ultimate responsibility.

Brennan's reaction to the serious accusations and public scrutiny, while somewhat slow in evolving, nevertheless was aggressive and highly responsive to the situation and very much customer-oriented. Indeed, the possibility exists that the positive and aggressive efforts of Sears to cope with a problem that is familiar to all consumers may presage a new and honest relationship of the repair industry in general with its customers. Is it possible that because of Sears's leadership, we as consumers will have a better stance with repair people in the future, that we can actually trust them?

If so, Sears's Brennan will have made an inestimable contribution to the economic rights of consumers. And Sears has the opportunity, if it can capitalize on it, of becoming the champion of consumer rights. Rather a heady possibility.

WHAT CAN BE LEARNED?

Learning Insight. *A heavy sales incentive program invites abusive practices in such consumer-service areas as health clubs, small loan firms, and repair businesses of all kinds.*

Although a firm may be tempted to motivate its employees to seek greater sales with various incentive programs, the end result in public scrutiny and condemnation may not be worth whatever increase in sales that might be gained. The very recent policy changes publicly announced by Sears's chairman Brennan for its auto-repair centers was long overdue. Policies of incentives and sales goals simply promote padded and phony diagnoses and bilking the consumer. Sears should have changed such policies years before but did this only grudgingly in 1992 as it faced a crescendo of complaints and investigations and a substantial loss of business. How can a firm that promotes its good customer relations have been so oblivious to the "occasions of sin" in a very susceptible area of its operation?

Learning Insight. *A firm and an industry need to recognize that long-standing practices on the borderline of good conduct may come under new and critical scrutiny by aggressive regulators, attorneys general, and consumer activists.*

The fact that a particular practice is long-standing—and presumably an accepted business practice—no longer guarantees freedom from hostile review and pressure to reform. In the language of the street: "Just because you always done it this way, don't mean it's right." And increasingly, such views are gaining many supporters.

Learning Insight. *Large corporations are particularly vulnerable to public scrutiny by activists, politicians, the media, regulatory agencies, and the legal establishment.*

The wiser course of action for such firms may well be to pursue a cautious approach in areas of potential controversy, even if short-term profits may have to be restrained as a consequence. Sears suffered a 15 percent decrease in its auto-repair business in the first week of bad publicity. Without immediate and drastic defensive reaction on its part, the loss could have been much worse.

FOR THOUGHT AND DISCUSSION

1. Most of the patrons of health clubs are educated and have fairly good incomes and jobs. How do you account for their being so susceptible to high pressure, fraud, and other abuses?
2. Amid the rather large number of small-loan firms, should not a consumer be able to shop around for the best deal, and thus escape the worst of the abuses mentioned in the chapter?
3. What is your opinion of the Sears auto-repair centers? Do you think their overcharging was less, worse, or about the same as their competitors? What led you to this opinion?
4. A common practice of repair people in all areas is to replace some parts that are still workable with new parts. This, of course, raises the price of the repair. But is this really such a bad practice—after all, the new parts should assure longer trouble free use of the car?

INVITATION TO ROLE PLAY

1. You are the chief executive of a chain of small-loan outlets. After hearing the bad publicity about the alleged practices of ITT's Consumer Loan Division, you want to be certain that your managers and employees are not guilty of similar practices. What policies might you establish to minimize abuses in the very susceptible small-loan business?
2. You are an executive assistant to Edward Brennan, CEO of Sears. He wants to institute sweeping reforms in the auto-repair operational unit. What arguments might you give him not to push the panic button, but to institute only very modest changes?

INVITATION TO RESEARCH

How has the Sears auto-repair scandal evolved since the first intimations were publicized in June 1992?

Three

CONCLUSIONS

21

Johnson & Johnson: Tylenol, A Shining Example of Responsible Business Conduct—and Yet . . . ?

It is a surprising anomaly, but perhaps it shouldn't be, given human nature, that a firm (or a person) can exhibit the most exemplary behavior toward others at one time, yet later fall to the lowest common denominator of conduct. In its handling of a catastrophe of no mean proportions, the criminal contamination of its highly profitable Tylenol capsules, Johnson & Johnson exhibited what has become a model for corporate responsibility to its customers, regardless of costs. Yet in a later day, the company has come under fire for price gouging for one of its cancer drugs.

THE PRELUDE

It is September 30, 1982. On the fifth floor of Johnson & Johnson's (J & J) headquarters in New Brunswick, New Jersey, Chairman James E. Burke is having a quiet meeting with President David R. Clair. The two top executives of the company liked to hold such informal meetings every two months. They would talk over important but nonpressing matters that they usually did not get around to dealing with in the normal course of events. Today, both men have reason to feel good, for J & J's sales and earnings were up sharply and the trend of business could hardly have been more promising. They even have time to dwell on some nonbusiness matters that sunny September morning.

Their complacency and self-satisfaction does not last long. Arthur Quill, a member of the executive committee, bursts into the meeting. Consternation and anguish flood the room as he brings word of cyanide deaths in Chicago that are connected to J & J's most important and profitable product, Extra-Strength Tylenol capsules.

THE PRODUCT

The success of Tylenol in the late 1970s and early 1980s had been sensational. It was introduced in 1955 by McNeil Laboratories as an alternative drug to aspirin and one that avoided the side effects of aspirin. In 1959, Johnson & Johnson acquired McNeil Laboratories and ran it as an independent subsidiary.

By 1974, Tylenol sales had grown to $50 million at retail, primarily achieved through heavy advertising to physicians. A national consumer advertising campaign was instituted in 1976, and this proved very effective. By 1979, Tylenol had become the largest-selling health and beauty aid in drug and food mass merchandising, breaking the 18-year domination of Procter & Gamble's Crest toothpaste. By 1982, Tylenol had captured 35.3 percent of the over-the-counter analgesic market. This was more than the market shares of Bayer, Bufferin, and Anacin combined. Table 21.1 shows the competitive positions of Tylenol and its principal competitors in this analgesic market. Total sales of all Tylenol products went from $115 million in 1976 to $350 million in 1982, a whopping 204 percent increase in a highly competitive market. As such, Tylenol accounted for 7 percent of all J & J sales. More important, it contributed 17 percent of all profits.

Then catastrophe struck.

THE COMPANY

Johnson & Johnson manufactures and markets a broad range of health care products in many countries of the world. Table 21.2 shows the various

Table 21.1 Market Shares of Major Brands—Over-the-Counter Analgesic Market, 1981

Brand	Percentage of market
Tylenol	35.3
Anacin	13
Bayer	11
Excedrin	10.1
Bufferin	9

Source: "A Death Blow for Tylenol?" **Business Week**, Oct. 18, 1982, p. 151.

Table 21.2 Contribution to Total Johnson & Johnson Sales Of Product Categories, 1983

Product Classification	Sales (Millions)	Percentage of Total Company Sales
Surgical and First-Aid Supplies	$1268	21%
Pharmaceuticals	1200	20
Sanitary Napkins and Tampons	933	16
Baby Products	555	9
Diagnostic Equipment	518	9
Tylenol and Variants	460	8
Other (includes hospital supplies, dental products, contraceptives	1039	17
TOTAL	$5973	100%

Source: After Its Recovery, New Headaches for Tylenol," *Business Week*, May 14, 1984, p. 137.

categories of products and their percentage of total corporate sales. In 1981, J & J was 68th on the *Fortune 500* list of the largest industrial companies in the United States, and it had sales of $5.4 billion. It was organized into four industry categories: Professional, Pharmaceutical, Industrial, and Consumer. The Professional Division included products such as ligatures, sutures, surgical dressings, and other surgical-related items. The Pharmaceutical Division included basically prescription drugs, while the Industrial area included textile products, industrial tapes, and fine chemicals.

The largest division was the Consumer Division, and this consisted of toiletries and hygienic products, such as baby care items, first aid products, and nonprescription drugs. These products were marketed primarily to the general public and distributed through wholesalers and directly to independent and chain retail outlets.

Tylenol was one of the major brands included in the Consumer Division. It is an acetaminophen-based or nonaspirin analgesic. It was the most profitable product for Johnson & Johnson in the early 1980s.

Through the years, J & J had assiduously worked to cultivate an image of responsibility and trust. Its products were associated with gentleness and safety—for all customers, from babies to the elderly. The corporate sense of responsibility fully covered the products and actions of any firms that it acquired, such as McNeil Laboratories.

THE CRISIS

The catastrophe started on a Wednesday morning in late September, 1982. Adam Janus had a minor chest pain, so he purchased a bottle of Extra-Strength Tylenol capsules. He took one capsule and was dead by midafternoon. Later that same day, Stanley Janus and his wife took capsules from the same bottle—both were dead by Friday afternoon. By the weekend, four more Chicago-area residents died under similar circumstances. The cause of death: cyanide, a deadly poison that can kill by disrupting the blood's ability to carry oxygen through the body, thereby affecting the heart, lungs, and brain. The cyanide had been used to contaminate Extra-Strength Tylenol capsules. Dr. Thomas Kim, chief of the critical care unit of Northwest Community Hospital in Arlington Heights, Illinois, noted, "The victims never had a chance. Death was certain within minutes."[1]

Medical examiners retrieved bottles from the victims' homes and found another 10 capsules laced with cyanide. In each case, the red half of the capsule was discolored and slightly swollen, and the usual dry white powder was replaced with a gray substance that had an almond odor. One of the capsules had 65 mg of cyanide—a lethal dose is considered to be 50 mg.

The McNeil executives learned of the poisonings from reporters calling for comment about the tragedy. Calls came from all the media, and then from pharmacies, doctors, hospitals, poison control centers, and hundreds of panicked consumers. McNeil quickly gathered information on the victims, causes of death, lot numbers on the poisoned Tylenol bottles, outlets where they had been purchased, dates when they had been manufactured, and the route they had taken through the distribution system.

After the deaths were linked to Tylenol, one of the biggest consumer alerts ever took place. Johnson & Johnson recalled batches, while consumers were advised not to take any Extra-Strength Tylenol capsules until the mystery was solved. Drugstores and supermarkets across the country pulled Tylenol products from their shelves; it soon became virtually impossible to obtain Tylenol anywhere.

In tracking down the mysterious contamination, it was quickly determined that the poisoning did not occur in manufacturing, either intentionally or accidentally. The poisoned capsules came from lots manufactured at both McNeil plants. Therefore, the tampering had to have happened in Chicago, since poisoning at both plants at the same time would have been almost impossible. The FDA suspected that someone unconnected with the manufacturer had bought the Tylenol over the counter, inserted cyanide in some capsules, then returned the bottles to the stores. Otherwise, the contamination would have been widespread, and not only in the Chicago area.

At this point, Johnson & Johnson was virtually cleared of any wrongdoing. But the company was stuck with having one of its major products publicly associated with poison and death, no matter how innocent it was. Perhaps the task of coping with the devastating impact of the tragedy

---

[1]Susan Tifft, "Poison Madness in the Midwest," *Time*, Oct. 11, 1982, p. 18.

would have been easier for Johnson & Johnson if the perpetrator were conclusively identified and caught. This was not to be, despite a special task
force of 100 FBI agents and Illinois investigators who chased down more
than 2000 leads and filed 57 volumes of reports.[2]

COMPANY REACTION

Johnson & Johnson decided to elevate the management of the crisis to the
corporate level. A game plan was developed that company executives hoped
would ensure eventual recovery. The game plan consisted of three phases:
Phase I was to figure out what had actually happened; Phase II was to assess
and contain the damage; and Phase III was to try to get Tylenol back into
the market.

The company that had always tried to keep a low profile now turned to
the media to provide it with the most accurate and current information, as
well as to help it prevent a panic. Twenty-five public relations specialists
were recruited from Johnson & Johnson's other divisions to help McNeil's
regular staff of 15. Advertising was suspended at first. All Tylenol capsules
were recalled—31 million bottles with a retail value of over $100 million.
Through advertisements promising to exchange tablets for capsules,
through 500,000 Mailgram messages to doctors, hospitals, and distributors,
and through statements to the media, J & J hoped to demystify the situation.

With proof that the tampering had not occurred in the manufacturing
process, the company moved into Phase II. Financially, it experienced
immediate losses amounting to over $100 million, the bulk of this coming
from the expense of buying unused Tylenol bottles from retailers and consumers and shipping them to disposal points. The cost of sending the tele-
grams was estimated at half a million; the costs associated with expected
product liability suits were expected to run in the millions.

Of more concern to the management was the impact of the poisoning
on the brand itself. Many predicted that Tylenol as a brand could no longer
survive. Some suggested that Johnson & Johnson reintroduce the product
under a new name to give it a fresh start and thus rid itself of the devastated brand image.

Surveys conducted by Johnson & Johnson about a month after the poisonings seemed to confirm the death of Tylenol as a brand name. In one
survey, 94 percent of the consumers were aware that Tylenol was involved
with the poisonings. Although 87 percent of these respondents realized that
the maker of Tylenol was not to blame for the deaths, 61 percent said they
were not likely to buy Tylenol in the future. Even worse, 50 percent of the

---

[2]"Tylenol Comes Back as Case Grows Cold," *Newsweek*, April 25, 1983, p. 16.

consumers said they would not use the Tylenol tablets either. The only promising result from the research was that 49 percent of the *frequent* users answered that they would eventually use Tylenol.[3]

The company found itself in a real dilemma. It wanted so much to keep the Tylenol name; after all, the acceptance had been developed by years of advertising. Now, was it all to be destroyed in a few days of adversity? On the one hand, if Tylenol was brought back too soon—before the hysteria had subsided—the product could die on the shelves. On the other hand, if Johnson & Johnson waited too long to bring the product back, competitors might well gain an unassailable market share lead. The marketing research results were not entirely acceptable to Johnson & Johnson executives. One expressed the company doubts: "The problem with consumer research is that it reflects attitudes and not behavior. The best way to know what consumers are really going to do is put the product back on the shelves and let them vote with their hands."[4] But what was the right timing?

Johnson & Johnson decided to rebuild the brand by focusing on the frequent users, and then to expand to include other consumers. It hoped that there was a core of loyal users who would want the product in both its tablet and capsule forms. In order to regain regular user confidence, television commercials were run informing the public that the company would do everything it could to regain their trust. The commercials featured Dr. Thomas Gates, medical director of McNeil, urging consumers to continue to trust Tylenol: "Tylenol has had the trust of the medical profession and a hundred million Americans for over twenty years. We value that trust too much to let any individual tamper with it. We want you to continue to trust Tylenol."[5]

Johnson & Johnson also tried to encourage Tylenol capsule users to switch to tablets, which are more difficult to sabotage. In an advertising campaign it offered to exchange tablets for capsules at no charge. In addition, it placed 76 million coupons in Sunday newspaper ads good for $2.50 toward the purchase of Tylenol.

Finally, a tamper-resistant package was designed to prevent the kind of tragedy that occurred in Chicago. Extra-strength capsules were now sold only in new triple-sealed packages. The flaps of the box were glued shut and were visibly torn apart when opened. The bottle's cap and neck were covered with a tight plastic seal printed with the company name, and the mouth of the bottle was covered with an inner foil seal. Both the box and

---

[3]Thomas Moore, "The Fight to Save Tylenol," *Fortune*, Nov. 29, 1982, p. 48.
[4]*Ibid.*, p. 49.
[5] Judith B. Gardner, "When a Brand Name Gets Hit by Bad News," *U.S. News & World Report*, Nov. 8, 1982, p. 71.

the bottle were labeled "Do Not Use If Safety Seals Are Broken." This triple-seal package cost an additional 2.4 cents per bottle, but Johnson & Johnson hoped it would instill consumer confidence in the safety of the product and spur sales. In addition, the company offered retailers higher-than-normal discounts—up to 25 percent on orders.

Consumers who said they had thrown away their Tylenol after the scare were given a toll-free number to call, and they received $2.50 in coupons too—in effect a free bottle, since bottles of 24 capsules or 30 tablets sold for about $2.50.

Over 2000 salespeople from all Johnson & Johnson domestic subsidiaries were mobilized to persuade doctors and pharmacists to again begin recommending Tylenol tablets to patients and customers. This was similar to the strategy initially used when the product was first introduced some 25 years before.

The Outcome

Immediately after the crisis, J & J's market share plunged from 35.3 percent of the pain reliever market to below 7 percent. Competitors were quick to take advantage of the situation. Upjohn Company and American Home Products Corporation were seeking Food and Drug Administration permission to sell an over-the-counter version of ibuprofen, a popular prescription pain reliever. Upjohn also granted marketing rights for its brand, Nuprin, to Bristol-Myers Co., maker of Bufferin, Excedrin, and Datril. Upjohn's prescription brand, Motrin—a stronger formulation than Nuprin—was generating some $200 million in 1982, making Motrin the company's biggest-selling drug. And lurking in the wings was mighty Proctor & Gamble Company (P & G), the world's heaviest advertiser. P & G was launching national ads for Norwich aspirin and was test-marketing a coated capsule containing aspirin granules.

Yet, there were some encouraging signs for J & J. *Psychology Today* polled its readers regarding whether Tylenol would survive as a brand name. Ninety-two percent thought Tylenol would survive the incident. This figure corresponded closely with the results of another survey conducted by Leo Shapiro, an independent market researcher, just two weeks after the deaths occurred, in which 91 percent said they would probably buy the product again.

Psychology Today, trying to get at the roots of such loyalty, roused comments such as these:

> A 23-year-old woman wrote that she would continue to use Tylenol because she felt that it was "tried and true."

A 61-year-old woman said that the company had been "honest and sincere."

And a young man thought Tylenol was an easy name to say.[6]

Such survey results presaged an amazing comeback. J & J's conscientious actions paid off. By May 1983, Tylenol had regained almost all the market share lost the previous September; its market share reached 35 percent, and it was to hold this until 1986, when another calamity struck.

New industry safety standards had been developed by the over-the-counter drug industry in concert with the Food and Drug Administration for tamper-resistant packaging. Marketers under law had to select a package "having an indicator or barrier to entry, which if breached or missing, can reasonably be expected to provide visible evidence to the consumer that the package has been tampered with or opened."[7] Despite toughened package standards, in February 1986, a Westchester, New York, woman died from cyanide-laced Extra-Strength Tylenol capsules. The tragedy of 3½ years before was being replayed. J & J immediately removed all Tylenol capsules from the market and offered refunds for capsules consumers had already bought.

Now the company made a major decision. It decided to no longer manufacture any over-the-counter capsules, because it could not guarantee their safety from criminal contamination. Henceforth, the company would market only tablets and so-called caplets, which were coated and elongated tablets that are easy to swallow. This decision was expected to cost $150 million. The president explained: "People think of this company as extraordinarily trustworthy and responsible, and we don't want to do anything to damage that."[8]

By July 1986, Tylenol had regained most of the market share lost in February, and it now stood at 32 percent.

INGREDIENTS OF SUCCESS AND THE CONTRAST WITH A. H. ROBINS

Johnson & Johnson, in its handling of the Tylenol problem, was truly a business success. It overcame the worst kind of adversity, that in which human life was lost in association with one of its products. In only a few months, it recouped most of its lost market share and regained its public image of corporate responsibility and trust. Admittedly, the injury to customers was by no means as great as that perpetrated by Robins and its Dalkon Shield; still, the public limelight was more intense and the trauma of the deaths greater because of the way they occurred. What accounted for the success of J & J in overcoming the adversity?

---

[6]Carin Rubenstein, "The Tylenol Tradition," *Psychology Today*, April 1983, p. 16.

[7]"Package Guides Studied," *Advertising Age*, Oct. 18, 1982, p. 82.

[8]Richard W. Stevenson, "Johnson & Johnson's Recovery," *New York Times*, July 5, 1986, pp. 33–34.

We can identify five significant factors:

1. Keeping communication channels open.
2. Taking quick corrective action.
3. Keeping faith in the product.
4. Protecting the public image at all costs.
5. Aggressively bringing back the brand.

Effective communication has seldom been better illustrated. It is vital to gain rapport with the press, to enlist their support and even their sympathy. And this is not easily done, for the press is inclined to sensationalize, criticize, and take sides against the big corporation. Johnson & Johnson gained the needed rapport through corporate openness and cooperation. In the early days of the disaster, it sought good two-way communication, with the media furnishing information from the field while J & J gave full and honest disclosure of its internal investigation and corrective actions. For good rapport, company officials need to be freely available and open to the press. Unfortunately, this usually goes against the natural bent of executives, so that a spirit of antipathy often is fostered—as it was with Robins, but not so with J & J during its time of greatest trial.

When product safety is in jeopardy, quick corrective action must be taken, *regardless* of the cost. This usually means immediate recall of the affected product, and such action can run into many millions of dollars. Even if the fault lies with only an isolated batch of products, a firm prudently may have to consider recalling them all, since the problem and danger can quickly become transferable to all items of that brand. Robins's grudging and delayed recall of the Shield simply exacerbated the problem and led to costs many times greater than would have occurred if the recall had taken place years before, when the problems were first brought to light.

Johnson & Johnson kept faith with its products and brand name, despite experts who thought the Tylenol name should be abandoned and that public trust could never be regained. Of course, the company was not at fault; there was no culpability, no carelessness. The cause was right. With Robins, the situation was vastly different: the company was culpable, with research carelessness heaped on callous disregard for real and potential health problems associated with the product. Admittedly, in keeping faith with a product, there is a thin line between a positive commitment and recalcitrant stubbornness to face up to any problem and accept any blame. Without J & J's faith in Tylenol, there would have been no chance of resurrecting the product and its market share.

Johnson & Johnson strove to protect its public image of being a socially responsible and caring firm. (The information box discusses *social responsibility* and presents the J & J credo regarding this.) If there was to be any chance for a fairly quick recovery from adversity, this public image had to

SOCIAL RESPONSIBILITY AND THE JOHNSON & JOHNSON CREDO

We can define social responsibility as the sense of responsibility a firm has for the needs of society, over and above its commitment to maximizing profits and stockholder interests. The following "Credo" of J & J illustrates the wide circle of corporate social responsibility that more and more firms are beginning to accept.

JOHNSON & JOHNSON'S CREDO[a]

We believe our first responsibility is to the doctors, nurses, and patients, to mothers and all others who use our products and services. In meeting their needs, everything we do must be of high quality. We must constantly strive to reduce our costs in order to maintain reasonable prices. Customers' orders must be serviced promptly and accurately. Our suppliers and distributors must have an opportunity to make a fair profit.

We are responsible to our employees, the men and women who work with us throughout the world. Everyone must be considered as an individual. We must respect their dignity and recognize their merit. They must have a sense of security in their jobs. Compensation must be fair and adequate, and working conditions clean, orderly, and safe. Employees must feel free to make suggestions and complaints. There must be equal opportunity for employment, development, and advancement for those qualified. We must provide competent management, and their actions must be just and ethical.

We are responsible to the communities in which we live and work and to the world community as well. We must be good citizens—support good works and charities and bear our fair share of taxes. We must encourage civic improvements and better health and education. We must maintain in good order the property we are privileged to use, protecting the environment and natural resources.

Our final responsibility is to our stockholders. Business must make a sound profit. We must experiment with new ideas. Research must be carried on, innovative programs developed, and mistakes paid for. New equipment must be purchased, new facilities provided, and new products launched. Reserves must be created to provide for adverse times. When we operate according to these principles, the stockholders should realize a fair return.

[a]*Source:* Company recruiting brochure.

be guarded—no matter how beset it was. Although the plight of Tylenol was well known, the corrective actions were prompt and thorough, and many people were thus assured that safety was restored. We should note here that for the public image to be regained under adverse circumstances, the corrective actions must be well publicized. Public relations efforts and good communication with the media are essential for this. Of course, it helps when the fault of the catastrophe is clearly not the firm's.

Johnson & Johnson did a superb job of aggressively bringing back the brand. In so doing, all efforts had to be coordinated: efforts to safeguard the public image had to be reasonably successful; the cause of the disaster needed to be conclusively established; the likelihood of the event happening again had to be virtually eliminated. Then aggressive promotional efforts could fuel the recovery.

Johnson & Johnson's efforts to come back necessarily focused on correcting the problem. Initially, it designed a tamper-resistant container to prevent the kind of tragedy that had occurred in Chicago. Extra-strength capsules were now to be sold only in new triple-sealed packages. Later in 1986, when another death occurred, the company dropped capsules entirely and offered Tylenol only in tablet form.

With the safety features in place, J & J then used heavy promotion. This included consumer advertising, with the theme of safety assurance and company social responsibility. J & J offered to exchange tablets for capsules at no charge. It offered millions of newspaper coupons good for $2.50 toward the purchase of Tylenol. Retailers were also given incentives to back Tylenol through discounts, advertising allowances, and full refunds for recalled capsules with all handling costs paid. These efforts directed to consumers and retailers alike bolstered dealer confidence in the resurgence of the brand.

RECENT DRUG PRICING ABUSES BY J & J?

In May 1992, publicity surfaced that Johnson & Johnson was guilty of "unconscionable" pricing of the cancer drug levamisole, used to treat colon cancer. The charge came from a distinguished physician and cancer expert, Charles G. Moertel of the Mayo Comprehensive Cancer Center, at the annual meeting of the American Society of Clinical Oncology. Under Johnson & Johnson's brand name, Ergamisol, levamisole costs patients $1250 to $1500 for a year's supply.

The controversy arose not so much from the absolute price of a lifesaving drug, but from its relative price to a 30-year-old veterinary version of the drug, which farmers use to treat their sheep for parasites. This version cost only $14. The dispute first came to light when an Illinois farmwoman, being treated for cancer, noticed her pills contained the same active ingredients she used to deworm her sheep.

Under sponsorship of the National Cancer Institute, Dr. Moertel and others found that levamisole, combined with a staple chemotherapy drug, 5-fluorouracil, was spectacularly effective in patients with advanced colon cancer, reducing recurrence by 40 percent and cutting deaths by a third. "It's an unequivocal success," he said. "We now have a therapy with a national impact" against the second-largest cause of cancer deaths, after lung cancer. "We were specifically promised that it would be marketed at a reasonable price."[9]

Johnson & Johnson defended its pricing of the consumer version of the drug thusly: "The price of the product reflects costly research over decades to determine possible uses in humans for other diseases."[10] J & J also pointed out that sales were less that $15 million a year, a relatively modest amount for a pharmaceutical product. At the same time, the company claimed to have partly backed over 1400 studies involving 40,000 patients in seeking new applications of the drug in humans.

Dr. Moertel dismissed Johnson & Johnson's justification for the high prices as necessary to meet the higher research and regulatory costs in preparing the drug for human consumption. He maintained that the National Cancer Institute, funded by American taxpayers, sponsored the studies. "The company just supplied the pills, which cost pennies." And he raised the question whether a new use for an old drug—a windfall—should justify a price surge: "Just because aspirin was found to improve your risk of heart attack, should you charge more?"[11]

The bad publicity now confronting J & J was not confined to the print media. TV news programs, such as *20/20*, soon featured this controversy, along with criticisms of drug pricing of the entire pharmaceutical industry. And the spokespersons for J & J and the other pharmaceutical companies hardly upheld their positions with conviction.

WHAT CAN BE LEARNED?

Any company's nightmare is that its product might be linked to death or injury. Such a calamity invariably results in fear and loss of public confidence in the product and the firm. At worst, such a disaster can kill a company, as happened with some canned-food firms whose products were contaminated with the deadly botulism toxin. We cannot forget the grudging demise of Chevrolet's rear-engine Corvair, whose lack of safety was the object of Ralph Nader's best-selling book, *Unsafe at Any Speed*, and we saw the delayed but serious consequences to Robins. Even at best, years of time and money invested in a brand may be lost, with the brand never able to regain its former robustness. In the throes of the catastrophe, J & J executives grappled with the major decision of abandoning the brand at the

---

[9] Marilyn Chase, "Doctor Assails J & J Price Tag on Cancer Drug," *Wall Street Journal*, May 20, 1992, pp. B1, B8.

[10] *Ibid.*, p. B1.

[11] *Ibid.*, p. B8.

height of its popularity. The decision could have gone either way. Now, with hindsight, the correctness of the decision not to abandon the product was unmistakably correct; but at the time, how was one to know? And this leads us to our first Insight.

Learning Insight. *In event of a catastrophe, heroic efforts may still save the brand, although the costs may be staggering.*

Even though J & J successfully brought back Tylenol, the costs were in the hundreds of millions of dollars. But the company size—over $5 billion in sales from a diversified product line—enabled it to handle the costs without jeopardy. A smaller firm would not have been able to weather this adversity especially without a broad product line like J & J's.

Learning Insight. *Whenever product safety is an issue, the danger of lawsuits must be reckoned with.*

As we saw with the Robins case, litigation brought bankruptcy and eventual takeover. Legal action finally was effective in curbing the company's abuses and procrastination in the absence of strong government regulation. This recourse upheld the rights of the general public, even though lawyers were perhaps the biggest beneficiaries. With J & J, the danger of litigation was muted, although hundreds of millions of dollars in lawsuits were still filed. But in the absence of corporate neglect, the swift constructive reaction, and the fact that the company could hardly have guarded against the actions of a madman, it escaped the worse scenario regarding litigation. Still, suits accused J & J of failing to package Tylenol in a tamper-proof container, and the legal expenses of defending itself were not inconsequential. The threat of litigation must be a major consideration for any firm today. Even if the organization is relatively blameless, legal costs can run into the millions. And no one can predict with certainty the decisions of juries.

Learning Insight. *Other firms may also be vulnerable to actions taken against the competitor.*

Although other firms in an industry stand to gain a competitive advantage during something like this, they and firms in related industries need to be particularly vigilant—because of the tendency toward "copycat crimes." By November, a month after the deaths, the Food and Drug Administration had received more than 270 reports of chemicals, pills, poisons, needles, pins, and razor blades in everything from food to drinks to medications.

Fortunately, no deaths resulted from these incidents. But FDA Commissioner Hayes worried: "My greatest fear is that because of the notoriety of the case and the financial damage to the company, someone else will take out his or her grudges on a product and do something similar."[12] Actually, the Tylenol case was not the first time products had been deliberately contaminated. Eyedrops, nasal sprays, milk of magnesia, as well as food and cosmetics have all been targets of tampering. An Oregon man was even sentenced to 20 years in prison for attempting to extort diamonds from grocery chains by putting cyanide in food products on their shelves.

Learning Insight. *It is possible to bounce back from extreme adversity.*

Certainly, one of the major things we can learn from this case is that it is possible to bounce back from extreme adversity. Before the Tylenol episode, this was not realized by most experts: the general opinion was that severe negative publicity resulted in such an image destruction that recovery could take years. The most optimistic predictions were that Tylenol might recover to a 20–21 percent market share in a year;[13] the pessimistic predictions were that the brand would never recover and should be abandoned. Actually, in eight months, Tylenol had regained almost all of its market share, to a satisfactory 35 percent. For such a recovery, a firm has to manifest unselfish concern, quick corrective action, and unsparing spending. And it must have a base of a good public image before the catastrophe.

Learning Insight. *A good corporate citizen's behavior may lapse. Good deeds and favorable publicity in the past do not assure freedom from future criticism.*

Recent accusations against J & J of "unconscionable" drug pricing quickly became widely publicized. On the surface, the position of J & J and its defense appeared highly vulnerable to such criticism: $14 for a sheep, $1,250 to $1,500 for humans whose lives are threatened. Where is the compassion and best interest of consumers that J & J had evinced some years before?

Perhaps there is ample justification for the company's position, but this is not understood by the press and in public opinion. The improved public image from the Tylenol troubles are quickly forgotten and replaced by pub-

---

[12]"Lessons That Emerge from Tylenol Disaster," *U.S. News & World Report*, Oct. 18, 1982, p. 68.
[13]"J & J Will Pay Dearly to Cure Tylenol," *Business Week*, Nov. 29, 1982, p. 37.

lic notions of company profiteering and price-gouging. Given its vulnerability to a hostile environment because of a dubious pricing strategy, J & J is well advised to marshal its justifications in far more persuasive terms than has happened as we go to press.

FOR THOUGHT AND DISCUSSION

1. Did J & J move too far in recalling all Extra-Strength Tylenol capsules? Would not a sufficient action have been to recall only those in the Chicago area, thus saving millions of dollars? Discuss.
2. How helpful were the marketing research survey results in the decision about whether or not to keep the Tylenol name?
3. "We must assume that someone had a terrible grudge against J & J to have perpetrated such a crime." Discuss.
4. What justification do you think Johnson & Johnson could offer for its levamisole pricing that would be generally acceptable to the press and public opinion?

INVITATION TO ROLE PLAY

1. Assume this scenario: it has been established that the fault of the contamination was accidental introduction of cyanide at the company plant. How would you as CEO of J & J have directed your recovery strategy? Be sure to give your rationale.
2. Assume the role of the executive responsible for the pricing of levamisole for treatment of colon cancer. What would you advise the executive committee regarding any pricing changes after the negative publicity in May 1992?

INVITATION TO RESEARCH

1. Has Tylenol been able to maintain its competitive position since the contamination crises. How has Johnson & Johnson done in recent years?
2. What, if anything, has J & J done regarding its pricing of levamisole (or Ergamisol) since May 1992?

22

Conclusions: What Can Be Learned?

As noted in the introduction, we are on the side of business. We want it to do a better job in its interface with society. All kinds of problems assail the firm that does not respond to the pressures of society. These include lawsuits, boycotts, governmental restrictions and regulations, and a besmirched public image. Although we have described a number of corporate misdeeds, we want to be more constructive than critical. We seek to identify how to avoid and how to cope with ethical and public-image dilemmas in the future.

INSIGHTS REGARDING OVERALL CORPORATE BEHAVIOR

Pervasiveness of Top Management Ethics

For better or for worse, the attitudes and actions of top executives—whether they be scrupulously honest and ethical or something far less—permeate an organization. The chief executive is the model. He or she sets the tone, influencing the behavior of the next tier of executives, and down the line to rank-and-file employees, although there may be an occasional exception or whistleblower. A number of cases have shown the contagious influence of a top executive who was more interested in short-term performance than in acting ethically: ITT, Beech-Nut, Union Carbide (Ohio Valley pollution), General Dynamics, and others.

Related to the top executive's influence over a company is the often mechanistic mindset of executive committees, which value the firm's immediate best interests over customer and employee safety, integrity, and environmental protection. We saw this in the Corvair case, where top GM executives sacrificed customer safety—sometimes even the safety of their own family members—in order to save a few dollars per car on a part that would have made the car more stable under extreme conditions. Acting alone, none of these executives would likely have made such an uncaring decision; acting as a group, the corporate bottom line was paramount. With its myopia, GM's groupthink could not recognize the potential negative long-term impact on the firm.

Dangers in Short-Term Profit Emphasis

Top management may not be directly involved in questionable dealings, but it promotes such behavior by strongly insisting on short-term profit maximization and performance goals. When these goals are difficult to achieve and not achieving them can be met with severe penalties, the climate is set for undesirable conduct: deceptive advertising, overselling, adulterated products (e.g., Beech-Nut's "apple juice"), and other illegal practices, such as bribery and price fixing (as in the electrical equipment industry case). We are not advocating that goals be toned down, that expectations be reduced, or that performance incentives should not be used. But the pressure by top management to reach those goals—accepting no excuses—can trigger unethical actions. This is especially likely in an organization where high moral standards and the customer's best interests are not the rule. We encountered this in a number of cases, particularly the General Dynamics, STP, and the S&L cases.

Top Management Is Ultimately Responsible

After catastrophes, but also after other corporate misdeeds, top management should not escape culpability, even though we have seen examples where this was done: such as in GM's Ralph Nader discreditation efforts, the electrical equipment industry's price-fixing conspiracy, and ITT's Chilean adventures. Blame-shifting by top executives is a repudiation of responsibility. No manager can escape accountability for the actions of subordinates.

With catastrophes, such as Bhopal and the Alaskan spill, the top executive should be actively and visibly in charge (even though, in the heat of emotion, officials in India were abusive to the CEO of Union Carbide). The presence of top executive Lawrence Rawl at the environmental disaster scene would have helped Exxon's public image and muted some of the criticisms regarding the company's carelessness and callousness.

The Fallacy of a "Follow-the-Leader" Syndrome

We saw several cases in which all (or most) firms followed their competitors in stooping to the lowest level of ethical and legal conduct: many members of the S&L industry, virtually all the firms in the electrical equipment industry during the price-fixing misadventure, and most of the defense contractors in the 1980s and before.

There are usually reasons given for following the herd: (1) since everyone else is doing it, it must be the thing to do, and (2) if we don't do likewise, we will be at a competitive disadvantage and our viability may even be threatened. Reflection shows the fallacy of such thinking. The herd or mob is seldom right and prudent; it more often exercises reckless abandon. Although unethical or illegal actions may escape detection or strong opposition in the short run, invariably such actions get their just desserts.

Attempts to Cover Up Are Invariably Found Out

Such coverups usually result in far worse consequences for the company than a forthright admission of blame. We saw this in the Beech-Nut and Dalkon Shield cases. With the Dalkon Shield, the prolonged denials and coverup compounded personal injuries and even fatalities—and led eventually to lawsuits that gutted the company. Even GM was guilty of a coverup when it ignored the safety reports on the Corvair and attempted to discredit its severest critic. Exxon, in the throes of its Valdez mishap, also yielded to the temptation to do some fingerpointing. It is human nature to try to blame someone else, or otherwise try to escape blame. But this is difficult to do today, with investigative reporting and a suspicious public.

Risks of Extreme Cost-Cutting

In prosperous times, many organizations succumb to frivolous spending and bloated staffs. In more sober times, cost-cutting prevails. Both extremes have dangers. Too much overhead and infrastructure can drastically affect profits, especially during lean times. But excessive cost-cutting may be even more perilous. We saw in the two major catastrophes, Bhopal and the Alaskan oil spill, that cost-cutting severely affected safety measures and contributed greatly to the gravity of the problem and the consequent handling of it.

During the rash of mergers and leveraged buyouts in the 1980s, the corporate raiders usually tried to cut operating costs to the bone in order to service the huge debt and spin off certain assets. During the recession of the early 1990s, management and technical staffs were sometimes cut back to the extreme in order to streamline operations and reduce overhead. In some cases, such severe retrenching curbed efficiency and innovation. Moderation seems to be desirable in controlling expense as in many other aspects of business.

Vulnerability of Highly Leveraged Takeovers

High leverage means heavy debt and interest costs. Overhead is increased, perhaps to perilous levels. A firm that can barely cover its overhead during good times is vulnerable when conditions change. The rallying cry for business takeovers was "synergy"—often expressed as "2 + 2 = 5." Thus, the idea that the combination of two firms is more effective than the firms as separate entities.

But, in the Campeau case, synergy was entirely lacking. Several factors reduce the possibility of synergy in many hostile takeovers:

1. Successful takeovers require good operating executives. Raiders such as Campeau, (probably) Goldsmith, and others, were adept at financial manipulations, but not so good at operating companies.
2. Subjected to severe cost-cutting, the acquired organization is often hurled into turmoil, with personnel running scared.
3. Retailing, in particular, presents unique working-capital problems because of the heavy buildup of inventory needed for Christmas business. This magnifies the financial demands on highly leveraged operations.

IMPORTANCE OF THE PUBLIC IMAGE

A firm's image—how it is viewed by its various publics—came under attack in many of these cases. General Motors; Union Carbide; Nestle; A. H. Robins, with its Dalkon Shield; Beech-Nut; some of the pharmaceutical companies, such as Burroughs-Wellcome and Hoffman-La Roche; the S&L industry; General Dynamics, Lockheed, and the defense industry; Exxon— all their reputations were besmirched by the publicity stemming from their misdeeds. Although we cannot identify the impact on sales and profits of a deteriorating image, we can speculate that there are serious consequences. Yet, many firms ignore their public image, take actions detrimental to such an important asset, or overlook the constraints as well as the opportunities that an image affords.

A bad reputation is difficult to overcome. It can affect the customer base, the quality of employees and executives, the cooperation of vendors and creditors, the surveillance of regulatory agencies, and not the least, the attention of the press. The press is both influenced by a firm's reputation and instrumental in creating it.

Power of the Press

We have seen the power of the media in a number of cases: General Motors, Union Carbide, Nestle, the Dalkon Shield, Beech-Nut, the pharmaceutical firms, the S&Ls, General Dynamics, Lockheed and the defense industry, Goldsmith's attempted takeover of Goodyear, the Exxon oil spill, and Johnson & Johnson's Tylenol. The media's power is most often wielded in a critical way: to hurt a firm's public image. The media can fan a problem or exacerbate an embarrassing or imprudent action. Its inclination is to emphasize the negative, since this is usually more sensational. In particular, with well-known firms, the media can trigger the herd instinct, increasing the number of people who are protesting and criticizing. But, it is also possible to use the media in a positive way, as Johnson & Johnson was able to do in its recovery from the Tylenol disaster.

We can make these generalizations regarding image or reputation:

1. A good image can be quickly lost if a firm relaxes its efforts to please customers and protect its caring position with respect to society and the environment.
2. It is very difficult and time-consuming to upgrade an image.
3. It is very easy to tear down a good image by a lapse of concern regarding customers, service, or the environment.
4. Large, well-known firms are particularly vulnerable to critical public scrutiny and must be careful to protect their reputation.
5. Marketing efforts, such as advertising, selling, product quality and safety, and pricing usually have the strongest impact on public image. They tend to be the most visible and the ones most susceptible to abuse and criticism.
6. The power of special interest groups—such as environmentalists and AIDS activist groups—is strengthened by media focus.
7. Public-image problems are seldom corrected by public-relations efforts. For example, public relations could do nothing for Nestle and Exxon, the pharmaceutical companies, or for the defense industry. An overall corporate commitment to correcting the problem must be taken—far beyond mere lip service or bought publicity.

INSIGHTS REGARDING SPECIFIC OPERATIONAL ASPECTS

Product Safety

A number of cases involved product or plant safety. In today's litigious environment, firms are particularly vulnerable in this area of their operation. They must be concerned with liability suits. Any hint of problems must be thoroughly investigated. Some notable firms, such as GM, Nestle, Dow Corning, and A. H. Robins, were negligent in this regard. When the worst-case scenario occurs, a firm must go for a salvage strategy: correct the situation, make restitution, admit any faults, recognize the likelihood that liability suits may damage the company. This course of action may be difficult to pursue, but the key objective should be to salvage the company, to leave its resources and its reputation in a position to climb from the depths. Robins did not do this, nor did many of the S&Ls. The other cases we examined did.

Any firm faced with heavy liability suits must recognize that its very viability can be in jeopardy. Obviously, a firm should try to avoid this situation in the first place, by minimizing carelessness or lack of concern, by investigating suspicions promptly and thoroughly (it helps here if the company encouraged good communications from its employees) and by being prepared to cooperate fully with the media and other investigators.

Vulnerable Pricing Practices

The "Robin Hood" philosophy of some drug firms (i.e., charging exorbitant prices for some popular drugs in order to subsidize other drugs and research) should be reevaluated. It is vulnerable to charges of profiteering and price gouging, especially when products essential to human welfare are involved. Not all critical charges are unjustified. With drugs, the issue can be emotional: how much profit should a drug maker seek on a product essential for health and even life itself, where the consumer has little choice?

Other pricing practices can also be criticized—for example, covering research and development (R & D) costs through pricing. Although this is common practice in the drug industry, other manufacturers consider such costs "sunk costs," not to be included in cost-plus pricing equations.

Where issues of public health and safety are involved, keeping costs and profit margins confidential may no longer be possible for drug manufacturers. With the press, government, and general public skeptical of industry pricing practices, perhaps a reassessment of pricing policies is due. Otherwise, drug firms are visible targets for criticism and regulation.

Collusion on pricing is so obviously illegal and easily prosecuted that one wonders how it ever happens. Price fixing is illegal under the first federal antitrust law, the Sherman Act of 1890. The simple act of conspiring to set prices or bids is all that needs to be proven; it does not matter whether competition was injured. Although the electrical equipment industry's price fixing, which was the most famous instance of this kind of conspiracy, occurred almost four decades ago, price fixing still occasionally occurs. With penalties quite severe and prosecution certain, there is no excuse for it.

Questionable Promotional Efforts

The temptation is to exaggerate a little, to "puff" a product's attributes just a little. Unfortunately, moderation is not always practiced. Mild exaggerations become outright deception. We found that in the STP's product claims, as well as in Beech-Nut's tacit acceptance of an adulterated product as pure apple juice.

False claims are eventually found out. With many products, false promises are quickly recognized by customers, who refuse to rebuy the product. But where such claims cannot be easily substantiated—with complex products, products with hidden ingredients, and ones whose benefits lie far in the future—the false promises are harder to detect. As we saw with STP, the malpractice can continue for years, until someone whistle-blows or some investigative body confirms the suspicions.

This suggests that consumers and purchasing agents alike should beware of the offer that is too good—as Beech-Nut did not do, ignoring the obvious clues.

Advertising statements, if well presented and attractive, should induce customers to purchase the product. But, if the expectations generated by the ads are not realized, there will be no repeat business. Repeat business is the very thing most firms seek: a continuity of business, which means loyal and satisfied customers.

Environmental Concerns

Several cases featured companies confronted with major environmental problems: Union Carbide, for example, in both the Ohio Valley and the Bhopal catastrophe, and Exxon in Alaska. From these disasters, we see the importance of environmental planning as one part of long-range strategic planning, and also the need for contingency planning for the worst-case scenario, unlikely though this might seem.

Worst-case scenario planning should not overlook product disasters. For example, Johnson & Johnson's Tylenol calamity was beyond what reasonable people would ever have expected, but contingency planning for a worst-case scenario would have made the company's reactions less stressful. Similarly, contingency planning by Robins might have saved the company from its unsuccessful, ill-fated attempts to cover up the Dalkon Shield's defects.

The power and influence of the environmentalists and their ally, a press that is often hostile to business, should not be lost on any business firm today. The remedy is not to assume a combative or adversarial stance, but to join the ranks of those who are concerned about the environment. After all, we live in one world. We have a mutual interest in preserving it for ourselves and our children, even if the bottom line of profits might have to be sacrificed a little.

Cautions in Foreign Operations

Many firms today do business worldwide. Although this presents great opportunities, it also poses some problems, some ethical dilemmas, and some opportunities for abuse. The most obvious abuse was ITT's interference in Chilean politics. ITT used such a heavy hand that the president of Chile, Allende, lost his life. Whether or not ITT can be directly blamed for this, few would accept the idea that corporate self-interest supersedes a foreign government's internal affairs. Such questionable practices have a critical effect on the image of the United States abroad.

Bribery of foreign officials, which came to light during the Lockheed and defense industry scandals, motivated the enactment of the Foreign Corrupt Practices Act of 1977, which made such bribery by U.S. firms illegal.

Union Carbide's acceptance of lower operating standards in its Third World operations led to the Bhopal accident—that and the company's laissez-faire policy of loose or nonexistent controls over its foreign managers and technicians. The lesson to be learned is that standards and controls must be even more rigidly applied in countries where workers and managers may be less competent than they are in more economically and educationally advanced countries.

The Nestle case raises the issue of promoting unsafe products in foreign markets. Nestle became the focus of strong and lasting criticism regarding its heavy promotion of infant formula in developing countries where sanitation was questionable and native mothers were prone to unsafe practices. Was it ethical for Nestle to seek a marketing advantage in such environments? Although there were compelling social arguments for doing what Nestle did, the crescendo of criticism forced the company to accede to the militants' demands.

We can also question the ethics of promoting the use of tobacco in foreign countries when the industry is under a health cloud here in the United States—indeed, most mass-media promotion of tobacco is banned. Is heavy promotion of what many consider an unsafe product ethical in light of a more easily influenced foreign user?

THE NOOSE TIGHTENS FOR QUESTIONABLE PRACTICES

Increasing Perils in Ghetto Dealings

We have seen two recent cases where targeting the ghetto with products that some saw as undesirable brought a crescendo of criticism. PowerMaster and St. Ides with strong beer and Uptown with cigarettes have been subjected to community and ministerial protests charging that business firms were foisting unhealthy and unsafe products on susceptible ghetto youth. The violence of the protests far exceeded anything the firms might have anticipated. The ability of black ministers to rouse the militancy of their parishioners is a power not easily countered by the business community. And government also was not hesitant to join the fray against the alleged perpetrators of abusive practices targeted at the ghetto.

The Tobacco Industry Is Particularly Vulnerable to Attack Today

Although the tobacco industry has been subject to criticism for over a hundred years, it is particularly ripe today, partly through changing social mores, partly through ever more corroborating research findings of the health risks in cigarette smoking, and, not least, through its own clumsy and self-seeking behavior.

The most recent round of highly-publicized criticisms involved targeting a specific brand to the black community. As it had with the strong beers, this community rallied to protest promoting an unhealthy product to a susceptible and easily influenced minority group.

Related to this round of denunciations was another event that received even wider attention: Joe Camel, the cartoon character in the promotion of Camel cigarettes, which somehow and without reasonable expectations found an almost unprecedented appeal—to children! The potential for such a beloved cartoon character to influence children to smoke was appalling and unacceptable to large sectors of American society, including the American Medical Association. The weak disclaimers of the R. J. Reynolds Tobacco Company that Joe Camel did not directly influence children to smoke, despite the fact that they widely recognized and admired the character, fell on skeptical and unaccepting ears. Yet the firm could not bring itself to pull the promotional campaign in the face of mounting public and governmental pressure.

Faced with increasing anti-smoking pressures in the U.S., the tobacco industry predictably turned its efforts overseas. Western Europe proved even more negative than the U.S. So Eastern Europe, the Far East, and developing countries became the most recent focus of attention and aggressive promotional efforts. Pressures to curb such efforts for an unsafe product were spewing forth in all parts of the world.

The tobacco industry continues to act like an ostrich with its head in the sand, despite overwhelming medical evidence that its product is indeed unhealthy, even deadly. Aggressive efforts by tobacco firms to push its opposition in any available direction smacks of selfish opportunism and disregard for health consequences in the crass pursuit of maximum profits.

Should not the tobacco industry finally recognize and admit the health risks of its product and stop the aggressive promotion? Related to these criticized promotional strategies is the sponsorship of such athletic events as the Virginia Slims Tennis Tournament, geared to healthy young women athletes but supported by a product deemed anathema to good health by medical experts and a substantial part of society. Were not these criticisms afflicting the tobacco industry really brought on by the myopia of the industry itself and its lack of social responsiveness?

Abusive Business Practices Today Face Ever Greater Risks for the Seller

We saw how high-pressure and abusive practices in the health club and small-loan industries have led to firms being targeted for legal action and adverse publicity by state attorneys general. No longer are such practices likely to be tolerated. Even if attorneys general do not get involved in the fray, investigative and consumer-relations reporters are quick to listen to and publicize consumer allegations of malpractice.

Just as we went to press, nationwide negative publicity surfaced about overcharges by Sears auto centers, perhaps the tip of the iceberg for similar abuses perpetrated by all sectors of the consumer repair industry. The threatened penalties for such alleged practices were severe indeed, and they included banning all Sears auto centers from doing business in the state of California. The ballgame is indeed changing in business dealings with consumers. *Caveat vendidor*, let the seller beware, is all the more operative today.

Firms Can Fall Rather Innocently into Denounced Practices

In view of the changed operating environment of today, a firm can innocently find itself in the critical public limelight over practices it had never realized could invoke such violent reactions. The makers of PowerMaster beer and St. Ides little thought that their marketing efforts would arouse such furor. Even R. J. Reynolds with its Joe Camel could hardly have predicted both the success and the hostility its cartoon character would foster. And Sears's top management was shocked by the furious condemnations of its auto-service operations, which had changed little in decades.

What is a firm to do? Can it possibly anticipate all the negative repercussions resulting from what it thought were legitimate and customary marketing practices?

Prudence would dictate management's approaching possible troublesome actions carefully and with input from experts in the field as to any possible negative reactions. Unilateral actions may result in an initial competitive advantage, but may hurt a firm's overall image and reputation.

Management's sensitivities to potential controversial areas should be given a much finer tuning than ever before. It helps if likely problems can be identified before they become serious, so that efforts can be planned to avoid them. Such efforts may involve a different brand name, a different targeting of customer groups, or less aggressive promotions. In some cases, the whole project may better be abandoned than risk confrontational publicity. Even past policies and practices may need to be reevaluated: their susceptibility to investigation and condemnation may be just around the corner.

Is such caution really warranted today? This is for each firm to judge. Do the gains outweigh the risks? Can we get away with this, or are we likely to be targeted? Certainly not all abusive practices will be uncovered by the press and by governmental investigators. But the consequences of being targeted may far outweigh any short-term profit-maximization. Top management may even save their own positions through more caution.

CONTROVERSIES

These are some of the controversies we encountered in the book:

- Jobs versus the environment, as in Union Carbide's polluting of the Ohio Valley. How far should we go in sacrificing jobs and economic benefits for a cleaner environment? There is no simple answer to this, nor one that everyone would agree upon, not even with cost/benefit analysis.
- Cost/benefit analyses lead to a host of disagreements, despite their facade of rationality. For example, are the costs involved in cleaning up factory pollution—involving massive investments in pollution control or plant shutdowns with consequent economic hardships— worth the benefits of a little better air quality? How do you put a dollar figure on "a little better air quality"? How much better should we demand? We saw a similar cost/benefit controversy with double-hulled tankers. The risk of oil spills would be somewhat reduced, but is the added cost and additional ship traffic a suitable tradeoff?
- Should multinational firms follow U.S. standards and policies abroad? This was an issue with Union Carbide at Bhopal and ITT in Chile.

While many maintain that domestic policies should prevail, others strongly disagree.

- How ethical are the Robin Hood pricing policies of the drug firms? Should firms charge exorbitant markups on some products to subsidize research and development for products that might benefit only a few people? Some critics have charged that the Robin Hood philosophy is only a fake rationale for abusive pricing.

- Do white-collar offenders get off too lightly? In most of the cases, the perpetrators received no prison sentences or fines. Even the light sentences that the price-fixing conspirators received were less than a pickpocket might expect. When top management escapes all legal blame in most cases, we're left to wonder.

- Even some laws and regulations are not without their critics—in particular, the Foreign Corrupt Practices Act, which prohibits payoffs to foreign officials by U.S. multinationals hoping to encourage purchases of their products and systems. Should the ethical standards of the United States be foisted on the rest of the world? How can U.S. firms compete equally with foreign competitors who have no such restrictions? When in Rome, should we not do as the Romans do?

- The age-old question, "Does the end justify the means?" was addressed with respect to the ITT case. The end, so ITT believed, was to protect its property from being taken over by a socialist Chilean government. Did this end justify trying to unseat the government of Chile? Some would maintain that the end never justifies the means, for where do we draw the line? Terrorists justify all their crimes against innocent humanity as their means toward the end of certain freedoms. But is this acceptable?

- How tolerant should we be of firms that are vital to national security? Can defense industry's abuses be tolerated because the companies are so important? Should we apply different standards of conduct and retribution to some firms than to others? Are there other options than rigorously punishing for major violations or "wrist slapping"? Closer monitoring and more careful auditing of defense contractors have been proposed, but the execution left something to be desired. But, is this a suitable option?

We confront a sample of socio-ethical issues without coming up with clear positions. Unanimity of opinion will probably never be obtained.

Sometimes, positions even fly in the face of majority opinion, such as when environmentalists demand things that will affect jobs in a particular community. The challenge of assessing the relative merit of various conflicting claims is a major one.

FINAL INSIGHTS

One Person Can Make a Difference

Sometimes, one courageous and dedicated person can make a difference in a company's conduct—even a nation's conduct, as with Ralph Nader. Nader was instrumental in ushering in a new social attitude of intolerance for companies that victimize the consumer and the environment. Some whistleblowers, such as Jerome LiCari, director of research and development at Beech-Nut, succeed in publicizing unethical corporate actions but gain little for themselves except travail. Sometimes private citizens take it upon themselves to protest and organize and use publicity—for example, West Virginia's Mr. and Mrs. Hagedorn, who finally pressured Union Carbide into cleaning up the Ohio Valley air pollution. Sometimes, a new management team or chief executive can foster a changed orientation. This was what some of the raiders promised during their takeovers. Alas, most of them proved more interested in personal enrichment than in improving socio-corporate relations.

One person can certainly make a difference in a negative way—for example, Harold Geneen of ITT, Andy Granatelli of STP, Charles Keating of the Lincoln Savings and Loan.

This Is an Era of "Caveat Vendidor": Let the Seller Beware

Thanks to Ralph Nader and other consumer activists, a new social attitude has emerged, "let the seller beware." This replaces the old philosophy of "let the buyer beware" that dominated the marketplace for many decades. The Yankee horse trader characterized that era of "let the buyer beware." In those days, shrewd purchasers might drive a hard bargain; less sophisticated purchasers were often victimized. At a time when a person's livelihood, and even very life, might depend on a horse, this aspect of business was not a matter to be treated lightly.

Nowadays, most businesses are concerned with fair treatment of their customers, if for no other reason than to maintain their positions in a competitive environment. Government agencies, the press, and the threat of legal action are all deterrents to less-than-desirable practices in the marketplace. Although abuses still creep in, they are seldom tolerated for long.

Adversity Need Not Be Forever

Most firms recover from their problems. Even Bhopal did not destroy Union Carbide, although it weakened it. Nestle had some years of combating worldwide criticism and boycotts, but this eventually passed. The pricing practices of the pharmaceutical companies still continue despite periodic flareups of criticism, and one wonders if there was any learning experience. But the industry is more conscious of public opinion and governmental scrutiny than it once was. Beech-Nut, ITT, STP, the electrical equipment industry, defense contractors—the firms incurred no permanent consequences although some executives were forced to retire, and perhaps harsher penalties should have been imposed. And Exxon's oil spill was barely a blink, despite the bad press and environmentalists' denunciations.

However, several cases showed more drastic and permanent consequences. Robins's incredibly bad handling of the Dalkon Shield disaster; harmful effects and the consequent flood of personal injury suits destroyed the company. Many of the S&Ls did not survive their rash speculations and their leaders faced jail terms. Some of the raiders, in particular Campeau, brought their acquisitions to bankruptcy. So, a firm cannot be assured that negligence or opportunism or simply bad luck will be readily overcome. But, it usually is.

Adversity can create opportunities. Johnson & Johnson found its public image even stronger as a result of its compassionate handling of the Tylenol problem. Some found that the S&L mess created financial opportunities for stronger and more prudent players. Even Goodyear, though it was sorely beset in fighting off Sir James Goldsmith, found the upsurge of public support reassuring for its long-term prospects.

Desirability of a Trusting Relationship

Perhaps the most important lesson we can learn from these cases is the desirability for businesses to seek a trusting relationship with their customers (as well as with their other publics, especially employees and suppliers). Such a trusting relationship suggests concern for customer satisfaction and fair dealings. The objective is loyalty and repeat business, a durable and mutually beneficial relationship, which is contrary to the philosophy of short-term profit maximization, corporate self-interest, and coercive practices with employees and dependent suppliers.

Such a philosophy and attitude must permeate an organization. It can easily be short-circuited despite pious public-relations statements if a general climate of opportunism and severe performance pressure prevail. Let's face it! Top management sets the tone. In the days before GM's confrontation with Ralph Nader, the tone of all auto manufacturers was not product safety. "Safety doesn't sell," was the traditional cliché of the entire industry. It took an aroused public and, finally, governmental pressure for car safety to assume a higher priority in auto manufacturing boardrooms. This was certainly not a trusting relationship, unlike the Tylenol case.

Such a trusting relationship should not be sought with consumers or final users alone. It should characterize the relationship between sales representatives and their clients, which suggests no exaggeration or misrepresentation, greater efforts at understanding customers' needs, and better servicing. It may even mean forgoing a sales opportunity when a customer's best interest may be better served by another product or at another time.

The trusting relationship suggests repudiating any adversarial stance with employees, with suppliers, and, beyond this, with the communities in which a firm does business. Easier said than done? Perhaps. But it is a constructive attitude waiting to be fostered. It reflects the growing attitude executives have of *symbiosis* between the firm and its various publics—that is, a relationship where each gains from the success and best interests of the other. There is a mutual stake in the overall product/company and its success. This can be extended to the corporate relationship with society: it should be a mutually beneficial relationship.

Such a relationship is conducive to good ethical conduct. It fosters a good reputation and public image. It insulates a firm from the worst of competitive battles. In the long run, is such a relationship of trust so difficult to accept?

DISCUSSION

FOR THOUGHT AND DISCUSSION

1. How would you combat a follow-the-leader attitude in your firm in an industry where questionable business dealings prevail?
2. Would you expect a trusting relationship to be effective in an industry—such as used cars, home repairs, and recreational land—where no repeat sales are likely? Why or why not?
3. You seek a symbiotic and trusting relationship with all your publics. Is it possible to please them all?

INVITATION TO ROLE PLAY

1. Your firm has had a strategy of bad rapport with the press. How would you attempt to improve this situation?
2. You are concerned about the air pollution your plant is generating. The lowest-cost estimate to correct the situation is $200 million. In the absence of any industry-wide standards, you worry that your unilateral action to clean up will jeopardize your competitive position. How would you handle this dilemma?

KING ALFRED'S COLLEGE

LIBRARY